*Missing Reels*

# Missing Reels

*Lost Films of American
and European Cinema*

*by*
HARRY WALDMAN

McFarland & Company, Inc., Publishers
*Jefferson, North Carolina, and London*

The photographs in this book are courtesy of the Museum of Modern Art, the British Film Institute, and Filmoteca Española. Internet site addresses were confirmed as of October 1999.

Brief quotations are provided from reviews published in *The New York Times, Variety, Harrison's Reports, Film Daily, Motion Picture Herald, Exhibitors Herald-World, Moving Picture World, Cine-Mundial, Mensajero Paramount* (1930–33), *Monthly Film Bulletin,* and *Close-Up* (1927–35).

*The present work is a reprint of the illustrated case bound edition of* Missing Reels: Lost Films of American and European Cinema, *first published in 2000 by McFarland.*

LIBRARY OF CONGRESS CATALOGUING-IN-PUBLICATION DATA

Waldman, Harry.
    Missing reels : lost films of American and European cinema / by Harry Waldman.
        p.    cm.
    Includes bibliographical references and index.

    ISBN-13: 978-0-7864-3777-1
    softcover : 50# alkaline paper ∞

    1. Motion pictures — Catalogs.    2. Lost films.    I. Title.
PN1998.W24    2008
016.79143'75 — dc21                                    99-88007

British Library cataloguing data are available

Cover image © 2000 RubberBall Productions

Manufactured in the United States of America

*McFarland & Company, Inc., Publishers*
    *Box 611, Jefferson, North Carolina 28640*
        *www.mcfarlandpub.com*

# Contents

# Introduction

The films discussed in this book are long lost, and their disappearance has left gaps in film history. This overview and examination of important missing films is an attempt to fill in the blanks and to present a more complete picture of what is missing from the cinema of America and Europe.

Like old baseball cards, pre–World War I films were made and released, then discarded after initial reception. Thus, we have the depressing fact that 80 percent of films from nearly all national cinemas of this era are no longer extant.

While no national cinema survived the war intact, some national industries suffered more than others. German productions (which were heavily influenced by Danish cinema), along with Italian and Austrian productions, took heavy blows because of the First World War. These national cinemas were also slow to recover.

Irish cinema was fortunate in one way: It became home for a time to Kalem, the first American company to film abroad, whose main director, Sidney Olcott, made spirited films about Irish life. Great Britain, which ruled Ireland at the time, produced thousands of silents; its films too vanished. In fact, British silent (and early sound) cinema is one of the least known of European cinemas.

From the war years to the transition to sound, the dispiriting trend continued: Two-thirds of the world's films from that era vanished. In the United States the number of films produced during this period was enormous. *Film Daily* alone, for instance, reviewed some 12,000 releases.

Unknown to most film enthusiasts are the prolific filmmaking efforts of some European states. On the Iberian Peninsula, filmmaking flourished. Hundreds of films were made in Spain, especially in the region of Catalonia, between 1897 and 1923, and its headquarters was Barcelona. In Lisbon (thanks to an influx of French filmmakers) silent filmmaking thrived in the period 1919–25, and revived in the early period of sound. But many of these films are long gone, too.

Swedish cinema had a golden age until it began emulating Hollywood in the early 1920s, and then Hollywood stripped it bare of its important filmmakers. Greek filmmaking in the 1920s flourished, but the coming of sound silenced that industry too—and most of the worthwhile Greek films disappeared. Dutch filmmaking, little known to the outside world, was extremely prolific in the silent era. It is only now becoming clear that Dutch film industry may have been the equal of any in Europe, the scope of its accomplishments matched only by modern Dutch filmmakers.

The introduction of, and the transition to, sound sent many of the world's studios into confusion, if not a panic, causing them to reshuffle projects in the works, add "sound" to silent films, and hire stage performers in their haste to put out talkies. The early sound films were deemed expendable in order to gain expertise in the new technology. And foreign-language productions, initially embraced by Hollywood companies in the film capital as well as in Europe—notably Paramount in Paris—suffered terribly. The productions were transitory, experimental efforts to hold onto world market shares until things stabilized or competitors dropped out.

The outbreak of the Second World War ended meaningful film production in Germany and most of Europe. From the period 1930–50, 15 percent of the films made in America and Europe are missing.

# Austria

A few months after the Lumière brothers' movies premiered in Paris, Eugene Dupont arrived in Vienna, bringing along movie shorts. He held the first film show in Vienna on March 27, 1896. The earliest Austrians to make films, beginning in 1902, were the documentary filmmakers Anton Kolm, his wife Luise Kolm (daughter of Louis Veltée, a film promoter since 1896), and their assistant Jakob Fleck. Their first important work, however, was *Von Stufe zu Stufe* (1908), which was the first Austrian fictional film. They made it in collaboration with the stage director Heinz Hanus.

In 1911, the Kolms and Fleck founded Wiener Kunstfilm, expanding beyond films of nonfiction and adaptations of fairground attractions to make farces and passion plays, often starring the stage actors Lotte Medelsky, Philipp Zeska, and the comic Karl Blasl. Until the outbreak of the war, Austrian movies relied on star power: popular singers, comedians, cabaret performers, stage actors, opera singers, and the operetta darlings Mizzi Gunther, Louise Kartousch, and Richard Waldemar, the opera tenors Hubert Marischka, Alexander Girardi, and Bernhard Baumeister (all in *Der Millionenonkel*, 1913).

By the time of the war, Austrians had made a great variety of movies, nearly 300 in all, but few were based on original material. The themes of these films were very broad, circumscribed by the needs of expression without sound, and borrowed from the traditional media of literature and operetta. Two of the country's earliest film stars were Liane Haid and Magda Sonja, and one of its most creative directors was the operetta librettist Felix Dörmann. Another filmmaker of note, Alexander Kolowrat, became known as the "film count," establishing his name as the producer nearly 150 films at his Sascha-Filmfabrik production company in the years 1912–27. He accounted for 15 percent of Austrian silents.

## Das Drama von Mayerling

(Karl Gerhardt and Hans Otto Löwenstein, 1919). Austria Film. **Script:** Fritz Lang. **With** Eugen Neufeld (Crown Prince Rudolf) and Midy Elliott (Mary Vetsera). A controversial film — the first to tell the story — made during the 30th anniversary marking the mysterious death (or disappearance, according to others) of Austria's Crown Prince Rudolf. It is a film that implies that the First World War might have been avoided if this man had come to rule an empire.

A man of intelligence, culture, purpose, energy, and standards, Crown Prince Rudolf was a liberal within a nest of ruling vipers. His intended reforms were seen as a threat to the position of the clergy and the power of reactionary forces in the Habsburg empire. Further, Rudolf's enemies feared that Emperor Francis Joseph might abdicate in his favor. In January 1889, in a hunting pavilion in Mayerling, 25 miles from Vienna, the 31-year-old Prince, and his companion, Baroness Maria Vetsera, were found dead. They had been under surveillance by the secret police.

The deaths were officially declared suicides by gunshot. Archduke Franz Ferdinand, a believer in the alliance between church and state, became heir-apparent to the Habsburg throne under the strongly conservative Emperor Francis Joseph I.

This film pins the blame for Rudolf's death on a group of aristocrats and allies within the church. Though made in the first year after the founding of the republic, it was immediately banned. It vanished. Six years later, the empire having been forever torn asunder by the war, Hans Löwenstein directed *Das Geheimnas des Leibfiakers Brattfisch (Coachman Brattfisch's Secret)* (with Zathonai and Maria Corda), a treatment of the same conspiracy theme, containing scenes from the 1919 film. He saw his 1925 film released.

## Durch die Quartiere des Elends und Verbrechens (Through the Quarters of Poverty and Crime)

(Robert Land, 1920). Micheluzzi-Film. **Script:** Emil Kläger. **Photography:** Otto Kanturek. **With** Alfred Gerasch, Walter Huber, Anna Kallin, and Armin Seydelmann. A dark, brooding four-reel (1,675-meter) social drama of the Vienna underworld thriving amidst urban misery, a standout example of the genre.

In 1928, Land, in Berlin, directed *I Kiss Your Hand, Madame*, starring Marlene Dietrich in just about the finest of her 20 or so silents.

## Einen Jux will er sich machen (He Wants to Have Fun)

(Emil Leyde, 1916). Robert-Müller-Film. **With** Ida Ribka (Mrs. Fischer), Poldi Müller (Marie), Leopold Strabmayer (Melchior), and Gustav Müller. A humorous three-reel tale, based on the 1842 dramatic comedy by Johann Nestroy (1802–1862), that signaled the demise of what were termed Austria's "grotesque comedies" of the prewar years. The production was a turn towards more sophisticated fare that shows how quickly confusing entanglements can develop, and that they do not necessarily come about with lies.

The action begins when the village spice shopkeeper asks his assistant to watch the place in his absence. Off he goes, moved by an urge for adventure, to the city. But the man comes upon brazen women, including the widow Mrs. Fischer, and the most embarrassing situations, which cause him to travel under an assumed name. In addition, his niece Marie shows up, having fled from her undesirable bridegroom. The matchmaking abilities of Mrs. Fischer and a rich inheritance help to straighten out all difficulties in the end.

This film's basis became the inspiration for Thornton Wilder's 1939 play *The Merchant of Yonkers* as well as his 1957 play *The Matchmaker,* the blockbuster hit *Hello, Dolly,* and Tom Stoppard's 1981 play *On the Razzle.*

## Die Gottesgeißel (The Scourge of God)

(Mihály Kertész, 1920). Sascha-Filmfabrik. **Script:** Ladislaus Vajda. **Photography:** Gustav Ucicky. **With** Lucy Doraine, Anton Tiller, and Svetozar Petrov. One of Kertész's earliest films after he departed Hungary, the 100-minute (six reels; 2,000-meter) spectacle (based on a Georges Ohnet work) is the followup to Kertész's *Der Stern von Damaskus* (1920).

The one-time lover of a struggling young artist who has harmed her in a fit or rage recovers from her physical wounds. At the same time, the young woman climbs the social ladder, becoming the owner of luxurious property. One day she meets the artist, now married, with whom she's still in love. When he doesn't yield to her advances — even as she threatens blackmail about his unsavory past — she becomes insane and dies of rejection.

## G'schichten aus der Steiermark (Stories from Styria)

(Hans Otto Löwenstein, 1929). Ottoton Film/Eagle Film. **With** Hilde Maria (Vroni), Anny Burg (Anni), Manya Mille, Karl Leiter (Hannes), Lois Gross (Lois), and Sepp Wendl (Sepp). A six-reel (2,000-meter) drama of the lives of servants living in Styria (or Steiermark), the region in central Austria whose main city is Graz.

## Inferno

(Paul Czinner, 1920). Pax-Film. **Script:** Czinner. **Photography:** Adolf Schlesinger. **With** Grete Lundt (Eve), Erik Schmedes (Ulrik), and Franz Herterich (Gerdner). One of Czinner's first films was this five-reel expressionistic drama (also called *Das Spiel mit dem Teufel* [*The Play with the Devil*]), which turned out to be the first such Austrian work and one of the country's most significant contributions to cinematic expressionism. Lundt plays the uninhibited wife murdered by her husband. In the film, "thousands of hands stretch out toward the newcomers," wrote a critic.

The production was made in Vienna, and is apparently based on Czinner's 1912 story, *Satans maske, groteske in einem akt ...* (*Satan's Mask, a Grotesque in One Act...*). According to the evidence, the film, which costars the opera singer Schmedes, was well received.

## Irrlichter der Tiefe (Illusive Lights of the Depth)

(Fritz Freisler, 1923). Friesler-Film. **Script:** Paul Fink. **With** Josef Peterhaus, Julius Strobl, Nora Gregor, and Ilse

Lorm. An early six-reel (2,300-meter) melodrama starring Nora Gregor, also called *Wankende Erde.*

## Lilith und Ly

(Erich Kober, 1919). Fiat-Film. **Script:** Fritz Lang. **Photography:** Willy Hameister. **With** Elga Beck (Lilith/Ly), Hans Marschall (Frank Landrow), Ernst Escherich (Mundarra), and Franz Kammauf. One of Lang's most forgotten fantasies is this Austrian work, made during one of his most productive periods, which was inspired by his travels to "exotic" regions of the East. Elements that Lang would later display in his German films are laid out here: magical spells, miracle-working stones from the Orient, vampirism, utopian discoveries and gentlemanly recklessness, and technical and supernatural force fields that bounce off one another. *Die Filmwelt* called Lang's film a "singular idea, and a beautiful direction" that "add up to a sensational film."

It centers on Mundarra, who is in love with the beautiful Ly, but she won't have him. To console himself, he sculpts her image, which he names Lilith. Landrow, his insomniac friend, discovers an Eastern parchment and ruby which can bring the inanimate to life. But there is a terrible secret at the heart of this tale, which was influenced by Wegener's *Der Golem* (1915).

## Der Millionenonkel (Uncle Moneybags)

(Hubert Marischka, 1913). Sascha-Filmfabrik. **Script:** Hubert and Ernst Marischka. **With** Alexander Girardi, Hubert Marischka, Hilde Radney, Marietta Weber, Leo Fall, and Bernhard Baumeister. The celebrated Girardi (then 63) and his company put together this memorable work, a five-reel adaptation of a 19th century operetta by Adolf Müller. The film became a tribute to Alexander Girardi, who reprises performances from 30 of his stage works. But the great star had this to say about the difficulties of acting in front of the camera: "I'll always think of you—Mr. Dentist."

The production, however, was a success in Austria and Germany. A critic wrote: "While we expected a potpourri from old operettas, we got nothing short of an operetta, with hit tunes, which delighted the ear and will certainly become popular from the cinema. The music, which lasted around two hours, was really long enough for two operettas. Exciting waltzes and dashing marches alternated, and one could literally feel the pleasure with which the gifted composer had approached his work."

That composer was Robert Stolz, who had been commissioned to compose the music for Marischka's silent medley of a film. Contrary to the usual movie music of that time, which was exclusively played by one pianist, it had to be incidental music for great orchestra this time. Therefore, Stolz used the established music of the corresponding works in the film and tied them together in his individual fashion, including *Der Verschwender, Brüderlein fein, Armes Mädel, Er und seine Schwester, Bruder Straubinger, Der Arme Jonathan, Der Zigeunerprimas, Mam'zelle Nitouche, Heisses Blut, Der Lustige Krieg, Der Künstlerblut Obersteiger, Der Vogelhändler, Der Bauer als Millionär, Fürstin Ninetta, Der Zigeunerbaron, Gasparone, Der Bettelstudent, Die Fledermaus, Heimliche Liebe, Die Jungfrau von Bellevil,* and *Mein Leopold.*

### Mit Gott für Kaiser und Reich (With God for Kaiser and Reich)

(Luise Kolm and Jakob Fleck, 1916). Wiener Kunstfilm. **With** Hermann Benke (Major von Hess), Josefine Josephi, Liane Haid, and Hans Rhoden. A sentimental four-reel work of propaganda that concludes it's possible to serve both god and country during the great conflict.

### Moderne Tänze (Modern Dances)

(1923). Filmwerke. **With** Anita Berber and Sebastian Droste. A scandalous one-reel (300-meter) documentary featuring the infamous Anita Berber, star of Berlin café society in the 1920s, and her partner Sebastian Droste. Berber (born in 1898) was one of the first nude dancers of the era and a most scandalous woman in Weimar Berlin. She and Droste preferred vice, horror, and ecstasy as the subjects of their dances, captured in this film, which confronted society with the topics of desire, love, dissipation, homosexuality, and drug use.

Berber began her career as a serious ballet dancer, but became known for her unconventional living, often seen in public in tuxedos and a monacle. Gossip and outrage followed her wherever she went. She died of tuberculosis in 1928.

### Musikantenlene

(Felix Dörmann, 1912). Vindobona-Film. **Script:** Emil and Arnold Golz. **With** Eugenie Bernay, Julius Brandt, Felix Brandt, Karl Schauer, and Ferdinand Stein. Also called *Roman einer Sängerin* (*Novel of a Singer*), this film helped make the name of Eugenie Bernay a household word. "This young lady," wrote a critic, "highly gifted artistically, surrounded by loveliness, possesses an uncommon talent, her supple figure is as if created for the movies, and her eyes take the place of a whole language." At performances of the 1,200-m film, Strauss's music was played, along with melodies by Philip Silber.

### Der Pfarrer von Kirchfeld (The Pastor of Kirchfeld)

(Luise Kolm and Jakob Fleck, 1914). Wiener Kunstfilm. **With** Max Neufeld (Pastor Hell), Hans Rhoden (Wurzensepp), Polly Janisch (Anna Birkmeier), and Lilly Károly. This became a well-received comedy based on Ludwid Anzengruber's story about the celibacy — or lack thereof — of a minister. What made the four-reel (1,500-meter) film popular was the fact that audiences were anticlerical and ready to laugh at the plot; the film's erotic scenes were enjoyed with a smirk while references to class evoked an immediate response.

In the comedy, one such scene concerns a working man who refuses money from a wealthy individual, saying, "Keen Bettler bin ich nicht" ("I'm not no begger"). Audiences responded warmly to the film's sense of human love, justice, and fine deeds, becoming irritated at hints of intrigue. This film allowed them to do what they wanted most: to laugh. The popular film also signaled the end of the practice of deliberately inserting stock landscape shots to offer the illusion of atmospheric adaptations. Instead, the actual, "wonderful nature shots" were a prelude to a whole series of similar Austrian films in the war years.

### Speckbacher

(Pierre Paul Gilmans, 1913). Jupiter-Film. **Script:** Gilmans. **With** Ferdinand

Exl (Josef Speckbacher), Hans Kratzer, Anton Ranzenhofer, Eduard Köck, and Josef Auer. Also called *Die Todesbraut* (*Death Bride*), the production is a one-hour (three-reel) drama of one of the nation's Tirolean leaders — others were Andréas Hofer, Joachim Haspinger, and Peter Mayr — who repelled the invaders from Saxony allied with Napoleon in the early part of the 19th century. The film was notable for its use of 2,000 extras, its historical costumes, actual weapons (from the Andréas Hofer Museum in Innsbruck), the decoration of many of the sets, and the staged battles.

### Das Spielzeug von Paris (The Plaything of Paris)

(Mihály Kertész, 1925). Sascha Film-fabrik/Phoebus Film. **Script:** Adolf Lantz and Arthur Berger. **Photography:** Gustav Ucicky and Max Nekut. **Design:** Arthur Berger. **With** Lily Damita (Lily), Eric Barclay (Miles Seward), Henry Treville (Viscomte de la Rochevaudray), Hugo Timing (theater manager), Théo Shall (Fournichon), and Hans Moser. Based on Margery Lawrence's novel *Red Heels*, this contemporary 150-minute (3,000-meter) Austrian-German production helped Kertész get to Hollywood.

The director "doesn't mince matters nor does he go out to find nasty situations or emphasize suggestiveness." Damita plays the gamin who becomes an exotic dancer in Vienna and Paris, where she is mistress to an aristocrat and the chief attraction of "Le Lapin Rouge" who gives it all up for the love of a young diplomat. Before she alters her life, she "strips consistently, but she wears her nakedness gracefully and without a sign of self-consciousness. She has ability which will raise her high in the profes-

sion without the need for nudity," wrote a critic.

The openly sexual film was called "excellent." The staging is "good and realistic. Cabarets, theaters, backstage, houses of the mighty, fishing village setting, and the like are ... included," wrote a critic. Interestingly, the theater manager, the viscomte, and a host of other parts "are admirably played by true artists, and, such being the case these days, their names are carefully withheld from billing."

Containing storm scenes that "are the best seen in some time," the film was released in Britain — but "in no way is this a British picture" came the disclaimer. There it was shown under the title *Red Heels*.

### Sterbewalzer (Waltz of Death)

(Felix Dörmann, 1915). Duca-Film. **Script:** Felix Dörmann. **With** Bertha Scrutin (Mascha), Eugen Jensen, Paul Richter, and Anton Garv. A three-reel (1,200-meter) romance, also called *Todeswalzer*, based on the director's 1907 libretto *A Walzertraum*, it is the tale of great love, renunciation, and voluntary death. The center of attraction is the daughter of a lawyer, who has to choose one of two husser officers for a husband. When she's ready, she will signal her intentions by asking the favored to dance a waltz. Her father, naturally, wants her to choose the richer man. The poorer one who is, naturally, the one she loves, makes the choice of committing suicide.

### Der Stern von Damaskus (The Star of Damascus)

(Mihály Kertész, 1920). Sascha-Filmfabrik. **Script:** Kertész and Ivan Siklósi. **Photography:** Gustav Ucicky. **With** Lucy

Doraine, Anton Tiller, and Svetozar Petrov. A 100-minute (six reels; 2,000 meter) drama based on a novel by Georges Ohnet, the film was one of Kertész's earliest in Austria, after his departure from Hungary. The production was photographed by the studio's chief cameraman, Ucicky, and featured a young Ivan Petrovich (then known as Svetozar Petrov). Equally unusual is the fact that the film had a sequel called *Die Gottesgeißel* (1920).

The story begins in Damascus, where a struggling young artist takes a mistress. But when she is forsaken, she avenges herself by taking in another man. When the artist surprises the pair, he wounds her in a fight. Sentenced to work at hard labor, he escapes, founds an artists school, and marries one of his pupils, an heiress to a fortune. While his life has turned for the better, the fate of the mistress is in question. The sequel concerns itself with her — and a bit more with the artist.

### Der Traum eines österreichischen Reservisten (The Dream of an Austrian Reservist)

(Luise Kolm and Jakob Fleck, 1915). Wiener Kunstfilm. A four-reel (1,500-meter) "tone picture," based on the well-known Carl Michael Ziehrer's operetta, that signaled the studio's desire to make patriotic films. When this film was shown, it was accompanied musically by the 40-man-strong Viennese Tone Art Orchestra (Wiener Tonkunstlerorchester) which allowed, in effect, a cinematically interpreted musical program. It had the critics writing, "We hear formally the gallop of the horse, the hurrah of the rider, the sound of the weapons, the thunder of the cannons fired at a distance."

Ziehrer (1843–1922) was a composer of dance music, at the same time becoming a top military bandmaster. Operettas appeared from 1866, with his most notable successes at the turn of the century. Few of his operettas are performed today outside of Vienna, though his marches remain popular. He was the last imperial and royal hofballmusikdirektor, succeeding the Johann Strausses in 1908.

### Der Verschwender (The Spendthrift)

(Luise Kolm and Jacob Fleck, 1917). Wiener Kunstfilm. **With** Marie Marchal (Cheristane), Wilhelm Klitsch (Flottwell), Hans Thoden (Valentin), and Liane Haid (Amalie). A two-part (1,800-meter and 1,600-meter) tale of a rich man's fall and redemption over a 30-year period, based on the Ferdinand Raimund's 1834 magical, allegorical, and instructive fairy tale as well as the popular opera. The most costly Austrian film of its day and one of the first big Austrian costumes films, the production brought stage magic to life on the screen. Just as important, it made Liane Haid, playing the wealthy, generous Flottwell's daughter Amalie, the first Austrian international star.

Until this film, Haid had played the type of Viennese girl full of youthful charm, a national type (trained as a dancer) who was graceful in movement. After a scintillating performance in the first part of the production, in which she is full of charm and grace, "she amazed as an aged family mother through the purity of her characterization" in the second part, wrote the critics.

### Von Stufe zu Stufe (From Step to Step)

(Heinz Hanus, 1908). Anton Kolm. Story: Hanus and Luise Kolm. **Photography:** Jakob Fleck. **With** Heinz Hanus

(Count Werner), Miss Steiner (Annerl), Claudius Veltée, and Rudolf Stiabny. This film inaugurated Austrian feature film production. Made by a director from Vienna's Renaissance Theater, it is an 800-meter tale of a girl from Vienna who is seduced by a raffish count. The production was shot on location, and contemporary dress was worn by the principals.

The story begins in the colorful bustle of the Volksprater, the well-known amusement park in Vienna. It leads Annerl from the shooting gallery to the milieu of the ruling class of the young count Werner to the castle of Waldheim. After many painful disillusionments through high-class society, the film takes her back to her home. Finally, wrote Hanus, "there is still a happy ending in the colorful hurly-burly life in the Park." One scene of this film survives.

### Wien im Krieg (Vienna in the War)

(Fritz Freisler and Heinz Hanus, 1916). Sascha-Meester-Film. **With** Paul Olmühl, Georg Kundert, and Erich Kober. Finding it impossible to import, let alone distribute, foreign films because of the world war, the Austrian production company backed the making of one of the earliest Austrian films shot on location, a 90-minute (four-reel, 1,800-meter) drama about the great conflict. "What is strikingly manifest from the picture is the love of the fatherland of the Viennese," wrote a critic, "their good-natured gaiety, which does not leave them under any conditions, and the prowess that is characteristic of the soldier in all love of life and geniality and inspires him to heroic deeds in the right spot and the right time" Another observer wrote of the film, "Dear fatherland, you need not worry — when you have such brave fighters, victory is ours."

### Zirkusgräfen (Circus Countess)

(Felix Dörmann, 1912). Helios Film. **Script:** Felix Dörmann. **With** Heinrich Eisenbackh (clown), Mizzi Telmont, Eugenie Bernay, and Felix Dörmann. A clown and his circus colleagues are the subject matter for this intimate, 900-meter tale directed by the highly regarded author, Dörmann. It describes the love of a clown for a beautiful, uninhibited performer. He gives up his life so that she might find a better life outside the circus by becoming the lover of a count.

# Belgium

In 1897, at the World Exhibition in Brussels, films were shown for the first time in Belgium. In 1908 Pathé sent Alfred Machin to the Belgian capital to set up the first studio within the country. Machin was the man behind the hits *La Fille de Delft, Suprême sacrifice, La Pie noir, La Légende de Mina Claessens, Bonaparte, le Bataille de Waterloo,* and *Maudit soit le guerre!,* often starring Blanche Montel, Fernand Gravey, and Albert Dieudonné.

By the First World War, the beginnings of several main trends of Belgium film production — chafing under the influence of French productions — became apparent: explorations, exoticism, ethnography; as well as folklore, or the observations of customs and traditions. Other sources from which inspiration was drawn included historic sites, landscapes, the picturesque, and tourism. During the war, Paul Flon and Henry A. Parys made their names at the Karreveld studio.

In 1921, Hippolye de Kempener, producer of the patriotic *La Belgique martyre* (1919), set up the Machelen studio (Belga-Films) and, in consideration of the local market, backed the making of coproductions, both French and Flemish, which became a natural approach to realizing ends. The studio's early directors included Jacques de Baroncelli, who made *Le Carillon de minuit* (1922) and Julien Duvivier, who made *L'Oeuvre immortelle* (1925).

## Belgique

(Paul Flon, 1920). **Script:** Flon. **Photography:** Freddy Smekern and Rader. **With** Maryse Talbot, Jimmy O'Kelly, Mylo, and Francis Martin. A hugely patriotic production that was shot with government and military support, the film was dedicated to Belgians who lost their lives in the First World War. The propaganda production, which was directed by a war veteran, evokes the horrors of the slaughter but also pays tribute to the pacifism of the industrial nation.

## Le Carillon de minuit (Chime at Midnight)

(Jacques de Baroncelli, 1922). Belga-Films. **Script:** J. Michel Lévy. **Assistants:** Henri Chomette and René Clair. **Photography:** Henri Barreyre. **Design:** Raoul Navez and William Lund. **With** Maggy Théry (Yanna), Loïs Stuart (Laura), Eric Barclay (Neel), Albert Sovet (Fred), Ferdinand Crommelynk, and Hubert Daix. One of the director's earliest efforts is this original, naturally photographed, and sensitively rendered Flemmish folktale of bourgeoisie life during the occupation of Flanders by the Spanish. It centers on the two children of an old violin maker.

Initially titled *La Tour de silence*, the film was apparently destroyed when the studio burned down. Baroncelli became known as a director who could work in almost any genre: melodrama, epic heroism, maritime, and bourgeoisie drama.

## Ce soir à huit heures (This Evening at 8:00)

(Pierre Charbonnier, 1930). **Script:** Charbonnier. **Photography:** Henri Stork. **With** Raymond Rouleau and Lucienne Lemarchand. This fresh and inspired short (shot in Gand, Belgium) shows the influence of the artist Félix Labisse — an admirer of Breughel and Bosch — and is the work of a gifted filmmaker who never made another film.

It is an ensemble of poetic sequences, called "very surrealistic": a bunch of oranges in Flanders Field; dozens of pairs of gloves floating on a creek on which bank two lovers can't stop kissing; and a vagabond motorcyclist being pelted with eggs. At one point, the male lover jumps from a bridge into the creek. Labisse as well as "baron" Mollet (a secretary to Guillaume Appolinaire) witnessed the film's shooting.

### Un Clown dans la rue (A Clown in the Street)

(René Leclère, (1930). **Photography:** Henri Barreyre. **With** Marcel Roels, Tony D'Algy, and Micky Damrémont. Filmed in the tradition of German expressionism and influenced by the most famous circus clown film of an era known for circus films — E. A. Dupont's *Variety* (1925) — this fully realized production is the sorrowful tale of a circus clown in search of love. it costars the handsome Hollywood expatriate D'Algy.

### La Famille Klepkens

(Gaston Schoukens, 1929). **Photography:** Paul Flon. **With** Toontje Janssens, Zizi Festeret, Julia Vanderhoeven, Francis Martin, Florence Nicole, and Rodolphe Verlèze. The director's *Nos peintres* (1923) was one of the earliest "films on art." This late 1920s production — inspired by Duvivier's *Le Mariage de mlle Beulemans* (1927) — was one of the earliest Belgian sound films, made in French and Flemish, and based on vaudeville writer Auguste de Hendrickx's hit comedy.

The production is a picturesque folktale about Belgian tradition. Starring the popular Janssens, the film is steeped in Brussels life, and was a huge hit just as the first talkies were arriving on the market. Its success was due in no small measure to its spirit of inventiveness, imagination, and an ingenious, working sound system and score that Schoukens wrote himself. Having established his name with this archetype of the popular Brussels film, Schoukens became a dominant Belgian filmmaker of the 1930s.

### La Famille Van Peteghem à la mer

(Isidore Moray, 1912). **With** Esther Deltenre and Gustave Libeau. The director, who filmed newsreel items and documentaries, was not content solely to film reality. As one of the pioneers of fiction films, Moray shot this impromptu sea sketch in color (in a process called "Kinemacolor," in red and green). It was his second film, based on the popular stage comedy *Zonneslag et cie*, and was seen by King Albert and Queen Elisabeth. The monarchs were reportedly duly impressed.

### Un Gamin de Bruxelles

(Francis Martin, 1923). Belga-Films. **Script:** Martin. **With** Martin, Suzanne Christy, William Elie, and Léo Ardel (the boy). Also called *Coeur de goose (Heart of Goose)*, this is a film without a rigid story, rather a look at a young protagonist at loose ends.

### Midi (Midday)

(Lucien Backman, 1929). A lifelike, witty report from the streets and dockyards of Brussels.

### L'Oeuvre immortelle (The Immortal Work)

(Julien Duvivier, 1925). Belga-Films/Van Hoven Consortium. **Script:** Duvivier and Maurice Widy. **Photography:** René Dantan and Henry Barreyre. **With** Suzanne Christy (Lucienne), Yvonne Willy, Jacques Van Hoven (Dr. Charles Bosquet), and Jimmy O'Kelly (Stéphane Manin). In the mid–1920s, Duvivier made a number of films (in France and Belgium) that have since vanished, and this period of his career has remained shrouded in mystery. One of these productions was this Belgian-Dutch production, a wrenching, emotion-filled tale about a physician who dedicates his life to finding a cure for tuberculosis, and a young assistant, the daughter of the woman he once loved, with whom he falls in love. She, however, falls for medical technologist Stéphane who discovers that the good doctor doesn't have long to live.

The film ends on the day the doctor discovers a cure — and dies of cancer. The production was initially called *L'Horrible expérience*.

### La Vie à l'envers (The Other Side of Life)

(Lucien Backman, 1930). An amusing work on the everyday movements of people.

# Denmark

In June 1896, at the Panorama on Copenhagen's Town Hall Square, Danes saw moving pictures for the first time. In September 1904 the first cinema in the country opened. It was called the Kosmorama and was situated in the fashionable part of Copenhagen's center. Usually, a showing consisted of three to four films lasting up to 45 minutes. First came a travelogue, then a dramatic film, and then one or two short comedies. Because of the noise from the projector (and to increase entertainment value), a pianist played while the films were running.

The first film pioneer in Denmark was Peter Elfelt (1866–1931), a photographer for the Royal Family who, in addition to films on royalty, specialized in films of the middle class and films about Greenland. His *Henrettelsen* (*The Execution*) (1903) was the first fiction film made in Denmark.

The first Danish film company, Nordisk Films Kompagni, was established in 1906 by Ole Olsen (1863–1943). Nordisk Films, which was the only Danish film company until 1909, cultivated the genres of melodrama, crime, light comedy, and the literary, and demonstrated a reputation for clear, crisp photography by such practitioners as Johan Ankerstjerne (1886–1959). The studio's melodramas often combined the erotic with the sensational. Light comedies included situation comedies, trick films, chase comedies, and comedies of destruction. In its first years, Nordisk broke out of the small Danish market by opening branches in Berlin (in 1906), London (1907), Vienna (1907), and New York (1908). Its success created a boom in the creation of other Danish studios. By the First World War, Nordisk Films was one of the world's largest film companies, and its focus was less the Danish audience and more the international market. Danish fiction films produced in the period 1896–1909 numbered around 250; travelogues, 450.

"Bigger is better" was the slogan for the period 1910–18 when Danish film took some important steps: A 3,000 seat cinema was built in Copenhagen, called the Paladsteatret (it was the largest in Northern Europe); the pianist was replaced by an orchestra; August Blom's *White Slave Trade* (1910) was the first film in Denmark to run more than one reel; Carl Th. Dreyer wrote a score of scripts before becoming a director; specially composed music (by Thorvald Rasch) was played for the first time, for *The Abyss* (1910), starring newcomer Asta Nielsen (1881–1972). Nielsen became world famous and the first European female movie star. Her film career — she made only 4 of her 70 films in Denmark — fell into three periods: a Danish period (1910–1911), her first German period (1911–1916), and her second German period (1919–1932). Her other Danish films were *The Black Dream, The Ballet Dance,* and *Towards the Light.*

Early Danish filmmakers included the prolific August Blom (1869–1947), the refined and stylistic Forest Holger-Madsen (1879–1943), the photographer Alfred Lind (1879–1959), writer-director Hjalmar Davidsen (1879–1958), the exacting A. W. Sandberg (1881–1938), as well as the up and coming Carl Th. Dreyer and Benjamin Christensen. In this period Danish filmmakers favored the psychological, the hallucinatory, and the ghostly, and began to use artificial lighting, which meant that they could film all year round. The first theoretical book on film came from the Dane Jens Locher in 1916, called *How to Write a Film.*

World War I proved fatal for Danish film companies, especially Nordisk Films: In 1917 Danish films were blacklisted by the Allied forces, who claimed that Germany had an interest in Danish film production. Furthermore, Germany forced Nordisk Films to sell its cinemas in Germany to Germans. Ufa, in fact, modeled itself after the giant production company. In the Danish silent period of the teens, 1,250 feature films were produced along with 550 travelogues.

Only 10 percent of Denmark's more than 2,000 silent films survive.

## Bryggerens datter (The Brewer's Daughter)

(Rasmus Ottesen, 1912). Scandinavian-Russian Trade Company. **Script:** Carl Th. Dreyer and Viggo Cavling. **Photography:** Adam Johansen. **With** Olaf Fönss, Emilie Sannom (Emma), Rasmus Ottesen, and Richard Jensen. This production represents Dreyer's first script turned into a film, and one of the most successful films by the Danish film pioneer Ottesen (1871–1949). Dreyer and his journalist friend Cavling (1887–1946) wrote the story in three days, earning 500 crowns. "The road to the cinema," said a biographer, "was henceforth open" to Dreyer, who wrote a score of scripts before becoming a director.

This first film treatment by Dreyer is an 800-meter tale of jealousy in which two men, one an upright worker, and the other a fickle, jealous type, vie for the hand of the beautiful Emma. The melodrama ends in the fashion of the day, by a mad pursuit that delivers the bad guy into the hands of justice. At the same time the film contains particular details demanded by producer Kai van der Aa Kühle (1879–1925), who was the son-in-law of the famous brewer Jacobson, founder of the Carlsberg company. The movie's main set piece is a brewery. One action scene makes use of a famous well located near Elseneur, and another scene has to do with horses barely escaping from a burning stable.

## Det Gamle Chatol (The Old Cabinet)

(Hjalmar Davidsen, 1913). Nordisk Films. **Script:** Carl Th. Dreyer. **Photography:** Louis Larson. **With** Maja Bjerre-Lind, Lauritz Lauritzen (Lt. Cecil Hoff), Ella Sprange (Clara Faber), and Aage Fönss (Lt. Arthur Rogers). Also called *Chatollets Hemmelighed* (*The Secret of the Old Cabinet*), the four-reel (1,200-meter) production is a psychological drama that represents Dreyer's fifth script in his career. Based on a story by Dreyer's journalist-colleague Viggo Cavling, it concerns the search by two officers for a hidden will. Containing action set in the mountains, a rescue of a child, and other "sensational incidents," wrote *Moving Picture World*, "the picture will please many."

## Gillekop (Tortuous)

(August Blom, 1916). Nordisk Films. **Script:** Carl Th. Dreyer. **Photography:** Johan Ankerstjerne. **With** Doris Langkilde, Frederik Jacobsen, Peter Nielsen, Johan Fritz-Petersen, Charles Wilken, and Gunnar Sommerfeldt. This drama represents Dreyer's last script before he became a director. Based on *The Unholy Genius* by Harald Tandrup (1874–1964), the 1700-m film was photographed by Nordisk's first great photographer and directed by the man who discovered Asta Nielsen. Director Blom was responsible for more than 100 silents in the period 1910–25, including *Atlantis* (1913), an early spectacle from Nordisk.

## Den Hvide Djævel (The White Devil)

(Forest Holger-Madsen, 1915). Nordisk Films. **Script:** Carl Th. Dreyer. **Photography:** Marius Clausen. **With** Carlo Wieth (Charles Herveau), Gerd Egede-Nissen (Clothilde de Nucingen), Johannes Ring (Baron de Nucingen), and Svend Kornbech (Jacques Collin). Also called *Djævelens Protégé* (*The Devil's Protege*), the film is a realistic social drama that Dreyer had the freedom to choose to script. His work is based on *Splendeurs et misères de courtesanes* by Honoré de Balzac.

The protagonist of the 1,100-meter film is the predatory and ambitious Jacques Collin (a character based on the real-life Vidocq, a reformed thief who founded the Sûreté, the early French detective agency).

## Lille Claus og store Claus (Little Claus and Great Claus)

(Elith Reumert, 1913). Danish Biograf. **Script:** Peter Nansen. **Photography:** Mads Anton Madsen. **With** Benjamin Christensen (Store Claus), Henrik Lamberg (Lille Claus), Robert Storm Petersen, and Peter Malberg. The well-known production is based on Hans Christian Andersen's disturbing 1835 story of the same name, which was one of his first works. The three-reel (850-meter) adaptation is also the first by Reumert (1885–1934) for the experimental studio whose most well-known filmmaker was Christensen. Their studio took care in making films (most notably Christensen's own 1913 film *Det Hemmelighedsfulde X* [*Orders Under Seal*]), becoming an exponent in the use of light and shadow and editing.

"In a village," goes the tale, "there once lived two men who had the same name. They were both called Claus. One of them had four horses, but the other had only one; so to distinguish them, people called the owner of the four horses, 'Great Claus,' and he who had only one, 'Little Claus.' Now we shall hear what happened to them, for this is a true story."

The film contains a wonderful plot, surprising developments, and sudden shocks as it relates how Little Claus, after losing his prize possession to his bullying rival, manages to outwit him. He becomes a wealthy cattleowner, while Great Claus, unwittingly, ends his own life. One of the earliest films by Christensen is representative of his, and Danish filmgoers', interest in man's darker, more unruly nature.

## Morfinisten (The Morphinist)

(Louis von Kohl, 1911). Scandinavian-Russian Trade Company. **Script:** Lily van der Aa Kühle. **Photography:** Alfred Lind. **With** Robert Schmidt, Lili Bech, and Albrecht Schmidt. The production company's first film (at 900-meters) was the ubiquitous cameraman-director Lind's earliest hit. It is the painful story of a drug user, his affair with a seductive woman, and his suicide. Viggo Cavling, the Danish journalist who often coscripted films with Carl Th. Dreyer, spoke to the attraction of drugs in his book *The Collective Spirit* (1926):

> The fact that people can become the slaves of stimulants which intensify, though but temporarily, their sense of creative activity, is really due to the peculiar satisfaction we experience in feeling the creative power at work within us. And if we cannot get it to work in any other way, we have recourse to alcohol, opium or hashish. The opium-smoker says good-bye to the world of automatism and goes off on a grand tour through the golden realms of fantasy, the wonder- land of the creative power. The word intoxication is used with reference to drugs, such as opium or morphia; but it applies also to the ecstasy of artistic creation.... The opium smoker's trance and the ecstasy of the artist at his work are but a sleeping and a waking form of the same thing. In sleep the result will be visions, phantoms, fantasy; waking, it gives us art, invention, new ideas, a moral exultation.

## Skæbnebæltet (Destiny's Skein)

(Svend Rindom, 1912). Gefion Film. **Script:** Rindom. **With** Benjamin Christensen, Karen Sandberg, Karl Rosenbaum, and Albrecht Schmidt. From the newly created studio Gefion came this 700-meter production that marked Benjamin Christensen's earliest screen appearance, having been encouraged to enter the medium by actor-writer Robert Storm Petersen. It is also an early work by Rindom (1884–1960), who later starred in Dreyer's *Du skal aere din hustru* (1925).

## Den Skønne Evelyn (Evelyn the Beautiful)

(Anders Wilhelm Sandberg, 1915). Nordisk Films. **Script:** Carl Th. Dreyer. **Photography:** Einar Olsen. **With** Rita Sacchetto, Henry Seemann, and Adolf Tronier-Funder. A 1,300-meter drama, also called *Pages from Her Life*, which is based on Viggo Cavling's story. It is one of the exacting director's earliest efforts, and represents another of Dreyer's early scripts for the medium.

### Spiritisten (The Spirits)

(Forest Holger-Madsen, 1914). Nordisk Films. **Script:** Holger-Madsen and Wilhelm Kienzl. **Photography:** Marius Clausen. **With** Marie Dinesen, Robert Schyberg, Carl Alstrup, and Vibeke Kröyer. This example of the director's interest in the fantastic, mysterious, and the hallucinatory (also called *A Voice from the Past* as well as *The Ghosts*) prefigured German expressionism and the 1920s films of Fritz Lang.

# France

World cinema was born in France during *La Belle Epoque*, when the Lumière brothers projected the first films to a paying audience in December 1895. Méliès quickly followed suit with his own movies; a short while later came Zecca and Alice Guy, as well as the enterprising Gaumont and Pathé when they set in place the foundations of their production companies.

The introduction of sound in Hollywood — especially its commercial possibilities — caught the French studios off guard, allowing American studios a chance to capture French filmgoers eager to hear films in their own language. In Hollywood, French-language films were the most important of of the film mecca's foreign-language productions. The mainstay of such productions, however, was Paramount's Joinville studio just outside of Paris, where the production of French-language features and shorts lasted nearly three years, during which the French studios played second fiddle, and catch-up, to the invading Americans. The prospective market was huge: 50 million speakers in France, Belgium, portions of Romania, Switzerland, North Africa, Luxembourg, Quebec province, and such cities as Barcelona, Madrid, New York, and New Orleans.

The list of stars Paramount had under contract was the longest outside of Hollywood. René Guissart, Louis Mercanton, Saint-Granier, and Yves Mirande headed the list of talented filmmakers signed by Paramount. The studio began by producing renditions of Hollywood films, and then original French features — especially boulevard comedies — and shorts. The 150 or so short films, notably the entertaining farces based on Georges Courteline's one-act plays, the musical sketches starring Yvette Guilbert, comedy shorts with Saint-Granier, early bits by Noël-Noël and Paul Colline, and comedies by Bernard Savoir, Willemetz, Saint-Granier, and Georges Rip, now nearly all lost, represent the most shorts made by any studio in France in the 1930s.

Paramount's efforts in Paris were a threat to the source of all this talent: French theater. The Comédie Française, for one, tried to fend off the film competition by decreeing that its members — one of the first to make the leap was Marie Bell — had to obtain permission to work in film. Otherwise the actors would be sued, perhaps barred from the theater. In addition, no more than one company member at a time could be in a film, and no one could be in a film whose story was adapted from a play in the repertoire.

Others objected to the concept of "filmed theater." It did little good, as theater people eagerly signed with Paramount in the French capital. As the debate on filmed theater rose to a crescendo, Louis Jouvet, after working for Paramount in Paris, directed his own version of *Knock* (1933), the play that would be his mascot for nearly 30 years. The following year the Comédie Française relented, allowing one of its productions to be transposed to the screen. It is a wonder that during these years Paramount in Paris could keep track not only of the filmmakers but of the films. Of the nearly 300 French-language productions that came out of Paris by Paramount, only three features — *Marius* (1931), *Topaze* (1932), and *Un Soir de réveillon* (1933) — are extant.

### Adémaï et la nation armée

(Jean de Marguénat, 1932). Paramount. **Script:** Paul Colline. **With** Noël-Noël (Adémaï) and Léonce Corne. Filmed in Paris, this 25-minute comedy marked the initial screen appearance of the rustic and naive character named Adémaï. He is a bit Chaplineque, with beard stubble, a pointed nose, small eyes, and a mild voice. His saving grace is his gentle manner and resourcefulness. Though he precipitates much trouble, he always comes to the rescue. In this film, the action takes place in the military because the French ministry has decreed that all civilians, including women, children, and old men, serve 21-day tours of duty — and Adémaï is a barracks instructor. The comic character formed the basis for several feature-length French films until after the Second World War. None of the films ever made it to the United States.

### Adémaï Joseph à l'O.N.M.

(Jean de Marguénat, 1933). Paramount. **Script:** Paul Colline. **With** Noël-Noël and Léonce Corne. A 15-minute Joinville comedy, the second in the series, about the bumbling Adémaï who is appointed to the post of weatherman at the Eiffel Tower.

### Ah! quelle gare! (To Which Station)

(René Guissart, 1932). Paramount. **Photography:** Ted Pahle. **Music:** Raoul Moretti. **With** Jeanne Boitel (Hélène), Milly Mathis (Agrippine), Armand Dranem (Tuvache), and Armand Lurville (Lescudier). A 65-minute original Paris comedy (initially titled *Pétoche* and *Ça roule...*) about a traveler sneaking aboard an overnight train. The culprit is found out, and the fun begins.

### L'Aimable lingère (The Polite Seamstress)

(Donatien, 1932). Paramount. An old baron, his son-in-law the count, and the viscount Gaston, who is the count's nephew, vie for the attention of the beautiful saleswoman of the town, Clara. Filmed in Paris, this risqué 30-minute short is based on the 1899 one-act comedy by Tristan Bernard. It is also known as *Chaque âge à ses plaisirs* (*Every Age to Its Pleasures*).

### A mi-chemin du ciel (Halfway up the Sky)

(Alberto Cavalcanti, 1930). Paramount. **Adaptation:** Cavalcanti. **Dialogue:** Georges Neveux. **Photography:**

Jacques Montéran and Ted Pahle. **With** Janine Merrey (Greta Nelson), Thomy Bourdelle (Jim), Marguerite Moreno (Mrs. Elsie), Enrique de Rivero (Fred Lintz), Raymond LeBoursier, and Jean Mercanton. This 87-minute Paris production, based on the much shorter *Half-Way to Heaven* (1929), takes place in a circus — a locale made world famous by E. A. Dupont's *Variety* (1925). The film centers on a young trapeze artist who falls in love with a beautiful member of the troupe, who happens to be another performer's girlfriend. He soon becomes the prime suspect in a murder. The film, released in Paris in June 1931, was snubbed because of its American setting and because director Cavalcanti cast his longtime friend, the heavily accented de Rivero, in the starring role.

## L'Amour guide

(Norman Taurog and Jean Boyer, 1933). Paramount. **With** Maurice Chevalier, Emile Chautard, and Jacqueline Francell. Filmed in Hollywood, this is the 80-minute version of *The Way to Love* (1933), also starring Chevalier. The comedian plays his characteristic American role, an upbeat Parisian bohemian who has only one goal in life: to be a tour guide in his beloved city. However, he becomes enmeshed in a love triangle. Production of the film became enmeshed in difficulties of its own. Two-and-one-half weeks into shooting, the costar of the English version, Sylvia Sidney, walked out of the picture. To make matters worse, other actors departed because of commitments elsewhere. Paramount signed on replacements and filming of both productions resumed, but when everything was over, Chevalier, irked about being typecast, signed with MGM.

As the only French film out of Hollywood in 1933, it was Paramount's last such production in Hollywood.

## Les As du turf (Aces of the Turf)

(Serge de Poligny, 1932). Paramount. **Script and dialogue:** Saint-Granier and Marc-Hély. **Photography:** Jacques Montéran. **Music:** Charles Borel-Clerc. **Design:** Henri Ménessier. **With** Josayne (Ginette), Paul Pauley (Lafleur), Alexandré Dréan (Papillon), Janett Flo (Lulu), Madeleine Guitty, and Jeanne Fusier-Gir. This 80-minute original Paris production (initially titled *Canari*) is Poligny's fast-paced racetrack farce, containing plenty of Gallic wisecracks. The story centers around characters named "Flower" and "Butterfly," Lafleur and Papillon, a pair of inveterate hangers-on whose financial and amorous adventures with Ginette and Lulu at the track reminded viewers of the more familiar Hollywood comedy team of Laurel and Hardy. The film was well received at its Paris premiere in March 1932. Released the United States in May 1935, it met this reception: "In view of the fact," wrote *Motion Picture Herald*, "that the greater part of the comedy lies in dialogue ... a knowledge of the language is practically a prerequisite to enjoyment of the film.... For [French-speaking patrons] the film contains considerable amusement."

## L'Athlète incomplet (L'Athlète malgré lui) (The Athlete Despite Himself)

(Claude Autant-Lara, 1932). Warner Bros. **With** Jeannette Ferney and Douglas Fairbanks, Jr. This 93-minute Hollywood French-language comedy about a mild-mannered college bookstore clerk who wins the girl by winning at track is based on Mervyn LeRoy's *Local Boy Makes Good* (1931), starring Joe E. Brown. Autant-Lara directed his film on the grounds of UCLA. Producer Irving Asher remembered Fairbanks's performance. "Nobody," he said, "would believe he was speaking such absolutely perfect French" when the film came out in Paris. The film's initial title was *Olympic 13 gagnant*.

## Avec l'assurance (With Assurance)

(Roger Capellani, 1932). Paramount. **Script and dialogue:** Saint-Granier. **Music:** Charles Borel-Clerc and Marcel Lattès. **Songs:** Saint-Granier. **Photography:** Fred Langenfeld. **With** Jeanne Helbling, Madeleine Guitty, Saint-Granier, André Berley, and Jean Mercanton. Another original Paramount production out of Paris, this risqué 84-minute slapstick comedy filmed at the French coast stars Saint-Granier as an insurance agent who finds the time not only to drum up business but to try out his would-be acting skills among the wealthy clientele at a hotel resort in Nice. "Until the fadeout," wrote the *New York Times* upon the film's release in 1935, "there is action, action, action. The excellent work of the leading players … is supported by a first-rate ensemble, embracing some of the prettiest young women yet seen on the French screen here."

## L'Aviateur

(William S. Seiter, 1931). Warner Bros. **Supervisor:** Jean Daumery. **With** Jeanne Helbling, Douglas Fairbanks, Jr. Rolla Norman and André Cheron. This 70-minute Hollywood French comedy is about a clerk who pens a book on aviation and then has to back up his claim to being an expert flyer. This "likely moneymaker" was touted for its flying gags, "as these are a welcome novelty," wrote *Variety*. Douglas Fairbanks, Jr. in his first French-langauge film, "speaks French very well for an American," noted the trade journal. The film is based on Warner Bros.–First National's hits *The Aviator* (1929) and *Going Wild* (1931), directed by Roy del Ruth and William S. Seiter, respectively.

## L'Avion de minuit (Midnight Plane)

(Dimitri Kirsanoff, 1938). Amical Films. **Script:** Kirsanoff and Louis Ténars. **Photography:** Enzo Riccione and Jacques Braun. **Design:** Aimé Bazin. **Music:** André Galli. **With** Colette Darfeuil (Colette), Abel Jaquin (Morel), Ginette d'Yd (Jacqueline), Jules Berry (Inspector Leroy), André Luguet (Carlos), Max Maxudian (Alberstein), and Georges Bever. Roger Labric's novel is the basis of this drama by a director who said, "le cinéma est un langage" and who had an instinctive understanding of the place of sound in film. In this late 1930s production, commercial pilot Morel and Colette fall in love during a stopover. She is careful to hide the fact that she is involved with a band of crooks, and succeeds in escaping from her dangerous friends in a shootout that eliminates the bad guys. This 90-minute film came after Kirsanoff's tragic, classic tale of an abduction and vendetta, *Rapt* (1934), called "a striking example of the suppression of superfluous words. Well worth seeing."

## Baleydier

(Jean Mamy, 1931). Braunberger-Richebé. **Script:** André Girard. **Dialogue:** Jacques Prévert. **Photography:** Roger Hubert. **With** Michel Simon (Baleydier), Josseline Gael (Lola), and Pierre Pradier (Petrequin). French filmmaking and marketing are deliciously critiqued from beginning to end in this 75-minute production. The story follows the rise to fame of a simple hairdresser's assistant. By winning a contest to head the cast in a picture, Baleydier goes on to become a star, with his girlfriend Lola along for the ride. His roles include playing Nero in a production directed by arty filmmaker "Petrequin." Shooting in a ridiculous manner, and including spectacular scenes of the fall of Rome, the fictional director emulates the outlandish and outsized Abel Gance. "The whole thing is fun for professionals," wrote a Paris reviewer.

## Bar du sud (Southern Bar)

(Henri Fescourt, 1938). **Script:** André Beucier. **Dialogue:** Jacques Chabannes. **Photography:** Raymond Agnel. **Music:** Jacques Dallin and Jane Bos. **With** Charles Vanel (Capt. Olivier), Tania Fédor (Elsa), Jean Galland (Arnold), Dolly Davis, and Lucien Galas. A wide-open-spaced tale set in North Africa, the film represented French cinema's attempt to locate its own wild west. But for the looming war that soon enough became a reality, French films might have had a whole new arena upon which to set their dramas. Charles Vanel plays a captain in the colonial intelligence service, on the trail of a superarms dealer. The twist in the 80-minute film is that the man in question (Galland) sends his beautiful wife (Fédor)—she believes him to be an oil prospector—to North Africa to find out what she can about the captain who is after him. The tables are turned when she falls in love with the tough-talking, horse-riding officer. "The story moves exceptionally well for a French pic," noted a critic. "Vanel is perfectly at home in a role like this."

## La Belle dame sans merci

(Germaine Dulac, 1920). Films D.H. **Story:** Irène Hillel-Erlanger. **Adaptation:** Dulac. **Photography:** Jacques Oliver. **With** Yolande Hillé, Daleyme (Lola de Sandoval), Denise Lorys (Countess d'Amaury, Jean Toulot (Guy d'Amaury), and Pierre Mareg. In this avante-garde and prefeminist tract by director Dulac and her longtime colleague Irène Hillel-Erlanger, the beautiful Lola has broken more hearts than she can recall. When she meets an old flame, the count d'Amaury, his son falls for her. At that point the count senses the dangerous passions that have come to life for everyone within his family—but he avoids making Lola the scapegoat in his efforts to ensure that no one gets hurt emotionally. Director Dulac favored the visual component of film over other elements of cinema—she characterized any film's story as a starting point, "a surface only"—and this 1,900-meter film bears her personal stamp. Prisms distort and multiply images in order to represent the character's mental states. Objects move, the camera moves with them—all novel effects in films at that time.

## La Belle marinière (The Beautiful Mariner)

(Harry Lachmann, 1932). Paramount. **Script:** Marcel Achard. **Photography:** Rudolph Maté. **Music:** Maurice Yvain. **Design:** Henri Ménessier. **Editor:** Jean Delannoy. **With** Madeleine Renaud (Marinette), Pierre Blanchar (Sylvestre), Rosine Deréan (Mique), and Jean Gabin (Pierre). An 80-minute original Paramount production out of Paris, the film was based on a 1929 play by Achard, and it represents Achard's fourth effort for the studio. Director Lachmann brought tenderness and humor to this romantic, insightful melodrama about the people whose lives center around a barge named "The Belle Marinière," which makes its way along the extensive river and canal systems of France. In this arena, one of the last in which life moves at a slower pace, love blooms (even as daily life and work intrude) between the handsome Pierre and the boat captain's daughter, Marinette. Her beautiful, younger sister Mique is also interested in Pierre.

## Le Beau rôle (The Good Act)

(Roger Capellani, 1932). Paramount. **Script:** Georges Rip. **With** Dranem, Edwige Feuillère, Léonce Corne, and Robert Arnoux. A 21-minute comedy sketch that has rising star Feuillère, in her fifth film for Paramount in Paris, playing a femme fatale to a crime boss.

## Big House (Revolte dans la prison)

(Paul Fejos and George Hill, 1931). MGM. **Dialogue:** Yves Mirande. **With** Charles Boyer, Mona Goya, André Berley, André Burgère, Rolla Norman, Georges Mauloy, Geymond Vital, and Emile Chautard, and Gustav Diessl. Filmed in Hollywood, this 95-minute French-language drama of prison tensions, a breakout, and a massacre in San Quentin is based on MGM's hugely successful *The Big House* (1930), starring Wallace Beery and Chester Morris, about which *Harrison's Report* wrote, "from the point of view of realism, few pictures ... can equal." The peripatetic Paul Fejos obtained the assignment after Jacques Feyder had dropped out. Their studio, led by Mayer and Thalberg, "was then the studio at the top," Fejos said, "not in art but at least in intelligence. I started working there, and the first picture I made was a picture which already existed in English ... and I needed to make this in French and German [*Menschen Hinter Gittern*]. Possibly the only interesting thing in it was that I imported for *Big House* an actor who afterwards became quite a potentate in Hollywood — Charles Boyer." The film's real stars were its contingent of European actors who rivaled any other cast put together on MGM's lot. After that effort, Fejos, who had worked in Hollywood for three years, left for Europe. As it turned out, his French and German versions of *Big House* were available for viewing only in Europe.

## Le Bluffeur

(André Luguet and Henry Blanke, 1932). Warner Bros. **Dialogue:** Luguet. **With** Luguet, Jeannette Ferney, Emile Chautard, and André Cheron. The studio's last French-language film out of Hollywood (it produced four French films in America, and three in Germany between 1930 and 1932) is an 80-minute comedy about a con man who convinces a would-be tycoon that there's a fortune to be made in rubber. It was based on WB–First National's *High Pressure* (1932), directed by Mervyn LeRoy, which *Variety* called "well-acted." André Luguet codirected the film because Henry Blanke was too anxious about handling the assignment on his own.

## Boudoir diplomatique

(Marcel de Sano, 1931). Universal. **With** Arlette Marchal, Tania Fédor, André Cheron, and Ivan Petrovitch. The French version of Mal St. Clair's *The*

The men in the prison in *Big House* (Paul Fejos, MGM, 1930). André Berley (center) and Charles Boyer (left).

*Boudoir Diplomat* (1930) was the sole French-language film out of Hollywood in which Universal invested any money; it backed the production of Françoise Rosay's *Papá sans le savoir* (1931) in Paris. This Hollywood film stars a singular foreign cast directed by Marchal's husband, the Rumanian-born, Paris-educated Marcel de Sano. He had come to Hollywood in 1929 only to commit suicide shortly after the film's completion. The film, initially titled *Amour sur commande*, was never released in the U.S. The Spanish version is *Don Juan diplomático;* the German, *Liebe auf Befehl.*

## Le Bouif au salon (Bouif at the Lounge)

(Louis Mercanton, 1931). Paramount. **Script:** Georges Rip. **Music:** Jean Lénoir. **With** Tramel. A 20-minute Paris short with Tramel in his most famous comic role, as Bouif, this time enjoying the pleasures of a running an auto dealership. Bouif, on a visit to a dealership, is asked by the owner, who is late for dinner, to take over for a spell — but to sell nothing and keep his mouth shut. Of course, Bouif luxuriates in the company of affluent buyers and boasts of his status until the owner makes a hasty return.

## La Brigade du bruit (The Noisy Gang)

(Louis Mercanton 1931). Paramount. **Script:** Paul Colline. **Music:** Calabreze. **With** Noël-Noël and Paul Colline. A 20-minute Paris comedy hit along the lines of the Keystone Cops, the short features a pair of well-known collaborators.

## Une Brune piquante (A Lively Brunette)

(Serge de Poligny, 1931). Paramount. **Script and dialogue:** Yves Mirande. **With** Fernandel and Noël-Noël. Filmed in Paris, this 17-minute farce, also called *La Femme à barbe* (*The Bearded Lady*), is about a traveling circus. In this charming sketch, Fernandel is a performer known for his ability to make any number of faces, "à la Fellini," as he later put it.

## Buster se marie

(Claude Autant-Lara and William Brophy, 1931). MGM. **Dialogue:** Yves Mirande. **With** Buster Keaton, Françoise Rosay, Jeanne Helbling, Mona Goya, Lya Lys, André Luguet, André Berley, Paul Morgan, and Rolla Norman. This is one of the least-known of Keaton's films, an 80-minute Hollywood comedy, based on Keaton's last silent film *Spite Marriage* (1929), in which he plays a tailor's assistant who rescues his bride — who has married him to spite another — from bootleggers and a sinking ship. The film contains a superlative cast, and Françoise Rosay is a standout. Assigned a role originally slated for an English acrobat, she practiced her scenes nightly in order to perform her comic part the way she saw it, matching the innovative Keaton — who was, in fact, the son of an acrobat — scene for scene. In one sequence, Keaton employs two dozen variations on the difficulty of getting the girl, who has drunk herself into a stupor, onto a bed.

## Calais-Douvres (Calais-Dover)

(Anatole Litvak and Jean Boyer, 1931). Ufa/ACE. **Script:** Irma von Cube,

Litvak, and Boyer. **Dialogue and lyrics:** Boyer. **Photography:** Franz Planer and Robert Baberske. **Music:** Micha Spoliansky and Hans-Otto Borgmann. **Design:** Werner Schlichting. **With** Lilian Harvey (Gladys), Rina Marsa (Claire), André Roanne (MacFerson), Robert Darthez (Jack), Armand Bernard (Jean), and Willy Rozier. Based loosely on Julius Berstel's play *Dover-Calais*, this comedy, which was filmed in Berlin, is the tale of a bet. A wealthy American, unlucky in love, hopes to cash in on his predicament by wagering $500,000 that for five years he can avoid entanglements with the opposite sex. To do that, he plies the waters of the English channel on his yacht (along with a crew of misogynists) and bars all women from the boat. Near the end of the term, he picks up a beautiful girl whose strength has given out trying to swim from Calais to Dover. When she boards, she identifies herelf as a reporter — and he, flattered, begins talking. The 87-minute operetta concludes with a carnival in Nice and an auto chase on the last day of the bet. In spite of many complications, MacFerson wins both his bet and the heart of the young woman. The tale was also filmed as *Nie wieder Liebe* (*No More Love*) (1931), directed by Litvak and starring Ufa's sturdy Harvey.

## Le Calvaire de Cimiez (The Cimiez Tribulation)

(Jacques de Baroncelli and René Dallière, 1934). Cinérêve. **Script:** Marie-Ange Rivain. **Music:** André Demurger and Edmond Lavagne. **Design:** Robert Gys. **With** Marie-Ange Rivain (Béatrice), Marie-Louise Sarky (Valentine), and Suzanne Bing. Henry Bordeaux's moving 1928 novel is the basis of this heart-wrenching, 80-minute tale of self-sacrifice.

The tale is set near a calvary in Cimiez. A calvary — "place of the skull" — is a statue of the crucified Jesus (as well as the site of the crucifixion outside Jerusalem); such statues are common at many crossroads in France. At such a crossroad, Beatrice has taken in the daughter of her cousin Valentine (who has become emotionally disturbed), despite the fact that she knows the father of the young woman is her own husband. Years later, when Valentine is sufficiently recovered to reclaim her daughter, Valentine hesitates. Understanding where her duty lies to a girl who does not know her, Valentine simulates an episode of madness, thereby losing a claim to her child.

## Camp volant (Temporary Shelter)

(Max Reichmann, 1932). Paramount. **Script:** Benno Vigny. **Music:** Francis Gromon. **With** Ivan Kowal-Samborski (Marco), Meg Lemonnier (Gloria), Jenny Luxeuil (Santa), Berthe Ostyn (Lydia), Lissy Arna, Thomy Bourdelle (Cesare), and Roberto Rey (Bobby Barnes). Paramount's 84-minute film, shot in Paris, was one of the earliest multilanguage (French, German, Spanish) productions, an experiment in sound that circumvented the need to film separate foreign-language versions of the same tale. The story was influenced by E. A. Dupont's famous circus drama *Variety* (1925), in which a murder is committed. In Paramount's film, a clown (Kowal-Samborski) loves a beautiful trapeze artist (Lemonnier). The clown is accused of provoking another member of the circus to commit suicide. Reichmann's film was promoted as *Marco, der Clown* in his native Germany because of the German-speaking Ostyn and Arna. It was called *El Payaso* (*The Clown*) in Latin countries because of the presence of the popular Roberto Rey. The language experiment was one of only two or three such efforts Paramount undertook in Paris.

## Le Cap perdu

(E. A. Dupont, 1931). BIP. **Script:** Victor Kendall. **Photography:** Walter Blakeley and Hal Young. **With** Marcelle Romée (Hélène), Harry Baur (Kell), Jean Max (Cass), and Henry Bosc (Kingsley). This 95-minute version of Dupont's British-made *Cape Forlorn* (1930), based on Frank Harvey's novel of the same name, is a stern tale of infidelity, evocatively photographed in the director's inimitable manner. On an isolated island, a dance-hall girl, married to the aged lighthouse keeper Kell, has an affair with Cass, his assistant, as well as with Kingsley, a shipwreck survivor. When the younger men get into a brawl over her, she shoots the lighthouse assistant, then discovers that Kingsley, whom she loves, is a fugitive from justice. The old man finally finds out — after which she is back in the dancehall, awaiting the release of her lover from jail.

## Caravane

(Erik Charell, 1934). Fox. **Supervisor:** André Daven. **Photography:** Theodor Sparkuhl. **Design:** Ernst Stern. **Music:** Werner Richard Heymann. **With** Annabella (Princess Wilma), Pierre Brasseur, André Berley, Charles Boyer (Lazi), Conchita Montenegro, André Cheron, and Carrie Daumery. The studio's second and last French-language film out of Hollywood is an extravagent, romantic 11-reel drama about an aristocratic woman who shares one wild night with a gypsy and his band. It was one of only two French-language films made in Hollywood in 1934.

Based on Fox's *Caravan* (1934, starring Loretta Young, Charles Boyer, and Conchita Montenegro) and featuring the best of Fox's Europa players, it was a "super-special" musical, budgeted at over $1 million, with 3,000 extras. The studio brought in stellar technical help and gave Charell the guiding hand. His background pointed to great promise. He had made his name as a theatrical producer of comedies and revues in central Europe in the early 1920s and came to America with Max Reinhardt in 1924 to stage *The Miracle*. He caught the attention of Hollywood with his first film, the epic Ufa production *Der Kongress tanzt* (*Congress Dances*) (1931). The musically inclined Charell saw his career nosedive after his Hollywood-made film was held up for several months — and then shown only in France.

## Le Cas du docteur Brenner

(Jean Daumery, 1932). First National. **Dialogue:** Paul Vialar. **With** Simone Genevois (Lottie), Jean Marchat (Dr. Brenner), Jeanne Brumbach, Maurice Rémy, and Louis Scott. A 75-minute melodrama, filmed in Berlin, that is based on Hollywood's *Alias the Doctor* (1932), directed by Michael Curtiz. It is the story of a surgeon who puts his livelihood in jeopardy when he takes the blame for a botched operation by his stepbrother.

## Le Centenaire (The Centenarian)

(Pierre-Jean Ducis, 1933). Paramount. **Script:** Noël-Noël and Robert Lavallee. **Music:** Jean Delettre and Raymond Wraskoff. **Photography:** René Colas, assisted by Kalinowski. **With** Noël-Noël, Léonce Corne, and René Génin. The film represented Paramount's last production in France in the 1930s. It was shot in the Eclair Studios (Epinay-sur-Seine) and released by Distribution Parisienne de Films. In this 35-minute comedy, a man who reaches the age of one hundred is feted by the townspeople. To the surprise of all, he (Noël-Noël) displays excellent physical health and great intellectual vigor.

## Champion de boxe

(Robert Bossis, 1932). Paramount. **Script:** Yves Mirande. **With** Robert Goupil and Edith Méra. A 30-minute comedy filmed in Paris, based on Mirande's one-act play of the same name, about a champion boxer and the femme fatale he cannot handle.

## La Chance (Luck)

(René Guissart, 1931). Paramount. **Supervision and script:** Yves Mirande. **Photography:** Ted Pahle. **Design:** Henri Ménessier. **With** Marie Bell (Tania), Françoise Rosay (Mrs. Mougeot), Marcel André (Dr. Gaston), Maurice Escande, and Fernand Fabre. An 80-minute takeoff on the chance of striking it rich in gambling, and on the need for luck in meeting the right person. Tania cannot stop herself at the baccarat tables until the middle-aged doctor Gaston saves her financially and emotionally. "The film is entertaining," wrote a critic

Noël-Noël as the 100-year-old man in *Le Centenaire* (P.-J. Ducis, Paramount, 1933).

upon the film's release in the United States, "and even those not so well versed in that language may enjoy some lovely views of the Riviera, inside and outside the casinoes." The film was an original Paramount production out of Paris, based on a play by Yves Mirande. When the Second World War loomed, director Guissart gave up filmmaking to become a casino director.

## Le Chanteur de Seville (The Singer of Sevilla)

(Ramón Novarro and Yvan Noé, 1930). MGM. **With** Novarro and Suzy Vernon. A tempestuous, romantic story of a convent girl who falls for a man of the world, this 105-minute French-language musical, filmed in Hollywood, is based on *Call of the Flesh* (*The Singer of Sevilla*) (1930), directed by Charles Brabin. The success of the production depended heavily on Novarro's reputation as the romantic hero of *Ben-Hur* (1925).

He repeated his role in the Spanish-language version, *Sevilla de mis amores* (1930).

## Le Chasseur de chez Maxim's (The Porter at Maxim's)

(Karl Anton, 1932). Paramount. **Script:** Paul Schiller. **Photography:** Harry Stradling. **Music:** René Sylviano. **With** Tramel (Julien), Mireille Perrey (Totoche), Marguerite Moreno (Miss Pauphilat), Suzy Vernon (Geneviève), Robert Burnier (Marquis du Vèlin), and Yves Mirande. A 65-minute comedy filmed in Paris that is based on the hugely successful 1920 play by the popular Mirande. It centers on Julien, a humbly married aristocrat who works as a porter in the evenings at the famous Paris restaurant so as to be near his mistress. "Mirande's dialog is exceeding witty," wrote *Variety*, and "the audience is kept laughing from end to end." Mireille Perrey, playing the part of the porter's mistress, "looks really good on the screen," wrote the trade daily when the film premiered in Paris in March 1933. The film was released in America two years later, at which time the *New York Times* noted that with but scant knowledge of the "plot, the spectators can write their own tickets without much effort.... There are many merry scenes, some fine views and excellent acting by all concerned, with special honors to Monsieur Tramel" as the chasseur. The film is one more example, scarcely noted at the time, of an original and successful Paramount production out of Paris.

## Chérie (Honey)

(Louis Mercanton, 1930). Paramount. **Dialogue and lyrics:** Saint-Granier. **Photography:** René Guissart. **With** Mona Goya (Olive Dangerfield), Marguerite Moreno (Mrs. Falkner), Saint-Granier (Charles Dangerfield), Fernand Gravey (Bobby), Marc-Hély (a detective), and Sunshine Woodward (Doris). An all-star cast is featured in this 80-minute light musical comedy, which is American in atmosphere and filmed in Paris. It is set in the South, where a brother and sister, the Dangerfields, face complications when they are forced to rent out their home to the rich northerner, Mrs. Falkner. "Production shows considerable improvement in the Joinville product," wrote *Variety* in January 1931, when the film premiered in Paris. "It is unquestionably the best yet out of Joinville and is very well received ... nicely acted all around ... Everybody gets a break and a gag ... Moreno is one of the few French stage actresses for whom the screen holds no pitfalls." Marc-Hély burlesques the part of a detective, Woodward a capitalist.

## Les Chères images (Costly Images)

(André Hugon, 1920). Pathé. **With** Maxa (Hélène Chantal), Eugéne Nau, Jean Angelo (Paul and André), and Paul Jorge. A 1,300-meter production based on Françoise Signerin's tragic novel about opposite twins, co-owners of a factory. When André decides to give up his post, he leaves Paul, who is married to Hélène and the father of beautiful little Colette, in charge. During a fireworks display, tragedy strikes: The little girl is burned alive, and Paul dies in an auto accident. The doctor convinces André to impersonate his brother and, improbable as it seems, he locates a lookalike for

Colette. But when certain photographs are discovered, the pretense collapses.

## La Chevauchée blanche (The White Cavalcade)

(E. B. Donatien, 1924). Films Donatien. **Script:** Charles-Félix Tavano and Donatien. **Design:** Donatien. **With** Lucienne Legrand, E. B. Donatien (the woodcutter), Jean Dax (the prince), and Kracheivsky. A sorrowful 1,700-meter tale of vengeance and horror set in Poland long ago. After his daughter is abducted by the son of a venerated prince, a woodcutter demands justice. When the prince refuses to believe him, the man takes matters into his own hands. He finds his daughter, who has been drugged and made to participate in an orgy. In anger, he takes her back, dragging her through the snow and killing her. To punish the kidnapper and his accomplice, he carries them to a ravine, where they all perish.

## Chien qui parle (Talking Dog)

(Robert Rips, 1932). Paramount. Script: Henri Duvernois. With Jeanne Fusier-Gir. A short Paris comedy from the distinguished and witty pen of Duvernois, based on his 1913 short story and popular 1928 play. A suspicious lover makes the most of man's best friend. He becomes aware of his mistress's duplicity through her dog's reactions to men's names he rattles off at random.

## La Cigarette

(Germaine Dulac, 1919). Film d'Art. **Script:** Jacques de Baroncelli. **Photography:** Louis Chaix. **With** An-

drée Brabant (Denise), Gabriel Signoret (Pierre Guérande), and Jules Raucourt (Maurice Herbert). A 1,400-meter drama that displays the singular filmmaker Dulac's interest in psychological suffering. Pierre, an archaeologist in his fifties, becomes disturbed when he overhears a comment about the difference in age between himself and his wife Denise. Convinced that his wife is having an affair with a younger man, he decides to end his own life. He draws inspiration from an Oriental tale about a betrayed sultan who found death by having poison poured into one of his 100 hookahs. Pierre poisons a single cigarette, and mixes it up with the others in a pack of cigarettes. At the fateful moment, however, his wife Denise lets him know that she saw what he did, and got rid of all the cigarettes. Their tenuous marriage remains intact.

Charles Ford wrote that Dulac "enveloped the protagonist [Gabriel Signoret] in a poetic, unreal atmosphere of soft-focus images whose delicacy of touch stunned" viewers.

## Un Client sérieux (An Important Customer)

(Claude Autant-Lara, 1932). Paramount. **Photography:** Michel Kelber. **Editor:** Autant-Lara. **With** Marcel Vallée (Alfred). A 30-minute Paris comedy based on an 1896 one-act play by Georges Courteline that combines two of Courteline's favorite themes — café life and the law. The playwright's sense of the frustrated "everyman" caught in red tape and the pomposities and stupidities of lawyers, judges, and courtroom procedures are the heart of this satire of justice. Café owner Alfred watches his business go downhill because one customer hogs the establishment. The man spends the entire day in the café, nursing a single drink while hogging the newspapers and cards, and other customers are staying away. Attempting to throw the man out, Alfred suffers a black eye. He files assault charges, and proves in court that the man has hurt his business. But Alfred suffers a fate familiar to Courteline's fans: He loses the case, thanks to wily lawyers, and is forced to pay court costs.

## Cœurs farouches (Fierce Hearts)

(Julien Duvivier, 1923). Celor-Films. **Script:** Duvivier. **With** Desdemona Mazza (Martha), Gaston Jacquet (Jean Loup), Rolla Norman (Landry), Jean Lorette (Vincent), and Cauvin-Vassai (Simon). An audacious tableau of peasant customs—harsh, brutal, and sincere—is recreated in this 1,800-meter renunciation of anything agreeable or pretty. Written in one evening, this story of four brothers who love the same woman was touted as forceful, daring filmmaking (shot in natural decors). It was also hailed for its excellent performances. But the work was rejected by the filmgoing public, and Duvivier abstained from making anything so sensitive for the next quarter century.

## Cognasse

(Louis Mercanton, 1932). Paramount. **Script:** Mercanton. **Dialogue:** Georges Rip. **Music:** Raoul Moretti. **Photography:** Harry Stradling. **With** Tramel (Cognasse), Thérèse Dorny (Mrs. Cognasse), Marguerite Moreno (a nurse), Robert Bossis, Georges Rip, and Jean Mercanton. This 95-minute film, veteran Louis Mercanton's last before his death in May 1932, was one of the finest of his distinguished career. It represents an original Joinville production. "As it is," wrote *Variety* when the film premiered in Paris in September 1932, "it shows no trace of unevenness, and is one of the best turned out here." Based on Georges Rip's popular play, Mercanton's film is a subtle political satire about the differences between talk and action. It reminded filmgoers of René Clair's instant classic, *A nous la liberté* (1930). Wallpaper factory worker Cognasse believes in the principles of socialism, or so he says, until he is promoted to factory boss. His head turned by his luck, Cognasse devotes his time to putting to rest his principles and picking up books about Napoleon—and worrying about the bottom line. The height of comedy is reached at a costume ball that Cognasse throws. He gets drunk and mournfully informs his wife that he is divorcing her, a la Josephine. Rip's "dialogue is delightful," wrote the *New York Times* on the film's release in America in April 1935, especially the line that drew the most laughs: "One becomes a conservative when saving money." "The scenes in the factory and the working-class quarter are convincing," continued the *Times*, and the acting of the ensemble "is worthy of the lead set by Tramel." The photography was also singled out for praise.

## Coiffeur pour dames (Ladies' Hairdresser)

(René Guissart, 1931). Paramount. **Script:** Paul Armont and Marcel Gerbidon. **Photography:** Enzo Riccione. **Music:** Claude Pingault. **Lyrics:** Fernand

Vimont and Didier Daix. **With** Mona Goya (Aline), Irène Brillant (Mrs. Louvet), Fernand Gravey (Mario), Nina Myral (Mrs. Gilibert), and Georges Mauloy. An excellent 80-minute musical comedy about Mario, a one-time farmhand and expert at clipping sheep who establishes a thriving beauty parlor in Paris, making good not only in business but also in the affections of his patrons. A string of beautiful women get into *his* hair. Censors trimmed the comedy to an hour for its American release in 1932. Thus the American reception: "Almost impossible," wrote *Variety*, "to judge the picture by its present appearance. It seems to be fairly interesting.... Gravey, in the title role, is surprisingly good. He proves himself a clever actor and one of the best bets Paramount has dug up on the other side." The actor sings several numbers, including the cute tune "Je Suis Coiffeur," and "is ably supported by some of the most comely French actresses seen on the screen here," wrote another reviewer about the original Paramount in Paris production. The film, based on a 1927 play by Armont and Gerbidon, was remade for a new generation in 1952 by Jean Boyer, a collaborator of Guissart's in Paris, starring Fernandel. Hollywood made a copy, *Shampoo*, in 1975.

### Construire un feu

(Claude Autant-Lara, 1927). **Script:** Autant-Lara. **Photography:** Maurice Guillemin and Henri Barreyre. **With** José Davert, Edmond Lartigaud, and Jean Leclerq. A medium-length, 600-meter, experimental filming of Jack London's esteemed 1902 short story, "To Build a Fire," with one character, told in a new and vital way. To present the nerve-racking tale of a man (played by Davert) facing the prospect of freezing to death in the Yukon — a silent story perfect for silent film — the director shot an unusual, complex series of frames with wide-screen processes and anamorphic lenses developed in the 1920s by Henri Chrétien — precursor technology to Cinemascope. The film's images are squeezed from side to side or top to bottom. Some frames contain one image; others are image combinations of different sizes arranged either horizontally or vertically; and still others are full-shots alongside close-ups, interior alongside exterior scenes, and positive shots next to negative shots ( which have to be spread across the length of a wall). *Close Up* (March 1931) wrote this about the film:

> The hunter, out in the snow. Fire of twigs. The snow falls off a tree. Fire of twigs — gone! Matches gone. Tiny images cluster round ... like grapes ... like bees buzzing at the lattice of consciousness. The temperature 90 degrees below zero. Temperature 105 degrees below. No titles or sound. Swarms of image bees informing the shape of the principal image. Abstract thoughts, emotions, memories: the overtones and undertones pictured round the picture. A tale recalled of a fellow hunter who felled an ox and crawled inside the carcass after necessary adjustments. (No detail spared: these are thoughts of a simple hunter who has disembowelled many a beast) The hunter thinks of his only companion, an alsatian. But the dog escapes in the tussle. The man thinks of those warmly in the hut, of hot soup turned by immense spoon. The dog (wedges of landscape) howls to the sky.

The film, which was shown for several months, appears to have been as great a viewing challenge as anything Abel Gance made at the time. It took a while to find a theater that would even show the film, and when contending exhibitors labeled the production "unfair competition," it was withdrawn from circulation. It vanished (some say it was destroyed) when Autant-Lara was in Hollywood in the years 1930–32. Stills survive.

### Conte cruel (Sardonic Tale)

(Gaston Modot, 1930). Natan. **Script:** Modot and Charles Spaak. **With** Modot. Longtime actor Modot's only directorial effort, and Charles Spaak's first script, is a medium-length sound film, an adaptation of a Villiers l'Isle-Adam's short story "La Torture par l'esperance" from his 1888 novel *Nouveaux Contes Cruels*. Taking place during the Inquisition, it is a psychological, surrealistic tale of terror about a rabbi branded "without faith." On the night before his execution, the rabbi imagines he can escape when he notices his cell door ajar. He heads for freedom, and his expectations soar. Only at the last minute does he sense "all stages of this fatal evening were an arranged torture, that of hope." The next morning he meets his fate at the *auto-de fé*.

### Contre-Enquête (Counter-Investigation)

(Jean Daumery, 1930). Warner Bros. **With** Suzy Vernon, Jeanne Helbling, Rolla Norman, Georges Mauloy, and Daniel Mendaille (Diamond Joe). This is a fast-paced 70-minute tale of a policeman who infiltrates a Chicago gang in order to identify a killer. The studio's first French-language production out of Hollywood, based on *Those Who Dance* (1930), starring William Boyd, played at Paris's Theater Folies Dramatiques in late 1930, and was, according to a critic, "well received, well directed and acted." It was appreciated because the genre of the gangster film was already one of the best advertised American products.

### Le Cordon bleu (The Blue Ribbon)

(Karl Anton, 1931). Paramount. **Supervision and adaptation:** Saint-Granier and Mary Murillo. **Script:** Tristan Bernard. **Design:** Henri Ménessier. **Music:** Francis Gromon. **With** Jeanne Helbling (Irma), Marguerite Moreno (Mrs. Dumorel), Madeleine Guitty (Célestine), Simone Héliard, Pierre Bertin (Oscar Ormont), Louis Baron fils (Barnereu), Marcel Vallée (Detective Dick), and Cora Lynn/Edwige Feuillère (Régine). An original 85-minute Paramount production out of Paris, based on the hit play by Tristan Bernard, the tale centers around beautiful divorcée Régine, who has several admirers. Their spirited adventures cause "very Frenchy mixups," wrote an American critic in Paris. *L'Echo* praised Anton's direction, the film's music and movement, and especially the "exceptional" acting. The *Journel des Nouvelles Littéraires* singled out Bertin for his remarkable dash as the young man Régine loves and the "pleasing and very elegant" Helbling as the other woman. But it was the young student from the Paris Conservatory, Edwige Feuillère, in her debut leading role, who carried the day. A star had arrived. In only her third film (performing under the pseudonym Cora Lynn so as not to draw attention to her association with the conservatory), she was hailed as "perfect, free, original, charming … a very fine comic ... in a great personal success."

## Côte d'azur (French Riviera)

(Roger Capellani, 1931). Paramount. **Script:** Benno Vigny. **Music:** Dickbee. **Lyrics:** Marc-Hély. **Photography:** Fred Langenfeld. **With** Simone Héliard (Hélène), Yvonne Hébert, Robert Burnier, Marcel Vallée, and Fanny Clair. This 103-minute musical comedy represents another original Paramount in Paris production. Hélène is a telephone operator on holiday on the famous French coast, where she finds romance. Capellani's film, loosely based on a play, contains scenes of the famous resort. It premiered in Paris in July 1932.

## La Couturière de Lunéville (The Dressmaker of Lunéville)

(Harry Lachmann, 1932). Paramount. **Photography:** Rudolph Maté. **Music:** Marcel Lattès. **Design:** Henri Ménessier. **With** Madeleine Renaud (Anna/Irène) and Pierre Blanchar (Claude Rollon). A 77-minute melodrama, this original Paramount production out of Paris is based on a well-known play by Alfred Savoir. The story begins a long way from the French capital and ends in the same country town, after scenes of Paris cabarets, banks, boudoirs, parks, and other attractions. Anna, a simple provincial dressmaker, falls in love with Lt. Claude Rollon. When he abandons her, she tries to kill herself. Failing at that, she leaves France for America. A decade later, as the great Hollywood star Irène Salago, she returns to her hometown and looks up Rollon (now a businessman). But he does not recognize her. At that point, she decides to make him

pay for the emptiness she has felt in the intervening years. The events that lead up to the "happy ending" are easy to follow, wrote the *New York Times*, "even without a knowledge of French, but speaking acquaintance with that language is necessary for full appreciation of the quips with which the dialogue is spiced." Technically, especially in its photography and action, the film was ranked as one of Paramount's finest out of Paris, and it was well received in Paris and New York. In 1935 Lachmann directed a Hollywood version of the Paris production called *Dressed to Thrill*, starring Tutta Rolf and Clive Brook. Maté was the photographer; Robert Kane, the producer.

## Criez-le sur les toits (Shout It from the House Tops)

(Karl Anton, 1932). Paramount. **Dialogue:** Saint-Granier. **Adaptation by:** Paul Schiller. **Music:** Charles Borel-Clerc. **Photography:** Otto Heller. **With** Paul Pauley (Martin Sr), Simone Héliard (Renée), Edith Méra, Robert Burnier (Martin Jr.), Saint-Granier (Jules Petipon), and Jacques Varennes. A 90-minute musical farce about a most unusual publicity campaign — to increase the appeal for "nudists' soap" — launched by the obsessed ad-man Martin Jr. The musical numbers are genuinely pleasing, wrote an observer, and many of the scenes highly amusing. The fine young Méra, who died before the film's release in the United States in 1935, plays an American soap buyer and speaks English. An original Paramount production out of Paris based on the play *It Pays to Advertise*, the film was one of Saint-Granier's last efforts for Paramount.

### Le Cycle du vin (The Wine Cycle)

(1931). Paramount. **Script:** Georges Neveux. **Songs:** Yvette Guilbert. **With** Yvette Guilbert. A 30-minute musical out of Paris featuring the legendary singer and performer doing a roundelay from her celebrated repertoire.

### La Dame d'en face (The Lady Across the Way)

(Claude Autant-Lara, 1932). Paramount. **Script:** Georges Rip. **With** Yvette Guilbert. A nostalgic musical short from Paris highlighting the talent of the great singer and the wit of the writer.

### La Danse nouvelle (The New Dance)

(Louis Mercanton, 1931). Paramount. **Script:** Georges Rip. **With** René Koval. The lugubrious contortions of modern dancing are put to the test by writer Georges Rip, who developed a high degree of proficiency at taking an actual event of the moment and stretching it to the point of absurdity. In this Paris short, patrons in a diner cannot help but notice a man making exaggerated movements. The man is irritated by an itch in the small of his back, but they assume something more topical: his movements are the latest steps in a dance craze. So they do the same.

### Dans une île perdue (On a Deserted Island)

(Alberto Cavalcanti, 1930). Paramount. **Script and dialogue:** Georges Neveux. **Photography:** René Guissart and Ted Pahle. **With** Enrique de Rivero (Davis), Danièle Parola (Alma), Marguerite Moreno (Mrs. Schomberg), Gaston Jacquet, Philippe Hériat, and Yvette Andréyor. This 86-minute Joinville production follows the story line of William A. Wellman's South Seas drama *Dangerous Paradise* (1930), starring Nancy Carroll and Richard Arlen. Both films are based on Joseph Conrad's steamy 1915 novel *Victory* as well as Maurice Tourneur's *Victory* (1919). On a small island near Malaysia, Alma, an orchestra violinist, meets Davis, who falls in love with her. Separated by a series of malevolent intrigues, they triumph after hair-raising adventures against an unscrupulous bunch of characters. One of Paramount's earliest productions in Paris, it was labeled amateurish because Moreno, in a tragic role, and de Rivero (a friend of the director's), in the heroic role, were miscast. Released in Paris in February 1931, the film should "probably written off as an early experiment," wrote *Variety*. "Whatever it can bring is gravy."

### Delphine

(Roger Capellani, 1931). Paramount. **Script:** Hans H. Zerlett. **Dialogue:** Jean Deyrmon. **Music:** Raoul Moretti. **Lyrics:** Saint-Granier. **With** Alice Cocéa (Colette Bernard), Henri Garat (André Bernard), and Clara Tambour (Delphine Chavannes). A 77-minute version out of Paris of Victor Schertzinger's one-hour Hollywood musical comedy *Fashions in Love* (1929), *Delphine* is the risqué tale of music-hall singer Colette and her friend Delphine, who head off for a series of romantic escapades.

### La Der des der (The Last of the Last)

(Jean Caret, 1932). Paramount. **Script:** André Hornez and Jean Deyrmon. **With** André Champeaux. In this 20-minute Paris comedy the group known as The Society of Nations has a special job: to select one soldier from a military regiment who will become the mate of a beautiful young woman. At the fateful moment, the young soldier wakes up and realizes that it is only a daydream.

## La Disparue (The Missing Woman)

(Louis Mercanton, 1931). Paramount. **Script:** Noël-Noël and Paul Colline. **With** Noël-Noël, Paul Colline, and Bach. A 13-minute comedy from Paris about a man (Noël-Noël) who tells the police commissioner (Colline) that his wife has disappeared. In this sketch, the character actor Bach plays the commissioner's dog.

## Un Drame au château d'Acre (In the Acre Chateau)

(Abel Gance, 1914). **With** Aurèle Sydney, Jeanne Briey, Maillard, and Jacques Volnys. This early effort by Gance, starring the up-and-coming Sydney, was shot in five days at a cost of 5,000 francs and was based on Gance's script *Les Morts reviennent-ils?*

## Echec au roi (The King Checkmated)

(Léon d'Usseau and Henri de la Falaise y de la Coudraye, 1931). United Artists. **Adaptation:** Robert Harari. **Photography:** Leo Tovar. **With** Françoise Rosay (Queen), Emile Chautard (King), Jules Raucourt, and Pauline Garon (Princess). The first sound film that the Hollywood studio released abroad is a 75-minute romantic drama about a king and queen at odds over whether the princess can marry a commoner. His majesty favors the union; her majesty does not. Based on Robert E. Sherwood's play *The Queen's Husband*, it was produced as the English-language *The Royal Bed* (1930). The French rendition is an excellent production, wrote *Film Daily*, and "the leading players have sensed the humor of the various situations." Shown in Chicago, the film, wrote one critic, surpassed anything turned out abroad at the time. The film is also called *Le Roi s'ennuie* (*The King Is Bored*); its working title was *Le Mari de la reine.*

## L'Emprise (Entanglement)

(Henri Diamant-Berger, 1923). Pathé. **Script:** Diamant-Berger. **With** Pierrette Madd (Jacqueline Dubreuil), Marguerite Moreno, Pierre de Guingand (Roger), Henri Rollan (Pierre Debreuil), and Marcel Vallée. An 1,800-meter melodrama by the underrated director who normally made revues and comedies starring Maurice Chevalier. This film is about compulsion. When her overbearing husband Pierre leaves for America, Jacqueline feels a sense of release. She begins to gamble madly and loses. The addiction is stronger than the will to resist, and the woman sacrifices almost anything to a passion that has staked a hold over her.

## L'Enigmatique Monsieur Parkes

(Louis Gasnier, 1930). Paramount. **Dialogue:** Jacques Bataille-Henri. **With** Adolphe Menjou (Courtney Parkes), Claudette Colbert (Lucy), Sandra Ravel, Emile Chautard, and André Cheron. This was the first of five French films that the studio produced in Hollywood. By contrast, in Joinville, France, from 1930 to 1933, it produced nearly 300. A drama about a country house jewel heist committed by two dashing thieves, the film followed on the heels of the studio's English-language version *Slightly Scarlet* (1930), directed by Gasnier and Edwin H. Knopf, and starring Clive Brook. Gasnier also directed the Spanish version, called *Amor audoz* (1930).

Praised by *Variety* for its "drawing room precision and chatter," the film found less favor with *Motion Picture News'* José Schorr, who had this to say in a review titled "*Un deluge de mots!*":

> Trop de mots et un jeu insuffisant rendent le premier film parlant français de Monsieur Adolphe Menjou ... assez insipide. La trame, un melodrame dont un bandit constitue le theme, aurant pu etre rendue emouvante si l'on s'était occupé de la direction autant que du dialogue. Menjou ne nous en ravit cependant pas moins, et Claudette Colbert lui apporte un appui très bon, mais sans passion. Les autres personnages sont bons, mais ne semblent pas bien adaptés à l'action. La mise en scène est attrayante et les voix excellentes. Si le français ne sont pas influences par le manqué de force de cette histoire. Ils aimeront ce film parlant.

### En zinc sec (In a Dry Bar)

(Louis Mercanton, 1931). Paramount. **Script:** Albert Willemetz. **With** Yvette Guilbert, Rivers-Cadet, and René Génin. A short nostalgic Paris musical, heavily promoted in early 1932 in the publication *La Rampe* (*Footlights*), with the great Yvette Guilbert singing forlornly of the past.

### Erreur de porte (Mistaken Door/ Wrong Door)

(Ferdinand Zecca, 1904). Pathé. **With** Breteau. Only a trailer survives of this excellently designed short hailed (at the time) as "the funniest picture ever seen." Originally called *Urgente bisogno* (*Urgent Business*), it was made by cinema's first "director of production."

At a railway station stands a countryman (Breteau) with a pained look on his face and holding his stomach. He asks directions. A baggage handler makes a vague motion of his head towards the left. The countryman heads towards a huge booth, opens the door, enters the room, and closes the door behind him. On the wall, to the left, is a phone; lower, a stool. Putting his food basket and umbrella on the floor, and looking a bit amused, even surprised, he takes off his shoes and climbs on the stool. Facing the camera, he undoes his belt, lowers his pants, and sits down. Once installed, he smiles, sighs with relief, and grimaces.

Outside the booth, a townsman impatiently waits to use the phone. Finally, the countryman comes out, visibly relieved. The irritated townsman, quickly enters the booth, and just as quickly exits. He takes out his handkerchief, pinches his nose, and gives the camera a look while grimacing. Then he takes a look in the direction of the countryman.

### Une Étoile disparaît (A Star Vanishes)

(Robert Villers, 1932). Paramount. **Script and dialogue:** Marcel Achard. **Music:** Lionel Cazaux. **Photography:** Harry Stradling. **With** Edith Méra (Liane Baxter), Suzy Vernon (Rosine), Rolla Norman (Roland Mercier), Marcel Vallée (Inspector Hulot), Paul Pauley, and André Brulé. Achard's second script for Paramount in Paris, but his first written directly for the screen (initially titled *Une Étoile est morte* and *Une Étoile s'éteint*). It turned out to be much more than just a star-studded vehicle. At 69 minutes, it was another original Paramount Joinville production. It was quickly labeled a hit, one of the best films turned out by the studio. Director Villers — Robert Wyler, brother of William — hit his peak with this comedy-mystery concerning the death of sultry film star Liane Baxter. "His direction and tempo place him at once among the best French directors," wrote *Variety*. An interesting footnote is that during the course of the story, Marie Glory, Madeleine Guitty, Henri Garat, Meg Lemonnier, Saint-Granier, Fernand Gravey, and Noël-Noël appear in anonymous bits. When a 74-minute version of the film reached the United States in 1935, the *New York Times* noted that "most of the light side of the action is supplied by the incredible antics of a detective [Inspector Hulot] whose stupidity and self-esteem exceed almost anything ever seen on American screens." In other words, screenwriter Achard had planted the first hints of a character he would later refine into Inspector Clouseau.

## Une Faible femme (A Weak Woman)

(Max de Vaucorbeil, 1932). Paramount. **Script:** Vaucorbeil. **Music:** Ralph Erwin. **With** Meg Lemonnier (Arlette Morand) and André Luguet (Henri Fournier). A 73-minute original Paramount Joinville production, based on Jacques Deval's comedy, about a widow unable to decide between two suitors — one a sportsman, the other an artist. The attractive Lemonnier, wrote *Variety*,

"appears to be putting on fashionable curves. Acting is satisfactory all round. Sets nice and photography good."

## Une Femme a menti (A Lady Lies)

(Charles de Rochefort, 1930). Paramount. **Adaptation:** Léopold Marchand and Hermann Kosterlitz. **With** Louise Lagrange (Annette Rollan), Jeanne Helbling (Anne-Marie) Simone Cerdan (Miriam Giverny), Alice Tissot, Odette Joyeux, Paul Capellani, and Georges Mauloy. Paramount's second French feature out of Paris was de Rochefort's debut effort at the Paris studio. The film is based on the 1929 Hollywood melodrama *The Lady Lies*. He shot it in two weeks, and it was interesting enough, especially since it starred former Hollywood actress Louise Lagrange, who was featured in Herbert Brenon's *Shadows of Paris* (1924) and *The Side Show of Life* (1924). In de Rochefort's film, which is set in Paris, she plays the woman in love with a widower whose two children reject her. Lagrange's name drew enough filmgoers to enable the film to recoupe its production costs in a week's run at the Vaudeville Theater in Paris.

## La Femme de la nuit

(Marcel L'Herbier, 1930). Braunberger-Richebé. **Photography:** L. H Burel and Nicolas Toporkoff. **Music:** Michael Lewin. **Design:** Pierre Schild. **With** Francesca Bertini (the princess), Jean Myrat (Jean), Antonin Artaud, and Marion Gerth. Based on Alfred Machard's novel of the same name, the 88-minute romance was released without the director's approval after he was denied permission to revise it at the last minute. The scintillating Bertini, star of the golden age of Italian cinema, is the woman of noble birth willing to give it all up for the French naval officer she has casually met at the gaming tables — and spent a night with. Moving from Paris to Monte Carlo to a Balkan kingdom, the story contains "all sorts of old-fashioned screen adventures," wrote the critics; Bertini "wears her elegant attire with considerable grace." The tale was also filmed in Berlin in German and Italian versions.

## La Femme poisson (The Fish Woman)

(Louis Mercanton, 1932). Paramount. **Script:** Marc-Hély. **With** Jeanne Fusier-Gir, Jean Mercanton, and Marc-Hély. A short comedy from Paris possibly about a homely fisherman's wife who refuses to listen to the arguments of a suffragette.

## La Fille des pachas

(Joë Hamman and Adrien Caillard, 1926). Films Borey. **Photography:** Jehen Fouquet and Henri Gondois. **With** Marguerite Madys (Zulika), Céline James (Khadidja), Hamman (Hubert), Henri Baudin (the pacha), and Camille Bardou (Ambara). Based on Elissa Rhaïs's 1922 novel of the same name about the images and roles of women in the North Africa, the production was shot with the support of the French military and Arabian leaders.

## Le Fils de l'autre (The Other One's Son)

(Henri de la Falaise, 1931). RKO. **With** Jeanne Helbling, Geymond Vital, Emile Chautard, and Carrie Daumery.

The studio's second French-language Hollywood production, an 83-minute film , was based on the spicy *The Woman Between* (1931), the story of a young man competing for the attention of his father's new wife. "The problem with the film," wrote *Variety*, "is that French people do not accept the idea of a man not caring enough for his wife to give her more than three minutes of his time on the day she returns from Europe." Nonetheless, the film, released by United Artists, found an audience in France — but not in the U.S. Its working titles were *Madame Julie*, from the play of the same name, and *Une Femme libre*.

## Le Fils improvisé (The Improvised Son)

(René Guissart, 1932). Paramount. **Script and dialogue:** Henri Falk. **Photography:** Ted Pahle. **Music:** René Sylviano. **Editor:** Jean Delannoy. **With** Florelle (Maud), Louis Baron fils (Léon le Bélier), Jackie Monnier (Fanny), Fernand Gravey (Fernand Brassart), André Brulé, and Saturnin Fabre (Mr. Brassert). Guissart's 84-minute comedy was a smash hit on its release in the French capital in late 1932. This original Paramount film out of Paris was one of studio's biggest successes, in no small measure due to the singular performances of Florelle and Gravey as well as the subject matter. As one of the finest comedies yet by Guissart, who had been a cameraman on *Ben-Hur* (1926), and graced by Pahle's excellent photography, the film looks at the foolishness of an old man (Baron fils) who believes that he has gained the love of a young woman (Florelle). Of course, she really loves another (Gravey), who is supposed to be her "son."

## La Flamme cachée (The Secret Flame)

(Musidora and Roger Lion, 1918). La Societé des Films Musidora. **Script:** Colette. **With** Musidora (Annie Morin), Jean Yonnel (Hubert Morin), Maurice Lagrenée (Armand), and Le Gosset. Codirected by one of the earliest French actresses (she was Irma Vep in Feuillade's serial *Les Vampires*, 1915-16), Musidora was called the "queen of cinema." In this four-reel drama (from Colette's second script for film) she plays an altogether different character: the young wife (of a rich man) in love with an impoverished student. In despair, she contemplates suicide. The film, which followed on the heels of *La Vagabonde* (1917), another tale of a woman in an unhappy relationship, was released by her own production company. Footage was incorporated into Musidora's compilation *La Magique image* (1951).

## La Foule hurle (The Crowd Roars)

(Jean Daumery, 1932). First National. **Script:** Seton I. Miller and Howard Hawks. **With** Jean Gabin (Joe Greer) and Helene Perdrière (Anne). Produced in Berlin, this French-language adaptation of Howard Hawks's crime drama *The Crowd Roars* (1931) is an 80-minute hybrid, consisting of long shots from the Hollywood production and original French-language close ups. Released in Paris, "the film does big business," noted *Variety*. "Stage show, weather and motor show, crowding Paris, all help."

## Franches lippées (Free Meals)

(Jean Delannoy, 1932). Paramount. **Dialogue:** Tristan Bernard. **Editor:** Jean Delannoy. **With** Alice Tissot (Mrs. Lemu) and Fernand Frey (Mr. Lemu). A 20-minute Paris comedy based on Bernard's 1928 one-act play, translated for its American readers as *Free Treat*, the short is a simple tale. After attending the theater, two well-off Parisian couples, the Lemus and the Lechapaus, get together for a late snack. The one problem is that Mrs. Lemu is tired of the other couple's stinginess. So she warns her husband, "you can't eat anything … Then they'll be obliged to pay because there will be two of them eating and only one of us." When the film was screened in Paris, it was coupled with Paramount's riotous Hollywood comedy about letting go, *If I Had a Million* (1932).

## Fumée noire (Black Smoke)

(Louis Delluc and René Coiffard, 1920). Parisia Films. **Script:** Louis Delluc. **Photography:** J. Schoenmackers. **Design:** Francis Jourdan and Kees Van Dongen. **With** Eve Francis (Gina), Dolly Spring (Betty), Paul Strozzi (Patrick), and Jean Hervé (Sidney). A psychological drama, the 1,400-meter film is a series of internal monologues on Delluc's favorite themes: an obsession with the unpleasant past and the confrontational interplay of past and present. After returning from the Orient, Patrick introduces his niece and nephew, Gina and Sidney, to opium. In a stupor, the boy dreams that he has killed a traveler, while the girl dreams of herself as a prostitute who has kidnapped her own brother. When they awake, they compare their dreams — and notice that their uncle is lying unconscious on the floor.

## Le Gendarme est sans pitié (The Officer Is Pitiless)

(Claude Autant-Lara, 1932). Paramount. **Photography:** Michel Kelber. **With** Ravet and Georges Cahuzac (Labourbourax). This 20-minute Paris satire on justice, based on Georges Courteline's 1899 one-act play of the same name, follows the travails of an everyman up against in the bureaucracy of the law, especially the unforgiving officer, named appropriately, Labourbourax.

## La Girouette sur la toit (The Weathercock on the Roof)

(Louis Mercanton, 1931). Paramount. **Script:** Georges Rip. **With** Tramel. A 30-minute comedy, filmed in Paris, apparently about a head of state who subjects prospective appointees to the "coup de crochet," or the kind of reception music-hall entertainers receive from the audience.

## La Grande mare (The Big Pond)

(Hobart Henley and Jacques Bataille-Henri, 1930). Paramount. **With** Maurice Chevalier and Claudette Colbert. Vivacious, sentimental, witty, this 78-minute French-language comedy out of Hollywood has the great Frenchman playing a tour guide in Venice who falls in love with an the daughter of a wealthy American chewing-gum manufacturer. (The film was based on Paramount's *The Big Pond* [1930], also directed by Henley and starring the same duo.) While Paramount had to tone down the English-language version, which involved the consumption of alcohol in the era of prohibition, not so that of the French

version. "If they go for this in France the way an audience of cosmopolitan French ... went for it at the premiere in the 55th St. Cinema," wrote *Variety*, it "will be more popular than the original.... From the canals of Venice to the chewing gum factory in America ... travels *La Grande mare*."

## Haï-Tang

(Jean Kemm and Richard Eichberg, 1930). BIP. **Script:** Ludwig Wolff and Monckton Hoffe. **Photography:** Heinrich Gärtner and Bruno Mondi. **Music:** Hans May. **With** Anna May Wong (Haï-Tang), Hélène Darly (Yvette), Robert Ancelin (Lt. Boris Ivanoff), Armand Lurville, and Marcel Vibert (the grand duke). This 80-minute French melodrama, which was filmed at Elstree Studios in Britain, is the French version of *The Flame of Love* (1930), also directed by the veteran Eichberg (1888–1953) — his career spanned the years 1912–1951 — and starring Wong. The exotic actress had left Hollywood at the dawn of sound films to work in Britain, where she also filmed a German version of the story *Der Weg zur Schande* (1930).

Wong plays a a cabaret performer in pre–Revolutionary St. Petersburg and Moscow who makes a fateful decision when her father is sentenced to death and a lover is exiled for the attempted murder of a high official. In the climactic scene, she is forced to turn to the grand duke who can save them. Taking off her gloves, she allows her coat to slip back from her shoulders — a signal that lingerie is soon to follow. By offering "her virtue on the altar of paternal love," wrote a critic, Haï-Tang "feels free to sacrifice her own life" after her father is set free: she takes poison to prove that she really loves another.

## Une Heure près de toi (One Hour with You)

(Ernst Lubitsch, 1932). Paramount. **Dialogue:** Leopold Marchand. **With** Jeanette MacDonald (Colette Bertier), Maurice Chevalier (Dr. Bertier), André Cheron, Pierre Etchepare (Adolphe), and Lily Damita (Mitzi). The director's first French-language film out of Hollywood is a rarity, a Lubitsch film that was never shown in the U.S. The 78-minute musical comedy about the absurd behavior of two elegant couples caught in intricate romantic tangles

Lily Damita and Jeanette MacDonald in *Une Heure près de toi* (Ernst Lubitsch, Paramount, 1932).

follows the outlines of Lubitsch's simultaneously filmed Chevalier-MacDonald romp *One Hour with You* (1932), which *Photoplay* called "a bit of naughty, but oh, so 'nize.'" Chevalier's character speaks to the audience in asides, asking its advice while relating his romantic predicaments, which mix song with dialogue. The action takes place in various locales, all luxurious.

In Paris, Colette and André are apparently happily married. Their idyllic state begins to crumble when André shares a taxi with a flirtatious lady. Arriving home, he discovers that his seductive cab mate is his wife's old school chum, Mitzi, who has arrived from Switzerland. Colette, meanwhile, has a

suitor of sorts in the person of André's best friend, the intense and inept Adolph. The stage is set for Colette's dinner party and dance.

Through trickery, Mitzi persuades Colette that another guest, Mlle Martel, is the one who has designs on her husband. She, Mitzi, will do Colette a favor by "rescuing" André from harm's way. In a sequence on the dance floor, Chevalier's face reflects the rapid transition from stern resistance to happy submission to Mitzi's advances. When Colette sees the two of them go off into the garden, she is so relieved that she even consents to dance with the ardent Adolph. The title song is begun by band singer Donald Novis, then sung in turn by the four principals describing the very different hours that each hopes to spend with the object of his or her affections. But when the party is over and André is nowhere to be found, Colette collapses in tears, consoled by Adolph. She is grateful for his concern and gives him a motherly kiss.

The next day, Mitzi's husband, Professor Olivier, starts divorce proceedings and arrives to confront André. Colette is shattered, but admits that she too has been unfaithful. She calls on the stunned Adolph to confirm the truth of their tryst. Behind her back, André gestures to Adolph to agree with everything Colette says. Now that Colette's own past has been established, she decides to forgive her husband, proclaiming there's "an Adolph for a Mitzi."

Stills: www.dandugan.com/maytime/f-onehou.html.

## Une Histoire de cirque

(Charles de Rochefort, 1930). Paramount. **With** Beby, Antonet, and Concho. A 15-minute short starring three renowned circus clowns of the era.

## Histoires de rire ( Joking )

(Jean Boyer, 1932). Paramount. **With** Fernand Frey, Nina Myral, Robert Goupil, Andrée Champeaux, Paul Pauley, Ravet, and Robert Sidonac. Three humorous sketches (20 minutes total) make up the Paris short. In the first, called Neiges Canadiennes (Canadian Snows), a young woman journalist investigates a bit of madness within an asylum; in Gratte-ciel (Skyscraper), a tramp offers his "chaplain services" to a bank; and in Ce sont des choses qui n'ar-

rivent jamais, which was inspired by a song by Boyer, two elderly servants reminisce by phone about the the the lost opportunities of their youth.

## Un Homme en habit (A Man in Swallowtails)

(René Guissart and Robert Bossis, 1931). Paramount. **Script and dialogue:** Saint-Granier. **Music:** Charles Borel-Clerc. **Photography:** Harry Stradling. **With** Diana (Gaby), Suzy Vernon (Germaine de Lussanges), Fernand Gravey (André de Lussanges), Jeanne Fusier-Gir, Louis Baron fils, Pierre Etchepare, Paul Pauley, Marc-Hély, and Pola Illéry (Totoche). A hilarious, original Paris hit, this 88-minute comedy based on Yves Mirande's 1922 stage success and the studio's Hollywood silent Evening Clothes (1927; directed by Luther Reed and starring Adolphe Menjou and Louise Brooks) takes place in the French capital. A man ends up there after an evening on the town, and at the end of his marriage, with only the formal clothing on his back. Newly signed Paramount performer Gravey (known in the United States as Gravet) plays the formally attired gentleman. With eight centimes in his pocket, he is on his own. His outfit leads him to a series of ridiculous adventures. He becomes an extra in a film, joins a funeral procession, becomes a member of a wedding party, and lands a job as a theater usher. In the happy ending, he reunites with his wife. "Above everything," wrote Variety, "tempo and ... dialog make the film.... Whatever may be this film's chance for adaptation in foreign languages, there is no question that French audiences will love it the world over."

## Un Homme heureux (A Happy Man)

(Antoine Bideau, 1932). **Script:** Jacques Bousquet. **Photography:** Paul Portier and Robert Tomatos. **Design:** Jean Laffitte. **With** Claude Dauphin (Claude), Alice Tissot, Suzanne Christy (Simone), Lucette Desmoulins (Lulu), Henry Bosc (Michel), and Jacques Bousquet. An 87-minute sexual romp about the shy young Claude who, unable to adequately express his love for Simone, asks Michel to do it for him. But his friend goes beyond the call of duty: he seduces Simone. Soon thereafter, she finds Michel in the arms of another young woman, breaks her engagement to him, and happily marries Claude.

## Les Hommes nouveaux (The New Men)

(Edouard-Emile Violet and E. B. Donatien, 1922). Dal Films. **Script:** Claude Farrère. **Photography:** Louis Dubois and André Dantan. **With** Marthe Ferrare (Christiane), Lucienne Legrand (Laure), E. B. Donatien (Amédée Bourron), Georges Melchior (de Chassagne), and Violet (de Tolly). A class-conscious work and diatribe against power and money, this trenchant 2,200-meter production is based on acclaimed novelist Farrère's 1922 novel of the same name. It centers on Bourron, one of the newly rich businessmen who has decided to expand his empire, in Morocco. To overcome bureaucratic procedures and expedite negotiations, he gets the help of an insider named Chassagne who, it turns out, was once in love with Bourron's wife, Christiane. When jealousy takes over, Chassagne is mortally wounded by Bourron. Bourron's daughter becomes aware of her father's ghastly nature, and rebels.

## Il est charmant (He Is Charming)

(Louis Mercanton, 1931). Paramount. **Dialogue:** Albert Willemetz. **Photography:** Harry Stradling. **Music:** Raoul Moretti. **Design:** René Renoux. **With** Meg Lemonnier (Jacqueline), Henri Garat (Jacques), Viviane Romance, Jean Mercanton, Armand Dranem, Louis Baron fils, The Mangan Tillerettes, Moussia, and Madeleine Guitty. Mercanton's 90-minute operetta was one of Paramount's biggest hits out of Paris in 1932. Initially titled *Paris, je t'aime*, this original Paramount production, based on Willemetz's spirited opera, centers around Jacques, a law student who would rather frequent music halls and spend time with the beautiful Jacqueline. The production's light and melodious music, the dancing and the nonstop fun (beginning with a girl disrobing), and its trick photography contributed to its being hailed an "unquestionable" success. The film, which made Garat a star, was censored in London, while for France "it is just a natural," wrote *Variety*. In the United States release a month after its Paris premiere, Garat and Lemonnier opened the French-language film by outlining the plot, such as it is, in English. Their film ends in a splendid marriage.

## Ils viennent tous, au cinéma (They All Go to the Movies)

(Henri Diamant-Berger, 1917). **Script:** André Heuze, and Diamant-Berger. **With** Mayol, Huguette Duflos,

Mistinguet, Maurice Chevalier, Gabriel Signoret, Jean Renouardt, André de Lorde. A boulevard revue (accompanied with spoken commentary and synchronized sound) that features some of the most celebrated performers of the era, directed by a man who (often working with Chevalier) helped make the genre popular in France. This series of sketches and pantomime was put together in the hope that it would attract a greater portion of the public (especially the "elite") to the cinema. Signoret and Renouardt play the characters Pierrot and Colombine; de Lorde the "Prince of Terror" because he was the recognized master of the Grand Guignol of horror pieces.

### L'Inconstante (The Fickle One)

(Hans Behrendt, André Rigaud, and Georges Root, 1931). Universal. **Script:** Hans H. Zerlett and Wilhelm Speyer. **Photography:** Willy Goldberger. **Music:** Theo Mackeben. **With** Danièle Parola (Gaby), Margo Lion, Georges Charlia (Georges), and Gaston Jacquet (Baron Max de Weissbourg). Produced in Berlin, this is an American-backed, "ultramodern" comedy about Gaby, a beautiful, high-class model wined and dined by the rich. Engaged to Georges, a good-natured and likable driving instructor, the vivacious model eventually settles down with her beau, but not before the denouement of the story, which, wrote a critic, "is effected in a rather dramatic way." The fast-paced, risqué 95-minute work is based on Wilhelm Speyer's novel *Ich geh' aus und du bleibst da*, and was also titled *L'Amour dispose* and *Je sors et tu restes là*.

### L'Indéfrisable (The Permanent Wave)

(Jean de Marguénat, 1931). Paramount. **Script:** Albert Willemetz and Saint-Granier. **With** Alexandré Dréan, Nina Myral, and Marcel Carpentier. A 15-minute comedy, made in Paris, about a long-suffering married man who seeks improvement in his life, particularly, his financial status, by having his shrewish wife "disappear."

### Invité monsieur à dîner

(Claude Autant-Lara, 1932). Paramount. **Photography:** Michel Kelber. **With** Georges Bever and Alice Tissot. A 15-minute Paris comedy based on Georges Courteline's 1905 drama of the same name.

### Iris perdue et retrouvée (Iris Lost and Found)

(Louis Gasnier, 1933). Paramount. **Script:** Marcel Achard. **Music:** Marcel Lattès. **With** Raymonde Allain (Iris de Persani), Edith Méra (Eve de Persani), Pierre Blanchar (Bernard Fontaine), André Brulé, and Jean Dax (Colin-Fouchet). Gasnier's 85-minute melodrama was one of Paramount's last French features out of the French capital. The original Paramount in Paris production, based on the novel by Pierre Frondaie, is about a woman who, discovering a secret about her brother, marries a man she does not love in order to shield her family's name.

### L'Ironie de destin (The Irony of Fate)

(Dimitri Kirsanoff, 1921–1923). Superfilm. **Script:** Kirsanoff. **With** Nadia

Sibirskaïa and Dimitri Kirsanoff. The Estonia-born Kirsanoff's first film, this 1,600-meter tale of lost opportunity (also called *Fatalité*) starring the exquisite Sibirskaïa came just before Kirsanoff's instant classic *Ménilmontant* (1924). A poor musician and a beggar, defeated by life, meet when they are old and recall their past without irony. An orphan working girl, she once lived on the same stair landing with him. He had a promising future as a sculptor but, unaware that she loved him, he was seduced by another woman. Their sad destinies were dictated by chance and unaffected by outside intervention.

Held for a year, the film played in a few Paris cinemas and lost money. But the film caught the attention of critics, who commented on Sibirskaïa's subtle performance, the exterior scenes in Paris, the simple story, and the absence of titles. The director favored experimental, precise imagery, design, and metaphor (along the lines of René Clair) to emphasize his poignant humanity, themes, and counterthemes in this sorrowful tale, which concludes with the lines, "After a life of misfortune, ironic Fate revealed to them the happiness that they had brushed against." Along with *Sables* (*Sands*) and *Brumes d'Automne* (*Autumn Fogs*), this film became part of the poetic quartet that signaled the director's rise in French cinema of the mid-to-late 1920s.

## Jenny Lind

(Arthur Robison, 1930). MGM. **Adaptation:** Hanns Kräly. **Dialogue:** Jacques Deval. **With** Grace Moore (Jenny), Françoise Rosay, Mona Goya, André Luguet, Georges Mauloy, and André Berley. A 92-minute French-language Hollywood production — the seventh of 13 such films in the studio's history — that is the story of the famous 19th-century Swedish soprano who on a yearlong American tour promoted by P. T. Barnum, realizes that love is at least as important as a career. The film was based on *A Lady's Morals* (1930), opera singer Grace Moore's first film.

European praise of the English-language vehicle convinced studio executive Louis B. Mayer that a French version, starring Moore, might also prove a success. When the idea was broached with Moore, she said, "But L. B., I speak so little French." Mayer reassured her, "I'm sending for the Jacques Feyders and Yves Mirande.... You'll be ready ... in two weeks." Françoise Rosay — who plays her rival in the film — coached Moore each evening on Molière. Said Moore, "I cut my teeth those two weeks on none but the poet himself." Then on the set, with Rosay keeping a "beady watchful eye on me through the screening lest I let one go unrolled," recounted Moore, "I relaxed through sheer astonishment and managed to turn in a much more natural and straightforward performance than I had given for the American screening." The French version was well received abroad — and never seen in America.

## Les Jeux sont faits (The Chips Are Down)

(Jean de Marguénat, 1932). Paramount. **Script:** Yves Mirande and Guillaume Wolff. **With** Noël-Noël, Alexandré Dréan, and Georges Bever. A 30-minute Paris comedy based on Mirande and Wolff's one-act hit of the same name.

## Laissez faire le temps (Let Time Deal with It)

(1932). Paramount. **Script:** Georges Rip and Jean le Seyeux. **With** Robert Arnoux and Yvette Guilbert. A 30-minute costumed comedy short and retrospective revue from the pen of Georges Rip that is a defense of French wit and grace — as opposed to invading American methods of the era — in the creation of a Paris musical. The legendary Guilbert sings from her repertoire and adds a touch of polish and delight in a sketch where she plays an 18th-century marquise standing before a mirror that reflects her image as the beautiful young woman she once was. Other scenes emphasize France's great historical figures and the vitality of the city of Paris. The Paramount short is also called *A la mode de chez nous (Our Way)*.

## Leçon du gouffre (The Lesson of the Abyss)

(Ferdinand Zecca and René Leprince, 1913). **Script:** Louis R. Rollini. **With** René Alexandré (Robert), Gabriel Signoret (Rochefort), Gabrielle Robinne (Gabrielle), Jeanne Grumbach (Anne), and Aimée Tessandier. In this honest and emotional tale of modern life, the beautiful Gabrielle, aware of her power over men, comes to renounce her own guile and a series of intrigues at coming into a fortune. After nearly being killed in a fall into an abyss, she interprets the incident as a "terrible warning," vowing to make for herself an honest life.

This four-reel (1,200-meter) drama containing scenes of intense eroticism was made by the film pioneer whom Georges Sadoul described as a "wily fox." It naturally appealed to French cinema pioneer Ferdinand Zecca, who shows what it took to "make it" in pre–World War I France. Moreover, it gave the filmmaker an enormous breadth of background material, and so much movement that filmgoers forgot that the camera itself doesn't "travel." Containing shots of village life as well as a tour of the city, the film came to be a virtual documentary of streets with horse-drawn carriages and motorcars, of bustling life, and most of all mood. Zecca moved to the even faster-paced U.S. in 1913 to supervise Pathé Exchange in New Jersey.

## La Lettre

(Louis Mercanton, 1930). Paramount. **Script:** Garrett Fort, Jean de Limur, Monta Bell, and Hermann Kosterlitz. **Dialogue:** Roger Ferdinand. **Photography:** René Guissart. **With** Marcelle Romée (Leslie Bennett) Paul Capellani (Maître Joyce), Hoang Thi The (Li Ti), and Jean Mercanton. A 70-minute melodrama based on Somerset Maugham's Singapore-based play about a letter that turns out to be the key piece of evidence in a crime of passion. Shown in Paris in March 1931, the film put Paramount on the spot. French filmgoers and critics took the studio to task for releasing a hybrid of Hollywood and Paris footage — exteriors from the Hollywood original and dialogue scenes shot in the French capital. More important, the fact that the blackmailer is Chinese aroused the ire of French audiences, who "consider the Chinese as honest," wrote an observer. "It is a good thing racial prejudices do not react similarly the world over." Still, Mercanton's direction and Guissart's photography were called adequate.

## Lopez, le bandit

(Jean Daumery, 1930). First National. **Dialogue:** Jacques Deval. **With** Gaston Glass (Pancho Lopez), Jeanne Helbling, Suzy Vernon, Geymond Vital, Rolla Norman, and André Cheron. The studio's first French-language film out of Hollywood is a 71-minute version of Clarence Badger's *The Bad Man* (1930), the tale of a Mexican bandit and the gang that restore justice to ranchers on the brink of ruin.

## Madame sans-gêne (Shameless Madame)

(Léonce Perret, 1925). Paramount. **With** Gloria Swanson, Charles de Roche-fort, Warwick Ward, and Emile Drain. This was the first French-American production, a 120-minute story of a washerwoman elevated to the nobility by Napoleon, based on Victorien Sardou's rich and humorous play. It offered a great woman's role. Sardou had written it for the famous 19th century French actress Rejane, and Hollywood star Gloria Swanson saw herself in the role of the indigent Catherine Hubscher and her rise to fame.

Though the idea for the film was enthusiastically received by French politicians, directors, designers, and actors, French film industry heads imposed a major condition—that a Frenchman

Gloria Swanson as the commoner who rises to the top in *Madame sans-gêne* (Léonce Perret, Paramount, 1925).

direct. Léonce Perret, who had worked in America, was chosen. He lent great authenticity to the historical drama by shooting in and around Napoleon's favorite residence and cast the film "impeccably," said Swanson, "and with a delicate sense for the international character of the production." At Compiegne, director Perret shot splendid scenes in Napoleon's own library, and he used the quill pen the emperor had used to sign treaties and blotted the ink with paper he'd used in his campaign chest in Prussia. At Fontainebleau Palace, they filmed in the Salle Henri II. In Louis XV's game room Perrot filmed a chess match on a set that the emperor of China had given to French royalty.

On April 17, 1925, *Madame sans-gêne* premiered in New York City. Gloria Swanson received a tremendous ovation: "Never has Broadway seen a splash as was given to this star," wrote a critic. "Her name in the largest electric letters ever given to an individual on Broadway decorate the facade of the Rivoli; the house is shrouded in the tri-color of France and the Stars and Stripes, and all the other buildings on both sides of Broadway from 49th to 50th streets are similarly decorated." In order that theatre owners be able to squeeze in five shows a day, Paramount subsequently trimmed the film from 11 reels to eight, which reduced the film to barely related scenes of Swanson in fabulous costume. In France it was shown uncut.

Stills:www.mdle.com/Classic-Films/PhotoGallery2/gloria8.htm.

### Magie moderne (Modern Magic)

(Dimitri Buchowetski, 1931). Paramount. **Dialogue:** Michel Duran. **Pho-** tography: Harry Stradling. **With** Lucien Galas (André), Fanny Clair (Jeanne) Gaston Jacquet (Stephan, the financier), Sunshine Woodward, and Madeleine Guitty (Mrs. Ridon). Also called *Télévision*, Buchowetski's 65-minute production — Paramount's thirteenth French film out of Paris and an early production with color sequences — is based on actual news of the era: the efforts of inventor Philo T. Farnsworth (1906–67) to bring electronic television to fruition. Though granted a patent for the new technology, the Utah-born inventor was eventually overshadowed and overtaken by corporate giant David Sarnoff and RCA.

In the French film, there is a happier ending. André lays claim to his great discovery — a technology to rival film — and to the fortune it promises. This is the production that led the critics to label Paramount's Paris studios a "Tower of Babel" because it was shot in Czech, *Svet bez hranic* (1931); Dutch, *De Sensatie der toekomst* (1931); German, *Welt ohne Grenzen* (1931); Italian, *Televisione* (1931); Polish, *Swiat bez granic* (1931); Romanian, *Televiziune* (1931); and Swedish, *Trådlöst och kärleksfullt* (1931). Perhaps in deference to RCA and Hollywood, Paramount released no version in the United States.

### Maquillage (Make-up)

(Karl Anton, 1932). Paramount. **Script, dialogue, and lyrics:** Saint-Granier. **Coscript:** Paul Schiller. **Colyricist:** André Hornez. **Music:** Marcel Lattès. **Photography:** Otto Heller. **With** Rosine Deréan (Ginette), Edwige Feuillère (Ketty), Milly Mathis, Robert Burnier (Bertini), Paul Pauley (Eugène Tapin), and Saint-Granier (Lucien Leroy).

Initially titled *Je t'attendrai* (*I Count upon You*), this 105-minute Paris comedy-drama is a greatly enhanced version of Paramount's Hollywood original *Behind the Make-up* (1930), starring William Powell and Fay Wray. That is especially true in the music and in the casting of the multitalented stars, notably Edwige Feuillère in her fourth Paramount production.

The plot concerns the song-writing clown Lucien who is swindled by Bertini, his partner, and nearly loses the affections of Ginette, the woman he loves, all the while hounded by the femme fatale Ketty. As a mixture of pathos and gags, the film was "conscientiously directed by Karl Anton who unrolls the milieu of the music-hall," wrote *Mon-Cine*. "The scenes are shot with a skilful dose of drama and comedy. Saint-Granier and Burnier are excellent; R. Déreán ... Pauley ... are equally fine." Feuillère, however, tops them all. She is, wrote *Le Journal*, the "perfect comedienne, fascinating, embodying the real femme fatale."

## Marions-nous (Let's Get Married)

(Louis Mercanton, 1931). Paramount. **Script, dialogue,** and **lyrics:** Saint-Granier. **Photography:** René Guissart. **Music:** Charles Borel-Clerc and Richard A. Whiting. **With** Alice Cocéa (Gisèle Landry), Marguerite Moreno (Mrs. Marshall), Helen D'Algy (Lolita), Véra Flory, Fernand Gravey (Francis Latour), Robert Burnier, Pierre Etchepare, and Jean Mercanton. A fine 103-minute Paris adaptation of *Her Wedding Night* (1930), which stars Clara Bow, this screwball comedy is simply about the complications married film star Gisèle and handsome Francis get themselves into. In a hurry to register at a hotel in a Balkan village, they unwittingly sign a marriage certificate. What follows is an endless series of gags until the happy ending. Shown in Paris in April 1931, the risqué film "means big business," wrote a critic. Guissart's photography was called "of Hollywoodian quality."

## Le Masque d'Hollywood

(Clarence Badger and Jean Daumery, 1931). First National. **With** Suzy Vernon, Rolla Norman, and Geymond Vital. The 77-minute caustic French-language musical, based on Mervyn LeRoy's *Show Girl in Hollywood* (1930), was the studio's second and last French-language film out of Hollywood. This rendition is stronger than the English version because the lead could sing better and the dialogue is smoother. In it, a New York girl named Dixie heads for Hollywood after leaving her boyfriend. She obtains a role in a film — written, ironically, by her former boyfriend. She finds trouble, on the set from a philandering director, and off the set when a friend nearly commits suicide, before she manages to get down to work and accepts a marriage proposal. Soon thereafter she abandons the city of stardom. The film mirrors veteran director Badger's sense of the crass world that was Hollywood. Ten years later Badger made his last film, an Australian production called *That Certain Something*, a production nearly identical in theme to his only foreign-language film.

## Le Meeting

(Louis Mercanton, 1931). Paramount. **Script:** Poulbot. **With** Jean Mercanton and Jean Bara. A 10-minute Paris comedy that features two well-known child actors putting to rest anything remotely serious.

### Ménages ultra-modernes (Ultramodern Couples)

(Serge de Poligny, 1931). **Dialogue:** Yves Mirande. **Photography:** Harry Stradling. **With** Noël-Noël, Marcel André, Yvonne Hébert, and Micheline Bernard. In this well-received 20-minute Paris comedy, two couples undo mix-ups they face at a hotel.

### La Mère Bontemps

(1931). Paramount. **With** Yvette Guilbert. A 15-minute Paris short, most likely based on an episode in Georges Neveux's play *Juliette, ou la clef des songes,* about a woman who dreams of another life for herself.

### Metteur en scène (The Picture Director)

(1930). MGM. **With** Buster Keaton (as Elmer Butts). The Hollywood-made film is the French version of the studio's first full-length Buster Keaton sound vehicle, *Free and Easy* (1930), about "Miss Gopher City," who achieves her dream of going to the film capital. Unfortunately, she's accompanied by her accident-prone manager. The film did a tremendous business when it premiered in Paris in late 1930 — Keaton was a huge favorite in France — but was criticized for its spare dialogue, few songs, and dependence on French and English subtitles. Further, its title implies a link with Keaton's late silent classics *The Extra* and *The Cameraman,* though this film was never shown in the U.S.

### Miche

(Jean de Marguénat, 1932). Paramount. **Script:** Marguenat. **Coscript:** Etienne Rey. **Music:** Charles Borel-Clerc. **Design:** Henri Ménessier. **Photography:** Jacques Montéran. **With** Suzy Vernon (Miche), Marguerite Moreno (Mrs. Sorbier), Edith Méra (Countess Kessera), Robert Burnier, and Armand Dranem (Damaze). A 90-minute romantic comedy based on the play of the same name by Etienne Rey, which revolves around the efforts of a young man and a young woman to arouse each other's interest. The simple tale is set among the slopes of Switzerland. "Exceptionally good French programmer," noted a Paris reviewer about the inexpensive, original Paramount production out of Paris. It was rated "an outstanding success" in its Paris run in April 1932. Released in the United States that December, the film contained censor cuts that had *Variety* urging distributors "to take a couple of hours off and do some more cutting to make the thing run smoothly."

### Mistrigi

(Harry Lachmann, 1932). Paramount. **Script and dialogue:** Marcel Achard. **Photography:** Harry Stradling. **Music:** Francis Gromon. **With** Madeleine Renaud (Nell Marignan), Simone Héliard (Fanny), Noël-Noël (Zamore), and Jean Debucourt. This 90-minute story of a rich woman who gives up everything for a poor opera singer was called "the first screen presentation ... of why Paramount in Paris has come to be an important film company. Because they ... are making pictures ... rather than worrying about American markets or opinions." The film remains noteworthy for its camerawork, called "beautiful in an obvious way, which is that much better [for the film]." Costing $50,000 to produce, the original Paramount Joinville production was projected in late 1931 as surefire box office in Paris. Lachmann incorporated an element of pathos into Achard's lighthearted farce while the great Madeleine Renaud, not always well-photogaphed in Paramount's Paris productions, was credited with her best effort yet, stage or screen. The film (Achard's third work for Paramount) reached the United States at 80-minutes in length in January 1933.

## Mon chapeau (My Hat)

(Jaquelux, 1933). Paramount. **Script:** Henri Falk. **With** Noël-Noël (Gregory), Marcel Dalio (Bokalas), and Jackie Monnier (Lolita). Slated to be a feature, this work out of Paris was turned into a short fantasy-comedy about a hat that enables any young man who wears it to win the girl of his dreams.

## Mon cœur balance (My Heart Wavers)

(René Guissart, 1932). Paramount. **Script:** Yves Mirande. **Assistant:** Maurice Moriot. **Design:** Henri Ménessier. **Photography:** Ted Pahle and Georges Benoit. **With** Marie Glory (Geneviève), Marguerite Moreno (Célestine), Noël-Noël, Hélène Perdrière (Henriette), and Diana M. Urban (Lulu). A 90-minute, rip-roaring romantic comedy with just the right kind of dialogue. Based on a play by Mirande, it follows the down-and-out ingenue Geneviève, whose life changes when she goes to work for, and then falls in love with, a young count.

While the outcome is never in doubt, the audience's interest is sustained by tangled alliances and complications caused by the count's two pseudosisters. *Variety* called this original Paramount feature out of Paris "unquestionably the best film of this type ever turned out of the Joinville studios, or any other here for that matter." Two months later, in February 1933, the *New York Times* rated it "one of the most enjoyable motion pictures ever submitted for approval and entertainment of the French-speaking population of New York." Further, the scenes in Paris and along the countryside through which the count's genuine sister (Mlle. Moreno) drives her old-fashioned automobile "give the audience a good idea of present-day France," wrote the *Times*, adding, the "photography is excellent."

## Monsieur Albert

(Karl Anton, 1932). Paramount. **Script:** Ernö Vajda and Benjamin Glazer. **Photography:** Rudolph Maté. **Music:** Marcel Lattès. **Lyrics:** Marc-Hely. **Design:** Henri Ménessier. **With** Betty Stockfeld (Sylvia Robertson), Noël-Noël (Mr. Albert), Louis Baron Fils (The King), Edwige Feuillère (Countess Peggy Riccardi), Armand Dranem, Vera Baranowskaïa (the Duchess), Georges Bever, and Jean Mercanton. Anton's 95-minute operetta is another example of the original nature of Paramount's French comedies out of Paris. Based on Vajda's story, the film is concerned with Monsieur Albert, a man of impressive bearing thought to be of aristocratic background. But Albert is something less and something more. The celebrated headwaiter at the Palace-Hôtel de Paris, he is a man who knows how to pronounce the phrases "Comment va madame la Marquise?" and "Comment sa porte le Comte?" Ambling cheerfully through the minor intrigues at a Swiss holiday hotel, making the most of his purported status, Albert tries to earn the love of the young American Sylvia Robertson. Fearing rejection (and recognized by a countess much smitten by him), he is afraid to admit to his livelihood.

The film was shot while Alexander Korda was shooting an English-language version in London (where Paramount also maintained a studio) called *Reserved for Ladies* (1932), starring Leslie Howard. The idea for making these sound films sprang from Harry D'Arrast's sophisticated and moving hit, *Service for Ladies*, produced by Paramount in 1927 and starring Adolphe Menjou. That film's Paris locale made it an ideal candidate for sound. Unlike the silent version, Paramount's Paris production ends with Albert winning the woman of his dreams even as he serves the main course at her engagement party to another man. Designer Ménessier gave great care to the film's locale, in Paris and abroad, while Maté's photography was rated at best indifferent. The film premiered in Paris in July 1932 and was called by *Mon-Cine* as "equally amusing" as D'Arrast's *Service for Ladies*.

Here is "an accomplishment of drollery … of humanity," wrote Julien Sorel in *Cinémonde*. "Noël-Noël plays Albert with "imagination and humor … Stockfeld is charming…. Feuillère is the spirited incarnation of the countess," wrote the critics. And Vera Baranowskaïa, the Russian actress who knew the entire repertoire of Chekov, was recalled years later by Feuillère as "another very strong actress" in the comedy.

## Monsieur le duc

(Claude Autant-Lara, 1932). Paramount. **Photography:** Michel Kelber. A Paris comedy sketch based on Georges Courteline's 1901 play of the same name.

## Monsieur le fox

(Hal Roach, 1931). MGM. **Script:** Willard Mack. **Dialogue:** Yvan Noé. **With** Lillian Savin (Woolie Woolie), André Luguet (Louis le Bay), and Barbara Leonard (Nedra). In 1931, Hollywood comedy filmmaker Hal Roach directed a half-dozen Spanish-language shorts featuring Laurel and Hardy and Charlie Chase. This is his one French-language feature, a 65-minute version of his own action-filled *Men of the North* (1930), billed as a romance of the French-Canadian wilds. Filmed simultaneously with his English version — but released afterwords — the French version, "with Hal Roach directing, and plenty of theatrical stuff," wrote *Film Daily*, "it should satisfy the thrill fans … scenery is excellent."

## La Montagne infidèle (Unfaithful Mountain)

(Jean Epstein, 1923). Pathé. **Photography:** P. Guichard. A medium-length, 600-meter documentary about the eruption of Mount Etna in June 1923. As the highest active volcano in Europe, it has erupted close to 100 times. The most destructive eruption occurred in 1169, when Catanai was destroy (with a loss of 15,000 lives), and in 1669 when more than 20,000 people perished. In spring 1923, Pathé commissioned the young Epstein to go to Sicily and record the latest geological events. Epstein shot the film (the fifth of his career) over several weeks. His film soon vanished, but he put his thoughts about the production into a book, *Le Cinématographe vu de l'Etna* (published 1926). In it he wrote, "On the screen, there is no still life. Objects have attitudes. The trees gesticulate. The mountains signify."

## Une Nuit à l'hôtel (A Night at the Hotel)

(Leo Mittler, 1931). **Script and dialogue:** Marcel Achard. **Photography:** Harry Stradling. **With** Marcelle Romée (Marion Barnes), Betty Stockfeld (Jennifer), Jenny Luxeuil, Willy Rozier (Emmanuel), Vera Baranowskaïa, Jeanne Boitel, and Marcel Dalio (Jerôme). This 85-minute comedy of manners is Achard's first work for Paramount in Paris. It is based on the novel by Eliot Crawshay-Williams, an emotional tale about Marion, who in a Riviera hotel falls in love with Emmanuel, a guest who commits suicide over their brief affair. The production contains fine scenes of the famous locale and engaging music.

## Nuit d'Espagne

(Henri de la Falaise, 1931). RKO. **Script:** Jean Daumery. **With** Jeanne Helbling and Geymond Vital. The studio's third and last Hollywood French-language production is a risqué 70-minute drama about a businessman who forgives his unsophisticated wife her year-long affair with a handsome Spanish bachelor. The film is based on *Transgression* (1931), directed by film pioneer Herbert Brenon.

## Les Nuits de Port-Saïd

(Leo Mittler, 1931). Paramount. **Script and dialogue:** Walter Mehring.

**Music:** Francis Gromon and Marcel Lattès. **Lyrics:** Georges Neveux. **Design:** Alfred Junge. **Producer:** Jacob Karol. **With** Gustav Diessl (Hans), Oskar Homolka (Winston Winkler), Marcel Vallée, Renée Heribel (Charlotte), Jean Worms, Armand Lurville, and José Davert. An 84-minute multilanguage melodrama, filmed in Paris, that centers around the niece of a cabaret owner. At an international port she finds love and intrigue that compel her to make a run for her life. This singular, original Paramount experiment in sound (begun by Dimitri Kirsanoff) was called *Die Nächte von Port-Saïd* in Germany and *Las Noches de Port-Saïd* in Spanish-speaking countries.

## Octave

(Louis Mercanton, 1931). Paramount. **Script:** Yves Mirande and Henri Geroule. **Photography:** Fred Langenfeld. **With** Noël-Noël (Octave), Marcel André, Yvonne Hébert, and Georges Bever. In this 28-minute Paris comedy of manners about infidelity, based on Mirande and Geroule's 1906 one-act play of the same name, Octave smokes out the identify of his wife's lover by feigning his own death at a party.

## Ohé! Ohé!

(Louis Mercanton, 1931). Paramount. **Script:** Georges Rip. **With** René Koval, Jean Mercanton, and Manuel Russell. A 15-minute Paris comedy sketch based on Rip's popular 1913 revue *Eh! Eh!*

## L'Ombre déchirée (Torn Shadow)

(Léon Poirier, 1921). Gaumont. **Script:** Jane Léon Poirier. **Photography:**

Jean Letort. **Design:** Robert-Jules Garnier. **With** Suzanne Desprès (Mother), Marguerite Madys (Cécile), Laurence Myrga, Jacques Robert, and Armand Tallier. A wrenching 1,800-meter fantasy that takes place on Christmas Eve. A poor woman who had been seduced and abandoned by a gypsy years earlier, begs for the life of her young, dying daughter. She asks Death to take her instead. The Angel of Death appears, and reveals to her what her daughter's life would be like if her wish is granted. Resigned, the mother lets fate take its course.

### On a volé un homme (Man Stolen)

(Max Ophüls, 1933). Fox-Europa and Erich Pommer. **Supervisor:** René Guissart. **Script:** René Pujol and Hans Wilhelm. **Music:** Bronislav Kapper and Walter Jurman. **Photography:** René Colas. **With** Lily Damita (Annette), Henri Garat (Jean de Lafaye), Fernand Fabre, and Nina Myral. Ophüls's first film after leaving Nazi Germany was this Paris production, a frothy 90-minute French-language mystery-romance. After being kidnapped, banker de Lafaye falls in love with the woman who is holding him ransom. The is film "was done by somebody who knows how to make films," wrote *Variety*. "It puts the regular run of local mades to shame ... Garat is the apex of the matinee idol type and Lili is something to look at." The photography is "worthy of the German origin of its sponsor," who produced one other film with Fox-Europa, Fritz Lang's *Liliom* (1934).

Lily Damita and Jean Garat in *On a volé un homme* (Max Ophüls, Fox, 1934).

## L'Ordonnance (The Orderly)

(Victor Tourjansky, 1920). Ermolieff. **Script:** Tourjansky. **Photography:** Joseph Mundviller and Nicolas Toporkoff. **Design:** Ivan Lochakoff. **With** Nathalie Kovanko (Jeanne), Alexandré Colas (colonel), Paul Hubert (orderly), and Henri Svoboda (Saint-Albert). Based on a dramatic short story (which takes place in 1890) by Maupassant, this is a carefully transposed, atmospheric 1,600-meter work. It begins with the funeral of the beautiful Jeanne, who has drowned herself. Her grief-stricken husband, a regimental colonel, reads her last letter to him. Her confession is then depicted on screen. It concerns a shocking revelation: her love affair with the handsome and gallant captain Saint-Albert. But her husband's orderly, finding out about the affair, exacts a heavy price for her silence: he rapes her. Unable to endure the shame, she ends her life. The film closes with a flashback to the husband finishing the letter and a dramatic scene in which he executes the orderly.

## L'Ouragan sur la montagne (Storm in the Mountain)

(Julien Duvivier, 1922). Geneva Films. **Script:** Duvivier and Philippe Amiguet. **With** Lotte Loring, Marie Pillar, Gaston Jacquet (Oscar), Camille Beuve, Emile Hesse, and Jean Stelli. An 1,850-meter production based on an original script, this experimental police production, shot in Germany, was the first French-German production of the postwar period. Duvivier shot it without knowing a word of German (though the lead actress is German) — and it inaugurated his international career.

## Papa sans le savoir (Father Unawares)

(Robert Villers, 1932). Universal. **Script and dialogue:** Yves Mirande and Gladys Lehman. **Photography:** Jacques Montéran and Emile Pierre. **With** Noël-Noël (Léon), Janine Merrey (Jeannine), Françoise Rosay, and Suzanne Delvé. Universal's $80,000, 103-minute moneymaker, filmed at the Eclair Epinay studios, was adapted by Mirande from his own play *Little Accident* and loosely follows the 1930 Hollywood film of the same name. Adding "brilliant French dialogue," Mirande created a tale about a young man (Noël-Noël) who's pressured by his family to forsake his poor girlfriend (Merrey) in order to marry an heiress, but he does the right thing when he finds out that his girlfriend has given birth. "Best actor in the whole show is the child," wrote *Variety*, "aged nine months at the time of filming, which makes a decided hit, resulting in beaucoup sniffling." The morally troubling comedy never made it to the U.S.

## Paramount en Parade

(Charles de Rochefort, 1930). Paramount. **Supervisor:** Elsie Janis. **Dialogue:** Saint-Granier. **Lyrics:** Jacques Bataille-Henri. **Editor:** de Rochefort. **With** Marguerite Moreno, Madeleine Guitty, Alice Tissot, Fanny Clair, Saint-Granier, Boucot, Elmire Vautier, The Mangan Tillerettes, and Maurice Chevalier. A 97-minute revue of Paramount's French stars of the era, begun by Louis Mercanton. The sketches, some in Technicolor, were filmed in three days and are a mix of Hollywood and Paris sequences, from the 24-member chorus known as The Mangan Tillerettes to Chevalier in a dance routine to what is reportedly the best sketch: a society event, seen at first glance from the perspective of the guests and then as the witty Saint-Granier (and de Rochefort) imagines it should have occurred.

## Pas d'histoires (Not History)

(Louis Mercanton, 1931). Paramount. **Script:** Georges Rip. **With** Paul Pauley. A Paris comedy short, evidently based on a sketch from Rip's 1928 revue *Tout Paris*, in which a magician resembles the longtime statesman Raymond Poincaré. In 1928 as premier of France, Poincaré managed a great and memorable feat, at least in the eyes of the ordinary man on the street: he stabilized the franc. In this topical satire, the magician, to the accompaniment of song and dance, achieves the stabilization in a more ingenious fashion. He conjures up a collection of rich men of history, from Midas on downward, who help in his economic goal.

## Passionnément (Passionately)

(René Guissart, 1932). Paramount. **Script:** Jean Boyer and Albert Willemetz. **Music:** André Messager. **Photography:** Harry Stradling. **With** Florelle (Kitty Stevenson), Fernand Gravey (Robert Perceval), Julien Carette (Auguste), Louis Baron Fils (William Stevenson), and Jean Mercanton. Based on Willemetz's 1927 three-act operetta, this is a sly 80-minute comedy (begun by Louis Mercanton before his death) about the manifestations of passion. It represents another original Paramount production out of Paris. American millionaire Stevenson arrives on the Riviera, but he is not on vacation. Instead, he is on business: to wangle young Frenchman Robert Perceval out of his Colorado estate because he believes there is oil on the property. He has brought along his pretty wife Kitty (disguised in a wig and blue glasses) because he is too jealous to leave her at home. The key to the American's plan is wine, which the Frenchman is known to enjoy. Ironically, it is the abstemious American who comes to enjoy it in such amount and variety that it alters his nature — for the better. He abandons his scheme. When he learns that his wife is having an affair with the Frenchman, it is of no matter to him. "Fair entertainment, and names sure to mean b.o. anywhere in French territory," noted a critic. The principals often break into song "with music rather too subtle for the screen." At the ending, a map of the locations of the wine-growing regions of France is displayed. Though Willemetz's operetta ran in New York in 1929, Paramount did not distribute *Passionnément* in the United States in the waning days of Prohibition.

## Le Père célibataire (The Bachelor Father)

(Arthur Robison, 1931). MGM. **Dialogue:** Yves Mirande. **With** Jeanne Helbling, Lily Damita, André Luguet, André Berley, Geymond Vital, André Burgère, and Marcel André. The Hollywood French-language comedy drama is based on a play about illegitimate children. Not surprisingly, it caused a ruckus at the Hays Office, Hollywood's official censor. It is a "very serious matter," Hays said, "to have one version for America and one for the continent." The Hays Office had hoped that filming of the stage production would be accepti-ble, it said, "if some irresponsible com-pany does not get a hold of it." Likewise, for continental distribution that might be fine too, but it was "not so sure about England. The picture is so full of broad remarks which I imagine the English speaking world will censor." While the English-language version, Robert Z. Leonard's *Bachelor Father* (1931), con-tains only the mildest hint of impropri-ety, the French version makes clear the out of wedlock status of the children grown to adulthood. The film was never released in the U.S.

## Le Père prématuré

(René Guissart, 1933). Paramount. **Script:** Henri Falk. **Photography:** Ted Pahle. **Music:** René Sylviano. **With** Edith Méra (Dolorès), Denise Dorian, (Suzy), Fernand Gravey (Edouard/Fred Puma), and Saturnin Fabre (Mr. Puma). This 75-minute original Paramount produc-tion out of Paris about conflict between father and son was the director's final film for the American studio.

## La Perle

(René Guissart, 1932). Paramount. **Script and dialogue:** Yves Mirande. **Photography:** Ted Pahle. **Music:** Claude Pingault. **Lyrics:** Jacques Monteux. **With** Suzy Vernon (Clotilde), Edwige Feuillère (Viviane Lancenay), Robert Arnoux (Jacques Surville), Armand Lurville (Veratcheff), and André Berley (Silberberg). Perhaps Guissart's best film for Paramount, this 92-minute original production was a high-water mark for the Paris studio. Jacques, a gem sales-man, aspires to become a successful and famous playwright. He seeks the hand of his employer's daughter, Clotilde Sil-berberg. When the young jewelry clerk is about to be fired, he accidentally swallows a pearl valued at 3 million francs. His boss sues for the pearl, Jacques refuses to hand it over, and it all becomes big news. A court rules that Jacques is not only not a thief, but that he has the right to refuse an operation to recover the pearl. Sud-denly a celebrity, Jacques does as he pleases, including flirting with the beau-tiful customer Viviane Lancenay. Now that he is the talk of the town, a play that he has written called *A Man Who Has Something in His Stomach* is produced in Paris, and it becomes a hit. When he wins the girl of his dreams, Jacques pro-duces the pearl. But it turns out that he had only faked swallowing it to make real his art.

Feuillère (in only her second star-ring role) "justifies the hopes placed in her." *Paris-Midi* and filmgoers found Mirande's dialogue zesty, Guissart's di-rection intelligent, Vernon exquisite, Berley a great talent, and the film irre-sistible. "It is easily arguable that any-thing so absurd is a waste of time, but French audiences do not think so," wrote the critic Herbert L. Matthews from Paris. "The producers here are tak-ing it for granted, anyway, that the pub-lic wants to be amused."

## Le Petit café (The Little Café)

(Ludwig Berger, 1930). Paramount. **With** Maurice Chevalier, Emile Chau-tard, André Berley, Tania Fédor, Françoise Rosay, and Yvonne Vallée. A smash 83-minute French-language musical — one of only five French-language films Para-mount ever shot in Hollywood. By con-trast, the studio produced 300 features and shorts in Joinville, France, in the same years. This film (which broke records in Paris) was the first film which Maurice Chevalier wanted to make in Hollywood. It turned out, however, to be his fourth film, made simultaneously with Berger's 72-minute English version, *Playboy of Paris*.

It is a remake of Max Linder's successful post–World War I French comedy about a waiter who inherits a fortune after he unwittingly signs a 20-year contract that commits him to a lowly job — by day. The only way he can enjoy his fortune is to become a playboy by night. While Linder's film failed in the U.S., Chevalier considered this French version, in which he sings a number of songs and does several comedy routines, a great success. "This is due in part," wrote *Film Daily*, "to the fact that the comedy is stressed more in the French version."

### Une Petite femme dans le train (A Little Lady on the Train)

(Karl Anton, 1932). Paramount. **Script and dialogue:** Saint-Granier and Paul Schiller. **Music:** Georges Van Parys. **Photography:** Fred Langenfeld. **With** Meg Lemonnier (Irène Pommerois), Edwige Feuillère (Adolphine), Henri Garat (Marcel), Pierre Etchepare, and Georges Bever. This 90-minute suspense thriller, an original Paramount production out of Paris based on a play by Leo Marchès, begins with a lie. In Paris, Irène Pommerois tells her husband she has to travel to Dijon on business, when, in fact, she wants to spend the night with her lover, Marcel, a public official. The next day, her husband reads the newspaper headline, "Derailment from Paris to Dijon. Numerous Victims," and rushes to find out what happened, accompanied by his mistress Adolphine. Shortly thereafter Irene shows up at home with Marcel. The two now have to concoct other lies to cover their tracks. "Henri Garat makes this go," wrote a Paris critic, "fully justified by his acting. He is exceeding well supported" by the charming and graceful Lemonnier. *L'Ami du film* singled out the "marvellous, brilliant, extraordinary" Feuillère, in her third film for Paramount. Anton's direction was called ingenious and well done, and he duplicated the effort in Paramount's little-known Czech version of the story, *Jsem devce a certem v tele* (1933).

### La Peur des coups (Afraid of Blows)

(Claude Autant-Lara, 1932). Paramount. **Photography:** Michel Kelber. **With** Fernand Frey and Henriette Delannoy. Autant-Lara's most well-known Paramount short from Paris, a 30-minute comedy about domestic friction based on George Courteline's 1894 one-act play of the same name. In the story, a woman knows her husband's weaknesses all too well, and, worse for him, how to exploit them.

### La Peur des histoires (Afraid of Trouble)

(1931). Paramount. **Script:** Georges Rip. **With** Marguerite Moreno, Paul Pauley, and Micheline Bernard. A Paris comedy short possibly based on a sketch from Rip's 1928 revue *Tout Paris* about the entertaining side of traffic congestion.

### Photogénies

(Jean Epstein, 1924). Films Jean Epstein. Shot in Paris, Epstein's 1,000-ft experimental, nonnarrative film (dedicated to Louis Delluc) helped to establish his reputation within the avantgarde. Taking ordinary newsreel footage, Epstein edited snippets of film to convey the sense of buried treasure within ordinary footage. Jean Mitry called it an "essay of pure cinema." Epstein showed his film once, then "dismantled" it. No one followed up on his ideas until Walter Ruttmann made *Mélodie du monde* (1930).

## La Piste de géants (Trail of Giants)

(Raoul Walsh and Pierre Couderc, 1931). Fox. **Photography:** Lucien Andriot and Arthur Edeson. **With** Jeanne Helbling (Denise), Gaston Glass (Colman), Emile Chautard, and Jules Raucourt. The studio's first French-language film out of Hollywood is a 97-minute version of Raoul Walsh's classic western spectacle, *The Big Trail* (1930), based on Hal G. Evarts's novel. The film premiered at the Max-Linder Theater in Paris.

## Plus fort que la haine (Stronger Than Hatred)

(Ferdinand Zecca and René Leprince, 1913). **Script:** Louis Z. Rollini. **With** René Alexandré (the painter), Gabriel Signoret, Gabrielle Robinne (Gina), and Aimée Tessandier. One of Zecca's last efforts, this three-reel (1,000-meter) color production about modernity (with scenes of Montmartre and its cabarets) is a lesson about life. The beautiful singer Gina, who is used to the adoration of the public, is pursued by a single-minded aristocrat. The unfortunate man, however, cannot consider marry her — never mind that she does not love him — because of family considerations. His suicide becomes news, and a satirical painting of his tomb by a young artist helps turn the unfortunate event into a scandal. Ridiculed in public, Gina vows revenge on the young artist by making him fall in love with her. But she bcomes caught in her own web when she falls for him.

## La Poule (The Hen)

(René Guissart, 1932). Paramount. **Script and dialogue:** Henri Duvernois. **Photography:** Fred Langenfeld. **Music:** Henri Christiné. **Design:** Henri Ménessier. **With** Arlette Marchal (Guillemette), Marguerite Moreno (Mrs. Hilmont), Madeleine Guitty, Edith Méra (Brigitte), Armand Dranem (Silvestry), and André Luguet. The 69-minute original Paramount production (based on Duvernois's popular novel of the same name) features some of the best-known French players of the era. It seems that the widower Silvestry, nicknamed "The Hen" because of his fussy preoccupation over his five daughters, especially their marriage possibilities, can't keep his nose clean. He is a mix of human qualities: honest, sincere, and devoted, and at the same time petty, vain, and gossipy. When the rich American Mrs. Hilmont invites the family to a month on the Riviera, the fun begins for the girls; trouble lies in wait for their father. Guissart's film, while not quite capturing the high-spirited source of the story, is "fairly bright and gay in spots," wrote *Variety*.

## La Pouponnière (The Nursery)

(Jean Boyer, 1932). Paramount. **Script:** Albert Willemetz. **Music:** Henri

Verdun. **Photography:** Harry Stradling. **With** Germaine Roger (Christine Delannoy), Françoise Rosay (Mrs. Delannoy), Robert Arnoux (Jean Moreau), and Julien Carette (a servant). Jean Boyer directed an 80-minute original Paramount comedy, based on René Pujol's operetta, about love blooming within the confines of a nursery.

## Pour vivre heureux (To Live Happily)

(Claudio de la Torre, 1932). **Photography:** Ted Pahle. **With** Simone Simon (Jacqueline Mauclair), Noël-Noël (Jean Mauclair), Pierre Etchepare, André Brulé, and Robert Bossis. This little-seen, gently cynical 80-minute comedy, an original Paramount production in Paris, is based on Yves Mirande's 1912 three-act stage hit, which was called "a brilliant idea of Molièresque gaiety." Jean Mauclair is in a struggling relationship with his art, his wife, and his life. An artist without pretensions, he finds himself outdistanced by colleagues and deceived by his spouse. One day he announces that he has had it with life, and he is going to throw himself off a bridge. Soon after he vanishes. Instantly, he is "discovered." His reputation soars, his pictures sell. There is even a Mauclair boom. His wife becomes rich by unloading onto the market not only his pictures but any number of false "Mauclairs." The artist, of course, has only faked his death. He attends his own funeral (it was not too difficult to come up with a body for the occasion) and finds his wife easily consoled, his friends pleased at the "boom." His scheme a success, he decides that since he is officially dead, happiness awaits in the country. A

few years later, however, things come to a head. An American in Paris announces a huge upcoming exhibition of Mauclaurs. To stop the fraudulent show, the happy painter reveals himself. Consternation follows, after which Mauclair returns to the country, and paints more Mauclairs.

## Prenez mes roses (Take My Roses)

(1930). Paramount. **With** Lucienne Boyer. A musical short from Paris signaling the screen debut of the sentimental singer.

## La Princesse aux clowns (The Princess and the Clowns)

(André Hugon, 1925). **Script:** Mary Murillo. **Photography:** Maurice Velle. **Design:** Jacques-Laurent Athalin. **With** Huguette Duflos (Princess Olga), Magda Roche, Charles de Rochefort (prince/clown), and Paul Franceschi. The moving eight-part, 2,700-meter production (based on the 1923 novel by Jean-José Frappa) is the tale of a Russian princess living in Paris after the Russian Revolution. Her life is transformed when she meets the circus clown Michaelis. Believing him to be Prince Michel, heir to the Russian throne — the resemblance is uncanny — she convinces him to return home. A sudden turn of fate, a counter-revolution, enables Michaelis to become king. But it turns out that he is not the real heir (who still lives), having acted so only because of his love for Olga. Yet when his heroism is established, he is annointed king — and marries Olga when the real prince steps aside. This extraordinary story was also filmed in an English version.

## Le Procès de Mary Dugan

(Marcel de Sano, 1931). MGM. **Script:** Becky Gardiner. **Photography:** Henry Sharp. **Dialogue:** Jacques Deval. **Design:** Cedric Gibbons. **With** Huguette Duflos (Mary), Françoise Rosay, Jeanne Helbling, Charles Boyer, André Burgère, Rolla Norman, Marcel André, Georges Mauloy, and Emile Chautard. The studio's eleventh French-language film out of Hollywood is a retelling of its first sound film, *The Trial of Mary Dugan* (1929), featuring Norma Shearer. This 100-minute drama features a stellar imported cast and the stunning beauty, Duflos.

De Sano was capable, perspicacious, and talked well of the project. "Everyone asked him for advice," recalled Françoise Rosay. Things started well, she said, then the director disappeared from the set. The studio went after him, and he would roll the cameras again, and then disappear again. "He was a real case," said Rosay. "He had stage fright." Not long after finishing the film — de Sano had also done the Spanish version, *El proceso de Mary Dugan* (1931) — the gifted director committed suicide. That, apparently, cast a long shadow on the film, and it was never screened in America.

## Quand monsieur voudra (When M'sieur Wishes)

(Jean Margueritte, 1932). Paramount. **Script:** Georges Dolley. **With** Robert Arnoux and Nina Myral. A short Paris comedy of manners very likely about a woman who seeks a divorce from the man she left years ago in order to marry a duke. The husband, a well-trained servant, gives his approval on the condition that his wife return to him for one night.

## Quand on est belle (When She's Pretty)

(Arthur Robison, 1931). MGM. **Script:** Yvan Noé. **With** Mona Goya (Peg), Lily Damita (Laura Murdock), Françoise Rosay, André Luguet (Brockton), André Burgère (Jacques), André Berley, and Rolla Norman. The 85-minute Hollywood French version of *The Easiest Way* (1930), based on Eugene Walter's play and the 1917 silent, is the story of the young woman Laura who, brought up in impoverished surroundings, gains the attention of her boss at the modeling agency. He offers her the works: luxury, money, anything else she wants — and a chance to have an affair.

Hollywood's official censor, the Hays Office, had, between 1927 and 1931, made it clear to interested studios that this particular storyline, while of ancient vintage, would run into trouble if it were filmed. So to avoid official censure, MGM soft-peddled the story in the English version — despite that the film was still banned in Ireland, portions of Canada, and was cut in Pennsylvania. But that was not the case in the French version, which, it turned out, is more in line with the nature of the source. The too-steamy film of "easy virtue," whose initial title had been *La Bonne vie*, never made it to American theaters.

## Quand te tues-tu? (When Do You Kill Yourself?)

(Roger Capellani, 1931). Paramount. **Script:** Saint-Granier. **Music:**

Charles Borel-Clerc and Marcel Lattès. **Photography:** Fred Langenfeld. **With** Simone Vaudry (Gaby), Madeleine Guitty, Noël-Noël (Léon Mirol), Robert Burnier (Viscount Xavier du Venoux), Armand Lurville (M. Meyse), Jeanne Fusier-Gir (Virginie), and Marc-Hély. One-time editor Capellani directed this 80-minute original Paramount production out of Paris that is based on a novel by André Dahl, the all-too-real account of a well-to-do viscount who cannot live without love. The film, which was released in the United States in 1932 to scant attention, features an impeccable cast that matched that of the Spanish version, *Cuando te suicidas?* (1932).

## Le Rebelle

(Adelqui Millar, 1930). Paramount. **Adaptation** and **dialogue:** Benno Vigny. **Photography:** Philip Tannura. **With** Thomy Bourdelle (General Platoff), Suzy Vernon (Marya Ivanova), and Pierre Batcheff (Boris Sabline). This 85-minute production (initially titled *Le Général*) is based on Louis Gasnier and George Cukor's *The Virtuous Sin* (1930), starring Conrad Veidt and Kay Francis. Paramount's fourth French film out of Paris is set in Russia, in 1914, when a young woman named Marya tries to save the life of her husband Boris, a pacifist medical student, because the First World War has forced him into the army. By joining a group of entertainers who perform for the fighting men, she hopes to meet and convince General Platoff, her husband's commanding officer, to pardon him for his refusal to take up arms. Premiering in Paris in September 1931, Millar's film was rated a "very fair programmer. Story clicking and technical

work very good, especially the photography," wrote *Variety*. "Either of the two main parts ... is a star role."

## Le Réquisitoire (Indictment)

(Dimitri Buchowetski, 1930). Paramount. **Script:** Benno Vigny, Hermann Kosterlitz, and Pierre Scize. **Photography:** Harry Stradling. **With** Marcelle Chantal (Lydia Alton), Fernand Fabre (Georges Sainclair), Raymond Leboursier (Bobby), Elmire Vautier, and Gaston Jacquet. Initially titled *Homicide*, this is the melodramatic 84-minute story of the idle, rich, and young Lydia Alton who accidently kills a policeman while speeding. During her trial for manslaughter, she falls for district attorney Sinclair. As one of Paramount's early French releases from Paris, the film was called "infinitely better in all respects than any other film yet made" in the studios outside of Paris. Whatever success it earned was entirely to Chantal who "steals the show" and moves "the sentimental French audience to the point where most of it is crying," observed a critic. "She dominates every scene with her cultivated acting and radiant appearance."

## Le Rêve d'Endymion (Endymion's Dream)

(Jean Caret, 1932). Paramount. **With** Boris Kniaseff and the Ballets Russes. This dance short from Paris stars the famous Russian-French dancer-choreographer and his company. Their ballet is based on the classical Greek myth about a young man who is kept immortally youthful and beautiful through eternal sleep, beloved by the goddess Selene, who comes to him every night in his cave. The short was filmed at the Forêt de Chantilly.

## Rien que des mensonges (Nothing but Lies)

(Karl Anton, 1932). Paramount. **Script:** Saint-Granier and Paul Schiller. **Music:** René Sylviano. **With** Marguerite Moreno (Mrs. Leverdier), Jeanne Fusier-Gir (Colombe), Robert Burnier (André Chevilly), and Armand Lurville. This was one of the funniest and last films produced by Paramount in Paris (also known as *Trois points c'est tout* and initially titled *Francs-maçons* and *Le Cercie viceux*). The 84-minute original story, based on a play, is nothing but a series of prevarications by the married man named André Chevilly. At the start, he claims to be a Freemason, a responsibility that necessitates his being away from home. After visiting his mistress and getting himself into trouble, he claims to be rich. That makes matters worse, so he lies again and gets into even more hot water. Moreno is the standout, giving one of her best performances as a music-hall entertainer in this moneymaking hit.

## Rien que la vérité (Nothing but the Truth)

(René Guissart, 1931). Paramount. **Script:** Paul Schiller and Saint-Granier. **Photography:** René Dantan. **Music:** Paul Barnaby. **Design:** Henri Ménessier and René Renoux. **With** Saint-Granier (Robert Barnet), Meg Lemonnier (Nicole), Armand Lurville (Ragnier-Lambert), and Pierre Etchepare. A diverting 92-minute screwball comedy from Paris that follows the story line of the studio's Hollywood production, *Nothing but the Truth* (1929), starring Richard Dix. But the French adaptation and treatment are different. Brazen Robert Barnet bets 250,000 francs that for 24 hours he will speak only the truth. He finds that not only is his bet in jeopardy but also his relationship with his girlfriend, Nicole. Excepting Chevalier's films out of Hollywood, Guissart's work became the biggest draw of its day when it premiered in September 1931 at the Paramount Theatre in Paris. "What makes the film move is the American tempo for gags," wrote a critic.

## Rive gauche (Left Bank)

(Alexander Korda, 1931). Paramount. **Supervisor:** Jean de Marguénat. **Adaptation and dialogue:** Benno Vigny. **Photography:** Ted Pahle and Harry Stradling. **Design:** Henri Ménessier. **Producer:** Robert Kane. **With** Meg Lemonnier (Lulu), Fanny Clair (Daisy), Henri Garat (Robert Delattre), Robert Arnoux (Alfred), and Jean Worms. This 95-minute, fast-paced, sophisticated, romantic comedy is a rendition of the studio's Hollywood version, called *Laughter* (1930), directed by Harry D'Arrast. It is about a young musician from Montparnasse who pursues the girl of his dreams to Rome, even after she weds a wealthy banker.

Korda's Paris film little resembles the Hollywood original in story or tone. Korda and Vigny made the French film their own by adding a more brooding atmosphere to their own story, reflecting their backgrounds in expressionistic German filmmaking. While the film is thus less humorous than D'Arrast's Hol-

Sacha Guitry as the man on the make, with Yvonne Printemps in *Roman d'amour et d'aventures* (Sacha Guitry, Eclipse, 1916).

lywood film, it is as sharply observed in the attitudes toward money and love. The film was shown to acclaim in Paris in October 1931.

## Roman d'amour et d'aventures (Story of Love and Adventure)

(René Hervil and Louis Mercanton, 1918). Eclipse. **With** Sacha Guitry, Yvonne Printemps, and Max Maxudian. This story of a young man on the make, which contains a commentator and personalities in the arts, science, and literature, resembles in approach and theme the kinds of films Guitry repeated in sound. Codirector René Hervil, a stage actor in Paris and in the provinces, made his film debut in 1912. He became well known in the 1920s as one of the greatest commercial film directors of the time. During the 1930s his *Le Mystère de la Villa Rose* was one of the first Franco-British double-cast talkies, and featured Arletty into her screen debut.

## Les Roquevillard

(Julien Duvivier, 1922). Pathé. **Script:** Duvivier. **Photography:** Albert Cohendy. **With** Jeanne Desclos (Edith), Nick Martens (Marguerite Roquevillard), Jeanne Kerwich, Juliette Verneuil, Jeanne Helbling, Georges Melchior (Maurice),

Maxine Desjardins (François), and Jean Stelli. A studied 1,950-meter production (based on the 1905 novel by Henry Bordeaux) that signaled Duvivier's interest in literary adaptations, the drama made Duvivier a favorite with the filmgoing public, and turned a profit for his investors. Though the protagonist, Maurice, comes from a tradition-bound family of magistrates, he falls in love with a married woman, Edith, and takes her to Italy. A scandal ensues — surprisingly, Maurice is accused of theft, not adultary — and Maurice's mother dies. Ashamed but innocent, Maurice is saved by the efforts of his father, François, who invokes the glorious and unassailable lineage of the Roquevillards.

## Sa nuit de noces (His Wedding Night)

(Louis Mercanton, 1931). Paramount. With Lucien Galas. A short, naughty Paris farce about couples who intend to exchange partners.

## Le Secret du docteur (The Doctor's Secret)

(Charles de Rochefort, 1930). Paramount. Adaptation: Denys Amiel. Editor: Roger Capellani. With Marcelle Chantal (Liliane Garner), Alice Tissot (Mrs. Reading), Odette Joyeux (Suzy), Max Maxudian (Dr. Brody), and Jean Bradin (Jean Colman). This 77-minute version of The Doctor's Secret (1930), which is based on a play by James Barrie, was one of Paramount's earliest films out of Paris. The tale was well-known in its day: An unhappily married woman runs away with her lover, only to see him die in an accident. She returns home distraught, trying to keep the affair and its aftermath a secret. However, as coincidence would have it, the doctor who had tried to save the man's life is also a friend of her husband's. Because of the beautiful and glamorous Marcelle Chantal's outstanding performance, her contract "should be one of Paramount's local assets," wrote Variety. The film "clicked" at its Paris premiere in October 1930.

## Le Seul bandit du village (The Only Rogue in the Village)

(Robert Bossis, 1931). Paramount. With Tramel and Georges Bever. A short Paris comedy that is based on Tristan Bernard's 1898 one-act vaudeville play of the same name about a baron who believes the baroness is having an affair with the only thief in the town.

## Le Sexe fort (The Strong Sex)

(1930). Paramount. With Saint-Granier, Marguerite Moreno, and Paul Pauley. A 10-minute Paris comedy likely based on Tristan Bernard's 1918 play about the lack of will in men. The tale points to a hitherto unimagined new order in the world, one in which husbands stay home, wives go to work, and women call men for dates.

## Si l'empereur savait ça! (If the Emperor Only Knew!)

(Jacques Feyder, 1930). MGM. Photography: William Daniels. Dialogue: Yves Mirande. With Tania Fédor, André Luguet, Françoise Rosay, and André Berley. The director's second French-language film out of Hollywood concerns itself with a subject he turned to often in his stay in America: the love between people of differing social status. The 90-minute drama about a dashing young peasant out to win the hand of a beautiful princess is a reworking of *His Glorious Night* (1929), based on Ferenc Molnár's play *Olympia*. André Luguet as the young hero is "very good, as usual," said a critic. "He's the best actor French legit has given the screen."

Feyder's version also revealed the great comedic talent of Françoise Rosay who, in the role of the beautiful heroine's mother, nearly steals the show. In one scene, for instance, she clips the end of a cigar with her finger-nail, lights up, and smokes. Feyder's handsome and lavish production, wrote *Variety*, is "unquestionably the finest French talker produced to date." Yet the film came under attack because "nobody can possibly enjoy this film without a full knowledge of French." Further, its atmospheric recreation of Paris life may have confused matters, since, supposedly, the action takes place in Vienna.

## Simone est comme ça (Simone Is Like That)

(Karl Anton, 1932). Paramount. **Script:** Yves Mirande. **Music:** Raoul Moretti. **Lyrics:** Jean Boyer. **With** Meg Lemonnier (Simone), Milly Mathis (Ernestine), Edith Méra, Pierre Etchepare (Max), André Brulé, and Henri Garat (André). An 86-minute original Paramount comedy filmed in Paris about two attractive people, Simone and André, who feel obliged to hide their feelings for each other. The film is based on Yves Mirande's hit 1926 three-act operetta, with music by Moretti.

## Le Soir des rois (Kings' Evening)

(Jean Daumery, 1932). Warner Bros.–First National. **Script:** Paul Vialar. **With** Simone Mareuil (Suzanne), Marie-Louise Delby (Lulu), María Dhervilly (the barones), Jacques Maury (Georges), Paul Vialar, and Jean Daumery. Based on Jerome Kingston's novel *Sinners All*, this 74-minute comedy was a rare American-backed French production filmed in London. It centers around an apparent crime. When Georges throws a Christmas party for old friends at his family estate, shady characters also show up. He soon discovers that the safe has been tampered with — and that his aunt's priceless necklace is gone. With his girlfriend's help, he unmasks the thieves and retrieves the jewelry — only to be surprised again. This version of *Help Yourself* (1932), directed by Daumery, was also called *Soyez les bienvenus*.

## Soyons gais

(Arthur Robison, 1930). MGM. **Dialogue:** Jacques Deval. **With** Françoise Rosay, Lily Damita, Mona Goya, Tania Fédor, Lya Lys, and Marcel André. This 88-minute freewheeling romantic comedy, the director's first (and the studio's fourth) from Hollywood is about divorcées who meet years later at a country party. The 88-minute film is a rendition of Robert Z. Leonard's entertainingly witty *Let Us Be Gay* (1930), adapted from Rachel Crother's stage play, which *Variety* called "strong on all counts, romance, comedy, human sympathy and gorgeous clothes against a glamorous setting." The French version was called *Gai, gai, démarions-nous* when shown in France.

## Le Spectre vert (The Green Ghost)

(Jacques Feyder,1930). MGM. **Dialogue:** Yves Mirande. **With** André Luguet and Jetta Goudal. The European director's first sound film was also the first French-language film out of Hollywood, based on Ben Hecht's story, which had been turned into *The Unholy Night* (1929), directed by, and starring, Lionel Barrymore. The 90-minute French version is a more atmospheric murder-mystery set in Britain. The film — its central metaphor is the London fog — was called "the mellowest of melodrama" by one critic, about an officer who is murdering fellow officers in order to inherit a fortune bequeathed to the regiment. The film was never released in the U.S. — it was slated only for export — but it came under attack in France, where law declared that a movie shot in America was anything but French, even if all the actors came from Paris.

## Sur le tas de sable (On the Sand Pile)

(Louis Mercanton, 1931). Paramount. **With** Jean Mercanton and Jean Bara. This 15-minute Paris comedy, based on a sketch by Poulbot, stars the two most touted French child actors of the era.

## Ta femme te trompe (Your Wife Deceives You)

(Robert Bossis, 1932). Paramount. **Script:** Jean Guitton. **With** Paul Pauley, Andrée Champeaux, Jean Guitton, and Georges Bever. This 30-minute comedy, written by a future member of the French Academy, is evidently about improper relationships, beginning with a doctor and his mistress having a spat and an author and his wife quarreling. The next morning the author's wife (Champeaux) wakes up in the bed of the doctor who, very respectfully, has passed the night in an armchair in the next room. Circumstances cause her to occupy the bed — until respect reaches the breaking point.

## Thérèse Raquin

(Jacques Feyder, 1927). DEFU. **Script:** Fanny Carslen and Willy Haas. **Photography:** Hans Scheib and Friedrich Fuglsang. **Design:** André Andréjew and Erich Zander. **With** Gina Manès (Thérèse), Jeanne Marie Laurent, Wolfgand Zilzer (Camille Raquin), and Adalbert von Schlettow (Laurent). Feyder's remarkable, 2,800-meter Franco-German production of Zola's timeless, psychologically intense tale of murder and guilt is a film that was said to have meshed well its atmosphere, narrative and stars. It became notable for the performance of the half–French, half–German cast members, notably Manès as the passionate young woman married to her cousin; Schlettow as the solid young man who transforms her life. Further, the tale incorporates up-to-date elements of automobiles and contemporary dress and a recreation (in Berlin) of the 1870s Paris street called Passage du Pont-Neuf. Jean Mitry called the film, for which Feyder wrote the titles, "one of the most uncompromising of the realist films and ... a masterpiece of French silent cinema." Released in the U.S. under the name *Thou Shalt Not*, it remains one of the most famous of lost films.

Gina Manès as the woman who inspires murder in *Thérèse Raquin* (Jacques Feyder, DEFU, 1928).

### Tobie est un ange (Tobias Is an Angel)

(Yves Allégret, 1941). SPDF. **Script:** Allégret and Pierre Brasseur. **Photography:** Henri Alekan. **With** Pola Illéry and Pierre Brasseur. Illéry's last film and photographer Alekan's first was reportedly destroyed in a lab fire in 1941.

### Le Tonnerre (Thunder)

(Louis Delluc, 1921). Alhambra Films. **Assistant director:** Jean Epstein. **Script:** Delluc. **Photography:** Alphonse Gibory. **With** Marcel Vallée (Mortimer), Lili Samuel (Evangéline), and Anna Widford. Based on Mark Twain's 1880 short story, "Mrs. McWilliams and the Lightning" (in France it was apparently called "Evangéline and the Thunder"), the film is a deliciously atmospheric burlesque about domesticity. The starting point is Twain's proposition that "The fear of lightning is one of the most distressing infirmities a human being can be afflicted with. It is mostly confined to women, but now and then you find it in a little dog, and sometimes a man." In actuality, Twain's wife, Livy, feared lightning—and her consternation was the inspiration for his tale.

The ever-careful Evangéline, at her "summer establishment," wakes up in the middle of the night to thunderous sounds. Afraid of what that means, she won't stay in bed, nor will she approach a window, wall, or an open door. She also believes it dangerous to sing or run water, and thinks that lit matches, woolen clothing, and open chimneys attract lightning, while cats are to be feared for their "electricity." One solution is to pray, another to decipher a German book on what to do in such a situation. The solution, according to the literature at hand, is to have her husband Mortimer protect the famly—by becoming an indoor lightning rod. He is made to stand on a chair wearing a fireman's helmet, saber, spurs, and ringing a bell. Passersby hear the racket coming from the house, and inform Evangéline and Mortimer of the truth to it all: that the sounds coming from afar are only celebratory fireworks.

## La Tournée verdure (The Greenery Tour)

(André E. Chotin, 1931). Paramount. Script: Georges Rip. With Marguerite Moreno. A 10-minute Paris satire evidently taken from a sketch from Rip's 1929 revue *A la mode de chez nous*, in which a guide expounds on history while taking a group through an orchard in flower. Sacha Guitry's treatment of historical characters is spoofed when the guide speaks of Louis Pasteur, Mozart, Napoleon III, and Charles Lindburgh as though Guitry's plays about them are their only claim to distinction.

## Toute sa vie (All Her Life)

(Alberto Cavalcanti, 1930). Paramount. Script and dialogue: Jean Aragny. Photography: Ted Pahle. With Marcelle Chantal (Suzy Valmond), Fernand Fabre (Jim Grey), Jean Mercanton (Jimmy), Pierre Richard-Willm (Stanley Vanning), and Elmire Vautier (Mrs. Ashmore). A 90-minute heartbreaker from Paris (initially titled *L'Appel du cœur*) that is based on the studio's Hollywood version, *Sarah and Son* (1930), starring Ruth Chatterton.

Chantal, one of the most glamorous screen actresses of her time, plays New York music-hall performer Suzy Valmond (she gets to render two songs in the film). Suzy is married to a violent man who abducts their infant son. She manages to go on with her life and achieves fame. But all the while her heart seeks only to locate her missing boy, Jimmy, who these many years was being raised by a wealthy English couple. Critical reaction to the Paris tearjerker was cool: "The sentimental French ... were expecting both mothers to make up and commune in their love of the child," wrote a critic at the film's Paris premier in November 1930. "Latter ending would have carried a considerable punch." Of the six foreign versions of the story Paramount produced, this one, shown in the United States in mid–1931 at 80 minutes, ranks as the best.

## Le Train sans yeux (Blind Train)

(Alberto Cavalcanti, 1925). Neo-Films. Script: Cavalcanti. Photography: Jimmy Rogers and Daub. With Gina Manès (Green Palma), Hanni Weisse, and Georges Charlia. This wild, improbable tale (based on a short story by Louis Delluc), one of Cavalcanti's earliest, is about the destructive power of passion. The American Green Palma, owner of a French bank, is rich, pretty, and coveted by a bank manager. She prefers another employee, but the manager gets him fired. He then heads by train to Cannes to find Green Palma. There she is the object of attention of several other men, including a blind scholar. The tale comes to a climax on the roaring train back to Paris, with the scholar finding himself in the engineer's seat!

The film was shot in Germany and then withheld from distribution because the producers could not pay their bills.

### La Traversé du Crepon (The Crossing of the Crepon)

(André Sauvage, 1923). A documentary short on mountain-climbing that was called at its release one of the "quality films that the commercial industry had not allowed the majority of the public to see" as well as among the "films of such value that they merit a second screening under the title of Cinema Classics."

### Un Trou dans le mur (A Hole in the Wall)

(René Barbéris, 1930). Paramount. **Assistant director:** Jean Cassagne. **With** Marguerite Moreno (Arthémise), Pierre Brasseur (Anatole), Jean Murat (André de Kerdrec), and Dolly Davis (Lucie). This 83-minute Paris comedy, based on Yves Mirande's popular 1929 play, was a milestone of sorts: it was Paramount's first film out of the French capital. Stage actress Moreno, in her film debut, lent her prestige and talent to play a countess unaware of a fortune buried within the walls of her prerevolutionary mansion. She was hailed as being in an "infinitely superior class to any other French actress of the moment." Her film differs entirely from Robert Florey's 1929 Hollywood production of the same name, a tale about spiritualism and mobsters. The Paris production was eagerly awaited, creating anticipation and a stir in the film world, which on June 7, 1930, called it a "rip roaring opening." *Variety* concluded, "the picture is fully up to the best standards of Hollywood."

### Tu seras duchesse! (You Will Be a Duchess!)

(René Guissart, 1931). Paramount. **Script and dialogue:** Yves Mirande. **Photography:** René Dantan. **Music:** Francis Gromon. **Design:** Henri Ménessier. **With** Marie Glory (Annette Poisson), Fernand Gravey (Marquis André de la Cour), André Berley (Mr. Poisson), Pierre Etchepare, Pierre Feuillère, and Sem (caricaturist). An exceptionally fine 85-minute original Paramount musical comedy from Paris about a rich, scheming, fish merchant who wants his charming young daughter Marie to marry a much older — and wealthy — duke. He intends to make this happen by first arranging for her to marry an impoverished and purportedly terminally ill marquis.

The Paris film "just evades being too naughty from the censor's standpoint, though the dialogue slipped through," wrote *Variety* from New York in May 1932. Three years later, this entertaining comedy reached U.S. screens again. Since it was still unsubtitled, the *New York Times* warned, "a knowledge of French is necessary for full appreciation of some of the finer points of this highly amusing production ... Guissart ... makes good use of the able actors at his command and keeps the picture moving smoothly."

## L'Uniforme

(Gaston Biasini, 1932). Paramount. **Script:** Henri Duvernois. **Photography:** Georges Clerc. **With** Fernand Frey (vagabond). A 30-minute comedy sketch from Paris (based on Duvernois's story) about the yearning for respectability. Taking part in a break-in, a Chaplinesque vagabond disguises himself as a policeman. As he suddenly feels the worthiness of the clothing he wears, his character changes. He is flattered when another policeman greets him, feels virtuous when he helps an old woman, and becomes outraged when insulted by a drunk. Brought back to reality when stripped of his uniform, he longs regretfully for the dignity he briefly felt.

## Les Vacances du diable (The Devil's Holiday)

(Alberto Cavalcanti, 1930). Paramount. **Adaptation:** Cavalcanti, Georges Neveux and Jean Aragny. **Dialogue:** Georges Neveux. **Photography:** Enzo Riccioni and Ted Pahle. **With** Marcelle Chantal (Betty Williams), Thomy Bourdelle (Mark Stone), Pierre Richard-Willm (Dr. Reynolds), Maurice Schutz (David Stone), and Jacques Varennes (Charlie Thorn). Based on Edmund Goulding's highly-rated *The Devil's Holiday* (1930), Paramount's French version from Paris is a morality play about a money-grubbing woman on the make who repents her ways. The story was showered with praise in its day. Pictures such as this, wrote a critic, "revive the drooping confidence in the screen as a mirror of things as they really are."

## Le Vendeur d'automobiles (The Car Dealer)

(1930). Paramount. **With** Saint-Granier. In this comedy short from Paris, Saint-Granier vainly attempts to become the top salesman of his dealership's latest models. He concludes the film with immitations of Maurice Chevalier, Raimu, Dorville, Max Dearly, and Maurice Rostand (son of the great Edmond Rostand).

## Le Vendeur du Louvre (The Salesclerk at the Louvre)

(Jean de Marguénat, 1932). Paramount. **Script:** Saint-Granier and Albert Willemetz. **With** Alexandré Dréan. A 12-minute Paris comedy in which a hick from the provinces is sold a bill of goods at the great Paris institution.

## La Veuve joyeuse (The Merry Widow)

(Ernst Lubitsch, 1934). MGM. **Adaptation:** Marcel Achard. **With** Maurice Chevalier (Danilo), Jeanette MacDonald (Missia), Danièle Parola (Dolores), Fifi D'Orsay (Marcelle), Marcel Vallée (Popoff), Pauline Garo (Loulou), Lya Lys (Maxim girl), André Cheron, and André Berley (General Achmed). The studio's thirteenth and last French-language film out of Hollywood is the consummate version of the selfsame director's historical musical romance *The*

Jeanette MacDonald as the widow, with Maurice Chevalier and Fifi D'Orsay in *La Veuve joyeuse* (Ernst Lubitsch, MGM, 1934).

*Merry Widow* (1934). Studio mogul Thalberg backed the making of the 105-minute French-language version to insure success in France, where Chevalier was more popular when he spoke in his native language. Further, Thalberg's investment of $50,000–$60,000 kept a number of production people on the Hollywood payroll.

Lubitsch, who directed only two French-language films in his career, shot the film simultaneously with the English version. He emphasized some scenes for the English-speaking audiences and played down others (notably eliminating any references to the French monar-

chy) for foreign consumption, but the results were a triumph. Further, the adaptation and dialogue made *La Veuve joyeuse* unique. Said Achard, "It does not have the feeling of a French version of an American production but rather of a French film."

Stills: www.dandugan.com/maytime/f-veuvej.html.

## Voici le printemps (Here's Spring)

(Louis Mercanton, 1931). Paramount. **With** Yvette Guilbert. A musical short from Paris with the legendary singer.

# Germany

In the years before the First World War, the Nordisk Films Company of Copenhagen had a dominant position in German cinema. As a result, the Scandinavian performer Asta Nielsen and the Danish-born director Stellan Rye became a natural part of German productions. Nielsen and Rye, along with Max Reinhardt and Paul Wegener, helped German cinema make the breakthrough to art.

"Thanks to Rye," wrote Georges Sadoul, "and the influence of Max Reinhardt, the German cinema was beginning to discover a style by turning towards legends of the Middle Ages, based on the splitting of personality, the power of fate, the sudden setting free of magical powers, the annihilation of apprentice magicians by obscure forces carelessly unchained."

Asta Nielsen's acting style from the beginning was characterized by sudden changes, from violent movement to standstill, almost a paralysis. In her autobiography she explains the origins of this method: "The opportunity to develop character and mood gradually, something denied the film actor, can only be replaced by a kind of 'auto suggestion' (or trance)." In Germany she was called "Die Duse des Films," a comparison to the Italian stage actress Eleonora Duse. Cinemas were named after her (there was even an Asta Nielsen waltz). She became a trendsetter in fashion. Her hairstyle — notably the two chignons around her ears — was imitated by young women in Germany and abroad.

Paul Wegener freed film from implied relationships to theater and literature, and discovered new camera techniques when he brought to the screen the supernatural, the fairytale, and the ballad, most evident in the Rye-Wegener-Seeber collaboration, *Der Student von Prag* (1913). It was one of German cinema's earliest horror-fantasies. Wegener recognized that the camera had to be "the real poet of film," while his theory of "kinetic lyricism" anticipated abstract filmmaking. Ethereal fantasy (a la the Brothers Grimm) was brought to life by German filmmakers, who were perhaps the first to commercialize sex and nudity, and sell it as art.

In 1917 Universum Film A.G. (Ufa) was formed, taking the assets in Germany of the Nordisk Films Company and patterning itself after the giant Danish organization. Wegener's artistic ambitions, his stress on the concept of illusion, and his leanings towards anti-civilization helped to make Ufa a national studio. Ufa's other great director was Ernst Lubitsch, who made his name by turning spectacle into drama and comedy into art.

During the transition to sound, Paramount was willing to go head-to-head with the highly regarded German studios for the German-language market: 64 million speakers in Germany, 7.5 million in Austria, 3.5 million in Czechoslovakia, a majority in Switzerland, and large percentages in Scandinavia and the Baltic states. It helped that the German studios, especially Ufa, had been caught unawares by the introduction of sound, and were slow in converting their studios to the new technology. In 1930 and 1931, Paramount shot 14 German films, two of which were directed by Alexander Korda.

## *Abel mit der Mundharmonika (Abel with the Harmonica)*

(Erich Waschneck, 1933). Ufa. **Script:** Manfred Hausmann and Walter Müller. **Photography:** Günther Rittau and Otto Baecker. **Music:** Clemens Schmalstich. **With** Karin Hardt (Corinna), Karl Schreiber (Abel), Heinz von Cleve (Patten), and Carl Balhaus. The camera's the thing in this ten-reel musical comedy (which was released after Hitler's rise to power). It is based on Manfred Hausmann's novel about an adventurous young woman, a balloonist and sea-farer, who attracts young men, especially one fine harmonica player and sailor.

In tune with Hausmann's novel, the director set the film in the north German lowlands, and it's an example of the loving attraction that German landscapes had to writers and directors. The production can lay claim to a series of remarkably effective wind-swept shots. It was also called *Eine Frau fällt vom Himmel.*

## *Abend ... Nacht ... Morgen (Evening ... Night ... Morning)*

(F. W. Murnau, 1919) Decla. **Script:** Rudolf Schneider-München. **Photography:** Eugen Hamm. **Design:** Robert Neppach. **With** Bruno Ziemer (Chester), Gertrud Welker (Maud), Otto Gebühr (the detective), and Conrad Veidt (Brilburn). This five-reel (1,700-meter) Decla detective film was the director's sixth film in his career, and is an example of a popular genre of the era. It is an American-style drama about a kept woman, a stolen necklace, and murder. It all takes place within a day and "seems to be an unconscious satire," said a critic.

## *Die Abenteuer eines Zehnmarkscheines (The Adventures of a Ten Mark Banknote)*

(Berthold Viertel, 1926). Ufa/Fox Europa. **Script:** Béla Balász. **Photography:** Helmar Lerski and Robert Baberske. **Design:** Robert Basilice and Walter Reimann. **With** Mary Nolan (Anna), Agnes Müller, Imogen Robertson, Walter Franck, Oskar Homolka (Hamel), Vladimir Sokoloff, Julius E. Hermann, and Karl Etlinger. Vienna-born scriptwriter and director Viertel made his mark with this story of a bit of currency, earned at the start by the struggling mill worker Anna. It then goes its accidental way from hand to hand through the social scene — from Anna's aged mother, to a thief, to a murderer — and the result is a kaleidoscopic, cross-sectional look at chaotic life in Berlin during the Weimar Republic.

Also called *Uneasy Money* and *K13513*, the six-reel (2,400-meter) picture found favor with the critics. *Filmtechnik* in Berlin called it "one of the most filmic ideas," a new twist in stroytelling in "horizontal action." Its many-sided variations led a New York critic to comment about "a dandy comedy incident near the finish" that brings the money back to Anna.

## Die Augen des Ole Brandis (Ole Brandis's Eyes)

(Stellan Rye, 1913). Deutsche Bioscop. **Script:** Hanns Heinz Ewers. **Photography:** Guido Seeber. **Design:** Rochus Gliese. **With** Paul Wegener, Alexander Moïssi, Grete Berger, Lothar Körner, Jean Ducret, and Eva Holländer. This mystical four-reeler represents one of Moïssi's earliest screen efforts, a collaboration by Rye and Ewers (1871–1943) that focuses on the psychological.

The hero, an artist (played by Moïssi), is the favorite of many women, especially one named Freda, though he pays her little heed. His life takes a surprising turn when a painting of his is stolen. After considerable trouble, he identifies the thief, an old man who is willing to give the artist anything to keep the painting. The artist wants only one thing — to be able to see people for what they really are. The old man hands him the material with which to accomplish the astonishing feat.

"The spectator," wrote a critic, "after seeing one or two transformations, begins to speculate on how this or that character is going to turn out. There is a ragged heroine who alone is good and true, and what she appears to be." Filmed along a beautiful mountain lake "with tremendous backgrounds and lovely bits of landscape, ilex trees, garden walks, marble steps, and the rough twists and bends of a hillside city's ways," the film was released in the United States "with no clue to the maker" and a warning that "the gallery will hardly understand the meaning of it all."

## Die Austreibung (The Expulsion)

(F. W. Murnau, 1923). Decla. **Script:** Thea von Harbou. **Design:** Rochus Gliese and Erich Czerwonski. **Photography:** Karl Freund. **Music:** Joseph Viet. **With** Carl Götz (Steyer), Eugen Klöpfer, Lucie Mannheim (Aenne), William Dieterle (Lauer), and Jacob Tiedke. This four-reel (1,550-meter) production, based on the disturbing play by Carl Hauptmann (who had died a year earlier), bears the influence of Swedish cinema.

With an emphasis on feeling, the director's 14th film in his career is an impressionistic, vividly designed work about a young woman, ambiguous about her heritage, who marries the hunter Lauer outside her immediate village — and pays a terrible price. "This is a film of distinction," wrote an observer, "in which one senses a love of art, a gift for conjuring up visual atmosphere, and the desire to create a means of artistic expression."

## Der Bittsteller (The Petitioner)

(Erich Engels, 1936). Terra Filmverleih. **Script:** Engles and Reinhold Bernt. **Photography:** Ernst Wilhelm Fiedler. **With** Karl Valentin, Liesl Karlstadt, Reinhold Berndt, and Lydia Methner. In the period 1932–37, Karl Valentin, who was known for his grotesque, comical movements, acted in a series of shorts directed by Engels, who also worked in the theater. This collaboration is a surprising and uninhibited 15-minute (400-meter) work when one considers the political and moral climate in which it was made. Produced in Nazi Germany, it is a sketch about a poor man who, after asking a rich man for a favor, receives a large amount of cash. The short film was withheld from circulation by Nazi censors until 1938.

### Der Blusenkönig (The Blouse King)

(Ernst Lubitsch, 1917). Union-Atelier. **Script:** Hanns Kräly. **Photography:** Kurt Richter. **With** Ernst Lubitsch (Sally Katz). Käthe Dorsch, Guido Herzfeld, and Max Zilzer. Lubitsch plays a skirt chaser; a sales assistant with his eye on the shop girls. When, out of habit, he ensnares the boss' plump daughter, the tables are turned on him: she wants to get married. Bur her father reads the situation to mean that Katz wants to marry into the business. So, to put him off, he offers Katz partnership in the firm. Katz immediately takes advantage of the situation by heading off to see the pretty supervisor of the manufacturing department. A surviving eight-minute fragment of this comedy indicates how the plot is resolved.

### Der brennende Acker (The Burning Field)

(F. W. Murnau, 1922). Goron-Deulig. **Script:** Willy Hass, Thea von Harbou, and Arthur Rosen. **Design:** Rochus Gliese. **Photography:** Karl Freund and Fritz Arno Wagner. **With** Werner Krauss (Rog), Lya de Putti (Gerda), Alfred Abel, and Eugen Klöpfer. This sober and poetic six-reeler is the director's 12th film in his career and an example of his vision of, and concern for, the natural world, which is symbolized by "The Devil's Field."

Beautifully designed by longtime colleague Gliese, the production is a drama of competing claims to a fortune in oil, where turbulence can be found within and outside the protagonists. Murnau's film, which he made after his astonishing *Nosferatu* (1921–22), attracted attention for its calm, snowy landscapes and comfortable interiors which contrast sharply with a nighttime oil well fire. "For the first time we saw the … marvellous sense of psychological intimacy fully recreated in a German film," wrote a critic. René Clair called the film "expressive about a natural nature." Two surviving reels attest to Murnau's sense of lighting, love of depth focus, atmosphere, and subtle understanding of character.

### Der Bucklige und die Tänzerin (The Hunchback and the Dancer)

(F. W. Murnau, 1920). Helios. **Script:** Carl Meyer. **Design:** Robert Neppach. **Photography:** Karl Freund. **With** Sacha Gura (Gina), John Gottowt (Wilton), Paul Biensfeldt, Anna von Pahlen, and Henri-Peters Arnold. Called a "production in which the characters are bathed in … atmosphere," the five-reeler was the director's fourth film in his career and an early example of his interest in the exotic and the erotic. It hints of the surreal, the influence of Reinhardt, and seems to have been inspired by Lubitsch's pantomime *Sumurun* (1920).

The unfortunate hero gives the woman he loves perfume from the Orient. But the scent is deadly to all but him. Containing masterly sets, a carefully studied depth of focus, and a mystery man, the film contains a "kind of psychic perfume like the scents the hunchback brought back from Java," wrote a critic.

Stills: www.fh-bielefeld.de/fb4/murnau/f_buckl.htm.

## Casanova wider Willen (Casanova Against His Will)

(William Brophy, 1931). MGM. **Adaptation:** Paul Morgan. **With** Buster Keaton and Françoise Rosay. This is the Hollywood German-language version of Keaton's final silent, *Spite Marriage* (1929), the story of a tailor's assistant who, married to an actress because she wants to get even with someone else, rescues his bride from bootleggers and a sinking ship.

The two stars reprise their roles from *Buster se marie* (1931), the romantic comedy highlighted by scenes of Keaton's trying to get the girl, who has drunk herself into a stupor, onto a bed. To achieve even greater verisimilitude, Keaton had taken the trouble to learn German in Berlin, and his studio promoted the fact that he "now speaks the tongue of Goethe and Schiller." Unfortunately, Keaton's knowledge of German was incomplete, as was demonstrated during the filming when he assumed his German lines corresponded to those in the French script he had already filmed. The German material, however, was full of obscenities — and the star was known to hate vulgarity. The whole mess was cleaned up before the film's premiere and, commented a reviewer in Berlin early 1932, Keaton "was amply repaid. His American accent is on the merry side and amuses the audience doubly because it is just how they imagined he would speak."

## Dämon des Meeres (The Sea Beast)

(Michael Curtiz, 1931). Warner Bros. **Script:** Ulrich Steindorff. **Photography:** Sid Hickox. **With** William Dieterle (Christoph), Lissy Arna, Anton Pointner, and Carla Bartheel. Completed in 14 days, this 75-minute German-language version of *Moby Dick* (1930), starring John Barrymore and Joan Bennett, was the third of five German films that the studio produced in Hollywood in the early 1930s.

With an imported German cast that worked daily until 8:00 P.M. and on Saturdays until sundown, it made use of the same costumes and sets as the English-language version. It follows Christoph — in this film his name has been changed from Ahab — after he returns home (minus a leg) to the consternation of his fiancée. Recalled Dieterle: "*Moby Dick* was the only story I did that I had known since childhood. I loved it. It was great fun. It had never been done in Germany. They didn't have the means, the big sailing ship, the whale. It was a sensation." The film was shown in Berlin in March 1931.

## Dann schön lieber Lebertran (Rather Than Even Cod Liver Oil)

(Max Ophüls, 1930). Ufa. **Script:** Ophüls, Emeric Pressburger, and Erich Kastner. **Photography:** Eugen Schüfftan. **With** Paul Kemp, Kathe Haack, Hanneelore Schroth, and Heinz Gunsdorf. Max Ophüls's first directorial effort was this 30-minute (605-meter) fantasy sound film based on Kastner's story *Emil and the Detective*. It is a serious comedy about a child who gets his wish: he changes roles with his parents, and gets to answer the question, "If the natural order of things is turned upside down … wouldn't life be more pleasant?"

Ophüls and Kastner show that change for change's sake may not be the wisest course. Better the familiar daily spoonful of cod liver oil than a host of new problems. Beware of change seekers, warn Ophüls and his collaborators in the Germany of 1930. "They come from the left and the right."

## …Denn alle Schuld rächt sich auf Erden (…All Guilt Avenges Itself on Earth)

(Stellan Rye, 1913). Eiko-Film/ Deutsche Bioscop. **Script:** Hanns Heinz Ewers. **Photography:** Paul Adler and Axel Graatkjaer. **With** Alexander Moïssi, Paul Wegener, Grete Berger (Grete), Hermann Seldeneck, and Paul Bildt. This four-reel social drama was acclaimed stage actor Moïssi's second for Rye. Grete Rothe, the daughter of a musician, is attracted to and seduced by Baron Rüttersheim. Cast out by her father and despairing of finding a job, she decides to throw herself into the water. By chance Baroness Rütthersheim comes across her path and offers her a job as a lady's companion. Unsuspectingly, Grete finds her seducer in the baroness's home. He starts a new affair with her and, once more, abandons her. Grete avenges herself on the baron's son Paul, who had become hopelessly infatuated with her. As the baron is demanding an accounting of her action from his former lover, "a shot resounds in a nearby room," wrote a critic. Paul, in deepest despair and unable to see any other way out, had killed himself.

## Es werde Licht! (Let There Be Light!)

(Richard Oswald, 1917–18). Oswald Films. **Script:** Oswald, E. A. Dupont and Lupu Pick. **Photography:** Max Fassbender. **With** Werner Krauss, Theodor Loos, Else Heims, Lupu Pick, Leontine Kühnberg, Heinrich Schroth, Reinhold Schünzel, Kurt Vespermann, and Ernst Pittschau. Director Oswald became a major director in Berlin in the teens and twenties, famous for films which combined sexual enlightenment with crime themes. The work that set Oswald on the way to commercial success was this daring, four-part educational work — a genre he created — that looks at sexual ethics, venereal disease, and prostitution. The film was based on ideas by Lupu Pick, and its episodes (each around 1,800-meter) also established the name of coscriptwriter Dupont. (Excerpts from the script can be found in Dupont's 1919 book *Wie ein Film geschrieben wird* [*How to Write a Film.*])

## Evinrude, die Geschichte eines Abenteurers (Evinrude, the History of an Adventurer)

(Stellan Rye, 1913). Deutsche Bioscop. **Script:** Hanns Heinz Ewers. **Photography:** Guido Seeber and Axel Graatkjaer. **Design:** Robert A. Dietrich and Rochus Gliese. **With** Paul Wegener, Alexander Moïssi, Grete Berger, Lyda Salmonova, Jean Ducret, Victor Colani, and Hanns Heinz Ewers. A shocking drama of social contrast that begins in the American West and moves to fashionable Berlin clubs, high-society drawing rooms, and elegant motor boats. In the prelude of the four-reel (1450-m) drama, we are introduced to the commotion and hustle and bustle of the American Wild West, in gold-digging country and the prairie where Wegener the protagonist finds himself. At the end of the film, he is just about where he began — and just as desperate — aboard a primitive barge.

## Ewig Dein (Forever Yours)

(Erich Engels, 1938). Terra Filmkunst. **Photography:** Edgar S. Ziesemer. **With** Karl Valentin, Liesl Karlstadt, Philipp Weichand, and Irene Kohl. A 555-meter short based on the play by Ferner and Neal.

## Der Fall Molander (The Molander Affair)

(G. W. Pabst, 1944). Terra Films/Prague. **Script:** Ernst Hasselbach. **Photography:** Willy Kuhle. **With** Paul Wegener, Harold Paulsen, Walter Frank, and Irene von Meyerdorff. Alfred Karrach's *Violin of the Stars* was the source for Austrian director G. W. Pabst's tale about a young violinist forced to pawn his pricelsss Stradivarius — and then questioning whether he is still a violinist. Pabst's last wartime film suffered a disputed fate: some claim the Russians seized, then released the film in Eastern Europe after the war; others that the film was destroyed at the postproduction stage when the lab was bombed; still others that it exists, unfinished, in an archive in Prague.

The subtext of the film is the need to face the truth about oneself, and perhaps with this work, the supposedly pacifist, leftist Pabst, was facing up to the reality of having lived and worked in Nazi Germany since the start of the war.

## Die Flamme (The Sweetheart)

(Ernst Lubitsch, 1924). Ufa. **Script:** Hanns Kräly and Rudolph Kurtz. **Photography:** Theodor Sparkuhl and Alfred Hansen. **Design:** Ernst Stern and Kurt Richter. **With** Pola Negri (Yvette), Hermann Thimig (Leduc), Alfred Abel, Hilda Wörmer, Max Adelbert, and Jacob Tiedke. Lubitsch's last German film, based on Hans Müller's impressionistic stage play of the same name, is an ambient 85-minute tale, set in a glowing mid–19th century Paris. The beautiful Yvette is caught between two men (her wealthy husband and a cousin who lusts after her) and a shady past that makes it difficult to function easily in bourgeois society.

Her story (in the American release, called *Montmartre*) concludes happily with the birth of a child; it ends in her suicide in the German version. For perhaps the first time in her career, Negri is a sweet, young, vascillating creature — she shows "nothing in the way of undress to compare with her revelations in ... more recent films" — and "belongs in the top class of our screen emotionalists," reported *Variety*. Lubitsch's film contains "moments of dramatic intensity, bits of comic by-play, and other directorial touches," noted the trade journal, "that come like a rush of fresh air after the conventional Hollywood-made pictures." One reel (20 minutes) of the vivid and chiaroscuro German version survives.

## Fräulein Julie (Miss Julie)

(Felix Basch, 1921). Art-Film. **Script:** Carl Mayer, Max Jungk, and Julius Urgiss. **Photography:** Julius Balting. **Design:** Robert Herlth and Walter

Röhrig. **With** Asta Nielsen, William Dieterle, Arnold Korff (the count), Lina Lossen (the countess), and Olaf Storm. An adaptation based on Strindberg's one-act classic whose creative force is the acclaimed scriptwriter Mayer. He favored films with no moral other than that which, wrote a critic, "is implied by the fate of its characters, and by the forces leading to that fate ... in which one may feel blind impulses welling from their springs of animal need and instinct." During a turn of the century's midsummer's eve, the daughter of the manor flirts with a class-envious groom, and the result is tragedy.

The five-reel work was one of Nielsen's last screen performances based on a work by Strindberg. "Her eyes," wrote a reviewer, "are the main thing.... Her abstract slenderness has the effect of a single, twitching nerve with a twisted mouth and ... burning eyes.... She can smile in a way that would oblige the police to ban" her work.

### Freies Volk (Free People)

(Martin Berger, 1924). Veritas-Film. **Photography:** Paul Holzki. **With** Camilla Spira, Albert Florath, and Mathias Wieman. This well-filmed antifascist drama, called "the first republican superproduction," symbolized the political turbulence of its time and was hailed as a "realm manual for social-democratic voters." Financed by the *Arbeiterbank* (*Worker's Bank*), and supported by Weimar trade unions and the Reichbanners, a political party, the film, wrote the critics, "speaks from the types which it reflects." It starred the young Wieman (as a struggling worker) in his debut picture. The outstandingly crowded eight-reel (2,500-meter) film came on the heels, as it were, of Berger's still more controversial short *Die Schmiede*.

Scenes of an anti–Semitic rally by the young Nazi Party induced the right-wing to call for an outright ban of this work, while the Communist press attacked it as "kitsch melodrama" that "conceals the revolutionary fight." Berger's admirers called him "a genuine and right people director ... on the world's stage the only courageous film director in Germany." When his film became a fiasco for the producers and creditors, Berger retrenched, continuing his career with safer subject matter.

### Gehetzte Frauen (Chased Women)

(Richard Oswald, 1927). Oswald Films. **Script:** Oswald, Herbert Juttke, and Georg C. Klaren. **Photography:** Edgar S. Ziesemer. **Design:** Gustav Knauer. **With** Asta Nielsen (Clarina), Gustav Froelich (Alexander), Alexander Murski (Count Corvin), Carmen Boni (Angelica), Kurt Gerron (Vladimir), Jacob Tiedke, and Olga Limberg. Based on Annie von Brabenetz's daring story "Brettlfliegen," the six-reel tale is about the nightclub performer Clarina who tries to shield her daughter from evil. "Movies and novels in that kind of world," wrote a critic, "can count on the interest of the public." The film, which "has given Asta Nielsen a great role," begins in an "interesting way, then looses itself in a rich sentimentality that always appeals to German-speaking audiences."

### Der Geizhals (The Miser)

(Franz Seitz, 1934). Bavaria Film. **Music:** Toni Thoms. **With** Karl Valentin, Joe Stoeckel, and Liesl Karlstadt. This 600-meter short (also called *Der Geizige*) based on Molière's comedy *The Miser* was made with Jewish backing in Nazi Germany. It was never released.

## Der Golem (The Golem)

(Henrik Galeen and Paul Wegener, 1915). **Script:** Galeen and Wegener. **Photography:** Guido Seeber. **Design:** Rochus Gliese. **With** Wegener (Golem), Carl Ebert, Rudolf Blümer, and Jacob Tiedke. This film was called by Henri Langois one of the "sources of Germany's national film art." The original filming of the clay creature brought to life by a rabbi to protect Prague's Jews is actually titled *Der Golem und wie er auf die Welt kam* (*The Golem and How He Came into the World*).

Wegener was the first modern German film actor and one of the great, early defectors from German theater. He had made his name as the conflicted Balduin in Stellan Rye's *Der Student von Prag* (1913), which was hailed as the first real auteur film. An early, great work, it signaled a new era in German film. Wegener matched that effort with his bold performance in this 1,250-meter mythical tale, which contrasts the character of the Golem and the naturalistic surroundings — medieval Prague with its ghetto is brought fantastically to life — in order to highlight horror and inhumanity. One still survives from this vivid, brooding, preexpressionist production, also called *The Monster of Fate*.

Wegener's 1920 rendition of the story, called *Ger Golem, wie er in die Welt kam*, differs from the 1915 version (although the Golem, played by Wegener, is almost physically identical in both versions) because of its expressionist sets, which imply a relationship to the physically imposing protagonist. In that film horror gives way to legend, terror to psychology.

One source claims that this lost film was rediscovered in 1958, but this appears untrue.

## Der Golem und die Tänzerin (The Golem and the Dancer)

(Paul Wegener, 1917). Union Film. **Script:** Wegener. **Photography:** M. A. Madsen. **Design:** Rochus Gliese. **With** Wegener, Lyda Salmonova, Erich Schönfelder, Emilie Kurz, Wilhelm Diegelmann, and Rochus Gliese (Golem). A fanciful, lighthearted tale about the inner workings of a film studio in which Salmonova, a regular cast member of Wegener's films, plays a dual role. In this four-reel production, the authentic myth of the Golem (played by Gliese and not Wegener) has been worked loose from its religious moorings to serve a variety of symbolic functions.

Poster still: www.scils.rutgers.edu/special/kay/backgroundgolem.html.

## Grafin Donelli (Countess Donelli)

(G. W. Pabst, 1924). Maxim Films. **Script:** Hans Kyser. **Photography:** Guido Seeber. **Design:** Hermann Warm. **With** Henny Porten, Paul Hansen, and Friedrich Kayssler. Pabst's second film in his career is an 81-minute melodrama, and the beginning of a long collaboration with Guido Seeber and Hermann Warm. Their film helped to revive the career of Germany's first superstar, Henny Porten, who in this production plays a widow in economic straits, helped by a man who commits a crime. Years later the truth comes out, and it nearly ruins their lives. Pabst's next film was the internationally acclaimed *Joyless Street* (1925).

## Die große Fahrt (The Big Journey)

(Lewis Seiler, 1931). Fox. **Script:** Florence Postal, Marie Boyle, and Jack Peabody. **Photography:** Lucien Andriot and Arthur Edeson. **With** Théo Shall (Colman) and Marion Lessing (Ruth). The studio's only Hollywood German-language production is a rendition of Raoul Walsh's 70-mm western pioneer spectacle (*The Big Trail*), and the first of its kind by the studio. The overwhelming and beautiful landscape and the "vastness of scene and gigantic idea," wrote one critic, "reminded [one] of the silent *Covered Wagon*." While not up to the English-language classic, which stars John Wayne (as Breck Colman), this version had a better reception than the studio's French, Spanish, or Italian-language renditions.

## Halblut (The Half-Caste)

(Fritz Lang, 1918). Decla-Bioscop, **Script:** Lang. **Photography:** Carl Hoffmann. **With** Ressel Orla, Carl de Vogt, Gilda Langer, and Paul Morgan. This Lang film is one of his earliest efforts, a tale of racial animosity surrounding a beautiful woman of mixed heritage. She is seductive, clever, enticing, promising love and bliss. Men want her, but not as a mate. The film ends, like many of Lang's later films, in tragedy.

In the four-reel (1,600-meter) production, exotic scenes of Mexican life alternate in sequence with glimpses of the fashionable life in European capitals. In an opium den, raw emotions combine with demoralizing influences to bring life to animated, if unreal, levels. "We see," wrote a critic, "the passions of the gamblers that turn the weakling into the criminal … we see the harmful influence of the servile half caste," played by Orla, who becomes a sexual slave.

"The film distinguishes itself," wrote a reviewer at a preview, "especially through its heightened dramatic handling from scene to scene." The "excellent direction and flawless technical treatment … mark it as a narrative film." But the film was trimmed on release, whereupon the same reviewer concluded, "the movie looks like something mass produced as opposed to something individually created." The production was one of Langer's last before her sudden death by influenza in 1920 at the age of 23.

Stills: alf.zfn.uni-bremen.de/~a14m/films/halbblut.htm.

## Das Haus ohne Fenster und Türen (The House Without Windows and Doors)

(Stellan Rye, 1914). Deutsche Bioscop. **Photography:** Guido Seeber. **Design:** Robert Dietrich and Klaus Richter. **With** Vladimir Maximoff, Theodor Loos, Friedrich Kühne, Rose Veldkirch, and Paul Biensfeldt. Rye's next to last film as director (with Veldkirch in her first film role) is a stylized detective and action thriller influenced by Max Reinhardt in its treatment of personality, emphasis on destiny, and concern with evil. It is mix of fantasy and reality set in secret tunnels, at masked balls, and within darkened settings. In this world in which nothing is clearly seen, the male protagonist finds himself tied beneath the blade of a pendulum and the heroine blindfolded on stage. They have to fight not only forces bigger than themselves but the darker forces of their own personalities.

Rye's final film of his short career was the satirical *Serenissimus lernt Tango* (*Serenissimus Dances the Tango*) (1914), written and directed in collaboration with Paul Wegener and starring Ernst Lubitsch. It was banned by the censors because it ridiculed an emperor. In 1914, during the First World War, the 34-year-old Rye was mortally wounded at Ypres. "The German cinema lost, with the refined Dane, one who had oriented it toward its national destiny," wrote a critic.

## Hedda Gabler

(Franz Eckstein, 1924). National Film. **Script:** Rosa Porten and Eckstein. **Photography:** Franz Stein. **Design:** Max Frick. **With** Asta Nielsen, Paul Morgan (Jürgen Tesman), and Gregori Chmara (Eilert Lövborg). A six-reel, 2,600-meter adaptation of Ibsen's 1890 classic that represents Nielsen's last work in a Scandanavian subject, as well as her last Ibsen silent. The film ends in the suicide of a woman who had great wealth but could attain none of her desires.

## Die heilige Flamme (The Sacred Flame)

(Berthold Viertel, 1931). Warner Bros. **Script:** Berthold Viertel. **Photography:** Frank Kesson. **With** Salka Steuremann (Mrs. Taylor), Dita Parlo (Stella), Gustav Froelich (Walter), Vladimir Sokoloff, and Anton Pointner. This seven-reeler, the fourth of the studio's five Hollywood German-language films, is a version of the 1929 tearjerker *The Sacred Flame*. Based on Somerset Maugham's play of the same name, it is tale of a disabled war hero who is mercifully killed by a family member. The film was produced in less than two weeks and premiered at Berlin's Marmorhaus-I.

## Der Herr der Liebe (The Master of Love)

(Fritz Lang, 1919). Helios. **Script:** Oscar Koffler. **Photography:** Emil Schünemann. **With** Carl de Vogt (Vasile Disescu), Gilda Langer (Yvette), Erika Unruh, and Lang. This harsh and unsettling tale was filmed in five days by the novice Lang. The "Master of Love" is a powerful landowner (or Boyer) in the Carpathians who knows only lust. He considers himself irresistible. So does his wife, Yvette. But when he has a fling with a maid, Yvette broods upon revenge, finding a willing door-to-door salesman. In unspeakable fury, her husband strangles her, and then shoots himself.

"The mileau and characterization require scenes of sensual brutal effects," wrote a critic. "The [1,400-meter] film is quite fascinating in its gripping dramatic power and the striking concision of the action." Carl de Vogt brought to the lead an "imposing appearance and powerful masculinity," while the gorgeous Gilda Langer was called a woman "with unprecedented delicate, refined, sharp sensual attraction."

Stills: alf.zfn.uni-bremen.de/~a14m/films/herr.htm.

## Herzog Ferrantes Ende (Duke Ferrantes's End)

(Paul Wegener, 1922). Ufa. **Script:** Wegener. **Photography:** Karl Freund and Reimar Kuntze. **Design:** Rochus Gliese and Walter Reimann. **With** Wegener, Lyda Salmonova, Paul Hartmann, Ernst Deutsch, Ferdinand Gregori,

Hannes Sturm, Hugo Döblin, Adele Sandrock, Wilhelm Diegelmann, Hertha von Walther, and Fritz Richard. A seven-reel (2,400-meter) drama which Henri Langois identified as one of Germany's and Wegener's great masterpieces. It was shown only in Russia.

## Ich heirate meinen Mann (I Married My Man)

(Emmerich W. Emo, 1931). Paramount. **Script:** Franz Schulz. **Photography:** Ted Pahle. **Music:** Richard Whiting and Charles Borel-Clerc. **With** Trude Berliner (Liane), Kurt Vespermann (Bob), Szöke Szakall (Adolphe), Miguel Ligero, and Igo Sym (Willy Carter). Based on Paramount's risqué musical comedy *Her Wedding Night* (1930), Emo's German rendition of a marital mixup, which was filmed in Paris, concludes in the Baltics.

## Die Januskopf (Janus Head)

(F. W. Murnau, 1920). Decla/Lipow Film. **Script:** Hans Janowitz. **Design:** Heinrich Richter. **Photography:** Karl Freund and Carl Hoffmann. **With** Conrad Veidt (Warren/O'Connor), Margarete Schlegel (Grace), Bela Lugosi (the butler), and Willy Kayser-Heyl. This film is an example of Murnau's ability to create theatrical avant-garde, á la Max Reinhardt, from a source that was probably not his right to adapt. Film historian Krakauer observed of Murnau's work that he had a penchant for blurring the boundaries between the real and unreal: "Reality in his films was surrounded by a halo of dreams and presentiments."

The six-reel (2,220-meter) production is a retelling of Stevenson's *The Strange Case of Dr. Jekyll and Mr. Hyde.* As the director's fifth film in his career, it was also called *Schrecken* and subtitled "On the Borders of Reality." His adaptation (for which he altered the protagonist's names to protect himself from legal proceedings) was praised especially for its crowd scenes and nightmare sequences.

## Jede Frau hat Etwas (Every Woman Has It)

(Leo Mittler, 1930). Paramount. **Dialogue:** Charles Rollinghof. **Photography:** René Guissart. **Music:** W. Franke Harling. **With** Trude Berliner (Olivia Dangerfield), Kurt Vespermann (Charles Dangerfield), Willi Clever (Burton), and Anni Ann (Cora). This 85-minute German-language film out of Paramount's Paris studios is a version of *Honey* (1930), directed by Wesley Ruggles and starring Nancy Carroll.

It is an example of Mittler's favorite subject matter: a comedy of manners, in this case centering around the humorous complications a brother and sister face when they try to rent their southern home to a northerner in order to raise money to care for their father. Troubles result when they take on the roles of butler and maid. This German-language film was a rarity for German audiences of the time because of its setting: America. Paramount's rendition needed that something special to carry the day, at least with the critics. *Variety* noted that "technically they did a good job in Joinville, but couldn't overcome the slim material and no outstanding actors. Germans have been making too many good musicals ... for anything not making the grade to stand up, especially when made by Americans."

## Kismet

(William Dieterle, 1931). Warner Bros. **Script:** Karl Etlinger and Ulrich Steindorff. **Photography:** Sid Hickox and John Seitz. **With** Gustav Froelich, Dita Parlo, Vladimir Sokoloff (Kasim), Anton Pointner, and Karl Etlinger. Meaning "fate," this version of the famous play of the same name was the studio's fifth and last German film out of Hollywood, the story of an Oriental magician who vanquishes an evil opponent. It was the director's third and last Hollywood film in his native language, shot in only two weeks with a stellar Berlin cast. The film was shown at the Marmorhous in Berlin.

## Der Knabe in Blau (The Boy in Blue)

(F. W. Murnau, 1919). Ernst Hoffmann/Victoria Film. **Script:** Hedda Hoffmann. **Photography:** Carl Hoffmann. **With** Ernst Hofmann (Thomas), Blandine Ebinger (gypsy), Margit Barnay (actress), and Karl Plathen. A fantasy inspired by the famous British painting, the five-reel film was Murnau's debut production of his 12-year career. The master filmmaker was a trained art historian whose painterly images were inspired by romantic, impressionist, and expressionist art. His films, however, display an antipathy toward expressionism's supernatural indulgences — a reaction due perhaps to Murnau's mentor, Max Reinhardt.

In this work, Thomas is the last in a long line of nobility, and wants to restore a measure of serenity to his life. He feels a strange connection between himself and the boy in blue in a painting, and has a dream in which the boy leads him to a hiding place. When he investigates the next day, he actually finds the legendary "emerald of death" which the boy is wearing on his chest. The stone, which always brings trouble to its carrier, was hidden by one of Thomas's ancestors. And true to the myth, Thomas is nearly destroyed by the jewel. But the love of a young actress saves him.

Stills: www.f h-bielefeld.de/fb4/murnau/f_kna.htm.

## Komödie des Herzens (Comedy of the Heart)

(Rochus Gliese, 1924). Ufa. **Script:** Peter Murglie. **Photography:** Theodor Sparkuhl. **Design:** Robert Herlth and Walter Röhrig. **Music:** Guisseppe Becce. **With** Lil Dagover (Gerda Werska), Nigel Barrie (Baron Vinzens), Alexander Murski (Count Inger), Ruth Weyher, and Colette Brettel. This drama, based on Sophie Hochstätter's *Maskenball des Herzens*, satirizes personal and societal mores. The dancer Gerta Werska loves Baron Vinzens, and a friendship develops between them. The baron, however, is interested in both Daisy and Inge, who are jealous of each other. After numerous amusing episodes, the baron receives the hand of Gerda, who happily gives up her art.

Scriped by F. W. Murnau and Gliese (thus the name "Murglie"), the six-reel (1,900-meter) film became a major producton of the year, and one that helped make the reputation of Erich Pommer, head of Ufa's three big production companies (Messter, Union, and Decla-Bioscop). As the man who helped elevate German film to the level of a serious artistic medium, Pommer was able to win German writers of stature over to the medium. (In this case, Murnau as scriptwriter was one of them.) And in his search for directors, he had a keen eye (his filmmakers included Ludwig Berger, Fritz Lang, Murnau, and Dupont)—as evidenced by the fact that Gliese did a fine job as director—and he knew how to keep them within his studio.

## Die Königsloge (The Royal Box)

(Bryan Foy, 1929). Warner Bros. **Photography:** E. B. Du Par. **With** Alexander Moïssi, Camilla Horn, and Sig Rumann. The studio broke new ground with this 80-minute German-language sound film from America. The production was shot in the Flatbush section of Brooklyn, at the old Vitagraph Studio, where John Bunny and the Talmadge sisters had made their first works. Based on Alexandré Dumas's work about a famous English actor, it was translated into German so that the well-known Moïssi could star. The film became the forerunner of the studio's half dozen German-language films out of Hollywood in the years 1930 an 1931.

In the popular work, Dumas relates the story of the English great actor Edmund Kean, who insults the Prince of Wales from the stage on seeing his beloved sharing the royal box with His Highness. "Moïssi incarnates Kean majestically," wrote a critic, "especially in scenes in which he plays Hamlet." The *Berlin Vorwarts* agreed in December 1929, writing, Moïssi "develops a wonderful theatrical grace. His intense voice loses hardly any of its charm. This Kean is a really great theatrical accomplishment." Despite the fact that the sound quality left something to be desired, the director, wrote *Film Daily*, "knows his Deutsch."

## Das Konzert (The Concert)

(Leo Mittler, 1931). Paramount. **Script:** Hans H. Zerlett. **Photography:** Enzo Riccione. **With** Olga Tschechowa (Maria), Karl Etlinger (Pollinger), Oskar Karlweis (Dr. Franz Jura), Ursula Grabley (Delfine), and Walter Janssen (Prof. Heink, pianist). Based on Hermann Bahr's 1910 play (which was a great box-office hit on the German stage) and Victor Schertzinger's *Fashions in Love* (1929), starring Adolphe Menjou and Fay Compton, Paramount in Paris shot this 74-minute German-language comedy. It "brings the first pleasant sounds from a Joinville production," wrote the Berlin critics in late 1931.

This rendition of a famed pianist's efforts to fend off his many admirers, especially the performance by Grabley (1908–1971) as the sexy Delfine, keeps the action going with "a certain compactness and rudeness that runs through all slapstick comedies in the German farce fashion." The singular Tschechowa, usually cast as a vamp, plays the musician's broad-minded wife. Berlin filmgoers pronounced the sound film a hit.

## Das Land ohne Frauen (Land Without Women)

(Carmine Gallone, 1929). Tobis. **Script:** Ladislaus Vajda. **Photography:** Otto Kanturek and Bruno Timm. **With** Conrad Veidt (Dick Ashton), Elga Brink (Evelyne Narnheim), Clifford McLaglen (Steve Parker), Grete Berger, Carla Bartheel, Kurt Vespermann, and Mathias Wieman (the American). This psychological action is a rather risqué early sound film from Tobis (produced by Pressburger), containing cries for whisky in German, and a song in English.

The 110-minute (nine-reel) work, described as a "25% sound" film, begins when the British, concerned about the population in Australia, send more than 400 women to the land down under. Elga, dubbed Bride number 68, attracts the attention of three men — and the tale ends in tragedy all around.

*Variety* wrote, "This is the first German picture that even suggests a talker. And it gives the first opportunity to judge whether the Germans are in a condition to produce talkers of international character. Judging by this effort they still have a lot to learn but there is no doubt that the Tobis equipment can turn out high-grade results. The chief trouble … was that the synchronized musical accompaniment was too loud in contrast to the dialog."

### Lebende Buddhas (Living Buddhas)

(Paul Wegener, 1923). Ufa. **Script:** Wegener and Hannes Sturm. **Photography:** Guido Seeber, Reimar Kuntze, and Josef Rona. **Effects:** Walter Ruttmann. **Design:** Hans Poelzig and Betho Höfer. **With** Wegener (Great Lama), Asta Nielsen, Käthe Haack, Gregori Chmara (Jebsun), Carl Ebert (Prof. Smith), Friedrich Kühne, Max Pohl, Heinrich Schroth, Hannes Sturm (Prof. Campbell), and Eduard Rothuser. Wegener's last production as author, director, and actor is the exotic story of Profs. Campbell and Smith who investigate a Tibetan sect that practices human sacrifice. Campbell saves a young woman from death and se-cures the sect's holy "Sutra." Smith, however, is captured by the Great Lama while a priest telepathically "steals" the girl's memories. The priest then follows Campbell and the girl to London to prevent him from decoding the Sutra. While Campbell deciphers the work, the Great Lama, stepping out of a wall painting, pulls Campbell, the girl, and the Sutra into the picture. In the temple of a goddess, Campbell is to be sacrificed but escapes. He is found, while the girl remains within the painting.

"The first three reels," wrote a critic, "have a quick tempo and rise to a blood orgy, with a temple celebration, masked temple dances, and crowd scenes." The five-reel (2550-m) tale (trimmed by 165-m and released as *Götter von Tibet/Gods of Tibet*) failed at the box-office because filmgoers rejected Nielsen in the role of a Tibetan.

### Leichtsinnige Jugend (Careless Youth)

(Leo Mittler, 1930). Paramount. **Story:** Hermann Kosterlitz and Benno Vigny. **Photography:** Fred Langenfeld and Friedl Behn-Gund. **With** Camilla Horn (Lydia Torn), Walter Rilla (Dan O'Bannon), and Vera Baranowskaïa. Filmed in Paris, Paramount's German film, also called *Frauen auf schiefer bahn*, was based on the Hollywood melodrama *Manslaughter* (1930), in which the woman protagonist commits a terrible road accident.

### Liebe auf Befehl (The Command to Love)

(Ernest Laemmle and Johannes Riemann, 1931). Universal. **Script:** Benjamin Glazer and Tom Reed. **Photography:** Charles Stumar. **With** Riemann (Attache), Hans Junkermann, Olga Tschechowa (Manuela), and Tala Birell. This 80-minute Hollywood German-language rendition of *Boudoir Diplomat* (1930) became the studio's only Hollywood work in the language. Featuring an imported cast and codirected by Carl Laemmle's nephew, it is the risqué tale of a handsome attaché who becomes romantically linked to the wives of two ambassadors, one of whom is his boss. The production was characterized by *Variety* as "the kind of story easier to swallow in German and fits better." *Film Daily* called it "pretty sophisticated fare ... should prove of interest to German audiences with the excellent calibre of the acting."

### Die Männer um Lucie (The Men Around Lucie)

(Alexander Korda, 1931). Paramount. **Supervisor:** Emmerich W. Emo. **Adaptation:** Benno Vigny. **Photography:** Harry Stradling. **Music:** Guy Zoka, Paul Barnaby, Ray Noble, Paul Maye, and Jane Bos. **Lyrics:** Vigny and Walter Mehring. **Design:** Henri Ménessier. **With** Liane Haid (Lucie), Trude Hesterberg (Lola), Oskar Karlweis (Karl), Walter Rilla (Robert), and Ernst Stahl-Nachbaur. This German version of Harry D'Arrast's *Laughter* (1930) is more in line with Korda's atmospheric and expressionistic French version *Rive gauche* (1931) than with the Hollywood original. Filmed in Paris and shown in Berlin, it is one of Korda's least known features.

### Marizza, gennant die Schmugglermadonna (Marizza, Called the Smuggler's Madonna)

(F. W. Murnau, 1921–22). Helios. **Adaptation:** Hans Janowitz. **Design:** Heinrich Richter. **Photography:** Karl Freund. **With** Tzwetta Tzatscheva (Marizza), Adele Sandrock (Mrs. Avricolos), Harry Frank (Christo), and H. H. von Twardowski (Antonio). This production (also called *Ein Schönes Tier, das Schöne Tier*) was the director's eighth film in his career and the first of his "peasant" films. Based on Wolfgang Geiger's story, it is the tale of a beautiful young maiden and the men around her. The five-reel (1,800-meter) adaptation and direction, wrote a critic, make "this complicated story ... quite a comprehensible film."

Stills: www.f h-bielefeld.de/fb4/murnau/f_mar.htm.

### Die Maske fallt (The Mask Falls)

(William Dieterle, 1931). Warner Bros. **Script:** Bradley King. **Photography:** Sid Hickox. **With** Lissy Arna, Anton Pointner, Carla Bartheel, Karl Etlinger, Ulrich Steindorff, and Salka Steuremann. This 70-minute feature, the second German-language film the studio produced in Hollywood, is based on the Mississippi drama *The Way of All Men*, and features a superlative cast of imports, most of them hired by Dieterle in Berlin. Filmed in less than two weeks on the set used for the English version, it was shown in Berlin.

### Meine Frau, die Filmschauspielerin (My Wife, the Film Star)

(Ernst Lubitsch, 1919). Union Film/Ufa. **Script:** Lubitsch, Erich Schönfelder, and Hanns Kräly. **Photography:** Theodor Sparkuhl. **Design:** Kurt Richter. **With** Ossi Oswalda (Ossi), Paul Biensfeldt, Victor Janson (Lachmann, the general director), Julius Dewald (Baron

Erich von Schwindt), and Hanns Kräly. The title of this this comedy tells it all. The three-reel (1,100-meter) production pulls pretense down from its pedestal and, in the usual Lubitsch fashion, points up the ridiculousness of the sublime.

Baron von Schwindt, on vacation in the Tirol, meets the alluring young Ossi. She's a diva (and has especially fine legs) but he imagines she's just a village girl. To get her way on the set, she turns it inside out and upside down; her director despairs of ever getting his film off the ground. Meanwhile, the Baron, a sworn enemy of modern women, falls in love with her when he sees her later on the screen. The star of the studio then turns her attention elsewhere — and becomes an even bigger "star": a baroness.

## Das Mirakel (The Miracle)

(Max Reinhardt, 1912). Continental Kunst-Film. **With** Maria Carmi, Douglas Payne, Florence Winston, Agathe Barescu, Ernest Matrya, and Ernst Lubitsch. Filmed on location around Vienna (at the Kreuzenstein Castle and the old church in Pechtoldsdorf), this was one of the most spectacular and evocative films of the period. The four-reel (1,460-meter) film was Reinhardt's first, based on Karl Vollmöller's London stage spectacle. It was financed by the American A. H. Woods. Also called *Sister Beatrice* and *The Miracle of Sister Beatrice*, the production, released in Berlin in 1914, with music by Engelbert Humperdinck, was an influence on the young Murnau.

The tale takes place in medieval Europe. In the sanctuary of a convent, a beautiful nun is swept off her feet by an ardent knight. She flees to the outside world, snatching the sculpture of Jesus as a child from the clutches of the Madonna in the cathedral. Unbelievably, the statue of the Virgin Mary comes to life and takes the nun's place. Death, however, follows in the nun's trail until, sadder but wiser, she returns to the convent. When the Virgin and Child are united, "the cathedral once more holds its most precious treasure ... and darkness falls. The end has come," wrote a critic.

Reinhardt made masterly use of light and shadow, inquisitors in black, a radiant nun on a white horse disappearing into the darkness, along with evocative forest, castle, church, and other scenes — evidence of the importance of natural settings and the sense of freedom and exploration inherent in exterior filming. By going beyond filming a stage play, Reinhardt produced expressionist theater, or theatrical avant-garde, a combination of mystery, fantasy, and whimsy with landscape, that had the New York critics calling his work "perhaps the most startling production ... that we have had" and "remarkable ... of great artistic merit."

Stills: *Moving Picture World* (November 23, 1912)

## Mordprozess Mary Dugan (The Murder Trial of Mary Dugan)

(Arthur Robison, 1930). MGM. **Script:** Becky Gardiner. **Photography:** Henry Sharp. **Design:** Cedric Gibbons. **With** Nora Gregor (Mary), Lucy Doraine, and Arnold Korff. This 115-minute, Hollywood-made German-language production represents the third of only four such productions in the studio's history, and it closely follows the 1929 Norma Shearer vehicle, *The Trial of Mary Dugan*, which was MGM's first talking picture.

Like the English version, it is straightforward, photographed theater about a prosecution and defense that alter their initial positions towards an accused murderer. At the Berlin premiere in February 1931, *Variety* wrote, "sound reproduction is distinguished and German dialog to the point and tense ... promises good box office returns." Another reviewer praised its "strong dramatic plot ... the audience was gripped and moved."

### Die Nacht der Entscheidung (The Night of Decision)

(Dimitri Buchowetski, 1931). Paramount. **Adaptation:** Benno Vigny, Martin Brown, and Louise Long. **Photography:** Philip Tannura. **With** Conrad Veidt (General Graf Platoff), Peter Voss (Boris Sabin), Olga Tschechowa (Marya Fédorowna), and Trude Hesterberg (Madame Alexandra). Buchowetski's Paris production, also called *Der General*, is based on Paramount's Hollywood melodrama *The Virtuous Sin* (1930). In contrast to the Hollywood original, the Paris film emphasizes the role of the commanding officer, well-played by the dashing Veidt, rather than that of young Marya trying to save her pacifist husband from a military firing squad during the First World War. Shown in Berlin.

### Die Nackte Wahrheit (The Naked Truth)

(Karl Anton, 1931). Paramount. **Script:** Paul Schiller. **Photography:** René Dantan. **Music:** Erwin Straus. **Design:** Henri Ménessier and René Renoux. **Producer:** Jacob Karol. **With** Otto Wernicke (Marengo), Oskar Karlweis (Bob Marr), Hans-Adalbert von Schlettow (President Wolter), Trude Hesterberg, and Jenny Jugo (Nicolette). A 76-minute risqué comedy made in Paris about the fundraising activities of the Association for Social Action Against Nudity. This film, in fact, has little to do, in story and tone, with the so-called Hollywood original, *Nothing but the Truth* (1929).

### Olympia

(Jacques Feyder, 1930). MGM. **Adaptation:** Yves Mirande. **Photography:** William H. Daniels. **Design:** Cedric Gibbons. **With** Nora Gregor (Olimpia), Hans Junkermann (Albert), and Théo Shall (Capt. Kovacs). This work was Feyder's Hollywood debut in German. An adaptation of Ferenc Molnár's satirical play *Olympia*, it is the story of a princess who falls in love with a commoner.

Shown at the the Gloria-Palast in Berlin, Feyder's 84-minute film makes sparse use of action and more use of dialogue than German audiences were accustomed to. He was criticized for filming theater: "Here is the place to say it with actions." Others hailed the director for his approach: "With rare certainty ... Feyder and his coworkers have struck the sphere of the Austrian court life.... Surprisingly well done." Further, "Olympia is played charmingly by the beautiful Nora Gregor."

### Prinz Kuckuck (Prince Cuckoo)

(Paul Leni, 1919). Gloria-Film. **Script:** Georg Kaiser. **Photography:** Carl Hoffmann. **Design:** Leni (interiors) and Otto Moldenhauer (exteriors).

With Niels Prien (Henry Felix Huart), Conrad Veidt, Olga Limburg, Magnus Stifter, Hanna Ralph, Marga Kierska, and Margarete Schlegel. Leni's tendency towards expressionism manifested itself in this juicy satire starring Prien as the notorious publisher nicknamed "Prinz Kuckuck." Based on Otto Julius Bierbaum's lengthy 1907 diatribe against Germany's political, economic, and social systems of the late 19th century, the film looks at the literary activity of a man whose opinions, actions, and life itself become stand-ins for a decadent society.

Leni's interior design, combined with the luminescence and chiaroscuro effects of the photography by Carl Hoffmann (1881–1947), brought to the fore his damning indictment of evil and inhumanity manifest in the period's mania for eroticism, its cultural turmoil, and lack of heroes. At the same time, the panoramic production seems to to have prefigured the realism of 1930s cinema. The six-reel (2,700-meter) production is sometimes referred to by the subtitle *Leben, Taten, Meinungen und Höllehfahrt eines Wollüstlings*.

## Prinz Sami (Prince Sami)

(Ernst Lubitsch, 1917). Union Film. Script: Lubitsch and Danny Kaden. Photography: Alfred Hansen. Design: Kurt Richter. With Ossi Oswalda (Maria), Ernst Lubitsch (Prince Sami), Wilhelm Diegelmann, Margarete Kupfer, Hanns Kräly, and Victor Janson. A 1,050-meter Oriental burlesque — one of Lubitsch's least known — with the popular Oswalda (1894–1948), as always, playing an imp and Lubitsch's female alter ego. One of the most important comic actresses of the era, Oswalda offered something rare — slapstick in Berlin.

## Die Privatsekretärin (The Private Secretary

(William Thiele, 1931). Greenbum-Emelka. Script: Franz Schulz. Photography: Otto Heller. Music: Paul Abraham. With Renate Müller (Vilma), Felix Bressart, Hermann Thimig, and Ludwig Stoessel. Fresh from making the musical hits *Love in Waltz Time* and *The Three from the Gasoline Station*, starring Lilian Harvey, Thiele directed one of the best of the then-popular genre of musical comedies. In fact, the action of the film is driven by the music.

His film stars a favorite of moviegoing audiences of the 1930s, the clean-cut Müller in a charming 100-minute romp about a stenographer on the make and "in a bit of undress," according to the reviews. "Miss Müller is easy to look at, which offsets her singing." However, "the ensemble singing is neat" within "strange modernistic German settings," and in the mob shots there are several unlisted characters who reportedly stand out. The production is also called *Sunshine Susie*.

## Rausch (Intoxication)

(Ernst Lubitsch, 1919). Argus-Film. Script: Hanns Kräly. Photography: Karl Freund. Design: Rochus Gliese. With Asta Nielsen (Henriette), Alfred Abel (Gaston), Karl Meinhard (Adolphe), Grete Dierks (Jeanne), and Heinz Stieda (the abbé). An adaptation of Strindberg's powerfully autobiographical *Brott och Brott* (*There Are Crimes and Crimes*), written in 1899, the production was called a "chamber film," a dark comedy of sin and retribution that takes place over two days. Set in Paris, it contains the director's singular trademark: an air of playfulness that makes sport of frailty.

Gaston, a playwright, has a mistress and a five-year-old daughter. On his great first night, with the public at his feet, he betrays his mistress by taking up with Henriette, the femme fatale and girlfriend of his best friend, Adolphe. He also wishes his daughter dead. The next day the little girl dies — and the playwright finds himself under suspicion for murder. In order to expiate his guilt for wishing the child dead — guilt is seen as its own retribution — Gaston suffers a breakdown. In the words of an abbé, "We are responsible for our thoughts, our words and our desires."

Gaston's breakdown leads him to realize that "Honor is a phantom; gold, nothing but dry leaves; women, mere intoxication." With his spirit in crisis, and the news that the girl died of a disease, the playwright makess a final adjustment between conscience and egotism. He heads to church to "have a final reckoning" with himself — and plans on going to the theater the following evening.

Lubitsch's five-reel (1,800-meter) film is an uncomplicated example of his feeling for an "American" approach to great dramatic art that did not, however, satisfy lead actress Nielsen. Their artistic differences became known when Nielsen said, "All the public wants is plot and thrill-packed films in the American style. The artist is allowed no time for the full dramatic development of a role, and if such time is allowed during the shooting, the director's scissors will cut away his best work as 'superfluous.'"

## Der Rodelkavalier (The Toboggan Cavalier)

(Ernst Lubitsch, 1918). Union Film/Ufa. **Script:** Lubitsch and Erich Schönfelder. **Photography:** Theodor Sparkuhl. **Design:** Kurt Richter. **With** Ossi Oswalda (Ossi), Harry Liedke, Ferry Sikla (Hannemann), Erich Schönfelder, Julius Falkenstein, and Lubitsch (Sally Pinner). Oswalda, the ever-popular Liedke, and Lubitsch romp in this three-reel (1,300-meter) romance of the outdoors. The pampered Ossi objects to marrying the man her father (commerical lawyer Hannemann) has selected for her. She cancels the wedding, travels to Krummhübel, where it's beautiful, where there is much snow, and where Pinner reigns. She pursues sport, and the father is powerless against that.

## Satanas

(F. W. Murnau, 1919). Victoria Film. **Script:** Robert Wiene. **Design:** Ernst Stern. **Photography:** Karl Freund. **With** Fritz Kortner (Pharoah), Ernst Hofmann (Jorab), Conrad Veidt (Lucifer), Margit Barnay, and Ernst Stahl-Nachbauer. A three-part, episodic work on the theme that evil does not beget good. The 2,600-meter production is set in Biblical times, the Renaissance, and during the Russian Revolution.

In all likelihood inspired by Luigi Maggi's *Satana* (1912), the early classic of the genre, as well as Griffith's *Intolerance*, Murnau incorporated sumptuous sets and wonderful photography to succeed "perfectly on the visual side," said a critic, creating scenes of "striking beauty." Only the second film in his career, Murnau worked with Max Reinhardt's favorite designer as well as scriptwriter Wiene — the (future) director of *Caligari*.

A fragment of 40 meters from the first episode (*Der Tyrran*) survives: the seduction scene between Fritz Kortner and Margit Barnay.

## Die Schmiede (The Smithy)

(Martin Berger, 1924). This left-wing short produced in Weimar Germany became part of the controversy it was covering. It was called a "great film about the proletariat" and the "class struggle" which starred amateurs. Director Berger submitted the script to German trade unions, which announced their support for the production. The newspaper *Rote Fahne* (*Red Flag*) denounced the exploitation of extras, while the Hugenberg newspaper *Der Tag* (*The Day*) called for the film's censure. At numerous showings the playing of the "Internationale" was banned. "So it is a fact that the film," wrote *Der Vorwarts*, "which depicts purely and simply a piece of the class struggle, truthfully and without exaggeration, has itself become part of the class struggle."

## Sehnsucht (Longing)

(F. W. Murnau, 1920). Mosch/Lipow Film. **Script:** Carl Heinz Jarosy. **Design:** Robert Neppach. **Photography:** Carl Hoffmann. **With** Conrad Veidt, Gussy Holl (duchess), Paul Graetz, and Helene Cray. A drama (also called *Bajazzo*) subtitled "The Story of the Suffering of an Artist," the five-reel (1,750-m) work was the director's third film of his short career. Set in Russia, it is the tale of a student-dancer who, while on a dangerous political mission, falls in love with a beautiful grand duchess (played by Veidt's real wife), and it ends in tragedy when he is imprisoned and she dies waiting for him.

## Die Sehnsucht jeder Frau (The Longing of Every Woman)

(Victor Sjöström, 1930). MGM. **With** Vilma Bánky and Joseph Schildkraut. The great Swedish actor-director made one foreign-language film during his American sojourn in the period 1924–1930. It is a 90-minute German-language production that follows the storyline of his only American sound film.

"A hit as a talker," wrote *Variety* of Sjöström's well-acted, directed, and treated English-language version, which was based on the play *They Knew What They Wanted*, though the film was deemed objectionable by the industry-appointed moralist William H. Hays. His German-language film (also called *Sunkissed*) is the story of a farmer who, on a visit to San Francisco, falls for an attractive waitress. Sending her a marriage proposal, he encloses not a photo of himself but of his handsome foreman. The heroine, offered a chance at a better life, accepts the offer. When she comes face to face with the truth, trouble develops within Sjöström's morally ambiguous world.

## Seine Freundin Annette (His Girlfriend Annette)

(Felix Basch, 1930). Paramount. **Story:** Hermann Kosterlitz. **Producer:** Paul Reno. **With** Lissy Arna (Annette Rollan), Fritz Delius (Robert Damartin), Hadrian M. Netto (Charles Tellin), and Philipp Manning. Paramount's production was the studio's first German-language film shot in Paris, in June 1930. It is also called *Die Frau, von der Man nicht Spricht* (*The Woman of Whom One Does Not Speak*), and is based on the Hollywood comedy-drama *The Lady Lies* (1929), the tale of a widower who upsets his children when he falls for another woman. The film was shown in Berlin.

## Sklaven der Sinne (Slaves of Sin)

(Carl Froelich, 1921). Decla-Bioscop. **Script:** Froelich and Walter Supper. **Photography:** Axel Graatkjaer. **Design:** Robert Herlth. **With** Asta Nielsen (Natasja Baraschkowa), Walter Janssen (Myschkin), Lyda Salmonova (Alexandra), and Alfred Abel (Parfen). Also called *Irrende Seelen* (*Wayward Souls*), this tale starring Asta Nielsen as the woman who chooses a life of luxury and debauchery was an early adaptation of Dostoyevsky's *The Idiot*. It is so called for the man named Myschkin who sacrifices his interests for Natasja. While in the middle of a series of intrigues and love triangles, Myschkin is in many respects a saint in a land where weaknesses of purpose, violence over trifles, lack of self-control, and futility lead to tragedy. These elements of Russian life — evident in the German culture of the early 1920s — are presented in the adaptation of the literary classic. The six-reel (2,800-meter) drama was highly acclaimed in its day.

## Ein Sommernachtstraum in unserer Zeit (A Midsummer Night's Dream in Our Time)

(Stellan Rye, 1913). Deutsche Bioscop. **Script:** Rye and Hanns Heinz Ewers. **Photography:** Guido Seeber and Axel Graatkjaer. **With** Alexander Moïssi, Grete Berger (Puck), Claus Clewing (Lysander), and Jean Ducret. A contemporary, fanciful adaptation of Shakespeare's comedy that represents a landmark in filmmaking, this rendition by Rye is least of all filmed theater. Rather, it was praised for its groundbreaking, harmonious interaction between form and content and for establishing its right to exist alongside theater.

Puck, the roguish spirit who causes all the transformations, becomes the symbol of the director's poetic mood, bringing into existence two complementary worlds: Oberon's spirit realm and the everyday world, with people full of various real and imaginary cares and sorrows. The film shows the dream of an old man who is expecting the arrival of the men engaged to his daughter and niece. In the dream, the lovers are chased by a leering Puck and the fairies. When he awakes, the old man believes his dream to be real, and goes in search of the lovers. He finds them innocently sleeping on the lawn.

The four-reel (950-meter) production was Rye's debut directorial effort (he also directed Ewer's stage version), and he shot it in Berlin following two screenplays he wrote for Wilhelm Gluckstadt at Denmark Film, in Copenhagen. Moïssi (who was born Moisiu to an Italian mother and Albanian father) had made his name on the (Reinhardt) stage in Vienna, Berlin, Prague, and St. Petersburg. He made three other films with Rye — all lost — and a total of seven silents and three sound films in his distinguished career.

## Sonntag des Lebens (Sunday of Life)

(Leo Mittler, 1930). Paramount. **Dialogue:** Béla Balász. **Producer:** Paul

Reno. **With** Camilla Horn (Betty Williams) and Willi Clever (David Stone). Paramount's 77-minute version of *The Devil's Holiday* (1930), a tale about a woman who tries to make amends for past deeds, is a Paris production whose "fundamental idea," wrote a critic, "is not bad." If it had been treated with more care and less haste, it might have been better received at the Titania-Palast in Berlin. Instead, Mittler's melodrama lacks attention to "correct German"— surprising considering of the reputation of the dialogue writer.

### Der Sprung ins Nichts (Half-Way to Heaven)

(Leo Mittler, 1931). Paramount. **Script:** Curt Alexander. **Photography:** Enzo Riccione. **Producer:** Paul Reno. **With** Cilly Feindt (Greta), Aribert Mog (Fred Lee), Sigurd Lohde (Jim), Hermann Blass, and Ida Perry (Mrs. Lee). Filmed at Paramount's Paris studios, this circus tale of heroism and murder has its roots in the hugely influential *Variety* (1925), directed by E. A. Dupont. The Hollywood source is *Half-Way to Heaven* (1929). It was shown in Berlin.

### Sturm über La Sarraz (Storm Over La Sarraz)

(Hans Richter, Sergei Eisenstein, and Ivor Montagu, 1929). **Script:** Richter. **Photography:** Edward Tissé. **With** Richter, Eisenstein, Walter Ruttmann, Béla Balász, and Leon Moussinac. At the 1929 Congress of Independent Films, held in Lausanne, the pretentious theme was the "Art of the Cinema, Its Social and Aesthetic Purposes," the bias was anti–Hollywood, and the best thing to come out of it was this eccentric sketch put together by left-wing filmmakers. It is a loopy two-reel comedy demonstrating how "Cinematic Art," suspended in place by "Commerce" and "Industry," is freed by "Independent-General" (Eisenstein). Director Eisenstein reportedly lost the film on the way back to Russia.

### Der Tanz geht weiter (The Dance Goes On)

(William Dieterle, 1930). Warner Bros. **Script:** Heinrich Fraenkel. **Photography:** Sid Hickox. **With** Dieterle (Dan Hogan), Anton Pointner (Diamond Joe), Lissy Arna, and Carla Bartheel. This 85-minute German-language film was the studio's first of five Hollywood German-language productions in the early 1930s. Its director made three of them. An atmospheric thriller (based on the studio's 1930 *Those Who Dance*), it reminded some of Josef von Sternberg's classic, *Underworld* (1927).

Dieterle shot his film quickly—in less than two weeks, in fact—using an imported German cast which he had recruited in Berlin. He stars as a purported gangster, out to avenge the death of his policeman-brother at the hands of a rival gang. *Film Daily* praised Dieterle for his direction and his acting. There was also surprisingly effective work by Pointner—"really splendid, his brutality nicely seasoned with comedy"—and by Bartheel. Since this was one of Hollywood's earliest German-language productions, it was, along with Jacques Feyder's MGM production *Olympia* (1930), eagerly awaited in Berlin. There the critics were more circumspect: "It is still an open question," they said, "whether it is worth while trundling a complete

German cast across an ocean and a continent to make a film among the hills of Hollywood."

### Tropennächte (Tropical Nights)

(Leo Mittler, 1930). Paramount. **Photography:** René Guissart. **Producer:** Paul Reno. **With** Dita Parlo (Alma). Paramount's 60-minute Paris production, based on Joseph Conrad's South Seas tale *Victory*, was one of the studio's rare German productions to make it to the U.S. *Film Daily* noted that this melodramic offering about an entertainer who is the object of attention of several men in the overheated South Pacific "can be followed very easily whether the audience understands German or not." Further, the film was promoted as a "German musical drama," though it contains only one song, and lead actress "is attractive and capable." While the film's tempo is more in keeping with the storyline, thus slower than its Hollywood counterpart, William A. Wellman's *Dangerous Paradise* (1930), starring Nancy Carroll, the langorous and humid background and action are duplicated in the Paris film.

### U 9 Weddigen (U-Boat 9)

(Heinz Paul, 1927). Story and **Script:** Paul. **With** Gerd Briese, Ernst Hofmann, Fred Solm, Hella Moja, Mathilde Sussin, and Fritz Alberti. A drama of warfare that, rare for its time, preaches reconciliation. With grim and realistic elements of warfare at sea, the German silent contains the germ of a love story in an attempt to compete with Hollywood.

It is set during the Great War, when a German woman married to an Eng-lishman must withstand the anxiety of seeing her son join the British navy. That brings back the terrible memory of the loss of another son at sea years earlier. But her second son, despite being wounded in battle, faces a kinder fate: He is nursed back to health by a German nurse, with whom he falls in love.

The 6,500-foot pro-peace film has "Some good war scenes with sinking of German submarine and English vessel carrying a big kick," noted *Film Daily*.

### Die verliebte Firma (The Firm in Love)

(Max Ophüls, 1931). DLS. **Script:** Hubert Marischka, and Fritz Zeckendorf. **Photography:** Karl Puth. **With** Gustav Froelich, Anny Ahlers, Lien Deyers, Leonhard Steckel, and Werner Fink. Max Ophüls's first German-language feature was a 70-minute forerunner to his classic *La Ronde* (1951). Though without the pathos, it was "the first film," said Ophüls, "where I felt myself driven ... my first attempt to imprint a rhythm to a film." The touching romance about filmmaking shows what happens when an entire film crew, on location in the mountains, falls in love with a beautiful stand-in.

### Von Morgens bis Mitternachts (From Morning to Night)

(Karlheinz Martin, 1920). **Script:** Martin and Herbert Juttke. **Photography:** Carl Hoffmann. **Design:** Robert Neppach. **With** Ernst Deutsch (the cashier), Erna Morena (the lady), Roma Bahn, Adolf Edgar, Hans Heym, and Heinrich von Twardowski. Adapted from the experimental stage piece by

Georg Kaiser, a well known German dramatist of the 1920s, this was one of the most radical and highly unusual expressionist productions of the era, a film that asks, "What is life? Is it nothing but a chase that goes on from morning to midnight, until the full span and meaning of a dream becomes real?"

The film is a work of extreme abstraction and stylization, both in appearance and acting, with dehumanized characters reduced to formal elements. The performers, who represent types, are striped with paint, and merge with the background decor. Everything comes out as grey on grey. These figures are defined by a few strongly stressed movements, with the rhythm of their existence located in their gestures. The five-reel (1,480-meter) production, upon which Martin's fame now rests, was briefly shown in Munich and Tokyo in 1922. The "coldness, numbness, and alienation," wrote a critic, that is the movie so distanced viewers that the production soon vanished.

Stills: www.dimos.de/arte/programm/f/vomobi.htm.

## Das wanderende Bild (The Wandering Image)

(Fritz Lang, 1920). May Film GNBH. **Script:** Land and Thea von Harbou. **Photography:** Guido Seeber. **With** Mia May, Hans Marr, and Rudolf Klein-Pohden. This Lang film represents his earliest collaboration with Harbou. Their 2,000-meter drama is part fantasy: At a snow-bound Alpine village, a stranger arrives who is able to cure a sick child. She departs just as quickly. The villagers take her to be a manifestation of the Virgin Mary.

## Weib im Dschungel (Woman in the Jungle)

(Dimitri Buchowetski, 1930). Paramount. **Dialogue:** Hermann Kosterlitz. **Photography:** René Guissart. **With** Charlotte Ander (Leslie Crosby), Ernst Stahl-Nachbaur (Robert), Erich Ponto (Joyce), and Philipp Manning. Filmed in Paris, this is the German version of *The Letter* (1929), directed in Hollywood by Jean de Limur and Monta Bell, and starring Jeanne Eagels.

This 61-minute rendition of W. Somerset Maugham's effective and serious tale of interracial love in Asia, though sporting a fine cast of character actors, met with a dismal reaction on release. German critics attacked "the careless direction ... the long drawn out and affected dialog," and the performance by lead actress Ander who "dared appear and bow before a [Berlin] audience hissing and howling."

## Welt ohne Grenzen (World Without Borders)

(Eugen Thiele, 1931). Paramount. **With** Anni Ann, Ida Perry, and Fred Döderlein (inventor). Little-known filmmaker Thiele directed in Paris Paramount's German rendition of the French-language *Magie moderne* (1931), a fictionalized story about the then developing mode of communications. Also titled *Television* at its Berlin release, the film represents one of the many versions of the story that Paramount produced in Paris.

## Wir Schalten um auf Hollywood (We're Switching Over to Hollywood)

(Paul Morgan and Frank Reicher, 1929–1931). MGM. **Adaptation:** Morgan.

**With** Heinrich George, Dita Parlo, and Nora Gregor. A two-hour German-language revue and adaptation of the studio's *The Hollywood Revue* (1929). This early sound film contains color sequences and features the studio's Hollywood imports, along with the studio's principals, Buster Keaton, John Gilbert, Norma Shearer, Joan Crawford, Marion Davies, and Laurel and Hardy, all apparently breaking out in German in the final number, "Singing in the Rain."

## Yorck

(Gustav Ucicky, 1931). Ufa. **Supervisor:** Ernest H. Correll. **Script:** Hans Müller and Robert Liebmann. **Design:** Robert Herlth. **Photography:** Carl Hoffmann. **With** Werner Krauss, Grete Mosheim (Barbara), Rudolf Forster (Frederich Wilhelm III), Jacob Tiedtke, Veit Harlan, and Walter Janssen. "The past is still very much alive in Europe," wrote a critic. This film "is able to portray it with a sense of reality, of sincerity, which it is hard for us to get in Hollywood."

It is a lavish, 102-minute psychological drama directed by the illegitimate son of Gustav Klimt — the Vienna-born Ucicky (1899–1961) began his career as the chief cameraman to Mihály Kertész at Sascha-Film in Vienna. The tale stars the established Krauss as the idiosyncratic Prussian general who, against the wishes of his King, France, and Napoleon, in 1812 signs a treaty with the czar and withdraws his forces from the soil of arch-enemy Russia.

"Compelling, especially because of the treatment," wrote *Variety*, the production "must have cost a pretty penny to do, there being quite a number of massive and beautiful sets and a big number of extras." As a film with real production value and such fine acting, "it can't be passed up," wrote a reviewer when it ran in New York in late 1932, even though it was released without English titles. "How marvelously Krauss speaks the German language," wrote the *New York Times.* "Krauss is alone on that still small plateau where once Mansfield and Salvini stood." As to the film's message, the "whole spirit of the film is militaristic. But on the other hand, Yorck is a rebel.... So there is something for democrat and monarchist."

## Zum goldenen Anker (The Golden Anchor)

(Alexander Korda, 1931). Paramount. **Script:** Marcel Pagnol, Ludwig Biró, and Alfred Polgar. **Photography:** Ted Pahle. **Design:** Alfred Junge and Vincent Korda. **Producer:** Jacob Karol. **With** Ursula Grabley (Fanny), Jabob Tiedtke (César), Mathias Wieman (Marius), Karl Etlinger (Panisse), Lucie Höflich (Honorine), and Albert Bassermann (Piquoiseau). Alexander Korda was behind the making of this little-known 82-minute German version of the classic *Marius* (1931), an original Paramount production shot in Paris in June-July 1931.

Also titled *Im hafen von Marseille*, his film closely follows the outlines of Pagnol's stage play and contains witty dialogue by Alfred Polgar. Korda, wrote a critic, "has well and neatly directed the picture and hit the right atmosphere, but he cannot refrain from stage technique.... Wieman is strong and ample. Tiedke is refreshingly true as owner of a pub and Marius' father. He unites humor and feeling." The well-photographed film premiered in Berlin.

# Great Britain

The first significant British production was R. W. Paul's *The Soldier's Courtship* (1896). In the early years of the new century, the films of J. Williamson, G. A. Smith, Cecil Hepworth, and George Pearson helped to popularize British productions, especially in the United States. Pearson noted of early British filmmakers that "he goes farthest who knows not where he is going." Early British filmmakers were, he said "explorers without map or compass, artisans striving step by step to find their art."

Early British film people experimented with extreme close-ups, cutting, and connecting film to tell a story. In the first known instance of a political motion picture photo opportunity, King Edward VII is reported to have stopped his entire royal procession so that the cameras could linger. The British film industry, while dominated by Hollywood, nonetheless set a standard in documentaries, beginning in the late 1920s. But on the whole, silent British films have remained in the dark, an ignored chapter of film history. Included are the early sound films of Michael Powell, many of which were produced and distributed by Hollywood studios.

## Annie Laurie

(Walter Tennyson, 1936). Mandover, Scotland. **Script:** Frank Miller. **Photography:** Jack Parker. **With** Will Fyffe (Will Laurie), Polly Ward (Annie), Bruce Seton, and Vivienne Chatterton. This musical comedy stars the hugely popular Fyffe whom many thought a finer entertainer than the better known Sir Harry Lauder. In this 82-minute production he plays a horse-drawn barge owner who finds himself overtaken by the technology of motorized boats. Out of work, he hits the road as part of a traveling show, accompanied by his adopted daughter, Annie. Their talent makes them rich — and leads to a discovery about Annie's true identity.

Will Fyffe's "bluff heartiness," wrote the *Monthly Film Bulletin*, "carries all before it."

## Auld Lang Syne

(George Pearson, 1929). Welsh-Pearson-Elder. **Script:** Pearson and Pat Mannock. Story: Hugh E. Wright. **Photography:** Bernard Knowles. **With** Harry Lauder (Sandy McTavish), Dorothy Boyd, and Pat Aherne (Angus). The production claims significance in that after it was completed, RCA synchronized six songs by the highly touted Sir Harry Lauder. That made the 75-minute (6,800-foot) film a production that could claim to be 20 percent sound, and permitted it to be marketed as an "All Singing Film."

A swan song to silent filmmaking in Britain, it is the tale of a conservative Scottish farmer (played by the famous Scots entertainer, Sir Harry, in his second film) who visits London, only to

Will Fyffe (Will Laurie) and Polly Ward (Annie) in the British classic *Annie Laurie* (Walter Tennyson, Mandover, 1936).

find that his son, who he imagined is a chemist, has become a boxer and that his daughter, who he thought is a nurse, is actually a dancer.

## *The Bells*

(Oscar F. Werndorff and Harcourt Templeman, 1931). BSFP. **Script:** C. H. Dand. **Photography:** Günther Krampf and Eric Cross. **Music:** Gustav Holst. **With** Donald Calthrop (Mathias), Jane Welsh (Annette), and Edward Sinclair (Sgt. Nash). One of the most unusual British films of the early era of sound was co-directed by the distinguished

emigré Werndorff, who had been the architect to Austria's last emperor and the designer of E. A. Dupont's classic tale of intrigue and murder, *Variety* (1925).

His film is as un–British as can be — an atmospheric fusion of the weird and fantastic, the romantic with the real. The subject matter of its source (Emile Erckmann and Alexandré Chatrian's 1869 play called *Le Juif Polonais*), combined with the talents of the filmmakers, resulted in a 75-minute expressionistic mystery centering on a murder of a Jew.

The protagonist is the reserved Mathias, a wealthy Alsatian burgomaster, who is also an innkeeper. Mathias is

Harry Lauder entertaining 'em at a New Year's Eve party in *Auld Lang Syne* (George Pearson, Welsh-Pearson-Elder, 1929).

ravaged by guilt and sleeps alone. On the evening of his daughter Annette's wedding — she is to inherit his fortune — he has a nightmare about a terrible event that occurred 15 years earlier. He has been called before the Court of Justice, the principal figure in a trial. We see his cheerful inn, with its blazing fire, spiced wine that warms visitors, along with the whistling wind and the drifting snow — none of it holds attraction. Staying for the night is a rich Eastern European Jew. When the visitor is in his sleigh, bells ringing and the snow falling, Mathias creeps up from behind and kills the man.

In his earliest British production,

esteemed Austrian photographer Grampf provided what were called unusual "eccentricities of lighting ... and dramatic effect," the lighting of the murder scenes bordering on the miraculous. Also for the first time in British sound films, a notable composer lent his talents to a production, by composing "Storm Prelude," "Wedding Feast," and other music.

### Born Lucky

(Michael Powell, 1932). Westminster Films. **Script:** Ralph Smart. **Photography:** Geoffrey Faithfull. **With**

Donald Calthrop (on left) is a burgomaster with a terrible secret in *The Bells* (Oscar F. Werndorff and Harcourt Templeman, BSFP, 1931).

Renee Ray (Mops) and John Longden (Frank). Powell's one-hour romantic comedy is the tale of a humble young woman's rise to fame. She's a music-hall performer interested in an aspiring playwright. Their attempts to make successes of themselves was called "ingenuous." Powell's treatment of this early film in his career shows "imagination," said a critic. Distributed by MGM.

### The Brown Wallet

(Michael Powell, 1936). Warner Bros. **Script:** Ian Dalrymple. **Photogra-**phy: Basil Emmott. **With** Patric Knowles (John Gillespie), Nancy O'Neil, Henry Caine, and Henrietta Watson. Just before rocketing to fame, Powell directed this 70-minute murder-thriller about a publisher in financial difficulty when his partner absconds with their funds. Gillespie is forced to turn for help to a wealthy aunt, but she spurns him. In trouble, he gets lucky — or so it seems — when he finds a stash of money in a wallet in a cab. That same night his wealthy aunt is poisoned, and he is accused of murdering her and rifling her safe. Dalrymple's script was called beautifully constructed, and it helped catapult him into such major works as *Pygmalion* (1938) and *The Citadel* (1938). In 1950 he produced *The Wooden Horse*.

## Bulldog Drummond

(Oscar Apfel, 1922). Hollandia/ Granger-Binger/Astra National. **Distributor:** W. W. Hodkinson: **Script:** Bernard E. Doxat-Pratt. **Photography:** Feiko Boersma, Jan Smit, and Max van Lier. **With** Carlyle Blackwell (Hugh Drummond), Evelyn Greeley (Phillis), Dorothy Fane (Irma), Horace de Vere (Peterson), and Warwick Ward. Containing a jolt a minute, this tale was the most acclaimed British-Dutch produc-

tion of its day, directed by an American. A faithful rendition of the 1921 stage hit *Sapper* by the prolific Herman Cyril Mc-Neile (1888–1937), it was a painstaking production in settings, props, and players, with action centering on an intrepid, breezy British adventurer (the Indiana Jones of his day) who, through countless, breathless, inextricable situations rescues a kidnapped wealthy American from the clutches of a wicked gang of international thieves.

The 6,700-foot film was called "one of the finest ... screened [in Britain}... there is no superfluous footage ... the thrills ... are effective ... and the English atmosphere ... wonderfully preserved." The concise and witty subtitles,

Carlyle Blackwell as the intrepid Bulldog will not remain tied up for long in *Bulldog Drummond* (Oscar Apfel, Hollandia/Granger-Binger/Astra National, 1922).

brilliant acting, the fresh femme fatale role, and the shocks, surprises, and action will make the picture a "winner anywhere." In New York, *Variety* noted that right through to the delirious ending, during which a diabolical doctor dies by one of his own "engines of torture," "so much happens and so swiftly … one is torn between a desire to laugh and an impulse to enjoy … it all." The production was also called *De Bloedhond van het geheimzinnige Sanatorium* (*The Bulldog of the Mysterious Sanitorium*) and *Het Geheimzinnige Sanatorium*.

## C.O.D.

(Michael Powell, 1932). Westminster Films. **Script:** Ralph Smart. **Photography:** Geoffrey Faithfull. **With** Garry Marsh (Peter), Hope Davey (Frances), Arthur Stratton, and Roland Culver. Based on a story by Philip MacDonald, Powell's film is about a young woman who, after her stepfather dies under mysterious circumstances, has to get rid of his body to avoid being incriminated in his death. When Frances discovers her stepfather dead in the library, she pays Peter Craven to help her hide the body. When the body turns up again at the scene of the crime, Frances is suspected of murder but Craven decides to find the real killer. The 65-minute film was distributed by United Artists.

## The Constant Nymph

(Adrian Brunel, 1928). Gainsborough. **Script:** Brunel, Alma Reville, and Margaret Kennedy. **Photography:** David W. Gobbett. **With** Ivor Novello (Louis Dodd), Mable Poulton (Tessa), and Benita Hume. Novello was called "the handsomest man in England." He and charming Poulton (in one of her last films) are in the first film rendition of the well-known 1924 theatrical drama by Margaret Kennedy (1896–1968) and Basil Dean (1888–1978), the tale of a temperamental composer who leaves his wife for a younger woman who is suffering from heart trouble. It contains the well-known line, "He tried to divide his heart and broke theirs." Shot abroad (in Austria) and at Queen's Hall, where Novello conducts a silent symphony, the 10,600-feet production was a fine success.

## The Fair Maid of Perth

(Edwin Greenwood, 1923). Anglia Films. **With** Russell Thorndike (Dwining), Sylvia Caine (Catherine), Lionel d'Aragon (Black Douglas), and Tristram Rawson (Gow). The adventure is based on Sir Walter Scott's invigorating novel of the same name. It concerns Katie Glover, the most beautiful young woman of Perth and the daughter of a clan leader. She is saved from an unscrupulous landowner by her beloved. Scott's work, which had helped to revive Highland culture, was highly popular in film treatments, including this 5,500-feet adaptation.

## The Fair Maid of Perth

(Miles Mander, 1926). DeForest Phonofilms, Scotland. **With** Louise Maurel. Based on Sir Walter Scott's novel, this version of the tale was filmed in Scott's homeland. In later years Mander became an actor, costarring, for instance, in *The Private Life of Henry VIII* (1933).

## Football Daft

(Victor W. Rowe, 1921). Broadway Cinema, Scotland. **Story:** James Milligan.

With Jimmy Brough and Alan Morton. Adapted from a comedy sketch, this production created quite a stir at Ibrox Park, in Glasgow, where the famous Alan Morton of the Rangers Football Club was seen "executing" his famous "Morton lob." In this comedy (also called *Fitba Daft*) a teetotaler mistakenly drinks whiskey (thinking it vinegar) after which he plays soccer. Morton needed several attempts at the famous kick before his scene was safely "in the can," after which he quipped, "must have my boots on the wrong feet." The 2,000-feet film ran for an exceptional six weeks at the Regent Cinema. It was reissued in 1923, then vanished.

## The Ghost Train

(Walter Forde, 1931). Gainsborough-Gaumont. **Script:** Angus MacPhail, Lajos Biró, and Sidney Gilliat. **Photography:** Lesley Rowson. **With** Jack Hulbert (Ted Deakin), Cicely Courtneidge (Miss Bourne), Donald Calthrop (Saul Hodgkin), and Ann Todd (Peggy Murdock). One of the most highly regarded of early British talkies, the 70-minute mystery-comedy-thriller (based on the 1925 play by Arnold Ridley) takes place in the middle of nowhere in the middle of the night. At an unidentified train station, where a small group of

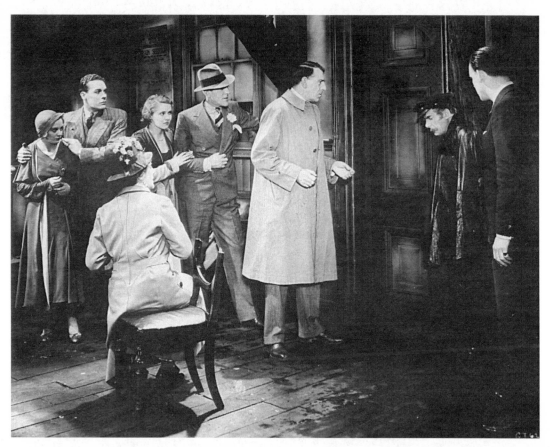

The spooked travelers await the news about the mysterious train in *The Ghost Train* (Walter Forde, Gainsborough-Gaumont, 1931).

travelers awaits the dawn. At midnight, so the rumor goes, a mysterious ghost train will pass by and anybody who set eyes upon it will be "struck dead." Stranded at this haunt are a fussy spinster, a couple on their honeymoon, a few salesmen, a doctor, and a detective (in disguise).

"In the waiting room," wrote *Bioscope*, "is some of the funniest stuff ever put over by an artist, British or foreign.... The atmosphere ... and brooding uneasiness ... is amazingly cleverly contrived." The result was that the film, shown in the U.S., was called one of the most gripping British films ever produced. "Clean, sharp, and with feasible development in the story," wrote *Motion Picture Herald*, " it represents one of the best British pictures of its particular type since sound." Five reels survive at the National Film Archive, London. A Dutch rendition, called *Spooktrein* (1939), directed by Karel Lamac, is extant.

### The Girl in the Crowd

(Michael Powell, 1934). Warner Bros. **Script:** Brock Williams. **Photography:** Basil Emmott. **With** Barry Clifton (David Gordon), Patricia Hilliard (Marian), Googie Withers (Sally), and Harold French (Bob). This rarity, a 50-minute quickie by Powell, is a comedy about the method a man employs to quickly and efficiently find a wife. Bookseller David Gordon's new wife Marian has never met David's friend Bob but by telephone advises him on how to meet a woman: by following the first attractive girl he sees. Unfortunately, that young woman turns out to be Marian and Bob is arrested. *Kino Weekly* called it an "amusing" production that, recalled Powell, "nobody ever saw."

### Gypsy Melody

(Edmond T. Gréville, 1936). British Artistic. **Script:** Irving Leroy and Dan Weldon. **With** Lupe Velez, Alfred Rode, Jerry Verno, and Raymond Lovell. French director Gréville (who was part English) formed a production company to make several films in Britain. In this 75-minute musical comedy, based on René Pujol's popular *Juanita* (1935) he captures the exoticism of a gypsy touring band, thanks to Hollywood star Velez as a dancer in love with a one-time captain of the guard (Rode) who is also a supreme violinist. "The music constitutes the film's major appeal," noted the *Monthly Film Bulletin*. Liszt's *Second Hungarian Rhapsody* "is extremely well rendered." The "charming country scenes and the general artistic background," said *Variety*, "make this pleasing light entertainment."

### The Harp King

(Max Leder, 1919). Ace Films, Scotland. **Script:** Leder. **With** Nan Wilkie (Cynthia) and W. R. Bell (John Davenport). A romance about a landowner's daughter in love with a musician, the five-reel (5,000-feet) production "exceeded all expectations," wrote the *Scottish Cinema*.

### The Heart of Midlothian

(Frank Wilson, 1914). Hepworth, Scotland. **With** Harry Buckland, Flora Morris (Effie Deans), Violet Hopson (Jeanie Deans), Alma Taylor (Madge), Stewart Rome (Ratcliffe), Cecil

Flora Morris and Violet Hopson are the sisters who fight an unjust law in *The Heart of Midlothian,* based on a tale by Walter Scott (Frank Wilson, Hepworth, 1914).

Mannering (George Staunton), Cyril Morton (Reuben), Harry Gilbey, and Warwick Buckland. An early Scottish hit, this work was adapted from Sir Walter Scott's story of the Porteous riot of 1736, in which are introduced the interesting incidents of the sisters Effie and Jeanie Deans. Effie is seduced while in the service of Mrs. Saddletree, and is imprisoned for child-murder, but Jeanie obtains her pardon through the intercession of the queen, and marries Reuben Butler.

A five-reel (4,300-feet) courtroom drama set in Edinburgh, it takes aim at the injustice of preserving old laws, in this case, one enacted in 1690 that put women on notice that concealment of pregnancy might be a crime punishable by death. Effie, the daughter of a farmer, has a child by an outlaw and is condemned to the gallows when the baby is stolen by the midwife's daughter. "The screen story is a powerful one," wrote *Moving Picture World.* "It is beautiful in setting, strong in types chosen, and so admirable is the construction that we are carried to the high points of gentle decrees."

Stills: *Moving Picture World* (May 23, 1914)

### The Hidden Life

(Maurits H. Binger and Bernard E. Doxat-Pratt, 1919–20). Anglo-Hollandia. **Photography:** Feiko Boersma. **With** Anna Bosilova/Annie Bos (Rose Arundel), Adelqui Migliar (Prof. Arundel), Renée Spiljar (Dora), Lola Cornero, Harry Waghalter (Godowski), Bert Darley (Capt. Robert Carey), Carl Tobi, Leni Marcus, Aafje Schutte, and Ernst Winar. Another intense, psychological British-Dutch drama (based on Robert Hichens and John Knittell's novel *Hidden Lives*) by the directors Binger and Doxat-Pratt. Its protagonist is Rose, wife of a career-conscious professor (his specialty is evolution), who has a fling with a soldier who was her childhood sweetheart. Their brief affair results in a child and alters the lives of those closest to them. The 1,550-meter production was called *Het Verborgen Leven* in the Netherlands.

### His Lordship

(Michael Powell, 1932). Westminster Films. **Script:** Ralph Smart. **Photography:** Geoffrey Faithfull. **With** Jerry Verno (Bert) Janet Megrew (Ilya Myona), Muriel George, and Ben Welden. Powell's

Annie Bos as the woman with a secret and Harry Waghalter as the man who will try to take advantage of her in *The Hidden Life* (Maurits H. Binger and Bernard E. Doxat-Pratt, Anglo-Hollandia, 1919).

most creative effort to date was this little seen romantic burlesque. Bert Gibbs becomes a Lord but agrees to pose as the fiancé of a movie star to please his mother. With scenes that feature a chorus of female reporters wearing horned-rimmed glasses and carrying oversized notebooks, the 75-minute film, a mix of satire and musical comedy, quickly vanished in the haze of quickies being churned out at the time. Distributed by United Artists.

## Huntingtower

(George Pearson, 1927). Welsh-Pearson-Elder. **Script:** Charles Whittaker. **With** Harry Lauder (Dickson McCunn), Vera Veronina (Princess Saskia), and Pat Aherne (John Heritage). In 1922, the prolific and versatile John Buchan (author of *The Thirty-Nine Steps*, 1915), wrote *Huntingtower,* which the critics called a "rousing good story, fresh in imagination and vigorous in treatment, with much humour blended in among the thrills." Five years later, on the 10th anniversary of the Bolshevik Revolution, Pearson directed a seven-reel (7,200-feet) adaptation that fused British and American filmmaking. Scripted and photographed by Americans, and co-starring an American, the film is an atmospheric morality tale of hostage taking and adventure centering around a white Russian saved by Scots.

When the quaint, middle-aged, retired Glasgow grocer Dickson McCunn — played by the popular Sir Harry Lauder in his film debut — sets off on a rhythmic walking tour of the lovely Scottish countryside, little does he realize what lies in store. He meets a mysterious stranger and becomes aware of the fact that a Russian princess is locked up in a castle. With the help of an incredible gang of Glasgow street urchins (the Gorbals Die-Hards), he mounts an audacious plan to rescue her (and her jewels) from closely guarded Huntingtower. The film is "curious," wrote a critic, "and not easy to review. Settings, exteriors, locations, cast, photography are all first class." However, Lauder's "mixtures of comedy and pathos are all there."

## In the Gloaming

(Edwin P. Collins, 1919). Broadwest, Scotland. **Story:** J. Bertram Brown. **With** Violet Hopson and Jack Jarman. In this 5,000-feet drama starring the popular Hopson, a speculator escapes jail, makes good abroad, and returns years later to find that his wife has wed her former lover.

## Kidnapped

(Alfred Werker, 1938). Twentieth Century–Fox. **Adaptation:** Sonya Levien, Eleanor Harris, Ernest Pascal, and Edwin Blum. **With** Warner Baxter (Alan Breck), Freddie Bartholomew (David Balfour), Arleen Whelan (Jean MacDonald), C. Aubrey Smith (Duke of Argyle), Reginald Owen, and John Carradine. Filmed in Scotland, this was one of the country's most ambitious productions to date. It is loosely based on Stevenson's classic adventure of a young man who sets out to claim his inheritance — and falls in with thieves and Scottish rebels. Master Balfour becomes part of the Scottish fight for freedom ( a storyline not part of Stevenson's novel) and his tale (which includes a subplot about a love affair) becomes one stamped with Hollywood's seal of approval. The flight across

Harry and the street urchins known as the Gorbals Die-Hards are on a rescue mission in a castle in *Huntingtower* (George Pearson, Welsh-Pearson-Elder, 1927).

the Scottish moors and hills while the red-coats are after the rebels for the murder of a tax collector — though telescoped to shorter scenes than in the novel — is the highpoint of the production.

## Kilties Three

(Maurice Sandground, 1918). Gaiety, Scotland. **Script:** Bernard Merivale. **With** Bob Reed and Rowland Hill. A daring war drama about an Edinburgh industrialist who weds a German nurse. She was once married to a German spy. The 5,800-feet production received little fanfare.

## The Life of Robert Burns

(Maurice Sandground, 1926). Scottish Film Academy. **With** Wal Croft. A biography of the great Ayrshire poet, the film was made on the 130th anniversary of his death. Londoner Maurice Sandground proposed the production to Scots entrepreneur Malcolm A. Irvine. The 7,600-feet film cleared its production costs of around £600 during the first week's showing at the Coliseum in Glasgow. The director recut and reissued the drama in 1928 under the title *Immortals of Bonnie Scotland*.

## The Life of Sir Walter Scott

(Maurice Sandground, 1926). Scottish Film Academy. A biography of the great novelist. Spurred on by the success of his *The Life of Robert Burns*, Sandground produced *The Life of Sir Walter Scott*, "an excellent and educational production," wrote a critic. The director reedited and reissued the 7,600-feet film in 1928 under the title *Immortals of Bonnie Scotland*.

## The Little Hour of Peter Wells

(Maurits H. Binger and Bernard E. Doxat-Pratt, 1920). Hollandia/Granger-Binger. **Script:** Eliot Stannard. **Photography:** Feiko Boersma. **With** O. B. Clarence (Peter), Adelqui Migliar (Pranco), Heather Thatcher (Camille Pablo), Hebden Foster (Capt. Faroa), Nico de Jong (Chief of Police Raoul Pablo), Willem Hunsche (King Enrico), Jan Kiveron, and Fred Homann. The British-Dutch production company's first effort was filmed in part in picturesque and beautiful Haarlem, "something out of Franz Hals," recalled O. B. Clarence.

In this romantic adventure (based on the 1913 novel by David Whitelaw), a young clerk and the beautiful Camille Pablo, the heroine (and daughter of a chief of police), get caught up in a devious, revolutionary, prewar plot centering on the murder of the king of Bragaglia and mysterious disappearance of the heir to the throne. With great crowd scenes, a coronation with trumpeters in brilliant uniform, and a museum in a park transformed into a palace, the spectacle was "everything that could be wished," said O. B. Clarence. In Holland the 75-minute (5,000-feet) film was called *De Heldendaad van Peter Wells* (*The Heroic Deed of Peter Wells*).

## The Little Minister

(Percy Nash, 1915). Neptune, Scotland. **With** Joan Ritz (Babbie), Dame May Whitty (Nanny Webster), Gregory Scott (Rev. Gavin Wishart), Fay Davis (Margaret Dishart), and Douglas Payne (Lord Rintoul). This first Scottish rendition of J. M. Barrie's popular and

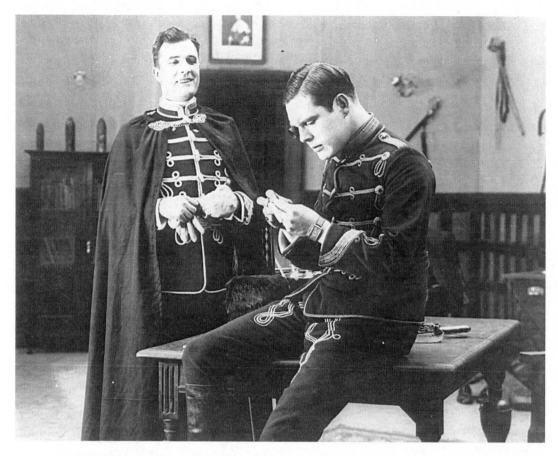

Hebden Foster (*right*) as the revolutionary leader in love with the daughter of a police chief in *The Little Hour of Peter Wells* (Maurits H. Binger and Bernard E. Doxat-Pratt, Granger-Binger, 1920).

moving 1891 novel and 1899 stage play is a 4,000-feet romance about a gypsy girl who is raised as the ward of a nobleman and who grows to love Gavin, the clergyman. In rural 1840s Scotland, Gavin Dishart arrives to become the new "little minister" of Thrums's Auld Licht church. He meets a mysterious young gypsy girl in the dens, and to his horror Babbie draws him into her escape from the soldiers after she incites a Luddite riot. But unknown to Gavin, Babbie is more than she seems. And they must overcome her secret, the villagers' fears of her, and worst of all, Gavin's devotion

to his mother's sensibilities, before they can openly declare their love.

The well-photographed film "follows the novel more closely than did the play, there being necessarily more opportunity for more diversified scenes," wrote a London critic. A great deal, for example, is made of Rintoul's rescue by Gavin. "The film version ... barely escapes being one of the best."

## *The Little Singer*

(Clarence Elder, 1956). Elder Films. With Louise Boyd, Campbell Hastie, Evelyn Lockhart, and Archie Neal. The film is a Scottish morality tale (based on Isabel Cameron's novel of the same name) about a young girl who wants to sing in St. Andrew Halls, in Glasgow, but whose family debts put her dreams in jeopardy. The one-hour drama failed to secure national release because of the unintelligibility of the Glasgow accent, though it was popular with local audiences.

## Lochinvar

(Leslie Seldon-Truss, 1915). Gaumont, Scotland. **With** Godfrey Trearle and Peggy Hyland. The first Scottish adaptation of Sir Walter Scott's stirring ballad, this romance relates the chivalrous heroics of a young knight. In the 2,100-feet production, he comes out of the west to rescue Ellen, the lady at Netherby Hall who is condemned to marry a "laggard in love and a dastard in war." On the night before her enforced marriage, Lochinvar persuades her to dance one last dance. Her young chevalier swings her into his saddle and makes off with her, before the "bridegroom" and his servants can recover from their astonishment

## Love, Life and Laughter

(George Pearson, 1923). Welsh-Pearson. **Script:** Pearson. **Photography:** Percy Strong. **With** Betty Balfour

Godfrey Tearle as Lochinvar and Peggy Hyland (*center*) as his love Ellen in the adaptation of Walter Scott's classic *Lochinvar* (Leslie Seldon-Truss, Gaumont, 1915).

(Tip-Toes), Harry Jonas, Frank Stanmore (balloon blower), Nancy Price, and Annie Esmond. To make this film, "we had risked our reputation and our resources," wrote George Pearson, "for the public might dislike its uncommon structure, and its queer mixture of imagination and realism." But this tale of a dancer who provides emotional support to a despairing young author turned out to be a beautiful, inspired, and ambitious work, one of the finest British silents. It bridges the passage from realism to fantasy, contrasting, among other things, the drabness of tenement life with the splendor of an open-air, night dance.

Its unusual aspects include subtitles against a pictorial background of soaring balloons, each encircling the face of a character in the fantasy, a number of color effects, and an unexpected ending. Thus the acclaim: The film "stands out as the greatest of British 'supers,'" wrote a critic, "if not quite an international masterpiece. The tempo and cutting are really brilliant." Balfour was called "the cleverest comedienne ... playing in British films." In a noteworthy scene that is set in a decorated dining room, Balfour is waiting for her friend to show up at the birthday party she has arranged for him. Unaware that he has taken his life, she excitedly receives a massage. At the moment she reads the note, the candles on the cake burn out, the streamers fall from the ceiling, and the light in the room dims. Everything suddenly appears cheap and out of place. Because of Pearson's 6,300-feet production, American films "have no advantage technically," reported one British reviewer, while "Pearson has made a film which," wrote the *Pall Mall Gazette*, "surpasses even the genius of D. W. Griffith." Years later, Pearson wrote, "were that film seen today, I should be the first to see its ... appeal to the emotions. On the stepping stones of past experiments, film technique has advanced to heights undreamed of by those who adventured when film was young."

## The Man Behind the Mask

(Michael Powell, 1936). Joe Rock. **Script:** Ian Hay, Syd Courtney, Jack Byrd, and Stanley Haynes. **Photography:** Francis Carver. **With** Hugh Williams (Nick Barclay), Jane Baxter (June Slade), Donald Calthrop (Dr. Walpole), Henry Oscar, Kitty Kelly, and Harry Carey. This 80-minute example of Powell's growing talent in the medium remains the most recent of his numerous lost films. On the night (at the masked ball) during which he plans to elope with the aristocratic June Slade, Nick Barclay is attacked by a mysterious man who assumes his identity. The man kidnaps June because she is in possession of the "Shield of Kahm." Since he immediately comes under suspicion for theft and abduction, Nick sets out to find "the man behind the mask," which leads him to a network of international thieves. "Technically," wrote *Monthly Film Bulletin*, "the film is excellent ... and the final scenes in the crook's house are impressive.... The director is to be most congratulated for having made what must be termed a good film out of very unlikely material."

*Opposite:* Betty Balfour as Tip-Toes, the dancer who rescues a despairing young author in *Love, Life and Laughter* (George Pearson, Welsh-Pearson, 1923).

Bernard Goetzke (*right*) arrives just in time to rescue Nita Naldi from the clutches of the man known as the "Fear o' God" in *The Mountain Eagle* (Alfred Hitchcock, Gainsborough-Emelka, Michael Balcon, 1926).

## The Mountain Eagle

(Alfred Hitchcock, 1926). Gainsborough-Emelka, Michael Balcon. **Script:** Eliot Stannard. **Photography:** Baron Ventimiglia. **With** Bernard Goetzke (Pettigrew), Nita Naldi (Beatrice), Malcolm Keen (Fear o' God), and John Hamilton (Edward). Hitchcock's second German film in his career (preceded by *The Pleasure Garden*, 1925) was his first thriller. Also called *Der Bergadler*— released in the U.S. as *Fear o' God*— it is a tale of a scandalous love affair among, of all people, the hillbillies of Kentucky. It was filmed in the Tirol. *Bioscope* praised Hitchcock for his "at times brilliant direction," though it found that the 7,500-feet film contains "an air of unreality."

The director's German-British period was an influence in the German pictorial style of his *Blackmail* (1929).

## Murder at Monte Carlo

(Ralph Ince, 1935). First National. **Script:** Michael Barringer. **Photography:** Basil Emmott. **With** Errol Flynn, Eve Gray, and Paul Graetz. Fresh from Australia, Flynn was cast in his first starring role in this tale of rivalry between two young journalists out to make a scoop of the death of a famous mathematician at Monte Carlo. They investigate the nerve-wracked professor's novel method of winning at roulette — as well as the foul deed. Flynn "gives a convincing performance," wrote London's *Picture Show*, while *Kine Weekly* called his effort "a high pressure portrayal." Within a year of making this 70-minute work, the young star was in Hollywood and heading the cast in *Captain Blood*.

## My Friend the King

(Michael Powell, 1931). 20th Century/Film Engineering. **Script:** Jefferson Farjeon. **Photography:** Geoffrey Faithfull. **With** Jerry Verno (Jim), Robert Holmes, Eric Pavitt (King Ludwig), and Phyllis Loring. Powell's 50-minute mystery concerns a young heir (Pavitt) to a throne who, on a visit to London, disappears. His whereabouts — and the nature of the kidnappers — become the concern of a good-hearted cabbie (Verno).

## Number Thirteen

(Alfred Hitchcock, 1922). W. and F. Film Service. **Script:** Anita Ross. **Photography:** J. Rosenthal. **With** Clare Greet and Ernest Thesiger. Also called *Mrs. Peaboby*, the film was one of Hitchcock's earliest directorial efforts, a comedy starring the stage actress Greet, known for portrayals of Cockney mothers. In mid-production, Islington studios closed down operations — and Hitchcock's film vanished. But the director didn't lose track of the star. He used her in *The Manxman* (1929), *Jamaica Inn* (1939), and other films.

## On Thin Ice

(Bernard Vorhaus, 1933). Hall Mark/Equity British. **Script:** Vorhaus. **Photography:** Eric Cross. **With** Ursula Jeans, Kenneth Law, Viola Gault, and Dorothy Bartlam. Vorhaus's first feature is a 62-minute melodrama about jealousy and blackmail within British high society. The film's settings, ranging from mansions to meadow to night club, were said to be "spectacular and picturesque."

## The Other Person

(Maurits H. Binger and Bernard E. Doxat-Pratt, 1920). Hollandia/Granger-Binger. **Script:** Benedict James. **Photography:** Feiko Boersma and Jan Smit. **With** Adelqui Migliar (the other man), Ivo Dawson (Andrew Grain), Zoë Palmer (Alice Dene), Arthur Pusey (Chris Larcher), Arthur Walcott (Reverend Dene), E. Story-Goften (Dr. Pess), Willem Hunsche (Amos Larcher), Nora Hayden (Dolly Banks), Annie Busquet, and Johan de Boer. Another British-Dutch psychological drama of revenge by Binger and Doxat-Pratt, based on the popular 1920 story of the same name by Fergus W. Hume (1859–1932). It is set in the village of Wichley, south of Devon, where squire Andrew Grain takes the advice of a spiritualist named Pess, who describes to Grain the "the other person," or spirit, who has a message for him.

The production became known for its experimental use of double exposures involving spiritualism. In the Netherlands the five-reel (1,525-meter) film was called *Onder Spiritistischen Dwang* (*Under Spiritualistic Coercion*). The following year Doxat-Pratt directed the well received *Fate's Plaything*, for Anglo-Hollandia.

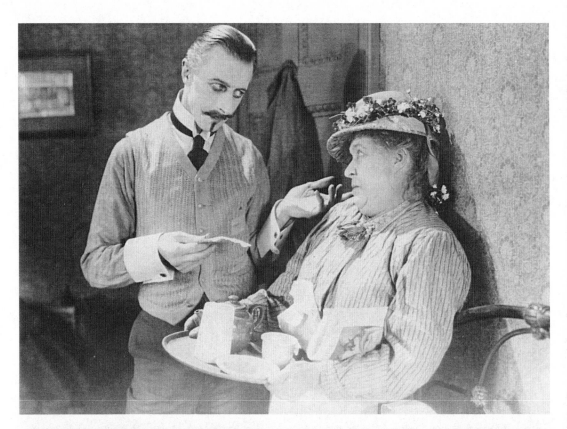

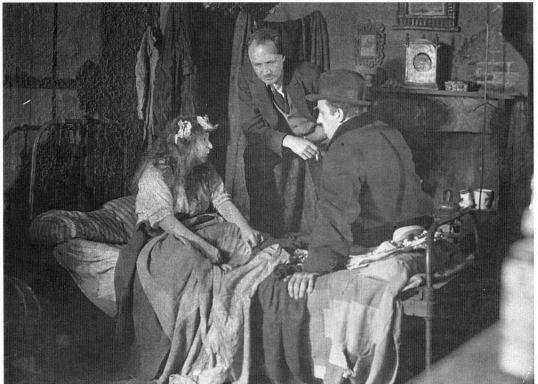

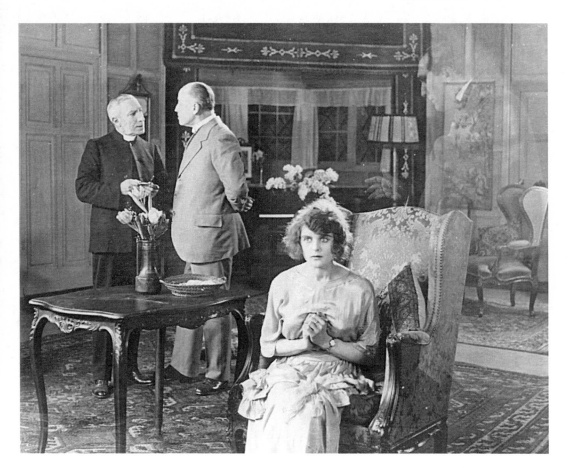

Arthur Walcott, Johan de Boer, Zoë Palmer and (*far right*) Adelqui Migliar as "The Other Person" (Maurits H. Binger and Bernard E. Doxat-Pratt, Granger-Binger, 1921).

## The Price of a Song

(Michael Powell, 1935). Fox British/Powell. **Script:** Michael Barringer. **Photography:** James Wilson. **With** Campbell Gullan, Marjorie Corbett, Gerald Fielding, and Eric Maturin. Starring the silent-screen veteran Campbell Gullan, Powell's 70-minute film was one of the earliest that he produced, a tale of an old man's attempt to commit the perfect crime. Here it is the murder of a songwriter for his inheritance.

## The Rasp

(Michael Powell, 1931). 20th Century/Film Engineering. **Script:** Philip MacDonald. **Photography:** Geoffrey Faithfull. **With** Claude Horton (Anthony), Phyllis Loring (Lucy), C. M. Hallard, and James Raglan (Alan). When cabinet minister John Hoode is murdered at his country house, his secretary, Alan Deacon, is the prime suspect and is arrested. Reporter Anthony Gethryn determines to unmask the

*Opposite top and bottom:* Scenes from Hitchcock's lost film *Number Thirteen* (Alfred Hitchcock, W. and F. Film Service, 1922).

real murderer. The nature of the film in which the murder weapon is a file, the victim is a cabinet minister, a newspaperman is involved, and the Scotland Yard crimefighters are seen as dimwitted put the spotlight on the director. Powell, in this 45-minute quickie, "has butted in on an American favorite theme," wrote a critic. He manages to keep the atmosphere "refreshingly English."

## Reveille

(George Pearson, 1924). Welsh-Pearson. **Script:** Pearson. **Photography:** Percy Strong. **With** Betty Balfour, Ralph Forbes, Frank Stanmore, and Steward Rome. Pearson's homage to those who made the supreme sacrifice during the First World War is more slice-of-life than plot, "merely the development of a theme," said the director, a "scrapbook of pictures of life caught in the living, no hero, no villain, no plot, no tying up loose ends."

The 8,400-feet tale — made on the tenth anniversary of the start of the great conflict — begins with the high hopes of a widow awaiting the return of three sons and a brother on Armistice Day. It ends with the sadness of Remembrance Day five years later. It has as its keystone "Two Minutes' Silence" for the dead. "I knew," wrote Pearson, "that … I was risking all to test my belief that the silent film could be freer in structure, and more effective when loosely-knit scenes could capture Wordsworth's 'homely sympathy that heeds the common life.'" The *Sunday Times* wrote, "This film may not be as great as *The Trojan Women*, but it is two thousand years nearer the human heart."

## Rob Roy

(Arthur Vivian, 1911). United Films, Scotland. **With** John Clyde, Theo Henries (Helen), Durward Lely (Francis Osbaldistone), and W. G. Robb. The first known feature-length film made in Scotland is this three-reel (2,000-feet) tale about the early 18th century Scottish hero, upon whose grave it reads,

> For why? Because the good old rule
> Sufficeth them; the simple plan,
> That they should take who have the
>    power,
> And they should keep who can.

The loose adaptation of Sir Walter Scott's well-known novel stars the actor John Clyde, who took the title role in a drama shot in fairly basic studio conditions at Rouken Glen on the southern edge of Glasgow.

## Secret Lives

(Edmond T. Gréville, 1937). Phoenix. **Script:** Basil Mason. **Photography:** Otto Heller. **With** Brigitte Horney, Neil Hamilton, and Raymond Lovell. French director Gréville, German star Horney, and Czech photographer Heller combined to bring to the screen a psychological tale of espionage set during the First World War — absent scenes of carnage — and without dialogue in more than half the 80-minute production. Making extensive use of camera angels and other tricks to present the emotional states of a number of French and German secret agents, the film was too abstract for most filmgoers, "though the story and much of the treatment is interesting," wrote a critic. It was released in the U.S. under the title *I Married a Spy*.

## She

(Will Barker and Horace L. Lucoque, 1916). **With** Alice Delysia (Ayesha), Henry Victor (Leo), Sydney Bland (Horace Holly), Blanche Forsythe (Ustane), and Hastings Batson (Billali). One of the earliest British features with lavish sets and mass crowd scenes was this production by Barker and Lucoque. It was also the first full-length British adventure, based on Henry Rider Haggard's thrilling 1887 Victorian novel, starring Delysia. The public had come to know her for her lovely body, "of which they have seen so much," it was said, in her fantastic revue and musical comedies.

The film's tale hinges on legend: Although aware that many of his ancestors have failed in the same mission, young Englishman Leo attempts to find the mysterious, beautiful, and immortal white queen who rules a lost African civilization.

He sets out on the quest aboard the deck of an African coaster, manned by dingy sailors. His triumphs over the aborigines involve a rescue of whites from drowning, combing through the grim cave of the Amhaggar and the underground palace of She, where reptiles of the most unpleasant kind are used for ornamentation and skeletons are as common as furniture. Whether in a

Alice Delysia as Ayesha and Henry Victor as the intrepid British adventurer in *She* (Will Barker and Horace Lisle Lucoque, 1916).

dusky ravine, a precipice, or facing the blazing fountain of the fire which turns She, after her bath, back to a woman 2,000 years old, the stalwart hero never wavers.

## Someday

(Michael Powell, 1935). Warner Bros. **Script:** Brock Williams. **Photography:** Basil Emmott and Monty Berman. **With** Esmond Knight (Curley), Margaret Lockwood (Emily), Henry Mollison, and Raymond Lovell. Based on Frank Lloyd's Hollywood drama *Young Nowheres* (1929), Powell's 70-minute romantic drama of tenament life is presented in entirely different fashion, in flashback. Curley Blake is a lift operator in a block of flats. He is in love with Emily, the cleaning girl. When Emily returns from a stay in hospital, Curley arranges to treat her to dinner in one of the flats. Unfortunately, the owner returns early. By surprising his girlfriend in the apartment of an absent tenant, Curley winds up in trouble with the law.

Powell's efforts to portray lower-class aspirations were brushed aside by the critics, who said "the theme deals with domestics and its suitability is confined mainly to picture-goers of that class." Still, "this is a pleasant unpretentious story pleasantly told."

## Someone Wasn't Thinking

(Bladen Peak, 1946). Scottish National Film. **Script:** Joseph McLeod. Narrated by McLeod, the film was the debut production of a new company, Scottish National Film Studios, launched in Glasgow in 1946 in celebration of cinema's 50th birthday and in reaction to what was seen as a national need. The critics had noted that "At the moment we find it impossible to produce feature films in Scotland in their entirety, having neither the personnel nor the equipment.... During the past twenty years Scotland has produced its own Talkie and Sound Recording equipment. It has made dozens of every kind of short film.... Producers have been working quietly on Industrial films, Musical and Dramatic shorts, and also sponsored films for Government departments. All are competent to turn out good work, and all have experience in every branch of film production. They have what the Americans call 'the know how.'"

With proper studio facilities and personnel, the production company was born. Its managing director was author, stage producer, and former BBC newsreader MacLead. The initial aim was to produce educational, scientific, religious, and shorts, with expansion to entertainment and full length feature films to follow. Their debut production (aptly titled) was shot in the center of Glasgow — and was the company's only film.

## The Star Reporter

(Michael Powell, 1931). Film Engineering. **Script:** Philip MacDonald and Ralph Smart. **Photography:** Geoffrey Faithfull and Powell. **With** Harold French (Major Starr), Spencer Trevor (Longbourne), Isla Bevin (Lady Susan Loman), and Garry Marsh (Mandel). Swift action and dialogue link a jewel robbery, blackmail, murder, and romance in another of Powell's trimmed-down crime dramas, at only 45 minutes, from his first year as a director. In this tale, Lord Longbourne is persuaded to steal his daughter's diamond and then claim the insurance money. Powell's "smoothness of direction and a crispness of acting and cutting" were credited for making the film and giving it the polish of a film costing 100 times as much. Distributed by 20th Century.

## A Study in Scarlet

(George Pearson, 1914). Samuelson. **Script:** Harry Engholm and Pearson. **Photography:** Walter Buckstone. **With** James Bragington (Sherlock Holmes), Fred Paul (Jefferson Hope), and Agnes Glynne (Lucy Ferrier). Pearson's film was a first on two counts: the first Sherlock Holmes film out of Britain, and the first screen version of Conan Doyle's first Holmes story. It is an exciting tale of Mormon mystery, murder, and implacable revenge, roaming over the American scene from the Rockies to Salt Lake (involving a wagon train), and finally to the suburbs of London, where a long and lean-figured, deer-stalker-hatted, cape-coated, and curved-piped Holmes solves a murder.

Filmed in Britain's Cheddar Gorge, a key early scene involves the rescue by the Mormons of a little four-year-old girl (played by the director's daughter Winifred) who is lost in the desert with her dying father. She grows into the heroine Lucy. One critic wrote: "One is filled with regret when this long film comes to an end."

## Thou Fool

(Fred Paul, 1926). Stoll, Scotland. This moving 5,100-feet drama, based on

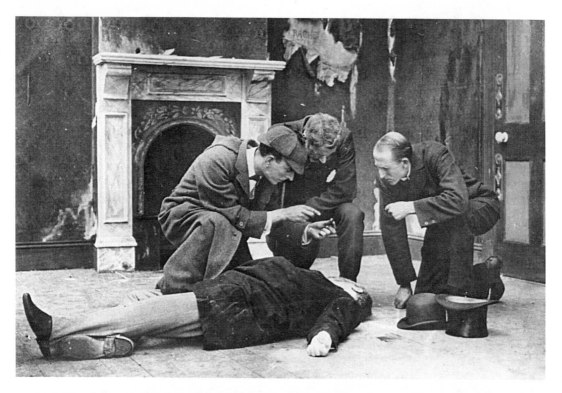

James Bragington, as Sherlock Holmes, looks upon a case in *A Study in Scarlet* (George Pearson, Samuelson, 1914).

the 1908 novel by John Joy Bell (1871–1934), makes clear the maxim, "There is that maketh himself rich, yet has nothing; there is that maketh himself poor, yet hath great riches." In Scotland, in the high moorland of Upper Lanarkshire, a woman struggles to make sure her only child will be able to get on in the world. At the center of the tale is the answer to his question, "When are ye goin' to tell me aboot my father?"

## Two Crowded Hours

(Michael Powell, 1931). Film Engineering. **Script:** Jefferson Farjeon. **Photography:** Geoffrey Faithfull. **With** John Longden, Jane Welsh, Jerry Verno, and Michael Hogan. Powell's debut film was this low-budget, 45-minute thriller about a detective on the trail of a murderer who was convicted by the detective's lover. The murderer is out for revenge on those who gave evidence against him. *Variety* called the film, whose editing was inspired by Soviet techniques, "just a quota quickie, but much better than … more ambitious pictures." Distributed by 20th Century.

## Was She Guilty?

(George André Béranger, 1922). Hollandia/Granger-Binger. **Script:** Maurits H. Binger. **Photography:** Feiko Boersma. **With** Jan Musch (Jones), Gertrude McCoy (Ruth Herwood), Norman Doxat-Pratt, Pierre Balledux (Ling Soo), Paul de Groot (John Herwood), Kitty Kluppell (Palmyra Hawks), Zoë Palmer (Mary), William A. Freshman (Bobby), Mari van Warmelo, Lewis Willoughby (George Midhurst), and Fred Homann. A sensationalist, upclose, British-Dutch production (also

called *Thou Shalt Not*) from Hollandia's Béranger and Binger, based on D. van Veens's story *Haar groote dag*. The film contrasts life in down and out East End London, including its public housing and opium dens, against wealthier, high strata environments elsewhere.

Well-off Ruth Herwood adopts Mary, the daughter of the thief Jones who had tried to rob her home. After her father is sent to Australia as punishment, the young girl grows up in splendor (and ignorance of her family) until her father returns, accompanied by Palmyra who is aware of "where he got his money." She has him blackmail Ruth Herwood and forces Mary to work for Long Soo, the "lecherous, treacherous" owner of a den of iniquity. When Jones is poisoned to death, Ruth is charged with murder.

The film found favor for its atmosphere. "From a scenic point of view," wrote a critic, "the feature is quite good. The exteriors are well done, whether studio or natural, and the interiors are often very beautiful." In Holland the five-reel (65-minute) film was titled *Gij zult niet dooden* (*Thou Shalt Not Kill*).

## The Wee MacGreegor's Sweetheart

(George Pearson, 1922). Welsh-Pearson. **Script:** Pearson. **With** Betty Balfour (Christina) and Donald Macardle (MacGreeger). Pearson's comedy was taken from two 1902 stories by the acclaimed Scottish author John Joy Bell. Shot in Scottish locations, including Edinburgh, Glasgow, and Bute, it is a merry 5,300-feet tale of two young lovers—a Glasgow lad and a harem-scarum lassie—always in trouble. MacGreeger is guileless but the fiery, irresistible Christina is not.

Gertrude McCoy (*left*), Lewis Willoughby (*second from left*), and Zoë Palmer in *Was She Guilty?* (George André Béranger, Granger-Binger, 1922).

## What Every Woman Knows

(Fred W. Durrant, 1917). Barker-Neptune. **With** Hilda Trevelyan (Maggie), A. B. Imeson (John), and Maud Yates (the countess). This romance was the first adaptation of James M. Barrie's play. The 5,100-feet tale takes place in Scotland, where plain Maggie Wylie's family, fearing she may become a spinster, finances young John Shand's stud-

ies in return for his agreement to marry her in five years. Recognizing his ambitions, Maggie helps to guide his career without his realizing it. He honors his commitment, even though he does not feel real love for her, as she does for him. Will he succumb to the wiles of young aristocratic beauty Sybil, or learn to appreciate Maggie's true worth? He learns about love only after he is elected to Parliament.

# Greece

The earliest Greek film is the 200-meter *Journal of the Olympic Games* (1906), produced by Gaumont. The father of Greek cinema was Evànghelos Mavrodimakos, who began distributing films within the country in 1908, while the first production company, Athene Film, was founded by the comedian Spiridon Dimitrakopulos in 1910. In 1911 and 1912, that production company produced four shorts starring Dimitrakopulos, and in 1914 produced the first Greek feature, *Golfo*, directed by Kostas Bahatoris. Other cinema pioneers include the Hungarian-born Joseph Hepp, a photographer who favored real-life dramas, and writer-director-producer Dimitris Gaziadis. who was influenced by German cinema.

In the late 1920s, when Greece had more than 200 theaters, Gaziadis set up Dag Films. He favored folklore in picturesque fashion, working with his brothers, the photographer Michael, production director Kostas, and lab technician Alexandré. Their films, numbering more than two dozen, revitalized Greek cinema. The transition to sound, however, resulted in a collapse not only of the Gaziadis's company, but of the Greek industry. In the period 1931–39, only 12 films were made within the country (some with Turkish or Egyptian assistance) — and nearly all have vanished.

## I apahidhes ton Athinon (The Ruffians of Athens)

(Dimitris Gaziadis, 1930). Dag Films. **Photography:** Michael Gaziadis. **With** Mary Sayiannou, Petros Epitropakis, Ioannis Prineas, Petros Kyriakos. This musical comedy became a fine success, establishing Sayiannou, of the National Theater, as the first Greek film star. The early "sound" film contains songs synchronized to lip movements.

## Astero

(Dimitris Gaziadis, 1929). Dag Films. **Photography:** Michael Gaziadis. **Script:** Pavlos Nirvanas. **With** Aliki Théodoridou. This melodramatic look at the lives and traditions of Greek shepherds (based on an original story by Nirvanas) became one of the first Greek films to be a hit abroad. More important, the 2,350-meter film, called "genuine and pure," inaugurated a highly profitable series of films for the producers.

The tale is set near the slopes of Helmos, where a pious father pries apart a young couple — his son and the young man's stepsister, the beautiful orphan and shepherdess Astero. Well-connected marriages are arranged for both, but at the last minute, the sensitive young woman bolts for the haven of the mountains. She nearly goes mad before all ends well.

## To ellinikon thavma (The Greek Miracle)

(Dimitris Gaziadis, 1921). **Photography:** Michael Gaziadis. **With** Maria Kroupenskaya and Agazaroff. The first important nonfictional film from Greece is this 2,000-meter romance starring Russian actors; it was filmed at the behest of the Greek government by new-comer Gaziadis, who had gained his film experience covering the Turkish-Greek war of 1919–21.

## Eros ke kymata (Love and Waves)

(Dimitris Gaziadis, 1927). Dag Films. **Script:** Dimitris Gaziadis. **Photography:** Michael Gaziadis. **With** Nikos Dendramis (Petros), Miranda Myrat (Rina), Emilios Véakis, Dimitris Tsakiris (Panos), Costas Moussouris, Yiorgos Pappas, Filio Naoum, Dina Sarri, and Orestis Laskos. A sentimental 8-reel silent that was the studio's first real hit, catching the fancy of the Greek public. The comedy stars a slew of excellent theatrical performers in their debut film, as well as one of the most beautiful women of the era, Dina Sarris ("Miss Greece"), and the poet Laskos. Shot around the tourist attractions of Athens, it's the story of a lover's quarrel between Panos and Rina. It seems that Rina has caught the eye of the suave Petros, causing Panos to become jealous. Everything works out well in the end.

## Filisse me, Maritsa (Kiss Me, Maritsa)

(Dimitris Gaziadis, 1930). Dag Films. Script: Dimitris Bogris. Photography: Michael Gaziadis. With Mary Sayiannou. Based on the comic operetta by Bogris about the beautiful Maritsa doing all she can to leave her confining village for the world of Athens, the film is another of Gaziadis's late silent films contains songs synchronized to lip movements.

## Golfo

(Kostas Bahatoris, 1914). Photography: Filippo Martelli and Nikos Koukoulas. With Virginia Diamanti (Golfo),

Dionyssios Venieris (Tassos), Olympia Damaskou (Starroula), and Yiorgis Ploutis. The first full-length Greek feature and one of earliest Greek films of merit is based on the bucolic five-act play by Spiros Peressiadis. Photographed by the Italian Martelli, the tear-jerker helped establish a genre whose subjects came from 19th century country life. One of the interesting aspects of the 1,200-meter tragedy is the costumes. Men wear tasseled caps and short white skirts (linen kilts) and white tights and black jackets. Their belts contain arsenals of pistols and knives; the higher their ranking, the more armor at their disposal. The women are beautiful and well dressed, especially the protagonist.

Tassos loves the beautiful and delectable Golfo, a young maiden of the mountains and daughter of Astero, but Stavroula also loves Tassos — and she does all she can to get him. She manages to woo him away from Golfo. Yet when Golfo finds out she cannot have the man she loves, she rejects a wealthy young suitor. Tassos returns to Golfo — only to find she has gone mad in his absence and taken poison. After she dies in his arms, the faithless young man commits suicide.

## Kain ke Avel (Cain and Abel)

(Kimon Spathopoulos, 1930). Dirmikis Bros. **Script:** Panayiotis Papatheodorou. **Photography:** Pavlos Dirmikis. **With** Kimon Spathopoulos, Andreas Evangeliou, and Anna Kiritsopoulou. A 2,600-meter tale set in a village in the provinces, the tragic film is about brothers vying for the love of a gypsy.

## O kakos dhromos (The Wrong Way)

(Ertogrul Muhssin, 1932). Iris Films.

With Marika Kotopouli and Kyveli. This adaptation of the passionate novel by Gregorios Xenopoulos was one of the first all-talking Greek features, a forceful and humorous musical brought to life by two great, elegant adversaries of Greek theater, Kyveli (1888–1978) and Kotopouli (1887–1954). It is the tale of two women who take different approaches to love. The risqué production was filmed in Istanbul by Turkey's foremost director of operettas. It was cut from over 100 minutes to 77 minutes for its U.S. release in 1936. Critics noted that the "old artifice of having plenty of music sounding in the background indicated that the producers were playing around with sound for the first time."

### Kerenia koukla (The Wax Doll)

(Michalis Glytsos, 1915–16). Asty Film. With Virginia Diamanti. Based on the 1909 novel and stage production by the great playwright Konstantinos Christomanos (1867–1911), this film was the first Greek production based on a stage production, as well as one of the earliest to contain scenes shot at the front.

### To limani ton dhakrion (The Port of Tears)

(Dimitris Gaziadis, 1929). Dag Films. Script: Gaziadis and Orestis Laskos. Photography: Michael Gaziadis. With Dimitris Tsakiris, Emilios Véakis, and Orestis Laskos. A rare Greek tale of social import based on the novel by Swedish writer Berndt Slovy, the 3,300-meter drama is about sponge divers who fall prey to smugglers interested in locating relics on the ocean floor.

### O Michael den ehi psila (Michael Doesn't Have Any Dough)

(Lykourgos Kalapothakis, 1923).

Photography: Joseph Hepp. With Michael Michael, Concetta Moschou, and Zaza Brillanti. Encouraged to take part in this short, two-part comedy, the comic actor Michael was responsible for the first commercially successful Greek film. In the film, he worked opposite two stars of the world of theatrical music.

### I bora (The Storm)

(Dimitris Gaziadis, 1930). Dag Film. Script: Pavlos Nirvanas. Photography: Michael Gaziadis. With Edmond Furst (Pavlos), Periklis Christoforidis (Andreas), Aliki Ieromimou (Maria), Dimitris Tsakiris, and Dita Parlo. Gaziadis's film, a powerful tale of a returning soldier who finds his wife has run off with another man, contains documentary war footage, the first use of such material in Greek film. In the tale, a soldier finds out he is indirectly responsible for the collapse of his marriage.

During the First World War, when Andreas and his comrade Pavlos are prisoners of war in Russia, Andreas tells his friend the most intimate details of his married life. Pavlos returns home from the war first — and looks up the wife, Maria. She falls in love with him. The drama is analogous to Leonhardt Frank's dramatic *Karl und Anna*, produced in the late 1920s, as well as the classic *The Return of Martin Guerre* (1982).

### O paliatsos tis zois (The Clown of Life)

(Nikos Metaxas and A. Kelafas, 1928) Acropolis Films. Script: Orestis Laskos. Photography: Dimitris Meravidis. With Kimon Spathopoulos and Katy Papanikolaou. The poet Laskos's first script for the medium, starring the stage performer who made a name for himself with his imitations of Chaplin. In his first film, Spathopoulos plays a tramp who falls for a woman with tuberculosis, and like the famous clown he sacrifices everything for her.

### Stella Violanti

(Yannis Loumos, 1931). Hellas Films. **Photography:** Jimmy Berlier. **With** Eleni Papadaki. Based on the 1909 novel of the same name by Gregorios Xenopoulos (the founder of 20th century Greek bourgeois drama), the sound film is one of the earliest such Greek productions, a description of mores on the harsh Ionian Islands and the setting for a doomed love affair — and the only film that the great stage actress Papadaki ever made. Stella seeks her own life, but comes into conflict with her tradition-bound, rich father who refuses to let her marry the man she loves, a telegraph operator. When her lover marries another, Stella dies of a broken heart.

### Tes moiras to apopaidi (Succession Abandoned)

(Dimos Bratsános, 1925). Ajax Film.

**Script:** Bratsános. **Photography:** Joseph Hepp. At 2,100 meter, this earliest Greek feature is a spectacular that helped set the tone and style for an important genre in Greek films: the emotional, staged melodrama, performed by nonprofessionals.

A child, abandoned by his mother in wartime, is raised by itinerants. He grows up to become rich and famous. A huge hit in Greece and abroad, including the United States, the film was shown regularly until 1950 — though the director profited little from it.

### O Villar sta gynaikeia loutra (Villar at the Old Age Spa)

(Joseph Hepp, 1924). **With** Nikos Sfakianakis (Villar). A short containing highly popular comic burlesques in which the Max Linder type character Villar makes do in an old-age spa. Nikos Sfakianakis, born in Crete, lived in Istanbul before making a career in Europe, in France in particular. He arrived in Greece in 1914, and became a variety star. He collaborated on a number of films with Hepp. He died forgotten.

# Hungary

One of the oldest and richest of film cultures, Hungarian cinema had its beginnings at the dawn of the century, when Béla Zitkovszky photographed *A Táncz* (*Dance*). In 1912 Mihály Kertész — in Hollywood he was Michael Curtiz — directed *Ma és holnap* (*Today and Yesterday*), one of Hungarian cinema's first full-length features, produced by Pro-

jectograph. During World War I, when the import of American, French and Italian films came to a halt, the absence of foreign competition worked in Hungary's favor. It led to an upheaval in Hungarian film production, and Hungary joined Denmark, the United States, Germany and Italy on the list of film-producing superpowers. In 1918 — within a single year — over 100 Hungarian feature-films were produced and shown to Hungarian and international audiences.

During this period, Jenö Janovics, an actor and theater director, rose to the front ranks as a filmmaker, as did Alexander Korda, Charles Vidor, Paul Fejos, Mihály Várkonyi, Paul Lukas, Béla Balász, Ica Lénkeffy, and Lajos Biró.

In 1919, Béla Kun's Communist takeover — he was a strong backer of nationalized film production — was followed by a violent counterrevolution, The country's best filmmakers, including Alexander Korda, the founder of Corvin studios, soon went into exile. Film production dropped to thirty films that year; only two are extant.

Of the 500 or so silent films produced in Hungary in the period 1912–1930, nearly all are gone. This includes two dozen films made in Hungary by Alexander Korda, as well as the films of Paul Fejos and Géza von Bolváry. The early careers of future stars like Vilma Bánky, Pál Lukács, Mihály Várkonyi, Franciska Gaál, Béla Lugosi, who all started in Budapest, are preserved only in a few hundred meters of fragmented sequences.

By 1930, when Hungarian cinema was at a standstill, Paramount briefly filled the gap, and beat everyone to the punch, by making two Hungarian sound films, both melodramas, in Paris. By inviting some of Hungary's best actors to Paris, the studio was acting on the supposition that Budapest audiences wanted, at least initially, to hear films in their own language. During the 1930s more than half of the features released within the country came from American studios.

The first sound productions made within Hungary were *A Kék bálvány* (*The Blue Idol*) (1931), directed by Lajos Lázár, and *Hyppolit a lakáj* (*Hyppolit the Butler*) (1931), directed by István Székely. Paul Fejos's *Tavaszi zápor* (*Spring Shower*) (1932) and Ladislao Vajda's *Magdát kicsapják* (*Magda Is Expelled*) (1938) have been called the finest prewar Hungarian films. A quarter of Hungary's pre–1945 sound films are gone.

## Ali rózsáskertje (The Rose Garden of Ali)

(Oszkár Damó, 1913). **With** János Doktor and Lajos Palágyi. **Photography:** Miksa Adler. Based on the novel by Géza Gárdonyi, Hungary's acclaimed provincial writer (in the best sense of the word) whose work is saturated with the culture of the countryside and the speech of its people. Damó's 75-minute (1,450-meter) adaptation was one of the longest Hungarian productions of its day.

## Arsene Lupin utolsó kalandja (Arsène Lupin's Last Adventure)

(Paul Fejos, 1921). **Photography:** Joseph Karban. **With** Gusztav Partos, Mara Jankovszky, Lajos Gellért, and Odön Bardi. Also called *Arsène Lupin's letztes Abenteur*, this early European adaptation of Maurice Leblanc's work is modeled after American serials. Lupin is a Raffles-type thief of Paris (pursued by the relentless Inspector Guerchard) who impersonates an aristocrat in order to make off with an art collection. He also finds love in the City of Lights.

## Bánk bán (Bánk, the Palatine)

(Mihály Kertész, 1914). Janovics-Film. **Script:** Jenö Janovics. **Photography:** László Fekete. **With** László Bakó

(Bánk), Mari Jászai (Gertrudis), Erszi Paulay (Melinda), István Szentgyörgyi, Mihály Várkonyi (Otto), Jenö Janovics (Tibore), Mihály Fekete (Mikhál bán), and Adorján Nagy (Endre). One of the most famous of early Hungarian silents, this production was also the first Hungarian film to be shot on location. The spectacular production includes scenes of a king's army marching over mountains. The publication *Nyugat* noted, "They did what they wanted with nature. An extensive landscape seen from above ... a sense of air and ... a perspective leading into the distance.... A wide hillside with a tiny corner of sky, lines of men trailing over the dark headland. A narrow strip of earth with the sky above filling the whole image." The film, which established the trend of the national-literary production, became Kertész' first commercial success, showing him to be an agile and eclectic master of the medium.

His film, which is based on the 1819 five-act classic of Hungarian theater by Joseph Katona (1791–1830), is an epic five-reel (1,500-meter) tale of cloak-and-dagger intrigue, revolt, and counterrevolt, taken from historical events. In 1213, while King Andreas II is away on a campaign, the German-born Queen Gertrudis becomes the victim of intrigue by the king's court representative, Bánk, who conspires to seize control of the kingdom. One plot element involves the seduction of Bánk's wife, Melinda. There is murder in both opposing camps, including the death of the queen.

Only a few stills from the film survive.

## Drakula

(Károly Lajthay, 1921). **With** Paul Askonas, Margit Lux (Mina), Karl Jotz, Myl Gene, Elemer Thury, Lajos Rethey, Oszkar Perczel, Paula Kende, Dezsö Kertész, Károly Hartvani, Lajos Szalkai, Aladar Ihasz, and Bela Timar. One of the earliest adaptations of Bram Stoker's classic 1897 novel was this unauthorized version, shot in Berlin, which preceded Murnau's now classic *Nosferatu: A Symphony of Terror* (1922).

Murnau's rendition, produced by Prana-Films, made headlines when Stoker's wife, Florence, sued the production company for copyright infringement. The German courts declared in her favor in 1925 and ordered the destruction of the negative and prints of Murnau's work. The production company then folded. Actor-director Lajthay's film, which was shown in Hungary, received little fanfare, but paid a price, too, when *Nosferatu* lost its legal battle: it was quietly withdrawn from circulation. It disappeared during the Second World War. *Nosferatu* (which almost became a lost film) was first shown in the U.S. in 1929.

## Egri csillagok (The Stars of Eger)

(Paul Fejos, 1923). Transylvania Films. **Script:** Fejos. **Photography:** Gyula Papp. Design: Istvan Basthy. **With** Mara Jankovszky (Eva), Zoltan Maklary (Istvan Dobó), Ili Takacs, and Gyula Stella. Paul Fejos based his most ambitious and crafted Hungarian film on Géza Gárdonyi's 1901 novel, *The Eclipse of the Crescent Moon.*

In the autumn of 1552, Captain Dobó and a handful of soldiers defend the fortress of Eger, the gateway to northern Hungary, from the expanding Turkish empire. The stirring, patriotic, and heroic film of Hungarian resilience, with a well-conceived plot and strongly-drawn characters, costars Fejos's wife as the great Magyar leader's lover.

Fejos had put the beautiful actress in five of his previous seven films — and therein, finally, lay the seeds of this film's demise. Fejos was a jealous man who had fought a number of duels over his name, his honor, and his marriage. When his exasperated wife left the set near the film's completion, Fejos abandoned the shooting, and shortly departed for a new life in the U.S. — where he obtained a divorce. His film then vanished.

### Egy fiúnak a fele (A Half of a Boy)

(Géza von Bolváry, 1924). Apparently based on one of the most popular novels by Kálmán Mikszáth (1847–1910), the anecdotal *Szent Péter esernyöje* (*St. Peter's Umbrella*) (1895), the film is the story of György, a poor, illegitimate boy who, growing up in an upper-class environment, must resolve questions about the meaning of identity and privilege and choose between inherited (but hidden) wealth and love for the beautiful Veronika, who is in possession of a miraculous item. While searching for one fortune, the young man finds another. The film displays the great author's compassion for (and his tragicomic descriptions of) the ordinary folk of the country. Central is the magnitude of their pretensions and the emptiness of their pockets.

### Egy nap a világ (The World Takes One Day)

(János Vaszary, 1943). **Photography:** Barnabás Hegyi. **Music:** Károly de Fries. **With** Lili Muráti, Antal Páger, Tivador Bilicsi, Mária Thay, Miklós Szakáts, and Piri Vaszary. Based on János Vaszary's work, this is a production that captured the fatalistic attitude toward life prevailing in Hungary during World War II. The film hit teams with an end-of-the-world mood and legendary interpretations by the two main characters, Muráti and Páger.

Newspapers preserved the story and contain a few scenes from the vanished film.

Stills: http://helka.iif.hu:8080/articles/prints/wake.hu.html; and http://helka.iif.hu:8080/articles/prints/images/1napav.jpg

### Az Ezüst kecske (The Silver Goat)

(Mihály Kertész, 1916). Kinoriport. **Script:** Aladar Fodor and Kertész. **With** Mihály Várkonyi and Léontine Kühnberg. This was the last, best adaptation of a work (of the same name) by Sándor Bródy (1863–1924), who was the first great Hungarian Jewish novelist. Handsome, bohemian, and a gambler, the author had an easygoing nature that was complemented by deep concerns with themes reflecting the injustice and unhappiness of the times.

In Budapest at the end of the last century, a young writer abandons his wife and their modest life for that of the world of politics, thanks to the appeal of a woman of the high society. The destruction of a pommel horse comes to symbolize the loss of his happiness.

Stills: http://members.tripod.com/~candide/1916_Az_ez_st_kecske.JPG.

## A Faun (The Faun)

(Alexander Korda, 1917). Corvin studios. **Script:** Ladislaus Vajda and Richárd Falk. **Photography:** Gusztáv Kovács. **Design:** László Márkus. **With** Gábor Rajnay, Deszo Gyárfás, Arthur Somlay, and Ica Lénkeffy. This is one of Korda's earliest efforts to bring literature to the screen, based on the humorous play by Edward Knoblock. about a demigod and his effects on the world. Lord Stonbury, a gambler in debt, has been dissuaded from attempting suicide by a faun. The young god offers him a deal: he will tell the aristocrat which horses to bet on — the faun knows a horse when he sees one — while the aristocrat will instruct him on how to be a gentleman (despite horns and a pointed nose) and to introduce him into society. As Prince Silviani of Sardinia, the faun demonstrates another great ability: to sense the true feelings within the people he meets — and to get them to admit, and then act on, their feelings. This leads to a great deal of romantic shuffling, love, and honesty, after which all is right with the world.

## Fehér galambok fekete városban (White Pigeons in a Black Town)

(Béla Balogh, 1923). Renaissance Film. **With** Dezsö Nagy and Artur Lakner. This film was proclaimed as one of the most notable of the era. The production attempts to give a feel of the harsh effects of runaway inflation on life in Budapest. It was directed by a theoretician who favored the dramaturgical and emotional powers of close-up, camera angle, and set-up, frame composition and cross-cutting.

## A Fehér rózsa (The White Rose)

(Alexander Korda, 1919). Councils' Republic. **Script:** Ladislaus Vajda. **Photography:** Gusztáv Kovács. **With** Maria Corda (Gûl-Bejáze), Gyula Bartos, Emil Fenyvessy, and Victor Varconi. A screen adaptation of the 1853 novel (translated as *Halil the Pedlar*) by Hungarian novelist Mór Jókai (1825–1904), the production was called a magical, timeless, Arabian Night–like tale of adventure in which the pedestrian rules of the ordinary world do not apply. It was one of the finest examples of the popularity of "Turkish" stories, in Hungary and abroad.

The film treats an episode of Turkish history in which Sultan Achmet III is dethroned in Istanbul (Stambul) by Janissaries led by an Albanian pedlar named Halil Patrona. In late September 1730, when the Sultan hesitates to take the field against the advancing Persians, his own people, led by the rough, outspoken, masterful Halil Patrona, unexpectedly, and amazingly, dethrone the Sultan. In his stead, Halil appoints Mahmud I as Sultan. Six weeks later, the masterful rebel-chief Halil becomes a martyr for justice: He is treacherously assassinated by the man whom he had drawn from obscurity to sit upon the throne.

While these incidents are true, what gives the film its feeling of the fantastic (and resemblance to *The Thousand and One Nights*) is the unique episode of Gûl-Bejáze — "The White Rose" — a veiled female slave. A 17-year-old beauty, she has been expelled from the Sultan's harem and auctioned off. "It was not the act of a wise man to pick up a flower which the Sultan had thrown away in order to inhale its fragrance," goes the tale, but that is what Halil does. Then he learns the terrible secret behind her expulsion.

## Fekete kapitány (The Black Captain)

(Paul Fejos, 1921). With Lajos Gellért, Mara Jankovszky, Gusztav Partos, and Odön Bardi. Also called Der Schwarze Kapitön, this is a surprising melodrama about a surprising subject from Hungary: police corruption in New York.

## A Gólyakalifa (The Nightmare)

(Alexander Korda, 1917). Corvin. Script: Frigyes Karinthy. Photography: Gusztáv Kovács. With Mártin Rátkai, Victor Varconi, Ica Lénkeffy, and Károly Huszár. This drama was adapted from the 1913 novel of the same name by Mihály Babits (1883–1941), who was one of Hungary's greatest humanistic Catholic writers of the century. "Apart from the artistic worth of his works," said a critic in the early years of the century, "he was a cultural fact, the new synthesis of the Hungarian and the European spirit and intellect." Babits often wrote about schizophrenia and other vagaries of the human soul, and this production signaled Corvin's attempt to bring to the screen the best of Hungarian literature.

This tale is a modern psychological nightmare and a delving into the unconscious. Its hero is a man who imagines a second life in his dreams. When he finally commits suicide in his sleep, it is nonetheless a shock to find the real-life hero dead in the morning. The tale is less a Hungarian version of Dr. Jekyll and Mr. Hyde than an exploration into the possibilities of the self.

## Göre Gábor kalandozásai (The Adventures of Gabriel Göre)

(Oszkár Damó, 1913). Based on the novel Göre Gábor bíró úr könyvei (The Books of His Worship Göre Gábor) (1892) by the acclaimed Géza Gárdonyi, the film is an example of writer-turned-director Damó's interest in social criticism. His film parodies, with mock-dialect and coarse humor, the narrowness of village life — a theme that Gárdonyi later disowned.

## János vitéz ( John, the Brave)

(Jenö [Eugen] Illés, 1916). With Alfréd Deésy and Kamilla Hollay. One of Jewish filmmaker Illés's nine films in 1916 and 1917, this production is also his most monumental, demonstrating his interest in high literary drama, as well as fantasy. It is based on the great 1844 narrative poem of the same name by the 22-year-old Alexander Petöfi (1823–1849), one of Hungary's greatest poets, who died fighting for his nation's independence.

The emotional folktale is a village tragedy with the message that one of the true happinesses available to mankind is the loving embrace of earthly beings. It centers on a young shepherd who, after being banished from his home and sweetheart, Iluska, encounters a series of adventuring before becoming a hussar and saving the beautiful daughter of the king of France. As a reward, the king offers him her hand, but János, true to the memory of Iluska, declines the gesture. Nonetheless, he is knighted. Returning home a hero, he discovers that Iluska has died. His ardor for her is so strong, however, that he follows her beyond the grave to Fairyland —

encountering giants and witches — and, by plucking a rose and dropping it into Fairyland's "water of life," Iluska is reborn. They become King and Queen of Fairyland.

Illés's only extant work is *Sulamith* (1916), which the director-cameraman-engineer, who also lived in Berlin, made in Hungary. Of his *John, the Brave*, only a few scenes survive.

## Jóslat (Prophecy)

(Paul Fejos, 1920). **With** Mara Jankovszky. Fejos's film is apparently based on a British drama about twin brothers in love with the same woman. Though the woman says she loves neither man (despite several love scenes), the men (who make it clear they dislike women) fight over her — and she resolves the issue (a happy ending being out of the question) by committing suicide.

## A Kacagó asszony (The Laughing Lady)

(Tibor Hagedüs, 1930). Paramount. **With** Gizi Bajor and Arthur Somlay. Paramount's second Hungarian-language film out of Paris was a melodrama based on the studio's *The Laughing Lady* (1930).

## A Kétarcú asszony (Two-Faced Woman)

(Géza von Bolváry, 1920). **With** Llona Mattyasovszky. After scripting three films for Béla Balogh, Bolváry directed this, his first film, called *Die Frau mit Zwei Gesichtern* in Germany. He later directed the explicit and harsh drama *Frauen, die Nicht Liebe Durfen* (1925).

## Lidércnyomas (Siege)

(Paul Fejos, 1920). **With** Margit Lux, Lajos Gellért, and Odön Bardi. This black comedy (also called *Halluzination*, as well as *Das Verbrechen des Lord Arthur Savile*) is an adaptation of Oscar Wilde's sly short story "Lord Arthur Savile's Crime."

At a party at Lady Windermere's, the young, handsome, and common sensible Lord Savile (who is shortly to marry) has his palm read by Septimus R. Podgers, the well-known "professional cheiromantist." He makes a shocking pronouncement: the aristocrat will commit murder. Stunned, Savile retreats in order to think things through. A man of action, he decides to take destiny into his own hands by going out and doing the deed. First, he postpones his marriage. In fact, he postpones his marriage twice, but his two attempts at murdering distant relatives, one by poison and another with a time bomb, go unrealized.. A failure at crime, he stands upon a bridge and vows to "let Destiny work out his doom. He would not stir to help her," at which point he spots Podgers — and heaves him into the water below. His destiny fulfilled — Podgers's death is ruled a suicide; he would be much missed in "cheiromantist circles" — Savile marries and lives happily ever after.

## Magdát kicsapják (Magda Is Expelled)

(Ladislao Vajda, 1938). Harmonia Film. **Script:** Károly Notí. **Photography:** István Eiben. **Design:** Márton Vincze. **With** Ida Turay (Magda), Piroska Perry (Headmistress), Klári Tolnay (teacher), Sándor Goth (professor),

Imre Ráday, George Nagy, and Antal Páger (Harvey). An exuberant tale adapted from Miklós Kádár's play about a 16-year-old in a Budapest business school for girls who finds out that actions can have unexpected consequences. Learning the art of letter-writing, the scrappy yet lonely Magda goes beyond mere practice to write her heart out to a fictitious businessman — Mr. Harvey of Liverpool — and then, just to see what happens, mails the correspondence.

Soon, a handsome young man by that name, accompanied by a relative, shows up at the school, where the atmosphere "is great fun," noted a critic, and Perry and Goth "are admirable. Schoolgirl part suits Ida Turay to perfection." Though Magda pays a price for her actions, she and her teacher are well compensated for their troubles. Acclaim came to the 80-minute film, which was directed by the son of the well-known screenwriter (and collaborator of Mihály Kertész and G. W. Pabst), Ladislaus Vajda. It was called "one of the brightest, cleverest and most amusing pictures made in Hungary thus far." It would be a while before that would be said of another film out of the country.

## Mesék az írógépről (Tales of a Typist)

(Alexander Korda, 1916). Corvin. **Script:** Korda. **Photography:** Arpád Virágh. **With** Lili Berky, Jenö Janovics, and György Kürthy. Adapted from the 1905 novel by István Szomaházy (also called *The Cable from the New York Express*), this three-reel (1,200-meter) film created a stereotype — a great favorite with Hollywood in the 1930s — about typists who dream about marrying upper management. While the middle-class fantasy is not new, in Hungary it was just more difficult to attain — and that made the film a hit.

## Az Orvos titka (The Doctor's Secret)

(Tibor Hagedüs, 1930). Paramount. **With** Gizi Bajor, Dezsö Kertész, Arthur Somlay, and Sándor Goth. A version of the tragedy *The Doctor's Secret* (1930), this was Paramount's debut Hungarian-language feature out of Paris. It costars Mihály Kertész's younger brother.

## Pán

(Paul Fejos, 1920). **With** Mara Jankovszky (Edvarda Mack) and Lajos Gellért (Thomas Glahn). In 1920, the Norwegian Knut Hamsun won the Nobel Prize in literature. Fejos's production was the first adaptation of Hamsun's great, lyrical, and tragic work *Pan* (written in 1894; translated in 1920), a tale of a loving couple whose never-consummated passion eventually leads to a very unhappy end. The modern story, which is an expression of the author's interest in irrational forces, is considered one of the great love stories in world literature, though only a dozen pages concern themselves with love; the rest is hatred. It's the kind of story that always attracted the volatile Hungarian director. The film stars his wife.

It begins when Lieutenant Glahn goes to an isolated isle off the Lapland coast for a summer to escape the social pressures of the developed world. There he rents a hunting lodge and meets the beautiful Edvarda, the lodge owner's daughter. Though she is attracted to the stranger, she repels his advances because she doesn't trust men. Soon, however, he shows her how beautiful love is and gains her affections. But Edvarda has a rival: her father's mistress, who has also attracted the lieutenant. Violence and worse come in to play when the lodge owner tries to get rid of the soldier.

## Pardon, tévedtem (Sorry, I Was Mistaken)

(István Székely, 1933). Hunnia Film. **Script:** Károly Nóti. **Photography:** István Eiben. **Music:** Miklós Bordszky. **With** Franciska Gaál, Paul Hörbiger, Szöke Szakáll, Sándor Goth, and Lili Berky. Produced by Joe Pasternak, and based on the stage hit by Lászlo Aladár, this musical by Jewish filmmaker Székely was one of the first international hits of Hungarian sound production. The 95-minute production features Gaál, one of Hungary's most charming actresses of the era. She plays the businesslike heroine in a romantic comedy of errors. She is backed by the comedians Szakáll and Hörbiger, recent German exiles, the former, a pantomime especially adept in the scene where he practices magic tricks; the latter playing a pianist mistaken by Gaál for a dilatory fiancé.

"There are many interesting views of the beautiful Hungarian countryside," wrote a critic, where Gaál is shown on horseback, "as well as of the capital city." Also called *Pesti Szerelem*, the production is an early example of how Hungary, for a brief period, absorbed artists fleeing Nazi Germany. Their talents were used that same year in a German-language version, called *Skandal in Bu-dapest*, directed by Székely and Géza von Bolváry.

## A Pénz (The Money)

(Sándor Pallós, 1919). **With** Lajos Gellért and Gyulá Bartos. Based on Gorki's 1895 short story *Tchelkash*, which is about his youthful experiences as a porter on the docks, the film looks at the "dumb and cruel savages" of the Russian masses. Gorki made them childlike and guileless, but moving in their frustration. He had lived with them in the "nethermost where there is naught but murk and slush," he wrote. Having heard their "harsh cry for life," he had "come up to bear witness to the suffering he had left behind."

The main character in the tale is the old-timer Grishka Tchelkash, well known to people at a port: he's a confused drunkard, yet at the same time a skillful, daring thief. He takes under his wings the impoverished Gavrila. They commit a crime, coming into a bundle of money. The old man feels for the younger man, perhaps recalling his own struggles to get out of unimagined poverty from a village from nowhere. But at the crucial moment, when they are set on splitting their loot, Gavrila imagines, "I'll give him … one c-rr-a-c-k over the head with the oar … take the money, and chuck him…. He's not the kind of man anybody would make a fuss about. No use to anybody. Who would stand up for him?" A fight ensues, and Gavrila smashes in the old man's head. Soon the rain and the spray wash away the red patch on the spot where Tchelkash has lain, washes away the traces of Tschelkash and the peasant lad on the sandy beach. And no trace is left on the seashore of the little drama that had been played out between two men.

As a tale of the soul of Russia, the film, which was made after the brief Communist rule in Hungary, vanished when the director, who intended to make a series of films based on Gorki's works, was murdered by Admiral Horthy's secret police.

### Sárga csikó (Yellow Foal)

(Félix Vanyll, 1913). Pathé. **Script:** Jenö Janovics. **Photography:** Robert Montgobert and Dezsö Polik. **With** Mihály Várkonyi (Laci Csorba), Mihály Fekete (Márton Csorba), Lili Hegyi, Andor Szakács (András Bakaj), Mihály Kertész, and Lili Berky (Erzsike Bakaj). Ferenc Csepreghy's highly popular, emotional drama about peasant life in the "pusta," the famous plains of Hungary, became the basis for this well-made three-reeler (1,540-meter), which became Hungarian cinema's earliest international hit—and one of Kertész's first films. It established stereotypes about the nation. From peasants' fringed, wide, flapping, white linen trousers to the method of rendering meat tender—keeping it under the saddle (as Hungarian horseman are said to have done for a thousand years)—this production presented "typical" details about Eastern European life.

The story concerns young love nearly torn asunder by the sins of the fathers. The film begins on the day Laci is to wed. His father Márton is on his way home, released after serving a 15-year jail sentence for a crime he didn't commit. On that same day he rescues his son's fiancée, Erzsike, from the river with the aid of a handsome bay colt. His homecoming breaks up the wedding party and creates near tragedy, for the crime of the bride's father, Andras, is exposed. In a drunken stupor, he had long ago killed a plainsman to get his horse. Yet in the end, there are no real villains in the tale: the wedding between Laci and Erzsike, the village beauty, takes place and at the fadeout everyone is content.

### A Senki fia (Nobody's Son)

(Mihály Kertész, 1917). Phoenix Films. **Script:** Ladislaus Vajda. **With** Ica Lénkeffy, Gyula Czortos, and Károly Lajthay. Another of Kertész's lost films, though stills survive.

Stills: http://members.tripod.com/ ~candide/1917_A_senki_fia.JPG.

### A Szentjóbi erdő titka (The Secret of St. Job Forest)

(Mihály Kertész, 1917). Phoenix Films. **Script:** Ladislaus Vajda. **Photography:** József Bécsi. **With** Lucy Doraine, Jenö Torzs, Dezsö Kertész, and Ferenc Peter. This was a popular and successful thriller, featuring the director's brother Dezsö, that signaled Kertész's desire to film subject matter that (although literary based) allowed wider freedom of treatment, while at the same time adhering to the legacy of national traditions. The production enabled Kertész to demonstrate his talent for vibrant composition and his well-known flair for tackling a tale of adventure and criminality. Scenes from this film are just about all that survive of Kertész's three dozen films at Phoenix.

Stills: http://members.tripod.com/ ~candide/1917.htm.

## Szenzacio (Sensation)

(Paul Fejos, 1922). **Photography:** Gyula Papp. **With** Mara Jankovszky, Leona Károlyi, and Antal Matany. Based on Pushkin's tragic short story *Pique Dame*, which takes place in the glittering world of 19th century St. Petersburg, the film is a satire on aristocracy and its absorption in gambling, duels (which director Fejos enjoyed taking part in), and fancy social affairs. It relates the tale of a Russian officer at the end of his rope: a compulsive gambler who pretends to fall for a beautiful young woman in order to gain from her grandmother, an old dowager (the Pique Dame), a magic formula for winning at cards.

## A Táncz (Dance)

(Béla Zitkovszky, 1901). **With** Lili Berky, Mihály Várkonyi, Lujza Blaha, and Sári Fedák. The first Hungarian film is a 27-minute production made up of one-minute reels, each a look at a different national folk dance. The film was made at the behest of Gyula Pekár, an expert on dance, and was directed by the chief projectionist of a cultural-scientific society (Urania Tudományos Szinház).

In 1899, with the support of the Hungarian Academy of Science, the Urania Hungarian Scientific Association was established. The association set up the Urania Hungarian Scientific Theatre, which then presented educational programs. "The theatre," read the notices, "gives lectures in the field of natural sciences as well as of civilisation, ethnography, arts, industry and technology, written by experts of the different areas, demonstrated by the methods of the theatrical stage, enhanced by projected colour photographs and decorations coupled with light-effects made possible by the latest achievements of modern technology."

The first publicly shown Hungarian moving picture, *Dance* was produced by that theatrical association. Its creator, Béla Zitkowsky, (1867–1930), was the association's ingenious photographer-technician. His film, which was shown on Urania's roof-terrace in the spring of 1901, starred the best-known stage actors. Zitkovszky was the creator and cameraman of numerous films, all lost.

Stills: www.filmkultura.iif.hu:8080/ articles/teaching/hundred.en.html; www.bgytf.hu/public/keletm/doc/96_18 _1k.html; *and* http://agy.bgytf.hu/public/keletm/doc/96_18_1k.html

## A Tanítónő (The Schoolmistress)

(Jenö Janovics, 1917). **Script:** Mihály Fekete. **Photography:** László Fekete. **With** István Szentgyörgyi (István Nagy), Mihály Várkonyi (István Nagy, Jr.), Ilonka Nagy, Aranka Laczkó, and Alajos Mészáros. Director of the National Theater of Kolozsvár, Janovics became interested in film when Pathé hired actors from his company. His film themes came from his stage repertoire.

This four-reel production is based on Sándor Bródy's 1908 topical drama of the same name. It is set in the early years of the century when most village peasants were exploited; they can only dream about achieving the lifestyles of their middle-class employers or of the chance to emigrate and start a new life. Containing a memorable female protagonist — a woman with sexual desires —

and a social conscience, the story became a classic of Hungarian literature.

### Yamata

(Alexander Korda, 1919). Councils' Republic. **Script:** Ladislaus Vajda. **Design:** László Márkus. **With** Gábor Rajnay (Yamata), Ila Lóth, Emil Fenyvessy, and Gusztáv Nándory. This sensational tale of a black slave's life — by implication, prerevolutionary, nonaristocratic life in Hungary — is a realistic look at revolt and murder. Yamata (played by the theatrical performer Rajnay) is mistreated by his master, and is taken under the wings by a young aristocrat. But he is then exploited in more subtle ways. Finally, implicated in a murder, he rebels, and is killed.

# Ireland

The history of cinema in Ireland is long and colorful. Dublin had its first public screening of films, from the Lumière Brothers, in April 1896. In February 1897 the first filmed Irish subjects were shown by one Professor Jolly in Dublin. They included items such as "People Walking in Sackville Street," "Traffic on Carlisle Bridge" and the "13th Hussars Marching Through the City." The first dedicated cinema, the Volta in Dublin's Mary Street, opened in 1909. James Joyce worked there at one time.

In 1910, Ireland became host to the Kalem company, the first American company to make films abroad. It was founded on an investment of $400 in 1907 by George Kleine, Samuel Long, and Frank Marion. Its name was based on the letters K-L-M. The two most important directors at Kalem were Marshall Neilan and Sidney Olcott, who shot a score of films in Killarney between 1910 and 1914. Olcott, it was said, "made a sincere effort to portray Ireland the Irish as he found them, and to deal sympathetically with their history." His inspiration was a series of Dion Boucicault plays that, because of their dependence on external effects, made them candidates for experimentation for longer film.

One of the stock company's main writers was the actress Gene Gauntier, known for her "working synopsis" of Kalem's *Ben-Hur* (1908). In fact, it was she who had encouraged Kalem to venture to Ireland. Kalem lasted as long as short pictures lasted. In 1915 it quit the business. That year Olcott shot three films on Irish soil for America's first film mogul, Siegmund Lubin (1851–1923), whose international film market was in jeopardy because of the war.

Among indigenous filmmakers the most important Irish production company from the early days was the Film Company of Ireland. Established by James Mark Sullivan in 1916, the company was inspired by Kalem's Irish success "to make Ireland known to the rest of the world ... to let people outside of Ireland realize that we have in Ireland others things than the dudeen, buffoon, knee breeches, and brass buckles."

Its principal director was the Abbey Theatre performer J. M. Kerrigan. In four years, he and his company, headquartered in Dublin, made nine shorts and five features, including the extant *Knocknagow* (1917) and *Willy Reilly and His Colleen Bawn* (1920). The Dublin fires of the "Easter Rising," in 1916, destroyed nearly all of the company's short films.

The first sound film shot in Ireland was Frank Borzage's *Song o' My Heart* (1930), starring the lyric tenor John McCormack. The film was a huge hit "far removed from Conn the Shaughraun business," said an Irish critic. *The Voice of Ireland* (1932) was Ireland's first indigenous sound film.

## All for Old Ireland

(Sidney Olcott, 1915). Lubin. **Script:** Olcott. **Photography:** George Hollister. **With** Valentine Grant (Eileen), Pat O'Malley (Myles), and Robert Rivers (Fagin). Olcott's three-reel production, which was his first for the American production company, brought him back to Ireland after Kalem folded. His film is a 19th century tale of personal heroics in the Irish struggle for liberty. "Its strongest bid for recognition is on the score of the fine locations," wrote *Moving Picture World*, especially the beautiful scenes around Black Rock Castle and the River Lee, "combined with a seemingly accurate portrayal of the Irish peasants." Valentine Grant was called by *Variety* "an ideal type for such a tale ... clever and impressive." The tale centers around Myles, an arms smuggler who is captured and imprisoned by the British.

The beautiful young Eileen helps him escape from his castle cell, killing two guards. After Myles finds safety in France, he sends for Eileen and her mother — and the struggle for Irish liberty remains unfinished.

Stills: *Moving Picture World* (July 24, 1915).

## Arrah-Na-Pogue (Arrah of the Kiss)

(Sidney Olcott, 1911). Kalem. **Script:** Gene Gauntier. **Photography:** George Hollister. **With** Jack Clark (Beamish McCoul), Gene Gauntier (Arrah Meelish), and Sidney Olcott (Shaun). This film was hailed as the best of its length to date — three-reels (3,000 feet) — and was the first American-backed production to have a musical score written for it, by Walter C. Simon. An adaptation of Dion Boucicault's 1864 romantic drama of the same name, it brought American director Olcott (not for the first time) to the attention of British authorities, who were reminded that unrest in Ireland lay just below the surface.

It is a tale set against the backdrop of the Irish rebellion of May 1798, which was fought by the peasants of Antrim in the north and Wexford and Kildare in the south. The drama concerns the mischievous Beamish, his involvement in Irish politics, and his exile from his sweetheart and homeland; as well as events surrounding his friend Shaun the postman, who is framed for a crime and sentenced to death. However, there is a happy resolution of the political intrigue — the rebellion posed a formidable threat, though it lasted only a month — and an end to lovers' quarrels.

## Bold Emmett, Ireland's Martyr

(Sidney Olcott, 1915). Lubin. **Script:** Olcott. **With** Jack Melville, Robert Rivers (Frealy), Sidney Olcott (Conn), Valentine Grant (Nora), and Laurene Santley (Mrs. Doyle). "It might be well to recorded," wrote *Variety*, "that Olcott is gradually assuming a position in the front rank of feature producers." His is a "picture with especial attention to details," noted the trade journal, a one-hour film that also brought him unwanted scrutiny from British authorities. With no doubt as to where his sympathies were, Olcott filmed a drama that recounts the daring exploits of an Irish hero: Robert Emmett, who, at 25, led the Rebellion of July 23, 1803, as well as the sacrifices of those closest to Emmett. He was the man who said, "Let no man write my epitaph."

Emmett is now considered one of the founders of Irish republicanism. Along with Wolfe Tone, he was inspired by the ideological underpinnings of the French Revolution. He believed that the British presence in Ireland was a divisive influence and that true equality and prosperity for the Irish people could only be attained in the context of an independent Ireland.

Olcott saw his film withdrawn from circulation in 1915 when British authorities claimed it was having a negative impact on recruitment in Ireland. Of Olcott's second film for Lubin, in which the "hills and dales of Ireland … carry the prettiest views imaginable," 18 minutes survive in the Library of Congress.

## Cruiskeen Lawn

(John MacDonagh, 1922). Irish Photo Plays Ltd. **Script:** John MacDonagh. **Photography:** Alfred H. Moise. **With** Tom Moran (Boyle), Kathleen Armstrong (Nora), and Jimmy O'Dea (Samuel). Ireland is a nation of horse lovers, and this tale of a racehorse that claims the Callahan Cup is an example of one of Ireland's popular myths. It was advertised as an "Irish story acted and directed by Irish people for picturegoers of the world, a tonic for jaded patrons who are clamoring for something different in photoplays."

A "great success," said the critics, the humorous five-reel (4,500-feet) tale was billed as the first "all Irish" feature to be shown in London. The longshot horse bails out its financially strapped owner (and allows him to win the hand of a girl, Nora) when it accidentally drinks the "elixir of life" (snake oil for rheumatism) that enhances its performance in the crucial race on the big day. The production was screened in the U.S. in 1925.

## The Fishermaid of Ballydavid

(Sidney Olcott, 1911). Kalem. **Photography:** George Hollister. **With** Gene Gauntier (Kathleen), Jack Clark, Arthur Donaldson, and Sidney Olcott. Director Olcott's simple drama is about a passionate Irish girl who falls for a visiting American, only to face rejection. The 1,000-feet tale was called "commendable on nearly every count" by *Moving Picture World*. Olcott shot the production in Ballydavid, in County Kerry, especially its "backgrounds … pleasing, fresh, and interesting." The "well-acted" story is "convincingly and clearly set forth. We understand and sympathize with it all," concluded the trade journal.

## Food of Love

(J. M. Kerrigan, 1916). Film Company of Ireland. **With** Kerrigan, Kathleen Murphy, and Fred O'Donovan. A 1,100-feet comedy "full of real Irish humor" whose resolution takes place in the "magnificent" scenery of Glendalough, County Wicklow.

## Four Irish Girls

(1916). Triangle Film Corp. **Script:** C. Gardner Sullivan. **With** Bessie Barriscale (Shammie), Margery Wilson, Aggie Herring, Alice Taffle, and Charles Ray (Richard). This sympathetic comedy-drama about Irish nationalism was produced shortly after the Easter Rising.

A group of orphaned girls and their elderly nurse live rent-free in a cottage located on the grounds of an estate far from Dublin that is bequeathed to an American. The oldest of the four girls falls in love with the young man who has come to inspect his property. She also gets caught up in the cause for Irish freedom after attending a secret meeting raided by the British. The work was praised for its subtitles and action which "bring laughs ... and make ... a delightful feature." The film is also called *A Corner in Colleens* as well as *Four Irish Girls in America.*

## Fun at a Finglas Fair

(F. J. McCormack, 1915). **Script:** Cathal McGarvey. **With** F. J. McCormack, Jack Eustace, John Connell, Frank Flannagan, Bob O'Brien, and Jack MacGarvey. This production is credited with being the first native Irish film, produced in order to win a three-guinea contest. It is a 1,000-feet comedy about two English crooks who, when they take up mischief in Ireland, receive their just punishment. Starring the great stage actor McCormack, the film was apparently shown once then destroyed by British soldiers in the Easter Rising of 1916. It "would have been a huge success," said an observer.

## A Girl of Glenbeigh

(J. M. Kerrigan, 1917). Film Company of Ireland. **With** Fred O'Donovan (Maurice), Kathleen Murphy (Kathleen), and Irene Murphy (Nora). A drama filmed amidst "superb Irish scenery," noted a critic, the four-reel (2,200-feet) production suggested the "great possibilities before" the Film Company of Ireland. "It is hoped that they will realize them.... They are a good crowd, good actors and good fellows."

## Ireland the Oppressed

(Sidney Olcott, 1912). Kalem. **Script:** Gene Gauntier. **Photography:** George Hollister. **With** Jack Clark (Marty), Alice Hollister (Peggy), Sidney Olcott (Father Falvey), John P. McGowan (British major), and Robert Vignola (the informer). "An Irishman is a good lover and a good fighter and the world loves him on both counts," said *Moving Picture World* at this film's premiere. Striking a ready chord, the film is a flashback to events of the mid–19th century (as told by old Marty at an Irish harvest celebration). A brave priest once took up the cause of struggling tenants thrown onto the streets by a brutal landlord. For his troubles he is imprisoned by the British. He is rescued, however, by an underground agrarian group (of which Marty was a member) called the "White

Boys." But then he is turned in by an informer, and saved, yet again, by a young girl who, for her involvement, is imprisoned for seven years by the British. The priest finds refuge in America.

At the conclusion of the flashback Marty reveals that the brave young woman of the story was none other than his wife. "The story is clearly developed and very effective," noted the trade journal. Playing one of the enemy is the versatile John P. McGowan, who had seen service as a dispatch rider in the Boer War. He turned actor because of his ability as a stuntman, wrote Terry Ramsaye. "He could shoot a rabbit on the run from the back of a galloping horse."

### The Irish in America

(Sidney Olcott, 1915). Lubin. **Script:** Olcott. **With** Sidney Olcott (Dan), Valentine Grant (Peggy), Laurene Santley, Arthur Donaldson, and Charles McCornell. Actor-director Olcott's three-reeler about an Irishman who makes good in New York and the West — the opening scenes take place on the Emerald Isle — and is joined by his sweetheart, is a simple enough story. But, wrote *Moving Picture World*, "so well has Mr. Olcott told it, endowed it with so much kindly feeling, unforced humor and real human nature, that it is thorough enjoyable from start to finish." The quiet beauty of Ireland is among the film's best features, noted the trade journal. This was the third and final film Olcott made for the production company in Ireland.

### The Kerry Gow (The Kerry Blacksmith)

(Sidney Olcott, 1912). Kalem. **Script:** Gene Gauntier. **Photography:** George

Hollister. **With** Jack Clark (Dan), Alice Hollister (Nora), Sidney Olcott, and John P. McGowan. Actor-director Olcott's production is based on Joseph Murphy's play of the same name, the often-told tale of the young woman who tries to fend off the intentions of her landlord. The plot of the three-reeler is but an excuse to present the film's embarrassment of riches — the romance between young lovers, the humor in everyday life, the attention to scenic detail, and the country's idyllic charm. These elements make the production "Irish, entirely Irish and nothing but Irish," stated *Moving Picture World*. "The Kalems have gone to Ireland and have brought back ... the true atmosphere and very real atmosphere of the Irish soil and the Irish heart."

Stills: *Moving Picture World* (November 9, 1912).

### The Miser's Gift

(J. M. Kerrigan, 1916). Film Company of Ireland. **With** J. M. Kerrigan (Ned), Kathleen Murphy (Dolan), and Fred O'Donovan. Set in Killaloe, in County Clare, this is an appealing two-reel comedy about a secret stash of money and the means used to find it. A girl and her lover know that her cheapskate of a father loves to drink. He also keeps his money in a secret place. In order to have him reveal the whereabouts of his fortune, they get him so drunk that when he imagines he has found a "leprechaun's gold," he'll hide it with his loot.

### The O'Neill

(Sidney Olcott, 1912). Kalem. **Photography:** George Hollister. **With** Jack

Clark (O'Neill), Gene Gauntier (Elinor), Sidney Olcott (the old man), Alice Hollister, and John P. McGowan. Based on the work *Erin's Isle*, Olcott's film concerns his favorite subject, Irish patriotism. O'Neill, an Irishman through and through, is on the run and with a price on his head. He is also a sort of Robin Hood whose life changes when he meets the beautiful Elinor. After a daring flight to the coast just ahead of the law, they marry and settle in France.

## O'Neil of the Glen

(J. M. Kerrigan, 1916). Film Company of Ireland. **Script:** W. J. Lysaght. **With** J. M. Kerrigan (Magroome), Nora Clancy (Nola), Fred O'Donovan, Brian Magowan (Don) and J. M. Carre (Tremaine). This three-reel (2,600-feet) production (an adaptation of Margaret T. Pender's story) was touted as the "first picture play by an Irish company with Irish actors in Ireland." It was also Kerrigan's debut as actor-director. Set in Ulster, Kerrigan's film centers around the murder of a man named O'Neil by his lawyer Tremaine. It appears that the lawyer committed the deed because he squandered his client's money. The film then traces the consequences for two lovers: O'Neil's son Dan and Tremaine's daughter Nola. The difficulties that separate the lovers evaporate when the tragic truth becomes known.

This "really first-class production," wrote the *Dublin Evening Mail*, "is sure to bring the work and players ... into the forefront of popularity." Filmgoers "will have the privilege of witnessing one of the finest cinematographic productions shown for quite some time."

## Puck Fair Romance

(J. M. Kerrigan, 1916). Film Company of Ireland. **With** J. M. Kerrigan (Jack) and Kathleen Murphy (Maureen). The annual Puck Fair, in Killorglan, County Kerry, is the setting for this agreeable romance in which an adventurer and artist meet and, each assuming the other owns land, fall in love. The 900-feet production was released in England as *A Romance of Puck Fair*.

## Rafferty's Rise

(J. M. Kerrigan, 1917). Film Company of Ireland. **Photography:** William Moser. **With** Fred O'Donovan (Rafferty), Kathleen Murphy (Kitty), and Brian Magowan (Hogan). This amusing, good-natured production had the critics praising the filmmakers for being "bold enough to go beyond the stereotyped two reels" when making a comedy. The three-reeler is based on Nicholas Hayes's popular play, *The Rise of Constable Rafferty*, about the efforts of an ineffectual member of the Royal Irish Constabulary to solve the case of a missing dog. A favorite of the ladies, the officer is only interested in becoming a sergeant.

"The film is typically Irish," wrote *Irish Limelight*. "The humor is clean and healthy, and of the most original type, the setting is of the beautiful scenery of the Dublin mountains, and the photography is as good as, if not better than, anything ... yet seen."

## Rosaleen Dhu (Dark Rosaleen)

(William J. Powers, 1920). Celtic Cinema Company. **Script:** William Powers. **With** William J. Powers and Kitty

Hart. Based on Joseph Denver's play of the same name, this nonpolitical production deals with the early days and incidents of the Land League. It gave Irish filmmakers great hopes for the future. Only the second work by Powers and his production, critics "were struck with wonder" at the mountain scenes, glen, and wooded landscape "so cleverly incorporated throughout the parts ... founded in Ireland."

The four-reel (4,000 feet) film takes place during the Land War in Connemera, in the years 1879–1882, when an Irish patriot is framed for murder. He is evicted and forced to find refuge in the Foreign Legion. In this desert arena (whose scenes were also praised for their verisimilitude), he finds salvation. He falls in love with a young Algerian who (improbable as it may seem) is an heiress to an Irish fortune. Director Powers died accidentally while filming *An Irish Vendetta* (1920).

### Shanachies Tales

(1916). Film Company of Ireland. A series of stories that center around the old Irish tale tellers known as Shanachies. Theirs was a tradition steeped in the art of storytelling and the magic of words in the Ireland of long ago. The Shanachie was the storyteller who went from house to house telling tales of ghosts and fairies, of old Irish heroes, and battles still to be won. One such Irish folktale concerns the giant Finn McCool (the Anglicized spelling of Fionn Mac Cumhail), the "Irish King Arthur" and one of the most celebrated heroes of Irish mythology.

One of the greatest of Celtic heroes received his education from the druid Finegas, who catches the Salmon of Knowledge and gives it to him to cook. Finn burns himself and sucks his thumb, thus acquiring all the world's knowledge. From then on he experiences a series of adventures involving hunting, fighting, sorcery, love, and passion. To solve any problem, all he has to do is suck his thumb. Finn also has numerous romances, but it is with a goddess that he begets his famous son, Oisín (Ossian). In a typical Celtic motif, Finn, after a titanic battle with the Scottish giant Ruiscare, does not die but only goes to sleep in a cave in the Cooley Mountains, waiting for the call to help Ireland in her hour of need.

Another tale involves how Cuchulainn, the Hound of Ulster, got his name. In ancient Ireland young children learned the game called hurling, which is played with a stick and a leather ball. The best by far at the game is Setanta, who could beat any team by himself. One day a man called Culann was watching Setanta playing and, impressed, he invited the young star to join him at dinner at his castle with his other guests. That evening, a fierce hound was guarding the grounds. When Setana arrives, the hound attacks, but Setanta strikes the leather ball at the hound and drives it down its throat, killing the animal. Culann is relieved that the boy was safe, but sad that his hound is dead. So Setanta says that he will guard the castle until Culann gets another hound. Since the Irish word for a hound is Cu (Coo), Setanta becomes known as Cuchulainn, the Hound of Culann, as well as the Hound of Ulster.

In addition, the Cooley Peninsula is the setting of one of Ireland's most famous stories, the epic saga of the "Tain bo Cuailgne" ("Cattle Raid of Cooley"), the folk tale of the single-handed battle between the hero, Cuchullain, the Hound of Ulster, and the armies of Queen Maebhe of Connaught, who is possessed by an insatiable desire to possess the legendary and mighty Brown Bull of Cooley.

## The Shaugraun

(Sidney Olcott, 1912). Kalem. **Script:** Gene Gauntier. **Photography:** George Hollister. **With** Sidney Olcott (Conn, the shaugraun), Gene Gauntier (Claire), Jack Clark (Capt. Molineaux), Robert Melville, and John P. McGowan (Corry Kinchella). Perhaps the most celebrated of Kalem's Irish films was this three-reel adaptation of the radiant 1874 classic play of the same name by Dion Boucicault (1820–1890). The film received one of the most glowing reviews of any Kalem production.

*Moving Picture World* wrote, "In the galaxy of features known as the O'Kalem plays, this production shines out with special lustre.... The Kalems have well-nigh touched perfection in the use they made of outdoor scenery ... one item in its program of uniform excellence." Photographed along the romantic coast of Beaufort, the film revolves around Conn, a lovable rascal who uses subterfuge, heroics, humor, and resourcefulness to thwart his enemies. When the villainy of the plotters, led by the corrupt Kinchella (he is trying to cheat his way to a fortune) is exposed and they are brought to justice, sweethearts are united. Olcott's exuberant and splendid melodrama offers realistic scenes of Irish life, particularly those of Irish huts and cottages. Olcott went to great pains in

one other respect. He retained playwright Boucicault's irreverent sense of humor in the subtitles. Summing up, the trade publication warned that "to chase ... such reels through the machine like so many ordinary releases would be a mortal sin in the catechism of motion pictures."

Stills: *Moving Picture World* (December 14, 1912).

## Stranger at My Door

(Brenden Stafford and Desmond Leslie, 1950). Leister Films, **Script:** Leslie. **Photography:** Stafford. **With** Michael Moore, Valentine Dyall, Joseph O'Conor, and Maire O'Neill. Also called *At a Dublin Inn*, this 80-minute, intricate noir thriller concerns a former commando who turns to crime in order give his girlfriend the luxuries she wants. He is unaware that she is being blackmailed.

## The Unfair Love Affair

(J. M. Kerrigan, 1916). Film Company of Ireland. **With** Kerrigan (Joe), Nora Clancy (Nora), and Fred O'Donovan (Fred). In this 1,800-feet comedy-drama, two men vie for the love of a woman.

## The Voice of Ireland

(Victor Haddick, 1932). **Script:** Haddick. **Photography:** Cyril Heath. **With** Richard Hayward, Victor Haddick, and Barney O'Hara. Ireland's first indigenous sound film is an overview of Irish art, entertainment, industry, sport, and landscape, with narration (in brogue) by Haddick and songs by Hayward. As a way to present Irish life and culture, a traveler is shown meeting folk dancers, horse breeders, fox hunters, and car racers. Naturally, he comes across beautiful Irish lakes and mountains. The *Belfast Newsletter* called the 50-minute production, which is absent sound effects or background music, a "close and expert study ... devoid ... of the stage Irishman."

### When Love Came to Gavin Burke

(Fred O'Donovan, 1918). Film Company of Ireland. With Fred O'Donovan (Gavin), Nora Clancy (Kate), Stephen Gould (John), and Brian Magowan (Jack). One of the production company's most highly regarded efforts was this rural drama exploring the nature of the Irish family. Stressing traditional Irish values, the emotional six-reel (3,700-feet) tale begins in the late 19th century when the beautiful Kate rejects the man she loves, the struggling farmer Gavin, for a more prosperous suitor. Her life as a wealthy woman, however, does not go as planned. As her daughter grows to maturity, history appears to be repeating itself. But this time, the former lover Gavin, having established himself as a man of means, intercedes. Fate brings him back to Kate and alters the destiny of Kate's daughter. Her daughter chooses her lover with her heart rather that with her head.

### Widow Malone

(J. M. Kerrigan, 1916). Film Company of Ireland. Called a "genuine Irish comedy" that was "an agreeable change from the ... knockabout comedies" of the period, the 1,200-feet film is about a little old lady who outwits two people trying to get hold of her money. She feigns poverty so as to thwart the intentions of a lawyer and a schoolteacher.

### A Woman's Wit

(J. M. Kerrigan, 1917). Film Company of Ireland. With Kerrigan, Kathleen Murphy, and Fred O'Donovan. A two-reel (1,700-feet), highly praised comedy.

# Italy

When, in 1905, Filoteo Alberini made *La presa di Roma* and Arturo Ambrosio (1869–1960) released his first two films (shot in the garden of his villa), the Italian cinema was born. In the period 1905–1931, Italian cinema produced nearly 10,000 silents. Nineteen came out that first year, the beginnings of a golden age of Italian filmmaking, especially as far as historical epics were concerned, which helped establish the names of directors Enrico Guazzoni (1876–1949), Mario Caserini (1874–1920), and Giovanni Pastrone (1883–1959). Major studios of the prewar period included Società Anonima Ambrosio and Itala Film in Turin and La Cines in Rome, as well as the modest family-owned Dora Film of Naples.

The number of Italian films produced increased steadily over the years:

120 or so in 1906; 180 in 1907; 625 in 1908; 825 in 1909; 870 in 1910; 1,125 or so in each of the years 1912, 1913, and 1914, when Italian production was dominating world markets. In 1915, more than 50 film companies in Rome, Turin, and elsewhere produced 1,500 films, ranging from historical subjects and short comedy and trick films that served as fillers between spectacles; highly romantic and passionate melodrama, usually set in contemporary aristocratic or upper-class surroundings; adventure, exemplified by the Za la Mort series of Emilio Ghione (1880–1930); and realist drama inspired by literature, whose practitioners were Nino Martoglio (1870–1921), Gustavo Serena, and Luigi Maggi (1867–1946).

Lost Italian films include documentaries from 1896 to 1930; the important genre of the diva-films produced between 1913 and 1928; works by the important authors and directors Carmine Gallone, Eugenio Perego, Mario Almirante, and especially Lucio D'Ambra (1880–1939; a filmmaker who has been compared to Ernst Lubitsch); and a wide array of films produced in the years 1924–1931, when major Italian filmmakers were forced to work abroad.

By the mid–1920s, the Italian industry was in decline. Fewer than 100 films came out in 1924; 40 in 1925 and 1926; 25 in each of the years 1927, 1928, and 1929. The year 1930 saw 13 silents, and finally in 1931, the last two silents of a glorious history. At the same time slow to make the transition to sound, Italian films were supplanted by American films.

By making Italian-language films in Paris, Paramount was not taking much of a risk, though it was acceding to Mussolini's 1929 government decree that films shown on Italian screens be in Italian. The American studio had a ready market in Italy, and the native industry was slow to adopt the new technology. At the dawn of sound, when Gennaro Righelli (1886–1949) directed the first Italian sound film, *La canzone dell'amore* (1930), Paramount had big plans for Italian-language productions, scheduling a dozen. To meet that end, it signed the most representative and experienced Italian performers and directors of the era, such as Oreste Biancoli and Mario Camerini. When the reviews on its earliest Italian films came in, however, the studio scaled back its efforts to seven features and one all-star revue. All the features were melodramas.

## *L'Aigrette (The Plume)*

(Baldassare Negroni, 1917). Tiber Film. **Script:** Lucio D'Ambra. **With** Hesperia, André Habay, Tulio Carminati, and Ida Carloni Talli. Director Negroni (1877–1948) had the title of count and was a scriptwriter who made his film debut before the First World War. He soon joined the ranks of the best Italian directors, thanks in part to this 2,225-meter adaptation of Dario Nicodemia's play, featuring the young and charming Carminati.

## *'A Legge (The Law)*

(Elvira Notari, 1920). Dora Film. **Script:** Elvira Notari. **Photography:** Nicola Notari. **With** Guissepe de Blasio (Tore), Carmela Bruno (Diana), Eduardo Notari, Rosè Angione (Rusella), Oreste Tesorone, and Silvia Simar. A 1,400-meter film shot on location in Naples that is a realistic and passionate critique of the era and a visceral work concerned with the plight of women and the underprivileged. It is based on a number of popular songs by E. A. Mario and Pacifico Vento.

Starring Naples singers, the film, a great success in its day, was directed by one of the unheralded creators of realist cinema, a woman who in the period 1906–1930 directed 60 features and scores of documentaries and shorts for her own production company of which her husband was photographer and son a key performer. The film was also called 'O festino e 'a legge (The Feast and the Law).

### Amleto e il suo clown (Hamlet and His Clown)

(Carmine Gallone, 1920). D'Ambra Film. Script: Lucio D'Ambra. With Soava Gallone and Luciano Molinari. Also called On with the Motley, this 1,950–meter comedy is based on a story by the multitalented Lucio D'Ambra.

### Amore rosso (Red Love)

(Gennaro Righelli, 1921). With Maria Jacobini, Oreste Bilancia, and Amleto Novelli. Starring Jacobini, the director's favorite actress, and the hugely popular Novelli — his eyes were hypnotic — in a 1,900-meter romance that was one of the highlights of the year in Italian cinema.

### A San Francisco (In San Francisco)

(Gustavo Serena, 1915). Caesar Film. Script: Arrigo Frusta. Adaptation: Salvatore di Giacomo. With Mercedes Brignone, Gustavo Serena, Carlo Benetti, and Camillo de Riso. One of strongest examples of social protest in early cinema, this 1,100-meter film (based on Giacomo's harsh work for the theater) became equally noteworthy for its violent contrasts in editing — something later found in Soviet and American films. It was made by a man who specialized in unflinching drama and who made artistic use of contemporary, everyday subject matter (in preference to the heroic, though he tended to favor the diva).

### L'Avventura del maggiore (The Major's Adventure)

(1913). Società Anonima Ambrosio. Ambrosio was the production company that specialized in historical films, and one of the first such films was this 125-meter tale. In Germany, it was titled Abenteuer des Majors.

### Il Bustino rosa (The Bustino Rose)

(1913). Società Anonima Ambrosio. Ambrosio's 200-meter historical drama, another early example of the genre by the pioneer film studio.

### La casa dei Pulcini (The House of Pulcinis)

(Mario Camerini, 1924). Pittaluga-Fert. Script: Camerini. Photography: Ottavio de Matteis. With Diomara Jacobini (Lauretta), Amleto Novelli (Count Landi), Rita D'Harcourt (the governess), Giuseppe Brignone, Franz Sala, and Armando Pouget. At 1,700 meters, this delicate film of psychology and atmosphere represents just about the last well-received Italian work from the silent era, written by Camerini.

## La cavalcata ardente (The Fiery Foray)

(Carmine Gallone, 1925). SAIC, Westli Film. **Script:** Galone and Giuseppe Forti. **Photography:** Alfredo Donelli and Emilio Guattari. **Design:** Filippo Folchi. **With** Soava Gallone (Countess de Montechiaro), Emilio Ghione (Prince Santafé), Gabriele de Gravonne (Giovanni Artuni), Jean Brindeau, and Edmondo van Riel. Costing 1.5 million lire, this was a sumptuous, patriotic, immensely successful 3,500-meter costume drama that tells an epic — and decadent — tale of the turbulent period of Garibaldi. In 1860, during the campaign to unite Italy, in the city of Naples, love, passion, and patriotism are brought to the fore.

The immense epic was a popular hit and an occasion of patriotic celebration, one of the few Italian films of note in the period 1924–28. Technical expert Gallone was a master crowd-handler, the De Mille of the early days of Italian cinema who found his forte in spectacle (though he also transferred to the screen masterpieces of Italian lyric theater). Half the footage of this 1925 film is extant.

## La donna bianca (The White Woman)

(Jack Salvatori, 1930). Paramount. **Script** and **dialogue:** Camillo Antona Traversi. **Photography:** Fernando Risi. **Design:** Paolo Reni. **Editor:** Jean de Limur. **With** Mathilde Casagrande (Leslie), Lamberto Picasso (Robert), Sandro Salvini (Mr. Joyce), Carlo Lombardi (Geoffrey), and Hoang Thi The (Li Ti). In its Singapore setting, Paramount's one-hour Italian film from

Paris is a faithful rendition of its dramatic, interracial hit *The Letter* (1929), starring Jeanne Eagels.

At the same time, the film is a hybrid: an early sound attempt to combine picturesque exteriors with the older, more familiar, and subtler stylistic elements reminiscent of silent filmmaking. Among the actors, one stands out. Casagrande, wrote a critic, while not quite disciplined enough and a bit too exuberant, displays her fine figure and uncommon dramatic qualities, especially in the efficacious, long discourse she gives at her murder trial. The other performers in the production, also called *Tragedie d'amore*, Picasso, Salvani, and Lombard remonstrate less well, or so reviewers felt at the time of the film's release in the Italian capital in February 1931.

## Il dramma di una notte (The Night's Drama)

(Mario Caserini, 1918). Gloria-Film. **Script:** Arrigo Frusta, Mario Caserini, and Fred Hardt. **With** Lyda Borelli and André Habay. A 1,500-meter work starring "the first diva of the cinema," Borelli (1884–1959).

## La fiaccola sotto il moggio (The Torch Under a Bushel)

(Luigi Maggi, 1911). An early 250-meter short by the early Italian filmmaker, called *Vengeance* as well as *La Torche sous le boisseau* in France.

## Fu Così che... (It Was Thus That...)

(Pietro S. Rivetta, 1922). The director wrote under the pseudonym Toddi, and he made more than a score of films in the 1920s — and all are lost. This 1,450-meter work is ranked as one of his best.

## Il giardino incantato (The Enchanted Garden)

(Eugenio Perego, 1918). F.A.I/Rinascimento. **Script:** Perego. **With** Pina Menichelli, Luigi Serventi, and Enrico Scatizzi. An adaptation of J. M. Barrie's well-known novel (also called *Il giardino delle volutta*). A 400-meter untitled negative survives, highlighting the femme fatale Menichelli.

## La Gioconda

(Eleuterio Rodolfi, 1916). **Script:** Arrigo Frusta. **With** Elena Makowska and Umberto Mozzato. An adaptation of Gabriele D'Annunzio's well-known drama that gives to ordinary events great passion, sinfulness, and all manner of spectacular embellishments. In the 1,400-meter tale, Lucio Settain, a sculptor, falls in love with, and under the spell of, the beautiful model, La Gioconda. The affair brings on tragedy: Lucio's suicide attempt; the near collapse of his marriage to Silvia; and worst of all, Silvia's horrific injuries, which come about when she confronts La Gioconda.

## Il girotondo degli undici lancieri (The Dance of Eleven Lancers)

(Lucio D'Ambra, 1919). Doremi Film. **Script:** D'Ambra. **Photography:** Umberto Della Valle. **Design:** Tito Antonelli. **With** Maria Corvin (Rosalla), Romano Calo (Prince Ludovico), Achille Vitti (the duke), and Rosetta d'Aprile. This celebrated light comedy by a specialist of the genre was hailed as a bril-liant cosmopolitan reflection on decadent art and society. The 1,900-meter film was also called *Il tenente dei lancieri*.

## Il grande sentiero (The Big Trail)

(Louis Loeffler, 1930). Fox. **With** Franco Corsaro (Colman). A rarely noted, Hollywood-made, Italian-language version of Raoul Walsh's *The Big Trail* (1930) — which was the first 70-mm film in the studio's history.

## Ivonne, la bella danzatrice

(Gustavo Serena, 1915). Caesar Film. **Script:** Arrigo Frusta. **With** Francesca Bertini and Gustavo Serena. Also called *Yvonne, la bella della "Danse brutale,"* the well-crafted 1,700-meter drama exemplifies the work of the prolific scriptwriter Frusta (1875–1965) and the great Bertini.

## Justice de femme!

(Diana Karenne, 1917). This 1,800-meter drama was directed by one of the legendary Italian movie queens, admired for her "great sensitivity, beauty, refinement, instinctive good taste, and mobility of expression," wrote a critic. She was able to express "through artifice as convincing as truth, grief, love, hate, fear, joy, the innermost feelings, the most secret impulses of the soul, each time creating a different face, heart, and passion." In a word, Karenne anticipated American publicity. She costarred in *Casanova* (1927). Her Italian work is also called *Giustizia de donna*.

## 'A Legge  see under A

## Maciste

(Vincenzo C. Denizot, 1915). **Script:** Gabriele D'Annunzio. **With** Bartolomeo Pagano. This was one of the first Italian productions out of America. A seven-reeler shot in New York and Europe, the film (based on the novel by Luigi Borgnetto) is a "modern-day" follow-up to Giovanni Pastrone's hugely successful 12-part *Cabiria* (1914). Pastrone, the inventor of the dolly for tracking shots, filmed the European portions. Pagano is the giant black slave called on to restore the rights of an aristocratic mother and daughter, and the film includes footage from *Cabiria*. *Variety* commented, "It's a great picture for one man … Pagano's work has never been equaled, let alone excelled, on the screen." In his career, Pagano (1878–1947) played the character Maciste in 25 films in the period 1914–1928.

## Maciste imperatore (Emperor Maciste)

(Guido Brignone, 1924). Pittaluga-Fert. **Story:** Pier Angel Mazzolotti. **Photography:** Massimo Terzano and Segundo de Chomón. **With** Bartolomeo Pagano, Elena Sangro, Domenico Gambino (Saetta), Franz Sala (Stanos), Lola Romanos (Cinzia), and Raoul Mayllard (Prince Ortis). One of Brignone's earliest efforts (he directed more than 50 films in the period 1915–58) and one of Pagano's last performances as the famous character who could match the feats of Douglas Fairbanks and Tom Mix.

The tale is set in the imaginary kingdom of Sirdania, where the regent Stanos intrigues against the legitimate heir to the throne, Prince Ortis. Maciste and his friend Saetta become aware of the brewing turbulence and come to the aid of the debilitated prince. The vicissitudes of life — and a great deal of action — leads to Maciste being proclaimed emperor, ending the reign of the puppet and his behind-the-scenes machinations, and restoring peace to the kingdom.

In Italy and to Italian-American audiences, the sumptuous production spoke more to reality than fantasy, offering a larger-than-life hero (the "Guitry with the biceps") alongside the popular Sangro (in the first of three Maciste films opposite Pagano). Six hundred and forty meters of tinted footage is extant from the 2100-meter production.

## La marcia nuziale (The Wedding March)

(Carmine Gallone, 1915). **Script:** Gallone. **Photography:** Domenico Grimaldi. **With** Lyda Borelli (Countess de Plessans), Amleto Novelli (Claudio Morillot), Leda Gys (Susanna Lechatellier), and Francesco Cacace (Ruggero Lechatellier). Borelli was touted as the "first diva of the cinema"— the type of woman tormented by passions — and was noted for her languorous pose, rapacious glance, and jerky movements. The film, containing some of the same themes from Gallone's *La Femme nue* (*The Naked Woman*) (1914), confirmed Borelli's extraordinary screen personality, as well as the great strength of the script, which was based on Henri Bataille's play about high society and a self-sacrificing woman.

One of Gallone's earliest efforts (in the years 1913–62, Gallone directed more than 150 productions), the film was one of the great successes of 1915–16, and it presaged Erich von Stroheim's stupendous Hollywood effort on the same story.

## Marthu' che ha visto il diavolo (Marthu Who Has Visited the Devil)

(Mario Almirante, 1921). Fert. With Franz Sala and Italia Almirante Manzini. A 1,400-meter tale of woe of which the first reel is missing. One thousand tinted meters survive, featuring one of the great stars of the golden age of Italian cinema, Itala Almirante Manzini (1890–1941).

## Mondo baldoria (Jolly World)

(Aldo Molinari, 1914). **Script:** Filippo Tommasso Marinetti. **With** Marinetti, Bruno Corra, Arnaldo Ginna, Giacomo Balla, and Emilio Settimelli. Called "the first futurist subject in cinema," this 900-meter avant-garde film expresses different ways of looking at life. In episodic form, the humorous work demonstrates such things as "How a Futurist Sleeps," "Morning Gymnastics," and a "Futurist Breakfast." In the portion "Searches for Inspiration—Drama of Objects," Manetti and Settimelli approach a set of objects and try to grasp their meaning. That's followed by a "discussion" between a foot, a hammer, and an umbrella. Later the futurists attempt a new way of walking while satirizing a "creditor's walk" as well as a "debter's walk." The film concludes with a "tea party" at which a number of women are seduced, an exhibition of "paintings ideally and outwardly deformed," and scenes of Balla falling in love with and marrying a sofa, after which a footstool is born.

## Monsieur la volpe (Mr. Fox)

(Hal Roach, 1931). MGM. With Franco Corsaro (Luigi) and Barbara Leonard. The 74-minute, Hollywood-made Italian-language adventure of the Canadian wilds, based on Hal Roach's *Men of the North* (1930), was released in Italy under the title *Luigi la volpe*.

## La morte piange, ride e poi … s'annoia (Death Weeps, Laughs, Then … Tires)

(Mario Bonnard, 1921). **With** Dolly Morgan. A 2,300-meter drama directed by the acclaimed actor Bonnard, who was often partner to the most famous divas of the period.

## Nelly la gigolette

(Emilio Ghione, 1914). Caesar Film. **Script:** Arrigo Frusta. **Photography:** Alberto G. Carta. **With** Francesca Bertini, Gustavo Serena, Emilio Ghione (Za la Mort), Alberto Collo (the banker), Carlo and Olga Benetti, and Baldassare Negroni. This four-part film (based on Giannini Anton Traversi's work) introduced to screen audiences the singular character Za la Mort (whose meaning is akin to Viva la Morte) and was Bertini's first film for Caesar Film.

Also called *La danzatrice della taverna nera* (*The Dancer from the Black Tavern*), it's the story of apache dancers who prey upon wealthy visitors to Italy. The 1,600-meter production revealed Ghione's ability to handle the dual roles of good guy and bad guy and confirmed Bertini's talent for melodrama.

## Nemesis

(Carmine Gallone, 1920). D'Ambra Film. **Script:** Lucio D'Ambra. **With** Soava Gallone. This light, 2,125-meter comedy reunited director Gallone and writer D'Ambra for one last effort before Italian cinema went into decline.

## Non e resurrezione senza morte (There Is No Resurrection Without Death)

(Eduardo Bencivenga, 1922). **With** Elena Sangro. A 2,050-meter drama with the rising star.

## L'oca alla Colbert (Goose à la "Colbert")

(Eleuterio Rodolfi, 1913). Società Anonima Ambrosio. The first comedy by the former actor Rodolfi is a 650-meter production that was shown in France and the United States.

## Paramount-Revue

(Charles de Rochefort, 1930). Paramount. **With** Carmen Boni, Nino Martini, Enrico Signori, and Romano Calo. A one-hour revue of Paramount's Italian talent in Paris.

## Perché no? (Why Not?)

(Amleto Palermi, 1930). Paramount. **Script:** Camillo Antona Traversi. **Photography:** Fernando Risi. **Design:** Paolo Reni. **Editor:** Helene Turner. **With** Maria Jacobini (Annette), Livio Pavanelli (Roberto), and Oreste Bilancia (Carlo). Paramount's first Italian-language production out of Paris was this 69-minute version of *The Lady Lies* (1929). It stars the well-known Jacobini

as the object of attention of a widowed attorney whose two children reject her.

In Rome in September 1930, the film was interesting enough to have critics noting that Palermi displayed a directorial flourish, but at times overplayed the comedy. The established lead actress and Pavanelli revealed through their performances a "grace and efficiency a bit declamatory but honest," while Bilancia's performance is on a par with the brilliant comedy manner that had made him a popular silent film star. "The entire cast is very competent," agreed *Film Daily*. "The production has lots of class.... Everything works out all right amid a lot of very clever comedy situations."

Francesca Bertini as the femme fatale in *Nelly la gigolette* (Emilio Ghione, Caesar, 1914).

## Perfido incanto (Perfidious Enchantment)

(Anton Giulio Bragaglia and Riccardo Cassano, 1916). **With** Lyda Borelli. This production was one of the world's earliest expressionistic films, now considered a forerunner of Wiene's *Caligari*

(1919). Starring the sophisticated Borelli, the 1,400-meter film, wrote a critic, is "a play of abstract rhythms." It was made in response to the 1916 "Manifesto of Futurist Cinematography," which called for a cinema of free expression and "analogies, simultaneity and interpretation of different times and places, musical researches, scenic states of mind, and dramas of objects." The directors' avant-garde *Il mio cadavere* (*My Corpse*) (1917) is also lost.

## Il ponte dei sospiri (The Bridge of Sighs)

(Domenico Gaido, 1921). Pasquali and Co. **With** Luciano Albertini (Roland), Carolina Withe (Leonora), and Antonietta Calderari. Based on a popular novel, this is a complex and ambitious four-part adventure, each episode a feature-length work: *La boca del leone* (*The Lion's Mouth*) (1,675 meters), *La potenza del male* (*The Power of Evil*) (1,700 meters), *Il dio della vendetta* (*The God of Revenge*) (1,925 meters), and *Il trionfo d'amore* (*The Triumph of Love*) (1,700 meters). Well told with climaxes that are well developed, the complete work contains stunts galore which, wrote an observer, "will only serve to increase the value of the picture" with popular audiences.

It begins when Roland the Strong marries Leonora, the daughter of Dandola, but he is soon imprisoned on charges of having murdered the lover of a Venetian courtesan. After five years, Roland escapes and sets off in pursuit of vengeance. Leonaora in the meantime has married Roland's rival Altieri, but her heart is still faithful to her first husband. In the end, Roland is avenged on all his enemies — they die various unpleasant deaths — and he is reunited with Leonora.

"Many of the settings are very fine and attention has been paid to well-known Venetian landscapes," wrote a critic. These include Doge's Palace, the Campanile of St. Mark's, and the Bridge of Sighs. In the long tradition of Italian film, the "crowd work shows skillful stage management."

## Povero bimbo (Poor Child)

(Emilio Graziani-Walter, 1916). Regina Film. A 500-meter work that got lost in the war years.

## Prelude à l'après-midi d'un faun (Prelude to the Afternoon of a Faun

(Roberto Rossellini, 1938). **Music** by Debussy. A short, erotic film inspired by Debussy's stirring late 19th century piece and Nijinsky's 1912 ballet of the same name, Rossellini's early work, a nonballet, was said to display a "revolutionary" vision of life by a director deeply impressed "by the water with the serpent slithering about ... and the dragonfly overhead." At that time in his life, said Rossellini, "I had a reputation of being a mad man full of dangerous ideas.... I was taken as a drop of vinegar in a salad."

## Ragazzo (Boy)

(Ivo Perilli, 1933). Cines. **Script:** Perilli and Emilio Cecchi. **Photography:** Massimo Terzano and Domenico Scala. **Music:** Luigi Colacicchi. **With** Costantino Frasca (the boy), Isa Pola, Giovanna Scotto (his mother), and Osvaldo Valenti. This unknown realistic sound film, which employed nonprofessional actors, was Perilli's first full-time directorial effort. The production was never allowed to be circulated, on orders of Mussolini. Worse still, the only known copy was destroyed when the Germans devastated Rome's Cineteca Nazionale in 1943.

Perilli had studied architecture, and began his film career creating sets and costumes on the early films of Brignone and Camerini. His first feature film, hinting at neorealism, is the emotional tale of a boy from the slums of Rome, orphaned by his father. The boy knows only gang life. He and his friends from the street enter a villa of which the mother is the caretaker, in order to steal. But at the last minute, the boy refuses to partake in the crime, and escapes. His life takes a turn for the better when he is introduced to the youth organizations sponsored by the government.

In the postwar years Perilli co-scripted *Europa 51, War and Peace, Barabbas,* and *The Bible.*

## Il re, le torre, gli alfieri (The King, the Towers, the Standard-Bearers)

(Lucio D'Ambra and Ivo Illuminati, 1916). **Script:** D'Ambra. As the most well-known scriptwriter of light comedy for Carmine Gallone and Augusto Genina, D'Ambra was called "the Goldoni of Italian cinema" because of the ingenuity of his narrative methods and rhythms, and his inventiveness in the use of sets and tricks. This multipart film, which is based on his novel, is a true Italian original: bizarre, extravagant, devilish, superficial, and filled with nudity. A caricature mixed with irony,

sentiment, and comedy, it was called "an important artistic and social event." It was described as a "sentimental comedy, rather ironic, rather sad, rather comic, rather old, rather new, rather true, rather false—like life." The production became an early international hit that D'Ambra characterized as a "modern *Iliad* played at the whim of a little Homer." It was said to have influenced Lubitsch in his operetta period, particularly his work *The Oyster Princess* (1920).

It also anticipated musical films. Its strength, like that of other original Italian films of the period (such as *Cabiria* and *Sperduti nel buio*), is that it led the world as an example (in this case) of the "silent musical" with nocturnal Strauss waltzes, princes and ambassadors from Lehár's operetta world, and ballet. The film's rhythm and variations of tone speak for themselves through the shooting and editing.

It featured professional actors alongside a well-known countess (Giorgina Dendice di Frasso), a marquis (Vittorio Bourbon del Monte), and a member of the Italian parliament—a sign of distinction that playwrights and famous performers wanted to impress upon their audiences. It did impress, for there was applause after each part of the film, noted a critic, "the first time ever this happened in the history of the screen."

## Il richiamo del cuore (The Reclaiming of the Heart)

(Jack Salvatori, 1930). Paramount. **Script** and **dialogue:** Oreste Biancoli. **Photography:** Fernando Risi. **Design:** Paolo Reni. **Editor:** Verna Willis. **With** Carmen Boni (Suzanne Sandi), Carlo Lombardi (Stanley), Sandro Salvini

(Ashmore), Alfredo Robert (Cyril), and Cesare Zoppetti. Filmed in Paris, Paramount's 83-minute Italian version of Dorothy Arzner's sensitive and moving *Sarah and Son* (1930) is, like the English-language version, a tear-jerker.

The attractive Carmen Boni took on the role that brought raves to Ruth Chatterton — that of a lonely, sensitive New Yorker who, after achieving operatic fame and wealth, lives only to locate a child of hers abducted at birth. When she locates him, "the complication then becomes one of rival claimants for the youngster's affections," wrote the *New York Times* in March 1931, "with mother love overcoming all obstacles at last." The plot's tones and touches attempt to elicit profound reactions in filmgoers, but the film, according to the era's critics, could have used more affective music and a faster tempo to match the moving story. Still, Paramount's Paris production, noted *Film Daily*, "should appeal to folks who know the language."

## La riva dei bruti (The Riverbank of the Violent)

(Mario Camerini, 1930). Paramount. **Script** and **dialogue:** Pier Luigi Melani. **Photography:** Fernando Risi. **Design:** Paolo Reni. **Editor:** Allison Shaffer. **With** Camillo Pilotto (Schomberg), Carlo Lombardi (Jones), Carmen Boni (Alma), Sandro Salvini (Davis), and Cesare Zoppetti. The established Mario Camerini directed a 73-minute film set in Malaysia, based on Joseph Conrad's harsh 1915 adventure story, *Victory*, and Maurice Tourneur's 1919 film of the same name.

The Paris melodrama, sometimes called *Domini senza dio* (*Dominions Without God*), contains some interesting particulars, especially a stark atmosphere and a dark vision of human relations. *Cinema Illustrazione*, in 1931, took the director to task, however, for failing to match his technically more artistic silent films, and Camerini, in reaction, turned down Paramount's offer to direct a second film in Paris.

## La rosa

(Arnaldo Fratelli, 1921). Tespi. **With** Bruno Barilli, Olympia Barroero (Lucietta), and Lamberto Picasso. Based on a short story by Pirandello, this is a delicate, psychological film about the young Signora Lucietta. On her way to start a new life after the sudden death of her husband, she meets on the train the handsome and engaging Fausto Silvagni. Arriving in Peola with her young children, the beautiful young woman is invited to an annual ball. She quickly captivates the hearts of her many admirers, including Fausto's. In a moment reminiscent of the judgment of Paris, she is presented with a rose and asked to toss it to the man she loves. That moment changes her life.

"A refined and delicate film which has not the perishable characteristics of nearly all the films of the time," wrote a critic, the 1,950-meter production seems to have been the Tespi studio's most worthwhile achievement. All of Tespi's films are lost.

## Santarellina

(Eugenio Perego, 1923). Lombardo Film. **Script:** Perego and Arrigo Frusta. **Photography:** Giacomo Bazzichelli. **With** Leda Gys, Silvio Orsini (Fernando), Lorenzo Soderni (Celestino Floridoro), and Carlo Reiter. This excellent comedy adaptation of Henry Meilhac and A. Milhaud's 1883 operetta *Mam'zelle Nitouche* (with music by Hervé) represents a rare hit during a period when Italian cinema was in decline, an attempt to outdo Caserini's well-received *Santarellina* of 1911.

The 1,400-meter production, which is set in the latter half of the 19th century, is the light-hearted tale of a young woman who becomes a overnight hit on the musical stage and, though betrothed to a stranger, winds up marrying the man she loves.

A critic of the 1920s said, "It is always a pleasure to write about Leda Gys.... One can find so much passion in her wide and bright pupils that her admirers' souls seem to be covered by dew made of light, the light of youth, of feeling, of intelligence. Leda Gys should not hide herself behind her modesty. We admit that from an aesthetic point of view she is just delightful, but today when the most exotic names of foreign artists are on everyone's lips, and on every theatre screen, it is a shame that an actress such as Leda Gys would not come to the forefront, in an extreme close-up, so to speak, when she has such a marvelous personality."

### Satana

(Luigi Maggi, 1912). Ambrosio. **Script:** Guido Volante. **Photography:** Giovanni Vitrotti and A. Scalenghe. **With** Mario Bonnard, Maria Cleo Tarlarini (Fiammetta), Mario Voller Buzzi (Jesus), Luigi Maggi, and Alberto Capozzi. A prelude to Griffith's *Intolerance* (1916), Ince's *Civilization* (1916), Tourneur's *Woman* (1918), and Dreyer's

*Pages from Satan's Book* (1918), Luigi Maggi's production is ranked as one of the most influential in Italian cinema. It's a wide-ranging, episodic spectacle, scripted by the well-known poet Volante (1876–1916) that recounts "the story of evil through the ages."

The 2,000-meter film opens with an all-too-brief glimpse of angels "on the plains of Heaven," followed by "The Rebellion" when Lucifer makes an onslaught on God's "impregnable towers," but is routed and expelled. Satan then enters the terrestrial paradise and transforms himself into a serpent. The winding of his uncoiled length upon the tree, "is a very fine piece of double exposure," noted *Moving Picture World*.

In the next reel, the Devil tempts Jesus in the desert and takes possession of Judas' soul. "The convulsion of the elements at the moment of crucifixion — the darkened heavens traversed by flashes of lightening — make a marvelous background to the terrible scene." In the third reel, the "evil genius," now a green-eyed monster disguised as a monk, invents absinthe, which leads generations into crime and death. The malevolent aspects of alchemy are made evident in scenes in a convent's laboratory, and are "particularly fine in their realism and novelty."

Finally, in the last part, which "takes us to the very heart of modern conditions," the "Red Demon," played by Bonnard in a top hat, is shown smoking, laughing, and assuming the guise of a millionaire captain of industry, a steel magnate.

With this film, director Maggi was acclaimed "an artist in the first flight" of filmmakers. He helped the young Italian cinema leap to the fore in examining issues of ethics, history, luxury, poverty, and inequality, all with a psychological underpinning and absent any preaching. "Too much praise cannot be given to pictures of this kind," concluded *Moving Picture World* in November 1913. "They justify the faith and hope in the higher possibilities of the moving picture." Sixty meters of the film survive.

Stills: *Moving Picture World* (January 18, 1913).

## Il segreto del dottore (The Doctor's Secret)

(Jack Salvatori, 1930). Paramount. **Script** and **dialogue:** Camillo Antona Traversi. **Photography:** Fernando Risi. **Design:** Paolo Reni. **Editor:** Merrill White. **With** Soava Gallone (Liliana Garner), Alfredo Robert (Dr. Brady), Lamberto Picasso (Giovanni), and Oreste Bilancia (Redding). Made in Paris, this 67-minute rendition of the 1930 Hollywood original features the great Soava Gallone in the only sound film she ever made.

The great silent-screen star returned to films after an absence of several years — her body of work containing numerous masterful performances — to play the anguished woman who wants to leave her husband for a lover, only to suffer tragedy at the last moment. Her performance fell short of expectations, according to the Rome publication *Cinema Illustrazione*. It made no bones about putting the blame on the director Salvatori when the film, edited by a fine Hollywood technician, was screened in February 1931.

## Sei tu l'amore? (Is It Love?)

(Alfredo Sabato, 1930). Italotone. **With** Louisa Caselotti, Alberto Rabag-

liati, and Enrico Armetta. The first Italian sound film to come out of Hollywood was this expensive 75-minute musical romantic comedy about a couple of down and out guys who save a woman from suicide. She goes on to attain fame and fortune. Costing $150,000 to produce, the film attracted a "greater throng," wrote the *New York Times*, than had ever been seen at the 8th Street Playhouse in New York.

## Sole (Sun)

(Alessandro Blasetti, 1929). Augustus Film. **Script:** Blasetti and Aldo Vergano. **Photography:** Giuseppe Caracciolo. **With** Dria Paola, Marcello Spada, Vasco Creti, and Vittorio Vaser. Blasetti's first film presaged the introduction of neorealism. It is a silent contemporary social drama about the draining and reclaiming of the Pontine marshes and waste land and the lives of those engaged in the effort at reclamation.

It was filmed at the instigation of Mussolini — in fact it was reviewed by Mussolini before its release — and helped to illustrate the so-called triumph of new ideas and the will to national progress. A success in its time, the film helped revive a moribund Italian cinema, giving special heart to producers.

Blasetti (called the "Don Quixote of Italian cinema") was praised for "the tight editing, the audacious framings, and his tendency to consider bodies and faces as a form of still life, as beautiful objects rather than as centers of emotion, passion, and suffering." By having his performers act with extreme restraint, Blasetti shifted interest away from the investigation and discovery of human nature to form and composition.

But *L'Imperio* pointed out that Blasetti's colleague, the antifascist writer Vergano (1891–1957), displayed a mentality that "still reveals ... democratic vices." Fifteen minutes of the film survive.

## Sperduti nel buio (Lost in Darkness)

(Nino Martoglio and Roberto Danesi, 1914). Catania. **With** Giovanni Grasso, Virginia Balistreiri, Maria Carmi, and Dillo Lombardi. Martoglio was a Sicilian journalist, poet, playwright, and theatrical director who made his film debut in Rome. In 1914 he went back home to found a production company. In Naples he adapted a play by Roberto Bracco to come up with what is now considered a classic, realist drama of poverty and unemployment. His film's dramatic theme, character, style, and acting marked a turning point in Italian production — a turn to human interest and truths. In telling a tale of parallel and contrast, the director made use of eloquent and evocative images, replacing the normal succession of captions common in films of the era.

In the slums of Naples, life is revealed for what it is by the contrast between the sunlit splendor of the streets and the darker luxury of the palace. In Naples, people live within cracked walls and walk on grime-filled streets. The very rich and the very poor are portrayed, and each group is explained in terms of the other.

Years later Henri Langois called the 1,800-meter film, which influenced Soviet filmmakers of the 1920s as well as postwar Italian filmmakers, "one of the greatest cinema achievements of all time ... bathed in light, a natural light that we have never seen in any film since." The film was stolen by the Germans during the First World War. Efforts to trace this early masterwork of Italian cinema have proved fruitless.

## La storia dei Tredici (The Story of the Tredici)

(Carmine Gallone, 1917). D'Ambra Film. **With** Lyda Borelli (The Duchess) and Ugo Piperno (Montriveau). Based on Balzac's *The Duchess of Langeais* (1834), this is one of D'Ambra Film's earliest productions, a startling tale of personal vengeance. The story is straightforward. The Duchess of Langeais, a figure of prominence in the French court, was at first devoted to her unfaithful husband. But inspired to flights of capriciousness, she became known as "the toast of Paris," juggling hearts wantonly. Then one day she encounters a strong, silent man (General de Montriveau), and a calculated flirtation with him develops into soul-searing love.

The 1,700-meter Italian adaptation takes place an island in the Mediterranean and in the convent of the Order of Barefoot Carmelites. Almost every religious house in the peninsula, or in Europe for that matter, was either destroyed or greatly affected by the outbreak of the French Revolution and the Napoleonic wars; but as this island was protected through those times by the English fleet, its wealthy convent and peaceable inhabitants were secure from the general worldly trouble and spoliation.

"The storms of many kinds which shook the first fifteen years of the nineteenth century," wrote Balzac, "spent their force before they reached those cliffs at so short a distance from the coast of Andalusia." But on the island, the hero, Montriveau, is seduced by a bored society coquette who uses religion as a "cold shower." She does so for a reason. After her husband had abandoned her, she vowed vengeance on other men. When their passion becomes too intense, Montriveau captures the duchess and threatens to brand her with an iron. The real about-face comes when the duchess falls in love with him — too late — and enters the convent.

The story was later filmed in Hollywood as *The Eternal Flame* (1923), directed by Frank Lloyd and starring Norma Talmadge.

### Televisione

(Charles de Rochefort, 1931). Paramount. **Script:** Michel Duran. **Dialogue:** Dino Falconi. **Photography:** Fernando Risi. **Design:** Paolo Reni. **With** Anna Maria Dossena (Jeanne), Silvio Orsini (André Leroy), Cesare Zoppetti (financier Steven), and Amina Pirani Maggi (Miss Ridon). Paramount's 66-minute Paris production, also called *La canzone del mondo* (*Song of the World*), is a semiserious tale of intrigue behind the invention of the electronic technology by a scientist named André Leroy and the young woman who saves the day.

The Italian film features the versatile, photogenic, and fine-speaking Maggi, whose beauty, voice, and comic streak had the critics proclaiming, "actresses like her are not found in abundance, for sure." An original Paris production in that there was no Hollywood original, the film follows the storyline of the often-filmed French-language *Magie moderne* and is the best version, reaching Rome in September 1931.

### Teresa Raquin

(Nino Martoglio, 1915). Catania. **Photography:** Luigi Romagnoli. **With** Maria Carmi, Dillo Lombardi, and Giacenta Pezsana. Another early realist drama by the highly acclaimed Sicilian playwright Martoglio in which the director evokes Zola's tale of murder and guilt in a psychological manner and through carefully crafted scenes. Composed of simple luminescent images, the film of verisimilitude was reportedly destroyed by the Nazis in 1944.

### L'ultimo dei Frontignac (The Last of the Frontignacs)

(Mario Caserini, 1911). Società Anonima Ambrosio. **Script:** Arrigo Frusta. **Photography:** Angelo Scalenghe. **With** Alberto Capozzi and Maria Cleo Tarlarini. This was an early, successful example of Italian bourgeois drama, based on Octave Feuillet's popular *The Story of a Poor Young Man*, which achieved fame because it was one of the first films in which players wear contemporary dress. The three-reel (1,000-meter) film features two of the earliest Italian stars.

In this tale of class conflict, in which a young man loses his fortune because of a sensational revelation, but gains something else, the love of a woman, the violent passion was said to be expressive of the Italian national character. The film was distributed in the United States, Great Britain, Spain, Germany, and Hungary. Until his death in 1920, the versatile Caserini made nearly 75 films, many of which added luster to Italian cinema.

### L'ultimo lord

(Augusto Genina, 1926). Films Pittaluga. **Script:** Genina. **Photography:**

**Maria Carmi is the woman who inspires murder in _Teresa Raquin_ (Nino Martoglio, Catania, 1915).**

Carlo Montuori and Vittorio Armenise. **With** Carmen Boni (Freddie Caverley), Bonaventura Ibañez (the Duke), Lido Manetti (Prince Cristiano), Gianna Terribili (the Princess), and Oreste Bilancia. Costing little to produce, this diverting comedy was one of the rare successful Italian productions of the period. Based on the 1925 comedy by Ugo Falena (who was inspired by Burnett's _Little Lord Fauntleroy_, 1886), the production concerns an old Italian nobleman, living in a splendid isolation in a villa, and a young relative come to visit.

After taking in his grandson — he has high hopes for the young lad — he has to readjust his thinking when the "he" turns out to be a granddaughter. She soon finds a lover.

Critics called the 2,200-meter film "perfect" and Boni's performance a "revelation." When sound came in, Genina shot the comedy under the title *La Femme en homme* (1931), also starring the charming Boni. One hundred and fifty meters of the sound film survives.

## La vacanza del diavolo (The Devil's Holiday)

(Jack Salvatori, 1931). Paramount. **Script** and **dialogue:** Dino Falconi. **Photography:** Enzo Riccione and Fernando Risi. **Design:** Paolo Reni. **Editor:** George Nichols, Jr. **With** Carmen Boni (Lina Hobart), Alfredo Robert (Edward Stone), Camillo Pilotto (Marc Stone). Maurizio d'Ancora (Robert Stone), Oreste Bilancia (Henry Carr), Sandro Salvini, and Cesare Zoppetti (Karl Thorn). Jack Salvatori's best effort out of Paramount's Paris studios is a well-acted, episodic production based on the money-making Hollywood original, starring Nancy Carroll as a young manicurist on the make who decides to make amends.

In the 71-minute Italian version, the ably attractive, coy Carmen Boni carries the film. "Taking it solely on its own merits," wrote *Film Daily*, the film "is a satisfying piece of entertainment and ought to have no trouble getting across its intended field." In Rome, the production was scrutinized under a harsher light, deemed "an Italian film, completely spoken, in which well-known actors have collaborated.... The study is notable for presenting in a clear fashion the characters' states of mind; but the word is there, ready to analyze that which the spirit of the cinema would leave to the public's fantasy."

## La vagabonda

(Ugo Falena and Eugenio Perego, 1917). F.A.I. **Script:** Colette. **With** Musidora (Renée Néré), Enrico Roma, Luigi Maggi (Maxim), Rina Maggi, and Ernesto Treves (Adolphe). Based on Colette's 1910 novel of the same name, the film represents Colette's first script for the medium. Containing few subtitles, it is a semiautobiographical tale of a music hall singer who is unable to accept love and eventually becomes disillusioned with her marriage. Colette had been a music hall entertainer in the period 1906–1910, and made that experience the central subject of her 1,000-meter story, which was filmed in Rome.

## La venere nera (The Black Venus)

(Blaise Cendrars, 1923). **Script:** Cendrars. **With** Dourga. Featuring a Hindu star of the Paris Opéra comique and directed by a well-known writer and poet, the film is a spoof of detective fiction. All the well-known sleuths of the day and some of their creators — Fantômas, Nick Carter, Arsène Lupin, Maurice Leblanc, Gustave Lerouge, Conan Doyle, Roulatabille (created by Gaston Leroux) — try, in Keystone Cops fashion, to solve the mystery behind the disappearance of two women.

The 1,250-meter film was shot in Rome and is based on the published script *La Perle fiévreuse* (*The Restless Pearl*).

tors of the day in a dramatic production made when such drama was in decline. With Italian producers scurrying to survive in a film market overwhelmed by American imports, Ghione tried to resurrect past glories by making the 2,700-meter thriller, and in the attempt brought back his most famous creation, Za la Mort.

## Il viaggio (The Journey)

(Gennaro Righelli, 1921). Fert. **Script:** Righelli. **Photography:** Massimo Terzano. **With** Maria Jacobini (Adriana Braggi), Carlo Benetti (Cesare Braggi), and Alfonso Casini (the doctor). Starring the director's favorite actress, the film is an early adaptation of a Pirandello story. When a widowed Sicilian, living as a recluse, learns she is dying, she goes on a trip accompanied by her brother-in law. She responds to life, enjoying herself for the first time in years — then commits suicide in Venice.

Righelli directed with great finesse and elegance, capturing the funereal atmosphere of Pirandello's novel. Jacobini and Benetti gave splendid performances, noted the critics, which assured the film's success.

## Za la Mort (Long-Live-Death)

(Emilio Ghione, 1915). Tiber Film. **With** Ghione, Kally Sambucini (Za la Vie), Alberto Collo, Floriana, and Diana D'Amore. Inspired by the examples of

Musidora in *La vagabonda* (Ugo Falena and Eugenio Perego, F.A.I., 1917).

## Via del peccato (Street of Sin)

(Emilio Ghione and Amleto Palermi, 1925). Ghione Film. **Script:** Palermi. **With** Soava Gallone, Kally Sambucini (Za la Vie), Ruggero Ruggeri, Gustavo Serena, Mario Bonnard, and Emilio Ghione (Za la Mort). Also called *Il cammino del peccato*, the film starred a dozen of the most popular Italian ac-

Emilio Ghione as the elusive bandit-hero in *Za la mort* (Emilio Ghione, Tiber, 1915).

the serial filmmakers Gasnier in New York (with his *Perils of Pauline*) and Feuillade in Paris, Ghione launched his own series (rather than serial), bringing to the fore the lean-faced, photogenic, romantic, and legendary criminal Za la Mort.

A mix of film invention and descriptions of milieux, the realist film — influenced by *Sperduti nel buio* (1914) and Neopolitan cinema — encompasses three episodes: *La banda delle cifre* (*Band of Figures*), *Za la Mort* and *Za la Vie,* and *L'imboscata* (*The Ambush*). In the famous character, violence lives side by side with noble sentiments. He resembles the gentleman thief Arsène Lupin. The first film in the series, said the critics, is a "tribute to the temperment of the acting of Ghione."

Ghione's highly regarded and popular detective series lasted into the 1920s and influenced film industries abroad. Ghione even published a novel, *L'ombra di Za la Mort* (*The Shadow of Za la Mort*) about his most famous screen creation. "I was a sentimental apache with a noble heart," said Ghione. "I lived amid violence but I hated ugliness; I loved flowers and the poor and could be tender at the right time and place." His partner is Za la Vie. They present a world of improbable and splendid adventures, and became one of the most acclaimed couples in international cinema.

# The Netherlands

The first Dutch film was made in 1896. By the turn of the century, the Mullens brothers (Albert and Willy) were promoting their "live shadows" in the low countries and making fully-fledged films rather than the usual shots of people leaving church and other clichés.

Dutch cinema reached its peak in the period 1912–1923, becoming as good as any filmmaking in the world. The nation's neutrality during the First World

War and the absence of foreign competition stimulated the native industry, which produced music-hall revues (accompanied by music), lively comedies, and, most important, intense sorrowful dramas. After the war, these kinds of productions continued to serve the native market as well as those abroad, notably the British market. Social dramas for the market in Britain were a mainstay in the years between the wars. Theo Frenkel, Maurits H. Binger and Alex Benno led the way.

The Netherlands' first movie mogul, Maurits Herman Binger (1868–1923) learned of the new phenomenon of "cinema" while in Paris perfecting his skills as a young printer and photographer. In 1912 he established the Filmfabriek Hollandia (Hollandia Film Factory) in Haarlem. His combination of energy, enthusiasm and keen business sense resulted in a well-oiled, highly productive film studio that produced (in addition to documentaries, shorts and industrials) between five and ten feature-length farces and dramas per year for an international market. Binger directed 40 films in his career, and the record number of films made by his studio remains unbroken in The Netherlands.

The studio's feature players included the exceptional Annie Bos, Beppie de Vries, Margie Morris, Lola Cornero, Willem de Meer, Adelqui Migliar (later Adelqui Millar), and the great Louis Bouwmeester and Louis Davids.

Filmfabriek Hollandia and Hollandia/Granger-Binger produced about 100 features during this period, more than half the Dutch output. Afterwards, wrote a critic, the country became "among the least significant where film production is concerned," although

Dutch theater turned into film became a success in the mid–1920s even in locations where there were no theaters in The Netherlands.

Dominated by American imports, the native film industry was forced to resort to a subspecialty, the documentary, to stay afloat. This was due in large part to Joris Ivens. During the transition to sound, Paramount in Paris filmed two productions in Dutch, a revue and a fictional tale (a semidocumentary of sorts) about a scientific discovery. By the mid–1930s, a large number of German directors and producers, including Kurt Gerron, found refuge in The Netherlands, adding life to the native film industry. Of the more than 300 silent fiction films which were produced in The Netherlands between 1896 and 1933, three-quarters are missing.

In addition, films of and about Amsterdam have been particularly popular; more than 1,000 nonfiction films with the city as a backdrop were made in the years 1896–1940. In the postwar years, the Dutch industry emphasized documentaries, a number of which have vanished.

### Aan Boord van de "Sabina" (On Board the "Sabina")

(Theo Frenkel, 1920). Amsterdam Film. **Script:** Frenkel. **With** Kees Lageman (skipper), Lily Bouwmeester (the daughter), Frits Bouwmeester, Jr., and Dio Huysmans. Also called *De Tocht met de Sabina* (*The Trip on the Sabina*), the film records the arduous lives of crew members, including the women, working on the barges and canals of the country. On board the barge "Sabina," the teenage daughter of the skipper catches the attention of two hired hands. When the man she favors commits a theft and is sent to jail, she takes his place pulling the boat. They unite when he is freed.

### De Aanranding op het Frederiksplein (The Assault on Frederik's Square)

(1919). Who plays whom in this production is unknown. Ads claimed a cast of "Dutch artistes." It is a farce that begins when Mrs. Jansen is accosted by Sintradelius, a notorious womanizer, on Frederik Square. He follows her home, where the situation becomes more dire because Mr. Jansen is away on business. Mina, the fishwife, is willing to act as a stand-in for 10 guilders. The two hatch a plan. Mina drinks a couple of glasses and Aaltje, the maid, turns on the gramophone. Then into this convivial atmosphere walks not the womanizer but Mr. Jansen. Mina takes him for the assailant, and throws him out — twice. After the confusion is cleared up, Mina receives her money for a job too-well done.

### Ah! ah! die Oscar! (Aw! Aw! That Oscar!)

Albert Mullens and Willy Mullens, 1904). Alberts Frères. **Photography:** Albert Mullens. In 1904, pioneer traveling exhibitors and fairground showmen Albert and Willy Mullens, who performed under the name Alberts Frères, began producing films. One of their half-dozen earliest comedies was this one (also called De Gevolgen van een huwelijksadvertentie [The Consequences of a Wedding Announcement]), which appeared a year before their more well known The Misadventures of a French Gentleman Without His Trousers at Zandvoort.

The brothers had an effortless visual flair for humor, with their films often ending in a chase. In this film, Oscar places an ad in the town newspaper: he's seeking a bride. Flooded with responses, he winds up fleeing from a host of eligible young women from Scheveningen. He's last seen scampering out into the country.

### American Girls

(Maurits H. Binger and Louis Davids, 1918). Hollandia. **Script:** Binger and Davids. **With** Beppie de Vries (Beppie Brown), Lola Cornero (Lola Brown), Margie Morris (Margie Brown), Paula de Waart (governess), Adelqui Migliar (Adelqui, the opera singer), Annie Bos (Anny, an actress), Louis Davids (Tinus, the private eye), Cor Smits (James Brown), Max van Gelder (impresario), and Jan van Dommelen. This light operetta (also called Amerikaansche meisjes) was one of the most well received Dutch comedies in its day, earning a five-week premiere. With accompanying musical selections by the multitalented Davids, it became one of the finest examples of Binger and his acting troupe's work, especially that of Davids playing an undercover detective who, in the course of his assignment, assumes a dozen disguises, from doctor to governess to pianist and streetsweeper.

In this convivial, naughty five-reel (2,200-meter) production, three rich Americans, loose in Amsterdam, bet the actress-girlfriend of a handsome young tenor at the Rembrandt Theater that they can win his attention.

They're outsmarted by the actress and her wily private detective — whose job it is to keep an eye on the unsuspecting opera singer.

## Amsterdam

(Henk Kleinman, 1928). Kleinmans Filmfabricatie. **Photography:** Andor von Barsy. A two-reel (850-meter) documentary look at the thriving city's architecture that represents the first Dutch experiment in sound. Also called *Een Filmreis door Nederland* (*A Film Trip Through Holland*), the production begins with the title "In film tempo through Amsterdam as a center of Art, Architecture, Business, and Industry." The panoramic production contains scenes of the Rijksmuseum, Rembrandtplein (Rembrandt Square), and St. Nichols Church, as well as scenes of the diamond industry, new apartment buildings, and the Jewish quarter of the city (along Jodenbreestraat). It also includes shots of the director shooting scenes at the Rembrandt Theater. In 1931, a 600-meter version of the film was released (with updated titles and the same background sounds).

## Amsterdam bij Nacht (Amsterdam by Night)

(Theo Frenkel, 1924). Dutch Film Co. **Script:** Frenkel and Herman Bouber. **With** Louis Davids, Heintje Davids, Willem van der Veer (Berend), Agnes Marou (Mrs. Berend), Kitty Kluppel (Stien), Carl Veerhoff (Dr. Gerard van Maanen), Jean Jensens (Mooie Louis), and Julie Roos. Beginning with documentary footage, the harsh six-reel (1,900-meter) melodrama, based on Bouber's play *Ronde Ka*, features the highly popular, many-sided Louis Davids playing himself and performing his famous folk street dances in the working-class Jordaan district of Amsterdam. "First a couple of picturesque views of Amsterdam from a bird's-eye view," go the titles, after which a clown draws back a curtain to reveal a slum at night. There a young doctor tends to Miss Stien, a poor woman of easy virtue, who has a broken leg. He falls in love with her, unaware that she is involved in a murder.

Dutch critics were quick to point out that "public house and nightlife as well as the pregnancy of an unmarried woman make this movie inaccessible to those under 18 years of age"; it is a story "set in the world of prostitutes and pimps." In the 1937 sound version codirected by Alex Benno, Davids is absent.

## Amsterdam in Woord en Beeld (Amsterdam in Word and Picture)

(Alex Benno, 1924). Actueel Film. **With** Alex de Meester (city guide), Jan van Dommelen, and Riek de la Mar-Kleij. A two-reel (580-meter) comedy about a group of tourists taking in the town by motorcoach — and a real-life look at the metropolis, including "well-known Dutch artists and various animals: cows, horses, pigs, dogs, sheep," wrote the critics. The visitors wind up in a traffic jam. During a tour that, among other things, takes them past Rembrandtplein, their guide tells them jokes about Amsterdam.

What made the film memorable was the fact that animal sounds were simultaneously piped into the theater.

## Amsterdam op Hol! (Amsterdam Running Riot!)

(Louis Chrispijn, Jr., and Léon Boedels, 1911). Filmfabriek Franz Nöggerath. **With** Isodoor Zwaaf. A combination fiction film and revue, this early Dutch production begins with the comedian Zwaaf sitting quietly in his apartment. He gets a phone call, and is told to hurry to the Flora Theater to take part in a last-minute revue. His race through town and to the performance turns humorous and exhausting. Appearing in the real-life revue scenes with him are Louis de Bree, Eduard Jacobs, Jan Biederman, and Marie van Rinko, among others.

## Aqua di Roma

(Boud Smit, 1962). Netherlands Ministry of Works. **Photography:** Anton von Munster and Jan Vonk. **Music:** Henk van Lijnschooten. A highly praised, 12-minute "camero" about the ancient city seen as leitmotiv of water: aqueducts, fountains, wells, street cleaners, and thirsty people. Containing no commentary, the gently humorous, swiftly edited, and keenly observed film "gets under the skin of a hot summer afternoon," wrote a European critic, "with remarkable accuracy."

## De Arnhemsche Medeminnaars (The Rivals from Arnhem)

(Alfred Machin, 1912). Hollandsche Film/Pathé. **Design:** Raoul Morand. **With** Léon Mathot. This Dutch-French production (also called De Medeminnaars van Arnheim and Les Rivaux d'Arnheim; English title, The Lock) was directed by the man many consider Europe's first filmmaker. Alfred Machin (1877–1929) was a Belgian-born director who made more than 150 films in his career. More than four-fifths of his films are lost.

Working at Pathé's Dutch branch, he made a smoothly told tale of joy and sorrow — much of which is in color. It concerns the brothers Hans and Pieter who, while visiting their great aunt, get into their first squabble — over their wooing of beautiful cousin Anna. She chooses Pieter, but Hans vows to disrupt the wedding. When Pieter least expects it, Hans sends him flying into a whirlpool in a river. However, he is rescued by people living along the water. When Hans is found guilty of attempted murder, Pieter goes to great lengths to get him a pardon. In the end, brotherly affection saves the day in this 265-meter work.

## Artistenrevue

(Alex Benno, 1925). Actueel. **With** Alex de Meester (the director), Isodoor Zwaaf (Flipje), Pauline Hervé/Pauline de Munnik, Césarine Speenhoff-Prinz, Marie Schafstad, Stella Seemer, Koos Speenhoff, Aida de Beau Clair, The Six Actueel Girls, Matthieu van Eysden, Adèle Boesnach, Eli Frank, The Bellings (jugglers), and The Casino Dancing Girls. Also called De Artisten-Revu and Revue artistique, this five reel (1,600-meter) farce, based on Michael Solser's Revue artistique, centers on Flipje — a man of a dozen occupations and even more failures — and his attempt to put together the best variety show in town. The skimpy plot served as an ample-enough reason to show off popular Dutch music-hall entertainers of the day. Critics called the farce "ultracomical in words and pictures."

## Attractive Archibald

(1912). Filmfabriek Franz Nöggerath. **With** Johan Buziau (Archibald), Jef Mertens, and Cato Mertens-de Jaeger. In a Dutch production shown only in Britain, the popular comedian Buziau plays a soldier assigned to work in the home of his colonel. In spite of his funny appearance, every young woman he meets fall for him. After a number of pratfalls, his commanding officer takes stern measures: he strips him of his uniform — the secret to his success — and throws him out of the house.

## De Avonturen van een Suiker-tante (The Adventures of a Sweet Aunt)

(1915). Filmfabriek Hollandia. Also called *De Suikertante*, the 250-meter comedy about a woman who decides it's never to late to get married — she places an ad seeking an eligible bachelor — was produced by Maurits H. Binger.

## Een Avontuur van een Abonné van de Stads-Editie (An Adventure of a Subscriber to the City Edition)

(Albert and Willy Mullens, 1909). Alberts Frères. **Photographer:** Albert Mullens. A reader of Haarlem's newspaper *Oprechte Haarlemsche Courant,* the city edition of the title, is the centerpiece of this farce by the early comedy filmmakers.

## Azor, de Hond van Alberts Frères als Politie (Azor, the Alberts Brothers' Policedog )

(Albert and Willy Mullens, 1907). Alberts Frères. **Photography:** Albert Mullens. A short comedy from the early comedy directors.

## De Bannelingen (The Exiles)

(Caroline van Dommelen and Léon Boedels, 1911). Filmfabriek Franz Nöggerath. **Script:** Caroline van Dommelen. **With** Caroline van Dommelen (Alexandra Iwanovna Medjanof), Cato Mertens-de Jaeger (Warwara Bogodouchow), Louis van Dommelen, Jef Mertens, Oscar Tourniaire, Jan van Dommelen, Jan Buderman, Anton Roemer, Manus Hulsman, and Wim Grelinger. Also called *De Verbanning naar Siberie* (*Banishment to Siberia*), this 50-minute (1,000-meter) film was made by one of the world's first woman directors.

Loosely based on the Oscar Wilde's first play, the 1880 four-act drama, *Vera, or the Nihilists,* it is about a young group of Russian revolutionaries, led by a woman, who plot to murder the czar. The nihilists are infiltrated by an aristocrat who notes, "This is the ninth conspiracy I have seen in Russia. They always end in a voyage en Siberie for my friends and a new decoration for myself." But the leader of the group falls in love with the czar and instead of killing him, commits suicide. Her last words are, "I have saved Russia."

## De Bertha (The "Bertha")

(Louis Chrispijn, Sr., 1913). Filmfabriek Hollandia. **With** Louis Chrispijn, Sr., and Christine van Meeteren

(Margaret). The golden period of Hollandia studios ran from 1912 to 1923, during which the actor-director Chrispijn and his wife Christine van Meeteren worked for the studio. This 925-meter film is the tale of heroic Margaret Verner, daughter of the captain of a ship called "Bertha." She is in love with a young inventor, and when she learns of a plot to sink the ship for the insurance money, the two of them play a crucial role in sending a telegraph that saves ship and crew.

The film was released in Belgium, and never shown in The Netherlands.

## Bleeke Bet

(Alex Benno and Ernst Lubitsch, 1923). Actueel Film. **Photography:** Max van Lier and H. W. Metman. **Design:** Piet Mossinkoff. **With** Alida Gijtenbeek (Bleeke Bet), Beppie de Vries (Jans), Rika Kloppenburg (Trui), Henriëtte Blazer (Ka), Piet Urban (Van Santen), Herman Bouber (Sally Matteman), Harry Boda (Ko Monjé), Kees Weerbenburg (Hannes), Jan van Dommelen (Tinus), Heintje Davids, and Louis Davids. Based on Herman Bouber's emotional 1917 play of the same name, Benno and Lubitsch's six-reel (1,750-meter) comedy-drama features the all-around entertainer Davids in one of his greatest successes. The film, one of Lubitsch's least known efforts, contains Louis Davids' famous street dance number "Radijs-Wats." Music and lyrics written by Davids — sung by a lecturer and often joined by audiences — accompanied the film's showing. Some scenes were filmed in Britain.

In this tale of intrigue, Van Santen is a miserly landlord who gouges his working-class tenants. He schemes to have his son, Hannes, marry Bet's beautiful daughter, Jans. The young woman, however, loves Ko. All's well that ends well when Van Santen and son disappear, and the lovers reunite. "Scenes of drunken fathers and drunken students," warned Dutch critics, "undermine parental authority."

Benno directed folksy comedy for his own company, Actueel Film, in the period 1921–1927, as well as for the Dutch Film Co., where Theo Frenkel also worked in the period 1924–1926.

## De Cabaret-Prinses

(Theo Frenkel, 1925). Dutch Film Co. **Script:** Frenkel. **Design:** Piet Mossinkoff. **With** Emmy Arbous (La Manuela), August van den Hoeck, Esther de Boer-van Rijk, Co Balfoort (Willem), André van Dijk, Jr. (Hendrik), Agnès Marou (Jeanne), Riek de la Mar-Kleij, and Jacques van Bijlevelt. A dark, six-reel drama of revenge that centers around the alluring dancer La Manuala and the brothers Willem and Hendrik who, in their search for love, nearly bring ruination upon their family. Also known as De Danseres van Montmartre, the production by the highly regarded Frenkel was the next-to-last work in his long career. The prolific Frenkel directed more than 200 films, in Britain, France, Germany, and Holland, in a 20-year career.

## Children of the Rhine

(Henry C. James, 1955). Netherlands Government Information Service. A ten-minute documentary about the lives of children on Rhine barges, made by a British director who was also responsible for the documentary *Rembrandt, a Man of Amsterdam*.

## De Damenscoupeur (The Ladies' Tailor)

(Maurits H. Binger, 1919). Hollandia. **Script:** Hans Nesna. **With** Cor Ruys (Jacques), Henny Schröder (Georgette), Jeanne van der Pers (Lily), Paula de Waart, Yvonne George, and Kitty Kluppell. Binger, who worked as a book printer, was Hollandia's finest director-producer. This is a rare four-reel (1,660-meter) comedy by the director and his studio about romantic and business entanglements centering around Jacques, the expert tailor at The Four Seasons fashion house who loves the owner's daughter, Lily. When Jacques' boss Georgette finds out — before he does — that he has won 100,000 guilders in the lottery, she fears he'll quit — and successfully schemes to sign him to a long-term contract. After he's collected his winnings, Jacques becomes a man about town — he especially likes entertaining the girls at the Café de Paris — but is limited in his actions by that binding contract.

In the cast was the beautiful, up-and-coming singer Yvonne George.

## Een Danstragedie

(Johan Gildemeijer, 1916). Rembrandt Film. **With** Adelqui Migliar (Mario), Meina Irwen (Meina), Piety en Jo Wigman (daughter), Christine Poolman (Mario's mother), Louis Gimberg, Caroline van Dommelen, Georgys (dance partner), and Piet Wigman. An eye-opening 1,700-meter drama about the struggle to realize one's dreams. It centers around the beautiful Meina, married to Mario, a musician. The crisis of their lives is precipitated when she announces her desire to become a dancer. Leaving her jealous and self-centered husband and their child, she makes a life for herself and establishes her name as an exotic, alluring, and scantily-clad performer of daring routines such as "Vision de Salome" and "Danse de Poignard." Only years later, when their daughter is dying, do they reconcile.

The notoriety of the lead and the unconventional plot had the critics bemoaning the production.

## Don Juan

(Léon Boedels, 1913). Filmfabriek Franz Nöggerath. **With** Willem van der Veer, Caroline van Dommelen, Tilly Lus, and Constant van Kerckhoven. One of the earliest adaptations of Molière's 1665 play about seduction and betrayal was this three-reel drama starring the excellent performer van der Veer — in one of his first films.

## De Drei Wensen (The Three Wishes)

(Kurt Gerron, 1937). Manenti Film Odeon/Roma. **Script:** F. Zeckendorff and Herman Bouber. **Dialogue:** A.H. de Jong. **Photography:** Akos Farkas. **Editor:** Jan Teunissen. **With** Annie van Duyn (Maria Scudo, the governess), Jan Teulings (Tino Murante), Mimi Boesnach (Cora Corelli), Jules Verstraete (the millionaire), Herman Bouber, and Kurt Gerron. Jewish actor-director Gerron, a costar in *The Blue Angel* (1929–30), in Brecht's original production of *The Threepenny Opera*, and a director at Ufa, brought to the screen, with some difficulty, this "charming and often original" comedy-drama (based on a fairy tale by the Brothers Grimm) about a millionaire who grants his governess three wishes. Maria's first wish is that he make her boyfriend a success. That done, her boyfriend takes up with Cora. Maria then requests that that woman becomes a successful opera star, but she still fails to get her boyfriend back. Even though a third try doesn't quite bring him back to her, the film ends happily.

Gerron filmed the lighthearted 82-minute production in Rome (the Italian version is called *I tre desideri*) and it claimed "splendid settings" and excellent editing, "which gives the picture a better pace than the usual Dutch productions," wrote a critic. Director Gerron, whose *Het Mysterie van de Mondschein Sonate* (*The Mystery of the Moonshine Sonata*) (1939) was the first Dutch detective film, died in Auschwitz.

### De Duivel (The Devil)

(Theo Frenkel, 1918). Amsterdam Film. **Script:** Frenkel. **With** Tonny Stevens (Earl Henri de Vere), Charles Mögle (J. Verburg), Annie Wesling (Henriëtte van Marle), Frits Bouwmeester, Jr., Cor Smits, Maurits Parser (Lablache), Herman Schwab, and Lous Korlaar-van Dam. A disturbing "docudrama" about the evils of gambling in which a young aristocrat is nearly brought to ruin by his "friend" Verburg. The film ends happily with the protagonist and his wife escaping to a better life in Canada. The four-reel (1,500-meter) production is also called *De Wraakzuchtige* (*The Vindictive*) as well as *In Duivelsklauwen* (*In the Devil's Clutches*).

### De Duivel in Amsterdam (The Devil in Amsterdam)

(Theo Frenkel, 1919). Amsterdam Film. **Script:** Frenkel. **With** Eduard Verkade (the Devil), Maggie Morris (Thérèse), Louis Bouwmeester (Van Rijn), Lily Bouwmeester, Jacques Reule, Mientje van Kerckhoven-Kling, and Louis Davids. Another Dutch tale of woe and warning from Theo Frenkel, this frightening film was based on the 1907 play by Ferenc Molnár, *Az Ordög* (*The Devil*). Satan (introduced in the prologue) leaves hell to do his malicious work on earth. He assumes the guise of Amsterdam citizens — whether gentleman, plumber, or gardener — to move among the unsuspecting. Appearing all of a sudden from a chimney or out of the ground, he exercises his work in the villas of the rich as well as the dwelling places of the poor; in the playground and in the store. He causes an accident in which a child is hit by a car and dies; induces a man to become addicted to gambling; and incites another to shoot a rival lover. At the end of the seven-reel (2,300-meter) drama, Satan, having done his work on earth, escorts three victims to hell.

### Eiland van Vertrouwen (Island of Trust)

(John Fernhout). Fernhout (1913–87) was the cinematographer of Joris Ivens's *The Breakers* (1929), *New Earth* (1934), *Spanish Earth* (1937), and *The 400 Million* (1938), and (under the name John Ferno) Raymond Spottiswoode's *The Fighting Dutch* (1943). He directed the documentaries *L'Ile de Pâques* (*Easter Island*) (1934), *Gebroken Dijken* (1945), and *Het Laatste Scot* (1945), and the shorts *Mercator* (1935), *A.B.C.* (1958), *Blue Peter* (1958), *Fortress of Peace* (1965), and *Delta Data* (1968). His *Sky Over Holland* (1967) received an Academy Award nomination as best short of the year. In 1971 he made *The Tree of Life.*

## Fatum (Fate)

(Theo Frenkel, 1915). Rembrandt Film. **Script:** Johan Gildemeijer. **With** Louis Davids, Henriette Davids, Louis Bouwmeester (Kobus Drost), Julie Frenkel-Meijer (Anna), John Timrott (Arend), Aaf Bouber, and Piet Fuchs. The debut film by the production company was a passionate, painful feature about a Dutch farmer who murders for love and ends with the talented Louis David's performance of a popular dance in the café Jordaans of Amsterdam.

Arend and Anna (both illiterate in highly educated Holland) are in love. When Arend is mobilized, Anna marries the rich farmer Kobus. When Arend returns, tragedy follows. Kobus kills Arend, and lands in jail for two years. Anna flees to Amsterdam, where Kobus eventually tracks her down in a dance hall. However, the shock of seeing her in such an place kills him at the moment he shouts, "Men, that is my wife." When the four-reel (70-minute) film (which costars David's wife Julie Frenkel-Meijer) was shown, the accompanying music came from the very typical Amsterdam barrel-organ.

## Gebroken Levens (Shattered Lives)

(Louis Chrispijn, Sr., 1914). Hollandia. **With** Annie Bos (Leida van Galen), Louis Bouwmeester, Sr. (Arie van Galen), Esther de Boer-van Rijk (Koos), Louis Chrispijn, Jr. (Max de Nessel), Coba Kinsbergen, Lau Ezerman, Mien Kling, Jan van Dommelen, Alex Benno, Barend Barendse, Louis Chrispijn, Sr., Willem van der Veer, and Fred Homann. A drama of injustice, the film was based on Otto Zeegers's 1911 play *Het Heilig Recht* (*The Sacred Right*). The four-reel (1,100-meter) production (also called *De Dochter van de Portier* [*The Door-Keeper's Daughter*] as well as *Heilig Recht*) starred three of the nation's best loved performers — Bouwmeester, Esther de Boer-van Rijk, and Bos — in the tale of an innocent man (and former officer) sent to jail for murder, and the subsequent impoverishment of his wife and daughter.

## Gegroet Mijn Limburg (Hello My Limburg)

(1955). Firma P. Pans. A one-hour color documentary about Holland's county of Limburg, focusing on daily life and industrial activity.

## Gloria fatalis

(Johan Gildemeijer, 1922). Munich Filmindustry/Rembrandt Film. **Script:** Gildemeijer. **With** Emmy Arbous (Sybil Mora), Gustav Semler (schoolmaster), and Mimi Irving. This was one of the first postwar Dutch-German productions — shot in Munich and released in 1924 — a six-reel (1,900-meter) drama of a woman giving up too much for her art. Also known as *Het Noodlot van den Roem,* it centers on the celebrated opera singer Mora who after falling in love and marrying a village organist and having a daughter, yearns for her earlier life. Her abandonment of her family leads to tragedy for all.

The tale was the sequel to Gildemeijer's popular *Gloria Transita* (*Faded Glory*) (1918), which was a tinted opera film — yellow for day scenes, blue for night — about the rise and fall of another beautiful opera singer which contains scenes from *Faust, I pagliacci*, and the climax from Verdi's *Rigoletto*.

### Gouda, het Hart van Holland (Gouda, the Heart of Holland)

(J. Kuysters, 1951). Views of the beautiful town of Gouda are presented in this 20-minute color documentary (in 16 mm) aimed at travelers.

### Helleveeg (Hellcat)

(Theo Frenkel, 1920). Amsterdam Film. **Script:** Frenkel. **Photography:** Dijkstra. **Design:** Theo van der Lugt. **With** Mien Duymaer van Twist (Jane), Co Balfoort (Willem Hendriks), Lily Bouwmeester (Louise), Frits Fuchs (Willem's brother), Theo Mann-Bouwmeester (Mrs. Van Wijck), Herman Schwab, and Johan Lüger. Another warning to Dutch men to beware of woman as vixen, especially the foreign kind, this four-reel (1,600-meter) production begins when the widower Willem Hendriks leaves the safety of Holland. He immigrates to California, leaving his daughter Louise in the care of the Van Wijck family. In charge of a nightclub, Willem meets Jane, the "hellcat" with an unsavory reputation. After they marry, he takes her back to Amsterdam where Jane, who had apparently reformed her ways, reverts to her former self. Willem begins drinking heavily, and she encourages him to buy a bar. There

Jane tries to offer Louise (who is engaged) to other men. But her brother-in-law sees in her only trouble, and while making an effort to protect Louise, he kills Jane. Saved, Louise reconciles with her fiancé and Willem gives up drinking.

### Holland Hails You

(1948). Fibo Beeldonderwijs. This 20-minute color documentary (in 16 mm) was one of the earliest of Holland's postwar films to offer general tourist information about The Netherlands.

### In Nieuwe Banen (In New Banen)

(Otto van Neijenhoff, 1951). A 45-minute color documentary (in 16 mm) by the prolific van Neijenhoff (1898–1977) about the development of industry in central Holland after the war. It was the first such film to look at the subject.

### Jimmy Walker

(Caspar Willers, 1962) A documentary about James J. Walker (1881–1946), the professional songwriter who turned politician and was elected mayor of New York City at the height of the jazz age, in 1925. As a dapper-dressed man-about-town he reflected much of its fizz, but with the Depression he lost popularity and, under investigation for corruption, left office in 1932.

### Kee en Janus naar Berlijn

(Alex Benno, 1922). Actueel. **Script:** Benno. **With** Adriënne Solser (Kee Mol) and Kees Pruis (Janus Mol). In this hugely popular comedy success of its day, long-married Kee and Janus, parents of two children and residents of the working-class Jordaan district of Amsterdam, win the lottery and head out of town. Their destination is Berlin where, they are told, everything is attractive and affordable. What they find are officious people who only give them trouble. They also lose most of their possessions, and in the end are relieved to make it back to Amsterdam. If ever they win money again, one place they'll never set eyes on again, they promise, is Germany.

Director Benno (born Benjamin Bonefang in Germany) shot the exteriors of this 1,500-meter film (also called *Kee en Janus in Duitschland*) in Berlin following the great success of *De Jantjes* (*The Jack-Tars*) (1922).

## Kee en Janus naar Parijs

(Alex Benno, 1923). Dutch Film Co. **Script:** Benno. **Photography:** Jan Smit. **Design:** Piet Mossinkoff. **With** Piet Köhler (Janus Meiblom), Adriënne Solser (Kee Mol), Sophie Willemse, Louis Richard, Kees Weerdenburg (Gerrit de Slome), Cor Weerdenburg-Smit (Griet), Johan Elsensohn (Hein Brommerd, alias de Jatter), Jan Nooij (Rinus Kous), Hans Brüning, Frans Meermans, André van Dijk, G. Caap, Beppie de Vries, and Alie Blanket. Seven years after Janus has died, his widow Kee decides to wed again. In the five-reel comedy, Kee marries Janus II — her new husband is also named Janus — and they plan to spend their honeymoon in the City of Lights. Once more, the team of Kee and Janus runs into trouble in a foreign city and, like the earlier adventure in Berlin, are happy to make it home in one piece — even if penniless. Still, they can regale their working-class friends with tales of having seen the Eiffel Tower and having been to the Moulin Rouge.

## Koolzaad (Rapeseed)

(1944). Macrofilm. In the Dutch province of Flevoland, this major agricultural product helped the country's economy during the closing days of the war. This documentary set the pattern for the Dutch industrial documentaries of the postwar years.

## Land in Nood (Land in Need)

(K. Visser, 1953). A two-reel (40-minute) color documentary (in 16 mm) about how the Dutch Society of Animal Protection rescued cattle during the terrible floods of 1953. This was one of a series of color documentaries on animal protection that Visser, based in The Hague, shot in the postwar years.

## De Leugen van Pierrot (Pierrot's Lie)

(Maurits H. Binger, 1920). Hollandia. **Design:** Theo van der Lugt. **With** Esther de Boer-van Rijk (Pierrot's mother), Henny Schröder, Adelqui Migliar (Pierrot), Renée Spiljar, Jan van Dommelen, and Martijntje de Vries. Based on the 1915 single-act play *Histoire d'un Pierrot* by Jacques van Hoven, this one-hour (1,200-meter) tale of sorrow was released two years after it was made, near the end of Binger's reign at Hollandia. Pierrot courts and marries Louisette. But his wife leaves him when she discovers that a former rival has pushed Pierrot into a life of dissipation. Only the help of Pierrot's fatherly good friend, Pochinet, helps him to reunite with his wife and son after six years.

## Levensschaduwen (Shadow of Life)

(Theo Frenkel, 1916). Amsterdam Film. **Script:** Frenkel. **With** Coen Hissink (Henri van Dijck), Mary Beekman, Cor Smits, Tonny Stevens, Balthazar Verhagen, and Herre de Vos, and Theo Frenkel, Jr. A four-reel (1,500-meter) drama about the unfairness of life. When company man named van Dijct is cheated out of a scientific discovery that can save his firm from bankruptcy, he reacts by killing his firm's manager. He is imprisoned for ten years, and the dire effects on him and his family take a lifetime to undo.

## Het Licht Brak Door (The Light Breaks Through)

(du Parant, 1954). Firma du Parant. Made ten years after the war, this 60-minute color documentary (in 16 mm) presents the camp life of displaced persons and indicates the help given to unfortunate victims. It was one of numerous films of the era dealing with the national effort at "social assistance."

## Liefdesoffer (Love's Sacrifice)

(Maurits H. Binger, 1916). Hollandia. **With** Annie Bos (Margareet Barker), Willem van der Veer, Lola Cornero, Pierre Mols, and Paula de Waart (Mrs. Miles). A four-reel (1,250-meter) production, also called *Het Offer van Margareet Barker* (*Margaret Barker's Sacrifice*), that is a lesson in love. It stars the popular Annie Bos as the impoverished woman who struggles to keep alive her marriage to a medical stu-

dent. His trip to South America, during which she is hospitalized, brings their marriage to a crisis: he returns with a girlfriend. In the painful conclusion, she lets go of her husband when she realizes he is no longer in love with her.

## Liefdesstrijd (Love's Struggle)

(Maurits H. Binger, 1915). Hollandia. **With** Annie Bos (Kate van Marlen), Willem van der Veer (Earl Alfred van der Loo), Florent la Roche, Jr. (Lt. Ruprecht van Halden), Paula de Waart (Kate's mother), Martha Walden (Alice), Jan van Dommelen, Christine Chrispijn-van Meeteren, Louis Chrispijn, Sr., Louis van Dommelen, and Fred Homann. A four reel (1,225-meter) drama of woe starring the popular Annie Bos as the woman caught between two lovers, a selfish aristocrat and a lieutenant. Her inability to see what's best for her leads to tragedy.

## Liefde Waakt (Love Wakes)

(Louis Chrispijn, Sr., 1914). Hollandia. **Script:** Simon Maris. **Design:** Theo van der Lugt. **With** Annie Bos (Jennie), Willem van der Veer, Christine Chrispijn-van Meeteren, Jan van Dommelen (Raymond), Jan Holtrop, Mien Kling, Alex Benno, Emile Timrott, and Marius Spree. A three-reel (925-meter) crime drama (also called *De Levende Mummie*) that centers on the model Jenny and a sculptor, Raymond, who loves her. The young woman's involvement with a gang of thieves leads to near death for her lover — entombment in a sarcophagus — before the happy ending.

## Limburg's Land en Volk (Limburg's Land and People)

(Herbert Leufkens, 1948). A 25-minute, postwar color documentary about the county of Limburg, focusing on its folklore and industry.

## Madame Pinkette & Co.

(Maurits H. Binger, 1917). Hollandia. With Annie Bos (Liane Fraser), Jan van Dommelen, Paula de Waart (Peggy), Adelqui Migliar, Cecil Ryan, Alex Benno, and Louis van Dommelen. A morality tale, based on Arthur Aplin's 1913 story *The Girl Who Saved His Honour*, about an adventurous young woman, Liane Fraser, a former telephonist and now manager of the fashion salon called Madame Pinkette. When the bookkeeper of the financially strapped salon is found dead in her apartment—Liane claims innocence—she is blackmailed. Most of the 1,200-meter production revolves around Liane's attempt to clear her name and save the saloon. She does this by taking a jockey's place and riding his horse to victory. Scantily clad women and a portrait of an unconventional marriage had the critics attacking the film.

## Made in Holland

(Max de Haas, 1951). Also called *Beautiful Things from Holland*, the short was directed by the prolific documentary pioneer who received an honorable mention at the Cannes Festival for his short *Jour de mes Années* (1960).

## Mooi Joultje van Volendam (Beautiful Juliet from Volendam)

(Alex Benno, 1924). Actueel Film. Script: Benno. Design: Piet Mossinkoff and Christiaan Lund. With Annie Bos (Juultje), Jan Kiveron (Sander), August van den Hoeck (Barendse), Remi Rasquin (Meesen), Pierre Balledux (Piet), Frans Bogaert (Rekveld), Marie Verstraete (Trees Barendse), Willem van der Veer (Willem Nijland), Johan Elsensohn (Toon), Arthur Sprenger, and Piet Fuchs. This was one of the most popular and successful Dutch features of the time, based on the 1920 play of the same name by Johan Lemaire. A six-reel (70-minute) Belgian coproduction about the trials and tribulations of the prettiest girl from a village who yearns for the gay life of Brussels, it starred the popular Bos in her last film role. The highly regarded Hugo de Groot composed the successful title song to the production, also called *Het Schone meisje van Volendam* and *La Belle de Volendam*.

## Mottige Janus (Scarface Janus)

(Maurits H. Binger, 1922). Hollandia. Script: Binger. Photography: Feiko Boersma. With Maurits de Vries (Janus Rechtsom), Meijer van Beem (Nathan), Kitty Kluppell (Lena Dorn), August van den Hoeck, Feiko Boersma, and Frits Bouwmeester. Based on a popular play by A. Weruméus Buning, the production was one of Binger's last (he died in 1923), after which Holland's most prolific studio went out of business. In this five-reel (1,450-meter) love story with an unhappy ending, Janus Rechtsom, nicknamed "Scarface," loves Lena, the girl next door. Although Lena once succumbed to Van Klarenberghe, she marries Janus. Not much later, he heads out to sea, leaving behind his wife and daughter. He returns three years later to find Lena married to her former lover. The shock drives him to drink, but things go awry for Lena as well, because Van Klarenberghe abandons her for another. Lena and daughter lead a sorrowful existence until a painful meeting reunites them with Janus. Lena dies knowing her daughter will be cared for by her father.

## Op de Wieken (Upon the Wing)

(K. Visser, 1954). This 30-minute color documentary (in 16 mm) presents information about the foddering of hungry birds during Holland's harsh winters.

## Paramount op Parade

(J. Weening and Ernst Lubitsch, 1930). Paramount. **With** Louis Davids, Theo Frenkel, Jr., Mien Duymaer van Twist, Charles Rogers, Lilian Roth, Jack Oakie, Zelma O'Neal, Warner Oland, William Powell, Maurice Chevalier, Evelyn Brent, Richard Arlen, Jean Arthur, William Austin, George Bancroft, Clara Bow, Mary Brian, Clive Brook, Nancy Carroll, Gary Cooper, Leon Erroll, Kay Francis, Mitzi Green, James Hall, Helen Kane, Dennis King, Abe Lyman's band, Nino Martini, David Newell, and Fay Wray. Filmed partially in Paris, Paramount's 110-minute (3,000-meter) Dutch musical revue features Theo Frenkel, Jr., the nephew of the well-known Dutch silent filmmaker, as well as the many-sided Louis Davids, the actor and composer of hundreds of songs, who sings "Tinus de verkeersagent."

## Het Proces Begeer (The Begeer Trial)

(Theo Frenkel, 1917–18). Amsterdam Film. **Script:** Frenkel. **Photography:** A. P. A. Adriaansz. **With** Jacques Sluyters (Jan Bolkestein), Willy Bruns (Marie), Annie Wesling (Toos), Chris de la Mar (Jan Hulsman), and Coen Hissink (Willem). This one-hour "docudrama" was released about a year after the events in question took place, based on the spectacular break-in of the Begeer Company, the well-known Amsterdam diamond concern. On the night of April 29, 1917, Jan Bolkestein, Willem Veltman, and Henri Klopper make their move, getting away with a stash in jewels. The police pursue them, but they vanish. Jan promises his girlfriend Marie, who was unaware of the crime, that he will make a new man of himself. They decide to marry. But before they do, the police capture the perpetrators. At the famous trial, the three are convicted and sentenced to six years behind bars.

The *Bioscop-Courant* called the tale an "Amsterdam sensation drama." The real Jan Bolkestein was called the "king of the Zeedlijk," a neighborhood in the city.

## Schakels (Links)

(Maurits H. Binger, 1919–20). Hollandia. **Script:** Binger. **Design:** Theo van der Lugt. **With** Jan van Dommelen (Pancras Duif), Adelqui Migliar (Henk Duif), Annie Bos (Marianne), Paula de Waart (Pancras' wife), Frits Bouwmeester, Jr. (Toontje), Jeanne van der Pers, Louis Davids (Jan Duif), Henny van Merle/Henny Schröder, Coen Hissink, Renée Spiljar, and Alex Benno. A surprising, upbeat feature based on the disturbing 1903 play by the highly regarded Herman Heijermans, whose favorite target was middle-class hypocrisy. Aside from *Op Hoop van Zegen* (*The Good Hope*), *Schakels* was the most often performed of Heijermans's plays. The 1,900-meter adaptation centers on what happens when Pancras Duif, the richest man in the area, decides to remarry.

Pancras Duif made his money the hard way: he earned it. Over a span of 25 years, from humble beginnings as a laborer, he worked hard, sacrificed, and saved. He was shrewd, and built a great iron works, called "The Link." Over the years he paid back his debts, helped others out of difficulties, including his son, a son-in-law, friends, and even a Jew or two.

Now, late in life, he is prepared to make his boldest move. His wife dead, he proposes to Marianne, his much younger housekeeper and caretaker, for her hand in marriage. His selfish, greedy, and self-absorbed children and their spouses — the heirs to his fortune — are aghast at the idea. And Marianne, though she cares for Pancras, rejects the offer because she has a child out of wedlock, and is a "woman with a past." While Pancras is ready to overlook such obstacles, Marianne knows that his children will do all they can to make her life miserable, if not stop the marriage. She decides to leave, but her son's illness brings her closer to Pancras who, despite opposition, keeps the mother and boy within his home. That's a surprisingly upbeat ending for a Dutch film of the era. In the original play, Marianne and child leave their benefactor to make their way in the hostile world.

### De Sensatie der Toekomst (The Thrill of the Future)

(Dimitri Buchowetski, 1931). Paramount. **With** Dolly Bouwmeester, Rolant Varno, Marie van Westerhoven, Charles Braakensiek, Johan Boskamp, Lien Deijers, and Hans Braakensiek. Paramount's only Dutch feature out of its Paris studio (also called *Televisie*) was one of the earliest Dutch sound films, containing the storyline and scenery of the studio's French-language *Magie moderne* (1931). In the 65-minute feature, a young man is nearly swindled out of his technological invention. The film is original in the sense that there was no Hollywood version.

### Vrouwenoogen (Women's Eyes)

(Caroline van Dommelen, 1913). Filmfabriek Franz Nöggerath. **Script:** Louis van Dommelen. **With** Caroline van Dommelen, Louis van Dommelen, Jan van Dommelen, Ansje van Dommelen-Kapper, and Cato Mertens-de Jaeger. A 900-meter work by one of the world's first woman directors that was called a "realistic biographical sketch."

# Portugal

In 1896, the Hungarian Erwin Rousby ventured to Portugal to show the first films in that country while Aurelio Paz dos Res was making the country's earliest shorts. By the end of the century Manuel de Costa Veiga had formed Veiga Portugal Film; the nation's second production company, Portugália Film, was founded five years later by João Freire Correia and Manuel Cardoso. These men were photographers, and their early films reflected their interest in cinematography. The first significant Portuguese film was *Os Crimes de Diogo Alves* (1910), directed by João Tavares for Portugália Film.

In 1917, Invicta Film studios, in Oporto, began film production. But it was not until after the war that Portuguese cinema underwent intensive development. Feverish activity possessed the centers of film production (especially at Invicta), which produced adaptations of the most popular and well-known 19th century Portuguese novels. Thus the best romances of Eça de Queroz, Camilo, Julio Diniz, and Manuel Pinheiro Chagas were translated to the screen. These efforts lasted until 1924, and "proved," wrote the critic Alves Costa, "that there was nothing to be feared in comparison with the current productions which arrived in Portugal from abroad."

The majority of films shown within the country from 1925 to 1930, however, came from Hollywood. In 1930, a renaissance of sorts occurred in Portuguese cinema. The Portuguese government legislated that no foreign phrases — not even a word — could be used in the titles of silent films or spoken in sound films shown within the country. That sparked the native industry, and set the competitive stage among foreign producers to make Portuguese-language films. The first sound film produced within Portugal was José Leitao de Barros's *A Severa* (November, 1930), backed by the German studio Tobis Klangfilm. Paramount in Paris, however, beat its German rival to the punch with Alberto Cavalcanti's melodrama *A Canção do berço* (1930). The studio followed with two other Portuguese-language films in Paris, *A Minha noite de núpcias* (1931) and *A Mulher que ri* (1931), comedies directed by Emmerich W. Emo. The moneymaking films were shown in Lisbon.

Though the talkies were a great success, they did not destroy the prestige accorded silent films. From 1911 to 1932, 67 silents (by the aforementioned studios as well as Lusitania-Film, Calde-villa-Film, Studio-Film, Iberia-Film, Fortuna Film, Enigma Film, Patria Film, and Lisboa Film) were produced within Portugal. Twenty-six were made by the French filmmakers Georges Pallu, Roger Lion, Maurice Mariaud, Mário Huguin, and Maurice Lauman, as well as the Italian Rino Lupo. Despite the fact that censorship existed, these filmmakers managed to get around it because they made their films within the country, whose fine climate was an added attraction to foreign filmmakers. Many of their films were shot "in the great studio which is Nature," wrote Alves Costa. "Herein lies the romance of Portugal's history of the cinema"— cinema which, during this period, took its "first steps towards world recognition." During the Second World War, Portuguese-Spanish productions accounted for a number of comedy hits and for most coproductions.

## *O amor fatal (Fatal Love)*

(Georges Pallu, 1920). Invicta Film. **Photography:** Albert Durot. **Design:** André Lecointe. **With** Alfredo Henriques, Clara Mussiana, Gastão Polónio, Duarte Silva, and María Emília Ferreira. Based on a story by Sérgio de Miranda, this four-part (2,000-meter) tragedy was made by Pallu made just before he made his classic *Amor de perdição* (*Ill-fated Love*) (1921).

## *Ave de Arribação (Migratory Birds)*

(Armando de Miranda, 1943). Cinelânda. **Photography:** Salazar Dinis. **Music:** Jaime Mendes. **With** Virgílio Teixeira (Marcos), Assis Pacheco, Leonor Maia, Maria Julieta, and Ricardo Malheiro. Filmed at sea, this neorealist drama about fisherman introduced to filmgoers the commanding performer Teixeira. This 114-minute film of adventure and love is set along the coast of the Algarve, and was directed by a man who knew the area well.

## Campinos (Fields)

(António Luís Lopes, 1932). **Script:** Lopes and María Helena Matos. **Photography:** Salazar Dinis. **With** Lopes, María Helena Matos, Rafael Lopes (the boy), Maria Lalande, Gil Ferreira, T. de Sousa, and Alvaro Negrão. This coming of age romantic drama, which was hailed for its outdoor footage, was just about the last Portuguese silent, though it was slated to be a sound film. Also called *Campinos do Ribatejo*, the production turned the young protagonist Rafael Lopes into a star. He "acted wonderfully and achieved a big success," wrote the critic Alves Costa.

## A Canção do berço (The Lullaby)

(Alberto Cavalcanti, 1930). Paramount. **Photography:** Ted Pahle. **With** Ester Leâo, Raúl de Carvalho, Corina Freire, Joaquim Alves da Costa, Alexandré Azevedo, and Antonio Sacramento. Cavalcanti's nine-reel (82-minute) production was Paramount's first Portuguese-language film out of Paris and represents Cavalcanti's only Portuguese film until his 1950s Brazilian films. The drama follows the heartfelt story of the studio's *Sarah and Son* (1930).

## O Comissário de polícia (The Police Commissioner)

(Georges Pallu, 1919). Invicta Film. **Photography:** Albert Durot. **Design:**

André Lecointe. **With** Rafael Marques (Sereno, the commissioner), Duarte Silva (Faustino), Maria Campos (Maria), Deolinda Sayal, Emília de Arbeu, Maria Oliveira, and Adolfo Quaresma. When French director Pallu signed a contract in 1918 with Invicta Film in Oporto, he helped put Portuguese films on the map, working in Portugal until 1925. One of his earliest productions for the studio was this burlesque, based on the late 19th-century satire of bourgeoisie manners by Gervásio Lobato. Lobato, as someone wrote, suffered from "comic hypertrophy." His work found the greatest favor when it ridiculed Lisbon society.

The four-reel (1,600-meter) film's text reflects the author's vital freshness and his rhythmic complications as it exposes the ridiculousness and prejudices of the urban middle class. That is made clear in the extravagances of the councilor Faustino who, though dominated at home by his wife Maria, is a womanizer. He chases the servants, all the while trying to pass himself off as a darling of a husband. The obvious truth, of course, made for laughter.

## O Condenando (The Condemned Man)

(Mário Huguin and Afonso Gaio, 1920). Portugália Film. **Script:** Gaio. **Photography:** Albert Durot and Ernesto de Albuquerque. **Design:** José Pacheco. **With** Joaquim de Oliveira (Lêndea), Maria Luísa Sampaio (Maria do Rosário), Virgínia Silva (Quitéria), Ana Pereira (Mariana), and Lina de Albuquerque (Josefa). Based on Gaio's 1916 play of the same name, the nine-reel film was one of the production company's major efforts and was codirected by a French filmmaker who had worked for Pathé.

## Fogo! (Fire!)

(Arthur Duarte and Alfredo Echegaray, 1949). Luso-Española. **Script:** Caridad Vega. **Photography:** Rafael Pacheco. **With** Raúl de Carvalho, Tony Leblanc (Juan), Nani Fernández, Emilio Arágon (Miguel), Teresa Casal (Elena), and Manolo Morán. A 104-minute Portuguese-Spanish drama filmed in Madrid, where it was called *Fuego!*, it's the tale of the heroic firefighter Juan and of his American-educated brother Miguel. Their love for the same woman leads to conflict — and to death.

## O Groom do Ritz (The Bellboy from the Ritz)

(Reinaldo Ferreira, 1923). Turia Pictures. **With** Aurèle Sidney, Alexandré Amores, Eduardo Graça, Luis de Magalhães, Alvaro Baptista, Alfredo Queirós, Lina de Albuquerque, and Beatriz Belmar. Based on the Spanish novella *El Botones del Ritz*, the sensationalist espionage tale starred the man who played the British man of justice, Ultus, and costarred a troupe of actors from the great film center of Barcelona. Taking place in a luxurious hotel, the five-reel tale of intrigue and double cross was shot in Lisbon.

## O Hóspede do quarto 13 (The Guest in Room No. 13)

(Arthur Duarte, 1946). Hermia Films. **Script:** Duarte and Eugène Deslaw. **Photography:** José Gaspar and Aquilino Mendes. **With** Alfredo Mayo (Duke of Gomara), Teresa Casal (Estela Nicolajeva), Rufino Ingelés (Eduardo), María Eugenia Branco (María Eugenia), and Esteban Amarante (Arriaga). A well-made 90-minute (2,500-meter) Portuguese-Spanish comedy-drama of intrigue and mystery filmed in Madrid, where it was called *El Huésped del cuarto no. 13*, the tale takes place in the Palace Hotel, where the Duke of Gomara resides. News from his American manager puts him in financial hot water. Also in the hotel is the daughter of the banker Arriaga, who's in love with him. Marriage offers a solution to the duke's problems. But when the banker's room is robbed, suspicion falls on the duke. His plans — and his future — appear to have suddenly gone up in smoke until the real culprits are captured. And then, when the wedding is back on track, comes more news from America.

## O Mais forte (The Stronger)

(Georges Pallu, 1919). Invicta Film. **Photography:** Albert Durot. **Design:** André Lecointe. **With** Pato Moniz, Duarte Silva, and Alfredo Henriques. This early effort by the French director Pallu (which came after *The Police Commissioner*) is a 1,500-meter drama in three parts, directed as a serial, with the popular theatrical performer and singer Henriques.

## O Milagre da Rainha (The Miracle of the Queen)

(António Leitão, 1930). Sociedade Universal de Superfilmes (SUS). **With** Fernanda Dinis (Queen Isabel), Armando de Carvalho (King Denis), Antonio Fagim, Lina Fontoura, Regina Fróis, and Heloísa Clara. Leitão's second film of his career was one of the last Portuguese silents, a rigorously constructed 1,800-meter tale evoking the figure and the reign of the great Queen Isabel (1271–1336), the sainted queen of the legend of "The Miracle of the Roses." Several important scenes were filmed in Coimbra.

Of Spanish birth (to the king of Aragon), Isabel marries at the age of 12 into the Portuguese royal house. There she endures an unfaithful and violent husband (King Denis), and turns her attention to works of piety at orphanages, hospitals, and the like. Assiduous in her concern for peace, she brings an end to a longstanding feud between her husband and her son, and just as important brings about a startling change in her husband's disposition before his death in 1325.

Isabel then becomes a Franciscan tertiary, adopting a simple life. In the last days of her life, she averts war between Portugal and Castile. After she dies in the town of Estremoz, near the Spanish border, miracles follow. Called "The Peacemaker" or "The Holy Saint," she is canonized in 1625.

### A Minha noite de núpcias (Her Wedding Night)

(Emmerich W. Emo, 1931). Paramount. **With** Beatriz Costa. Director E. W. Emo, who filmed Paramount's German-language musical comedy *Ich heirate meinen Mann* (1931) in Paris, retained the risqué elements in this 99-minute Portuguese-language version (also produced in Paris) that featured the newly discovered Beatriz Costa.

### A Morgadinha de Val-Flor (The Heiress of Val-Flor)

(Ernesto de Albuquerque, 1921–24). Briga Film. **Adaptation:** Augusto de Mello. **Photography:** de Albuquerque. **With** Auzenda de Oliveira, Maria Pia de Almeida (Mrs. Condessa), Maria Sampaio, Maria Santos (Luis Fernando), Erico Braga, Henrique Alves, Teixera Soares, and Arthur Duarte. A 2,150-meter high romantic comedy based on the popular 1870 five-act drama by the prolific Manuel Pinheiro Chagas, the film stars a troupe of theatrical performers from Lisbon.

### A Mulher que ri (The Woman Who Laughs)

(Emmerich W. Emo, 1931). Paramount. **With** Raúl de Carvalho and Joaquim Alves da Costa. A Portuguese-language comedy that is similar in style and content to Paramount's Spanish-language musical comedy *Lo mejor es réir* (1930), which Emo directed and Florián Rey supervised. This film is perhaps Paramount's most creative Portuguese feature from Paris, only loosely based on Harry D'Arrast's Hollywood hit *Laughter* (1930).

### Não há rapazes maus (There Are No Bad Children)

(Eduardo García Maroto, 1946). Lisboa Film. **Assistant Director:** Julio Buchs. **Story:** Armando Vieira Pinto. **Photography:** César Fraile. **Music:** João Mendes. **With** Raúl de Carvalho (Father Américo), Maria Lalande (María), Antonio Silva, Maria Matos, Assis Pacheco, and Carlos Otero. Called *No hay chicos malos* in Spain, the 98-minute (2,700-meter) film, photographed by the excellent cameraman Fraile, is a moving melodrama of hope, as personified by the emotional performance by Carvalho.

## Nua (Nude)

(Maurice Mariaud, 1931). Tágide Film. **Story:** Alberto Castro Neves. **With** Eduardo Malta, Saur Ben-Hafid, Rosa Maria, Tomás de Sousa, Dina Vilhena, and António Leitão. This was one of the last Portuguese silents, starring the well-known artist Malta and the exotic Ben-Hafid, who was called "a débutante with natural and valuable qualities." In the 91-minute action-packed adventure, which was filmed on the north coast, Ben-Hafid appears as a naked and quite alluring vampire.

## Quando o amor fala... (When Love Speaks...)

(Georges Pallu, 1921). Invicta Film. Made the same year Pallu made *Amor de perdição* (a three-hour Romeo and Juliet–like landmark of Portuguese cinema and one of the most beautiful films of the silent era — shown in the U.S for the first time in 1997), the production was one of Pallu's shortest (800-meter), which probably accounted for its limited distribution and subsequent disappearance.

## O Rei da força (The King of Strength)

(Ernesto de Albuquerque, 1922). Enigma Film. **Story:** Fernando Machado and Ruy da Cunha. **Photography:** de Albuquerque. **With** Ruy da Cunha, Lina de Albuquerque, Alvaro Baptista, Carlos Machad, and Amélia Perry. An eight-reel, Hollywood-style adventure that aimed to expose the great qualities of the star athlete and competitor Cunha, based on episodes from his life in the circus.

## A Sereia de pedra (The Siren of Stone)

(Roger Lion and Virginia de Castro e Almeida, 1922). Fortuna Film. **Adaptation:** Alberto Jardim. **Photography:** Marcel Bizot and Daniel Quentin. **With** Maria Emília Castelo Branco (Maria), Gil Clany (Léonore), Max Maxudian (Pedro), Arthur Duarte (Miguel Alves), Nestor Lopes (Claudio L'innocent), Francisco Senna (Fragoso), and Manoël Grillo (the bullfighter). Based on de Castro's spiritual classic of morality and righteousness, called *Obra do demónio* (*Work of the Demon*), the star-studded film was one of Portuguese cinema's most ambitions of the era. As the brain-child of de Castro, it was the first of two films that she and French director Lion collaborated on in Portugal. (Their second was *Os Olhos da alma* [*Eyes of the Soul*], 1923.)

This seven-reel (1,600-meter) production was their best collaborative effort, a beautiful, well-acted, and technically proficient production filmed in Tomar, Portugal. It was released in 1923 in France as *The Phantom of Love*. It was a huge hit, hailed for its originality and imagery, its perfection and accomplishment. When Virginia de Castro died, a prize for the best Franco-Portuguese production was created in her honor.

## O Suicida de boca do inferno (The Suicide of Hell's Mouth)

(Ernesto de Albuquerque, 1923). Enigma Film. **With** Alvaro Baptista (Humberto de Gusmão), Lina de Albuquerque (Maria Luísa), José Clímaco (João), Amélia Perry (Rosa), Maria Sampaio, and Júlio Branco. A highly ambitious, popular, complicated, eight-reel police drama, encompassing, love, hate, intrigue, and revenge — in a word, a battle between good and evil.

## Tempestades da vida (Life's Turmoils)

(Augusto de Lacerda, 1923). Invicta Film. **Supervisor:** Georges Pallu. **Script:** Lacerda. **Design:** André Lecointe. **With** Lacerda (Pedro Arrais), Brunilde Júdice (Rosa), Fernando Pereira (Joáo Maria), Aldina de Sousa (Túlia), Duarte Silva, and Alfredo de Sousa (Damião). A singular work of the era shot on location among fisherman at Póvoa de Varzim on the north coast of Portugal. Examining regional characteristics, the 2,500-meter film was made by a man of the theater who doubled as a man of letters. His effort was supervised by Invicta's top director, Pallu.

## A Tormenta (Tempest)

(Georges Pallu, 1924). Invicta Film. **Script:** Paulo Osório. **Photography:** Albert Durot. **Design:** André Lecointe. **With** Maria Clementina, António Pinheiro, and José Soveral. This production was Pallu's last Portuguese film, a little-seen 2,000-meter melodrama that signaled the end of an era in Portuguese filmmaking.

## Toureiros por amor (Bullfighters for Love)

(Alexandré Amores, 1930). Reporter X Film. **Photography:** Augusto Ribeiro Seabra. **With** Francisco Machado, Benjamin António Machado, and Julieta Palmeiro. An eagerly awaited, spirited, late Portuguese silent comedy, this film is about two bullfighters, Pato and Patochão, who approach the opposite sex as if doing battle in the ring. Amores's 1,000-meter attempt to create a comic duo was praised for its imagination.

## O Trevo das quatro folhas (The Four-Leaf Clover)

(Chianca de Garcia, 1936). Sonarte. **Script:** Garcia, José G. Ferreira, and Tomás Ribeiro Colaço. **Photography:** Garcia. **Music:** Frederico de Freitas. **Design:** Keil do Amaral and Bernardo Marques. **With** Beatriz Costa (Manuela/Rosita), Nascimento Fernandes, and Procópio Ferreira (Juca), Waldemar Mota (soccer official), and António Sacramento. This comedy was Garcia's first sound film, a 3,000-meter production that mocks the intensity with which Iberians respond to soccer. The production brought together the popular Iberian performers Fernandes and Costa and the great Brazilian comedian Ferreira.

## Ver e amar! (To See Is to Love!)

(Chianca de Garcia, 1930). Sociedade Geral de Filmes. **Photography:** Manuel Luís Viera. **With** Heloísa Clara, Erico Braga, Celeste de Oliveira, Alberto Rebelo, Mário Fernando, and Augusto Santos. The director's first screen effort "permits us to entertain great hopes for the future," wrote the critic Alves Costa. It is the work of one of the "young cineastes who, full of courage and faith, have made their debut in the difficult craft of creating images in movement."

This production, a likable, unpretentious 2,150-meter romantic parody of Hollywood methods (which includes a potshot at *Ben-Hur*), takes place during the carnival at São Luís. It stars the debutante Clara and the veteran stage performer Braga in one of the last Portuguese silents. Their film was made in the year Portuguese cinema was experiencing a rebirth.

## A Vida do soldado (The Soldier's Life)

(Anibal Contreiras, 1930). Lisboa. With Perpetua. Made by an amateur, the documentary was one of Portuguese cinema's last silents and one of the significant half dozen Portuguese films of the year. At 2,600-meter, it records the lives of Portuguese recruits.

In the Portugal of 1930, every physically fit man of 20 was obliged to enter the army. The film looks at the men from the Portuguese provinces who have to leave their families, their fiancées, and their homes and go to Lisbon to carry out their military service. For many of these young men, it is their first significant venture outside their native villages. The film documents (at times in romantic terms) their arrival in the capital, their first contact with big buildings, large avenues, traffic, policemen; in short, urban chaos. After their initial cultural shock, they begin life in the barracks and take part in the various exercises which continue for weeks and months until the end of military obligation.

Well photographed, this production signaled the arrival of a promising new director, though the attempt to mark an important trend in Portuguese filmmaking was overtaken by events. "Countries with a limited production can never throw themselves into cinematic realizations of superfilms," wrote the critic Alves Costa. "For these countries, pure or romantic documentary films are the ideally cinematographic forms to employ, and those that have the greatest guarantee of an artistic and commercial success." Nonetheless, the transition to sound overwhelmed the last Portuguese silents, and Contreiras' film vanished.

## Vida nova (New Life)

(Nascimento Fernandes, 1919). Portugal Films. **Script:** Ernesto Rodrigues, F. Bermudes, and João Bastos. **With** Fernandes and Amélia Pereira. This vaudeville comedy was advertised to the public in bold headlines that read, "Nascimento is in Portugal." The three-parter (2,600 meters) has the popular Barcelona actor-director Fernandes going through all sorts of trials and tribulations, including a boxing match, to win the girl of his dreams. Hugely popular in its day, the film vanished when Portuguese films went into decline in the mid–1920s.

## A Volta de José do Telhado (The Return of José do Telhado)

(Armando de Miranda, 1949). **Story:** Miranda and Gentil Marques. **Photography:** Aquilino Mendes. **Music:** Jaime Mendes. **Design:** Manuel Lima. **With** Virgílio Teixeira, Milu (Zara), Leonor Maia (Joaninha), and Juvenal de Araújo. Director Miranda dared to film a historical adventure about a legendary 19th century bandit and popular hero of the downtrodden at a time when his nation was under one-man rule. The lead role in the two-hour (10-reel, 3,500-meter) drama is played to the hilt by highly regarded Teixeira. The character's call to stand up to injustice was a critical failure in autocratic Portugal, where it was labeled, "By no means a shining work."

# Spain

Fructuoso Gelabert and Segundo de Chomón were responsible for the first fictional films in Spain, in the late 1890s. The region of Catalonia, whose principal city is Barcelona, was the mainstay of filmmaking in the years 1897–1923: nearly 500 films were produced in the 25-year period. Literary adaptations of works by Angel Guimerà and Jacinto Benavente and others dominated the early years of the century — and would make quite a retrospective today.

Cinematic tales of folklore and melodrama were important in the 1920s, especially those made by Florián Rey, José Buchs, and Benito Perojo. In September 1929, at the Barcelona Coliseum, Spanish filmgoers heard their first sound films. There was a ready market in the major cities of Barcelona, Madrid, Bilbao, Zaragoza, Valencia, and Sevilla, with theaters equipped for sound. One of the earliest sound films released in the country was Paramount's Hollywood musical *Innocents of Paris* (1929), starring Maurice Chevalier. But the film was in English.

In order to better attract Spain's filmgoing public of more than 100 million (not to mention sizable audiences in Mexico and Argentina), Hollywood studios turned out Spanish-language productions. Paramount turned to making Spanish films closer to Spain — in Paris. It produced 20 features and shorts, combining comedy, melodrama, and song. Further, Paramount had an ace up its sleeve: Argentine tango singer Carlos Gardel, whose popularity created an instant audience for Spanish-language sound films. Gardel was already a superstar, and his Paris films only increased his stature — and Paramount's revenues — throughout the Spanish-speaking world.

After Gardel's death in 1935, Argentina, often emulating Paramount's production style, became a prime exporter of musical comedy throughout the continent. Next to its French productions, Paramount's Spanish films were its best out of Paris. A rare extant production from Paris: *Melodie de arrabal* (1933).

## Agustina de Aragón

(Florián Rey, 1928). Victoria. **Script:** Rey. **Photography:** Alberto Arroyo. **Design:** Gonzalo de Picola. **With** Marina Torres (Agustina), María Luz Callejo (Santica), Manuel San Germán, and José María Alonso. A patriotic, stirring tale of resistance and heroism, the film is set in the Napoleonic era, in 1808, when the inhabitants of Zaragoza, in the region of Aragon, stave off the French invaders. How they retain their freedoms is due to the efforts of the central figure, a humble woman named Agustina, who is able to move among the French invaders and pass information along to the Spanish defenders. A 30 minute portion of film is extant.

## Amar es sufrir (To Love Is to Suffer)

(Domènec Ceret and Joan Solà Mestres, 1916). Studio Films. **Story:** Lola

Paris. **With** Josep Font and Consuela Hidalgo. A 1,350-meter drama from a story and script by the multifaceted Lola Paris, the film, which was shot in Barcelona, is the tale of an orphan girl raised in a wealthy family whose fortunes change during wartime. Amidst suffering, the young girl finds love.

### Una aventura de cine (A Cinematic Adventure)

(Juan de Orduña, 1927). Helios Film. **Script:** Wenceslao Fernández Flórez. **Photography:** Alberto Arroyo. **Design:** José María Torres. **With** Elisa Ruiz Romero (Alicia), Aurira Ruíz Romero (Aurora), and Juan de Orduña (Gustavo). Cofounder of the production company Goya Films with Florián Rey, Orduña made his debut as a director with this comedy, his only silent.

### Los Bohemios (Bohemians)

(Ricardo de Baños, 1905). Gaumont. Directed by the brother of Ramon de Baños, this is one of Ricardo de Baños's first films, a well-known short, light operetta that was synchronized during projection with sound (from a gramophone, billed as a "chronophone system," behind the screen). Filmed at the Comedy Theater, the 100-meter film (a Spanish cousin of Puccini's *La Bohème*) centers around familiar scenes of the characters, artists, and poets of boundless hopes and empty pockets in Barcelona. The film, which was a big hit in Spain and South America, contains the famous quip by one bohemian to another, "Yo le empujo" ("I will push you") (into doing something).

### El botón de fuego (Button of Fire)

(Joan María Codina and Joan Solà Mestres, 1919). Studio Films. **With** Bianca Valoris, Silvia Mariategui, Anita Stephenson, Suzanne Roumestan, Josep Balaguer, and Julia de la Canyera. The 10-episode (7,000-meter) serial was one of the last such serials out of Barcelona. It centers around a secret society—the Button of Fire—which seeks revolution within the country. After the assassination of a high military official, a famous detective is set loose to identify the radicals behind the killing. A battle between the military and the revolutionaries concludes the serial, and the last episode, called *Justicia*. Other episodes: *Ordenes secretas, Charito la billetera, Amor y fanatismo, Condenado a muerte, El poder del enemigo, En el castillo de Irving, En poder una secta, Herido de muerte,* and *La lucha por la libertad.*

### Boy

(Benito Perojo, 1925). Goya Films. **Script:** Perojo. **Photography:** Albert Duverger. **Design:** Pierre Schildknecht and Georges Jacouty. **With** Juan de Orduña (Boy), Suzy Vernon (Beatriz), Maurice Schutz, and Joaquín Houyez. A dramatic yet sentimental tale of Spain's former greatness as exemplified through the life of a young man, nicknamed "Boy," from the start of his military career at a naval academy to his tragic death. Also called *El Marino español* (in Argentina) and *Grand gosse (Big Kid)* (in France as a three-part serial), the studio's second film, which was shot in Paris, is based on the novel by Luis Coloma.

A full-blooded young man who

leads a care-free life, for whom country and church are means to an end, and which includes a murder charge for which he is found innocent, the young protagonist is forced to wrestle with issues of morality and materialism as he slowly grows to maturity. Religion is emphasized in the production (understandable since the source is the work of a priest), and as the film approaches the end "Boy" becomes the patriot ready to die for God and Spain. The final scene finds his estranged father and stepmother standing in reverence with their son's broken-hearted sweetheart before his tomb. Orduña was praised for his performance, and it established his name.

## Buenos días

(Florián Rey, 1933). Paramount. **Photography:** Harry Stradling. **Design:** Jaquelux. **With** Imperio Argentina (Carmen) and Rafael Jaimez (Luis). This 14-minute original musical production from Paris (based on a story by Jesús Rey) is an intimate look at the relationship between two young performers, a singer and her accompanying pianist. It also represents Florián Rey's only directorial effort in Paris for Paramount.

## Un caballero de frac (A Gentleman in a Tailcoat)

(Carlos San Martín and Roger Capellani, 1932). Paramount. **Script:** Saint-Granier. **Adaptation:** Honorio Maura. **Photography:** Ted Pahle. **With** Roberto Rey (André de Dussange), Rosita Díaz Gimeno (Susana de Dussange), Gabriel Algara (Pierre), Luis Llaneza (Buffetaut), Carlos Martínez Baena, and Gloria Guzmán (Totoche).

The 100-minute tale out of Paris tells the story of an apparently well-to-do aristocrat who suddenly finds himself with nothing but a set of evening clothes. It demonstrates what a man can do when he applies himself.

Also called *Un Hombre de frac,* this Spanish-language musical comedy is loosely based on two sources: Luther Reed's silent *Evening Clothes* (1927), starring Adolphe Menjou, and Yves Mirande's 1922 play *L'Homme en habit.* Ray's performance earned star status and the film, shown in Los Angeles and in Latin areas, was a huge hit.

## El caballero de la noche

(James Tinling, 1932). Fox. **Adaptation:** José López Rubio. **Music:** Troy Sanders. **Photography:** Sidney Wagner. **With** José Mojica, Mona Maris (Lady Elena), and Andrés de Segurola. A stylish, Hollywood-made Spanish version of *Dick Turpin* (1925), which had been directed by John Blystone, featuring the great Tom Mix. In this work of picturesque garments, luminous atmosphere and colors, beautiful women, gallant men, and all kinds of dramatic romance — one of only two Spanish-language Hollywood films released in 1932 — is famed Mexican singer Mojica as the late–18th century masked English bandit Dick Turpin, whose deeds once charmed many a youngster.

The hero, wrote *Cine-Mundial,* "is … generous, kind, very highly polished, for the greatest pleasure of the ladies, although such a bandit may be more legendary than real." He lives on his own income — any real criminal instinct on his part would have assured failure for the film — and dresses better than the impeccable Andrés de Segurola. The hero, continued *Cine-Mundial*, "will not defraud his admirers, he will honor his type, escape the hangman's noose, marry the beloved of a hated aristocrat, sing beautiful songs, and call a thief the one who circulates in the saloons and lives by cheating the humble." Shown in New York in late 1932, the action film outshined the British version, *Dick Turpin* (1933), starring Victor McLaglen.

### El Caín moderno

(Antonio Cuesta, 1913). Cuesta preferred to shoot films of actual events, such as bullfights, but often turned to fiction films such as this contemporary tale of fratricide.

### Carceleras (Jailers)

(Segundo de Chomón, 1910). Chomón and Fuster. **Photography:** Chomón. Chomón, who became known as one of Spain's great trick-film artists, was the first voice of Spanish cinema. He began his career in 1901 as a cameraman and technical director. From 1906 to 1909, he directed in France, hired by Pathé to compete with Méliès. From 1913 to 1924, Chomón made films in Italy as well as in France. He worked on about 500 productions in his career.

In the thriving film center of Barcelona in 1910, Chomón produced a series of comic operettas, melodramas, and fantasy films such as this early, well-received 150-meter mystery drama (based on the light operetta by Ricardo Flores), and the first version of the story. It contains a bit of animation.

The film is set in Cordoba, where the talk of the town is the upcoming marriage of Gabriel and Lola. But when Gabriel is implicated in the murder of Pacorro, a troubadour invited to helped celebrate the upwedding marriage, all bets are off. The minstrel man, it soon turns out, was also interested in Soledad, Lola's sister. Gabriel is carted off to jail, but Soledad feels a responsibility to him, and knows he is innocent. She attempts to clear his name and save him from a life sentence. The actual murderer turns out to be Jesús, another troubadour who was in love with her.

### La carta (The Letter)

(Adelqui Millar, 1930). Paramount. **With** Carmen Larrabeiti (Leslie Bennett), Carlos Díaz de Mendoza (George Nelson), and Luis Peña (Mr. Joyce). The Spanish version of *The Letter* (1929), starring Jeanne Eagels, is based on Maugham's 1925 novel and 1927 play. Paramount's Paris drama was a hit with Latin audiences, reported *Cine-Mundial* in April 1931.

### La casa es seria (The Serious House)

(Louis Gasnier and Jaquelux, 1933). Paramount. **Script and lyrics:** Alfredo Le Pera. **With** Carlos Gardel, Imperio Argentina, and Lolita Benavente. An original production out of Paris, this 20-minute risqué musical comedy is about an innocent woman (Argentina) lured by Gardel to a house of ill repute. Gardel sings the emotional and sensual tangos "Recuerdo Malevo" and "Volvió una Noche."

### Cascarrabias (Grumpy)

(Cyril Gardner, 1930). Paramount. **With** Ernesto Vilches, Carmen Guerrero, Delia Magaña, and Andrés de Segurola.

One of the studio's earliest Spanish-language films from Hollywood, a large-scale romantic production that introduced to the American filmgoing public one of Spain's eminent stage actors. Based on *Grumpy* (1930), which had been directed by George Cukor and Cyril Gardner, the film centers around a famous English lord and criminologist whose house is robbed. Vilches, noted *Variety*, put his talent to work and "achieved wonders in the film." The sufficiently complicated mystery signaled the coming of age of "genuinely good Spanish-language films" and was a moneymaker.

## Castillos en el aire (Castles in the Air)

(Jaime Salvador, 1938). Edward Le Baron Productions. **Story:** Salvador. **Adaptation:** Miguel de Zárraga, Jr. **With** Cristina Tellez, Rafael Alcalde, Pilar Arcos, Andrés de Segurola, and Emilia Leovalli. The hope was that this 84-minute production would be the beginning of a series of Hollywood-made Spanish-language films that would catch the attention of Hispanics.

In this story about the glamorous world of filmmaking, a shy European stenographer wins a trip to Hollywood. On the way to her "Castles in the Air," she becomes romantically involved with a bank clerk passing himself off as a Russian prince. "Without pretension of a great spectacular, but mounted with propriety and luxury that entertains," wrote *Cine-Mundial*, the film "makes an hour and a half pass pleasantly."

## Cerveza gratis (Free Beer)

(Fructuoso Gelabert, 1906). Empresa Diorama. **Story:** Gelabert. **Design:** Vicenç Raspall. **With** Joan Morales (the painter), Josep Yepes, José Vico, and Antoni Estrada. A short, well-received comedy by the multitalented Gelabert, one of the founders of Spanish cinema. In a Barcelona bar, a poor painter is mistreated when his friend is unable to pay for a drink. Thrown out, he gets even by painting a sign announcing "Free Beer" and hanging it outside the establishment. A riot ensues. The 130-meter film was popular enough to be exported and shown in France and Portugal.

## Chéri-Bibi

(Carlos Borcosque, 1931). MGM. **Script:** Miguel de Zárraga. **Design:** Cedric Gibbons. **With** Ernesto Vilches, María Fernanda Ladrón de Guevara (Cecilia), María Tubau, and Tito Davison. An 80-minute, Spanish-language Parisian murder mystery unique in that in Hollywood it preceeded the making and release of the English version, *The Phantom of Paris*. The slated star of the English production, Lon Chaney, who had only one sound film to his credit, died of cancer in 1930, and that put the film on hold. His replacement, John Gilbert, wound up taking his cues from the star of the Spanish film, who plays the magician Chéri-Bibi. Through a series of complex tricks—including a Houdini-like escape, chains and all, from prison—he convinces the authorities that he is not the killer of his fiancée's father. Because the Spanish production was produced first, it went unreleased in America so as not to distract attention from Gilbert's vehicle. *Variety* wrote, "It isn't Gilbert that makes the picture, it makes itself."

## La chica del gato (The Cat's Girl)

(Antonio Calvache, 1926). Film Numancia. **Script:** Calvache. **Photography:** Armando Pou. **Design:** José María Torres. **With** Josefina J. Ochoa (Gaudalupe), Elena Salvador (Chuncha), María Mayor (Eufrasia), and Consuelo Qiujano (Nena), Carlos Handt (Sigmundo), Fernando Díaz de Mendoza Serrano (Barcaza). This highly popular comedy of the era is based on the hit play by Carlos Arniches.

In the poor section of Madrid, the gamin Guadalupe, accompanied by her cat Pablo and her bird Crispín, is picked up by a family with a disreputable background. They intend to use her in their schemes, but she resists, despite their threats, and flees. Dying of hunger and cold, she and her animal friends sneak into the house of Mr. de Barcaza. Discovered, she reveals her sad history, and is offered work by the beautiful Nena. Guadalupe soon finds out that Nena is being wooed by the not very likable Sigmundo, a German manufacturer. Worse, he threatens trouble if Nena doesn't agree to marry him. But fortune takes a turn for the better when Guadalupe — thanks to her cat — discovers that Sigmundo is already married. Nena is off the hook, and Guadalupe and her friends find a permanent home.

## La ciudad de cartón (Cardboard City)

(Louis King, 1933). Fox. **Story** and **supervision:** Gregorio Martínez Sierra. **Adaptation:** José López Rubio and John Reinhardt. **With** Catalina Bárcena, José Crespo, Andrés de Segurola, Janet Gaynor, Roland Young, and John Barrymore. One of the studio's more clever and satiric Spanish-language comedies, this was Martínez Sierra's first original production from Hollywood and one of Catalina Bárcena's best films. It pokes fun at Hollywood mores. More important, Bárcena again revealed herself to be a great actress. She plays the woman about to marry an American rancher, but in a train accident she loses her memory. She is then mistaken for the "great European star" who, unidentified, had died in the crash. The emotionally dramatic, unforeseen events that follow become the basis for the film, which takes on a measure of verisimilitude when a welcoming committee of actual Hollywood stars greets the "foreign celebrity" in perfect Castilian. "A great film," wrote *Cine-Mundial*, "a great role ... and a new success."

## El cliente seductor (The Handsome Customer)

(Richard Blumenthal, 1931). Paramount. **Supervision:** Florián Rey. **With** Imperio Argentina, Maurice Chevalier, Rosita Díaz Gimeno, Carmen Navascués, and Carlos Martínez Baena. An original 20-minute short that promoted Paramount's superstars in Paris, especially Chevalier and his recently completed Hollywood comedy, *The Smiling Lieutenant* (1931), directed by Ernst Lubitsch. Chevalier plays a dashing Spanish-speaking boulevardier romancing three lovelies at a café in sunny Paris. The short was shown in Madrid in February 1932.

## Codicia (Greed)

(Joan María Codina and Joan Solà Mestres, 1918). Studio Films. **Design:**

Alfred Fontanals. **With** Bianca Valoris (the Marquessa), Lola Paris ("Turquoise"), Maria Alvarez de Burgos (Rosalinda), and Carmen Rodríquez (Mrs. Tobiche). A 14-episode (10,000-meter) adventure serial, inspired by French models and produced in Barcelona on a grand scale. The tale of an avaricious noblewoman includes an escape by airplane.

## El código penal (The Criminal Code)

(Phil Rosen, 1931). Columbia. **Script:** Matías Cirici Ventalló. **Photography:** Joseph Walker. **With** María Alba, María Calvo, Julio Villarreal, and Ramón Peon. The studio's second venture in Spanish-language films, shot in Hollywood, is a brutal prison drama about a young man who, railroaded into jail by a corrupt D.A., commits a murder. As one of four low-budget Spanish-language films, each a moneymaker, that the studio produced in 1931, the drama is a rendition of Howard Hawks's *The Criminal Code* (1931), which *Variety* wrote, "can play to any type of audience: they'll understand it and talk about it. A corking picture." It was the same for the ten-reel Spanish version. "The studio hit the mark plentyfully," commented *Cine-Mundial*.

## El comediante

(Ernesto Vilches, 1931). Paramount. **Script:** Vilches. **With** Vilches, Angelita Benítez, and María Calvo. This film represents Spanish actor-director Vilches's attempt to take charge of his work in Hollywood, where he was unsatisfied with his assignments. He plays a famous actor who attracts the atten- tion of the daughter of a rich English-woman. The photogenic star is, wrote *Cine-Mundial*, "well modulated" in his performance. Vilches, however, thought differently. "The producers don't know my character," he said. "They don't know how to exploit me. Now they have given me a vaudeville work, lightweight and agreeable. Any actor could do the work." After this seven-reel effort, Vilches returned to Spain.

## Conoces a tu mujer? (Do You Know Your Woman?)

(David Howard, 1931). Fox. **Script:** Matías Cirici Ventalló. **Dialogue:** Nicolas Jordan de Urries. **With** Carmen Larrabeiti, Antonio Reveles, Manuel Arbó, Anna María Custodio, and Miguel Ligero. This spicy Hollywood-made seven-reeler, a Spanish-language societal comedy with a North American theme, is a rendition of William K. Howard's highly amusing *Don't Bet on Women* (1931), the tale of a seductive woman who teaches men a thing or two about being so-called lady killers. "I recommend the film," wrote the *Cine-Mundial* reviewer, "and applaud the actors."

## La cruz y la espada (The Cross and the Sword)

(Frank Strayer, 1934). Fox. **With** José Mojica, Anita Campillo, and Juan Torena. "There are instances that result in no mistakes," wrote *Cine-Mundial* about this tuneful Spanish-language drama of Franciscans establishing missions in early 19th-century California. It was based on an original idea by theater and screenwriting veteran Miguel de Zárraga and signifies his most lasting contribution to Hollywood and Spanish film.

The popular Mexican tenor Mojica, singing as only he could, is the young Franciscan with a devilish temptation for a 17-year-old Spanish beauty. The young priest is on the verge of giving up his vows in order to marry her, but she's promised to another, and never suspects the tragedy that is about to unfold. "Even those not familiar with the language of Cervantes," wrote the *New York Times*, can enjoy the numerous songs of all types in which Señor Mojica displays his virtuosity, and follow the romantic story." First screened at the Teatro Variedades in New York, the film became one of Fox's biggest Spanish-language moneymakers. It realized "a dream that appeared impossible a few years ago," wrote *Cine-Mundial*, "the creation of a legitimate cinema for us; nothing less than in Hollywood." Fox apparently intended to trade on the film's success by making an English version, but did the next best thing, releasing the Spanish-language film with English subtitles.

## Cuando el amor rie (When Love Laughs)

(David Howard, 1930). Fox. **Script:** Jules Furthman. **With** José Mojica, and Mona Maris. This Spanish-language operetta, translated by Francisco More de la Torre, is a remake of Joseph Franz's *Love Gambler* (1922). Set in Spanish California, the 75-minute Hollywood film stars the highly original Mexican tenor Mojica as a swashbuckling, singing, cowboy lover who has his eyes on a "spitfire" college graduate. "The Latins are learning," wrote *Variety*. "This one is an original ... with sure-fire appeal."

The film ranked alongside *El precio de un beso* (1930) as one of Fox's early foreign-language hits. In Spain, it was called *Ladrón de amor*.

## Cuando te suicidas? (When Do You Kill Yourself?)

(Manuel Romero, 1932). **Script:** Saint-Granier. **Adaptation** and **dialogue:** Claudio de la Torre. **With** Imperio Argentina (Gaby), Fernando Soler (Xavier du Venoux), Carmen Navascués (Viuda), José Isbert (Petavey), Carlos Martínez Baena (Abraham), Enrique de Rosas (Moisés), and Manuel Russell (León Mirol). The story of an aristocrat who threatens to kill himself unless he finds love, Manuel Romero's 81-minute film, representing his first effort for Paramount in Paris, is an example of his impeccable sense of casting. The young Mexican actor Soler is the lovelorn young viscount, and Imperio Argentina matches him as the woman who saves his life. Shown in Madrid in April 1932 and in Los Angeles in early 1933, the comedy-drama is an example of the original work produced by Paramount in Paris.

## Cuentos baturros (Aragonese Peasant Stories)

(Domènec Ceret, 1915–16). Studio Films. **With** Ceret. A series of burlesque sketches starring a well-known Barcelona comic. Totaling 17 sketches in all, the series ran more than 20,000 meters, making it the longest series in the Barcelona studio's history. It includes the episodes *Teléfono improvisado, Las elecciones de Villagiloca, El gordo de Navidad, Tio Isidro en carnaval, La ciencia* *comprometida,* and *El héroe de Villa-giloca.* The film was popular enough to be shown in Portugal and Latin America.

## El cuerpo del delito (Body of Crime)

(Cyril Gardner, 1930). Paramount. With Ramón Pereda, Andrés de Segurola, Antonio Moreno, María Alba (Miss Delroy), María Calvo, Carlos Villarías, and Barry Norton. Not counting the musical revue *Galas de la Paramount* (1930), this nine-reel film represents the studio's earliest Spanish-language production out of Hollywood — though not a film for purists of pronunciation, noted the Hollywood periodical *Cinelandia.* The outline of the story is similar to the studio's *The Benson Murder Case* (1929). A man is murdered, and four people become suspect. By the end, the interlocking themes of evasion and culpability — always interesting in any of S. S. Van Dine's Philo Vance stories — gives viewers their money's worth. *Cine-Mundial* observed, "The first of the ... Spanish films by Paramount is deserving of fame."

## La danza fatale

(Josep Togores and Ramón de Baños, 1914). Argos Film. **Script:** Togores. **Photography and editing:** Ramon de Baños. With Pastora Imperio, Consuelo Soriano, Domènec Ceret, Emma Mariotti, José Vico, and Edouard Girardier. A tale of three young women forced to go into hiding after the death of their gunrunning father. One becomes a singer in a music hall, the second an artist, the third a lover of a nobleman. When their identities are exposed, tragedy ensues. The 1,200-meter Barce-lona melodrama was begun by the young and exacting writer Togores (1893–1970) and never finished to his satisfaction.

## De frente, marchen (Forward, March)

(Edward Sedgwick, 1930). MGM. **Script:** Salvador de Alberich. With Buster Keaton (Elmer Stuyvesant), Juan de Landa (Sgt. Grunon), and Conchita Montenegro. This 80-minute Holly-wood-made Spanish version of *Dough-boys* (1930) is one the great comedian's earliest sound films. Having spoken Spanish for the first time in MGM's highly praised *Estrellados* (1930), Keaton plays the eccentric, a delicious type of Andalusian, in the U.S. Army because his chauffeur has enlisted. It was hugely popular.

## El diablo del mar (The Sea Devil)

(Juan Duval, 1936). Theater Classics. **Script:** Duval. With Ramón Pereda, Movita Castañeda, Carlos Villarías, and Barry Norton. Barcelona-born Duval (1899–1954), wrote the *New York Times,* came up with "another of those stories about a white man (Ramón Pereda) 'going native' after having been cast away on a delightful South Sea Island." There he encounters danger in the form of a giant sea creature and, of course, the charming daughter of an island chief. Duval shot the 65-minute film in Hollywood simultaneously with his English-language *Devil Monster.*

## El dios del mar (The Sea God)

(Edward Venturini, 1930). Paramount. **Adaptation:** Josep Carner Ribalta.

**With** Ramón Pereda (Ahab), Rosita Moreno, Julio Villarreal, and Manuel Arbó. An eight-reel Hollywood-made Spanish version of the graphic *Moby Dick* (1930), which *Harrison's Reports* labeled, "gruesome at times, fantastic at others, yet in all this is excellent entertainment." The studio's sixth Spanish-language film out of Hollywood brought stardom to the modest Pereda, playing the tragic figure who returns home minus a leg but vows to kill the great sea beast. The rest of the cast shared in the success of the moneymaking film.

### Doña mentiras (The Lady Lies)

(Adelqui Millar, 1930). Paramount. **With** Carmen Larrabeiti, Félix de Pomès, Miguel Ligero, Carmen Moragas, and Helen D'Algy. One of Paramount's earliest Spanish adaptations from Paris, based on the English-language hit *The Lady Lies* (1930), is the tale of a widower who tries to court a young lady over the objections of his children. At its debut screening, the film was called "a step forward" because of the "excellence of the production." However, the theatricality of the performers, save for the excellent Miguel Ligero, dismayed some viewers, as did the Castilian. Nonetheless, the film was a moneymaker.

### Don Juan de Serrallonga

(Ricardo de Baños and Alberto Marro, 1910). Hispano Films. **Script and photography:** de Baños. **With** Cecilio Rodríguez de la Vega (Joan) and M. Dolors Puchol (Joana de Torrellas). Also called *Los bandoleros de las Guillerías*, the historical drama, which was shown in a four-part series, was the first feature shot in Spain. It is based on the 19th-century classic by Víctor Balaguer (1824–1901) about the famous 17th bandit of the Guillerías. A magnificently ambitious, dynamic, and picturesque production, especially in the natural mountain settings, the 1,200-meter film became a model of composition, achieving a popularity equal to the stage production, and vindicated de Baños' faith that the story was cinematic.

### Don Quijote de la Mancha

(Narcís Cuyàs, 1910). Iris Films. Script: Cuyàs. From the land of its origin came the earliest adaptation — by a Barcelona studio— of a small portion of Cervantes's masterpiece and the country's noblest literary heirloom. The demented old crusading "knight" with a passion for chivalry and justice and his faithful companion Sancho are briefly brought to life in an episode based on chapters VI and VII of the novel, called "The History of the Curious-Impertinent."

It is the sad tale (read to Quixote and Sancho by a curate) of two close friends, Anselmo and Lothario, and Anselmo's beautiful young wife, Camila. Not quite at ease in his marriage, Anselmo asks Lothario to test his wife's faithfulness. Lothario in vain attempts to dissuade his friend from a scheme that Anselomo realizes too late is foolishness. Ironically, each of the three protagonists is aware of what the other is doing, yet none can stop the fatal outcome. Anselmo's "impertinent curiosity" is proof that one should never look a gift horse in the mouth and that the axiom "seeing is believing" is not a foolproof way of testing reality.

## Don Quintín el Amargao

(Manuel Noriega, 1925). Atlántida. **Script:** Carlos Primelles. **Photography:** Luis R. Alonso. **With** Juan Nadal (Don Quintín), Josefina Tapias, and Pedro Elviro. Based on the 1925 play by Carlos Arniches y Barrera, Antonio Estremera, and Jacinto Guerrero, the film concerns itself with an arrogant and bitter man, an *amargao*, who is hated and feared. Convinced that his baby daughter isn't his, Don Quintín abandons her in a sailor's cabin, and twenty years later, his mind no less at ease, he sets out to find her.

A high point of the tale takes place in a café where Don Quintín is sitting with a few friends, and his daughter — a young woman whom he doesn't recognize — is at another table with her husband. Arrogantly spitting out an olive pit, he hits her in the eye. Without a word, the couple gets up and leaves. As Don Quintín is basking in his bravado, the husband returns — and forces him to swallow the pit. Later on, the old man combs the town for the young man, seeking revenge, but instead discovers the identity of his daughter, who is happy and pregnant.

Luis Buñuel codirected a sound version in Madrid in 1935 and filmed it again in Mexico in 1951 under the title *La hija del engaño* (*Daughter of Deceit*).

## Dos mas uno, dos (Two and One, Two)

(John Reinhardt, 1934). Fox. **Adaptation:** José López Rubio. **With** Rosita Moreno, Valentin Parera, Andrés de Segurola, and Carmen Rodríguez. This Hollywood-made Spanish-language comedy-romance is based on the 1928 silent *Don't Marry*. "A new succcess," wrote *Cine-Mundial* about the efforts of a protofeminist fending off the overtures of an archaeologist. She tells him his taste in women is bad — and to take a look instead at her older cousin. Moreno exhibits her flair for dance "in one of the most interesting episodes," said a critic. More important, the sequence of events on the eve of his marriage to the cousin reveals the real relationship between the two women. The film played in Madrid and at the Teatro Campoamor in New York. An incomplete print exists.

## Dos noches (Two Nights)

(Carlos Borcosque, 1933). MGM. **Adaptation:** Miguel de Zárraga. **With** José Crespo (Boris), Conchita Montenegro (Sandra), and Manuel Noriega. The 62-minute Spanish version of *Revenge at Monte Carlo* (1933) was the studio's last Spanish-language production from Hollywood. It was billed as an "emotional love picture" and filmed in five days. It follows the circuit of life of an agreeable Russo-Spanish soldier of fortune who tries to restore a deposed European leader to power while chasing a beautiful French dancer. He foils the plots of a renegade band of emigrés, resists machinations by agents of the new government, and nearly loses his life.

*Cine-Mundial* singled out the director for his "extraordinary judgment." His was an example of Hollywood's picking up the pace of Spanish-language film production while throwing less money at it. After playing abroad, the film, released in America by Fanchon Royer Productions, was shown at the

Teatro Variedades in New York. An incomplete print is extant.

### En cado puerto un amor (In Every Port a Love)

(Marcel Silver, 1931). MGM. **Script and Supervisor:** Edgar Neville. **With** Conchita Montenegro (Elena), José Crespo (Jack), and Juan de Landa. A vivid, refined, and ironic 91-minute, Hollywood-made Spanish version of Sam Wood's rough, ribald, and risqué *Way for a Sailor* (1930), starring John Gilbert. Advertised as "the drama of dramas," the story concerns a seaman who tries the win the favors of the woman he loves. "Extraordinary event," reported *Cine-Mundial*, "you have to see the film because it's well done."

### En cuerpo y alma (Body and Soul)

(David Howard, 1931). Fox. **With** Jorge Lewis (Ted), Anna María Custodio (Clara), and José Alcantara (Phillip). Based on the studio's *Body and Soul* (1931), this 100-minute Hollywood movie featured a cast and crew from Barcelona and Madrid. The production, wrote *Cine-Mundial*, "is about one of those juvenile idylls they never realize." Phillip, who has left his wife, Clara, and Ted join the air force during the First World War. The action centers around their trying to shoot down a German dirigible, which *Cine-Mundial* described as "excellently filmed … agreeably spectacular." The drama then concerns the surviving flier who falls in love with the wife of his dead friend.

### Eran trece (There Were Thirteen)

(David Howard, 1931). Fox. **Adaptation:** José López Rubio. **Photography:** Sidney Wagner. **With** Manuel Arbó (Charlie Chan), Raúl Roulien (Max Minchin), Luana Alcañiz, Anna María Custodio (Elena Potter), Blanca de Castejón, Carmen Rodríguez, Carlos Díaz de Mendoza, Miguel Ligero, and Juan Torena (Dick Kennaway). Showcasing imported talent, this nine-reel production was the first, and only, Spanish film out of Hollywood about the famous sleuth. Based on *Charlie Chan Carries On* (1931), it features the genial detective-philosopher who says, amongst other things, "Man should never hurry except to catch a flea." His services are engaged in Honolulu after a Scotland Yard detective, hired to locate a killer, is himself shot. It seems that of the original thirteen tourists on a round-the-world trip, three have been eliminated on route: one in London and two in Paris. So the ingenious Chan, hoping to unmask the culprit, accompanies the remaining ten to San Francisco.

### Espérame (Wait for Me)

(Louis Gasnier, 1932). Paramount. **Supervisor:** Florián Rey. **Script and lyrics:** Alfredo Le Pera. **Photography:** Harry Stradling. **Songs:** Pilar Arcos. **Music:** Marcel Lattès. **With** Carlos Gardel (Carlos de Acuña), Goyita Herrero (Rosario), Matilde Artero (Pepita), and Lolita Benavente (Juanita). In this 70-minute feature, Carlos Gardel stars in his second Paris production as a highly acclaimed Buenos Aires cabaret artist who tries to win the heart of young, rich, and mysterious society woman Rosario. Veteran director Gasnier's compendium of Argentine and Spanish folklore, filmed over a three-week period, came in for praise. "Considerable attention has been devoted to the settings of this familiar story," wrote the *New York Times*. "The scenes of the masked ball and in the popular cafés are particularly interesting. There is an abundance of comic incidents in this otherwise highly sentimental tale." The great Gardel sings four numbers: the rumba "Por Tus Ojos Negros" ("For Your Black Eyes"), a *zamba*, and two tangos.

## Fabricante de suicidos (Maker of Suicides)

(Francisco E. Riquelme, 1928). Hispano American. **Script:** Riquelme and Francisco Elias. **Photography:** José Gaspar Serra. **With** Pedro Elviro. A comedy filmed in Barcelona.

## La fiesta del diablo (The Devil's Holiday)

(Adelqui Millar, 1930). Paramount. **Script:** Edmund Goulding. **With** Carmen Larrabeiti (Hallie Hobart), Tony D'Algy (David Stone), Félix de Pomès (Mark Stone), Amelia Muñoz, and Miguel Ligero (Charlie Thorne). Made in Paris, this 93-minute Spanish version of *The Devil's Holiday* (1930) takes a melodramatic look at an opportunistic young woman named Hallie Hobart, who tries to make amends for past deeds. It was called pleasant enough by *Film Daily*.

## 48 pesetas de taxi (A Taxi Fee of 48 Pesetas)

(Fernando Delgado, 1929). Hispano Fox. **Script:** Delgado. **Photography:** Enrique Blanco. **Design:** Agustín Espí. **With** Erna Becker, Ricardo Nuñez, Carmen Tierra, and José Isbert. Filmed in Madrid, this production was one of the last silents from Spain. It was also the first Spanish film to satirize Hollywood Westerns. One sequence, which takes place in a saloon frequented by cowboys, tramps, and the sheriff, caused the production to be labeled obscene and banned in Barcelona.

## Fuerza y nobleza (Strength and Nobility)

(Ricardo and Ramón de Baños, 1917). Royal Films. **Photography:** Ricardo and Ramón de Baños. **Design:** Brunet and Pons. **Titles:** Joan J. Junceda. **With** Jack Johnson, Lucille Johnson, Nicolás Perchicot, Francesco Aguiló, Miguel del Llano, Fernando Delgado, and Ticia Lombia. Made during the apogee of Spanish serials, this was a well-received, popular feature (by a Barcelona studio) with a real black man as the hero. Patterning his role after the Italian superhero Maciste, the world-famous boxer Jack Johnson (who had fled America on morals charges) plays an ironman and superhero in an imaginary land. He becomes embroiled in a complex series of adventures and intrigues when he tries to help reinstate rightful heirs to the throne. His wife, the gentle Lucille Johnson, is the princess-ballerina in distress. The four episodes of this little-known 8,000-meter production are titled "El Testamento de un príncipe," "Entre fieras," "El Film revelador," and "Jack Johnson, justiciero."

## Fútbol, amor y toros (Soccer, Love and Bullfights)

(Florián Rey, 1929). Selecciones Nuñoz. **Script:** Rey. **Photography:** Alberto Arroyo. **Design:** Paulino Méndez. **With** Ricardo Núñez (Ricardo), Blanca

Rodríguez (María), Carlos Rufert, and Modesto Rives. A comedy, synchronized to music and sound, about the three great passions of Spaniards: love, bull-fighting, and soccer. A former bull-fighter (Ricardo's father) and a one-time soccer star (María's father) are the agents who unite their children in love.

### Galas de la Paramount (Paramount Galas)

(Edward Venturini and Geoffrey Shurlock, 1930). Paramount. This 79-minute all-star Hollywood revue of Paramount's Spanish contract players was one of the studio's rare foreign-language revues from the film capital. Included in the film, which follows the outlines of *Paramount on Parade* (1930), are the enchanting Rosita Moreno, the great Ernesto Vilches, and newcomer Ramón Pereda acting as masters of ceremony to an aggregation of sketches and musical numbers.

### La Gitanilla (The Little Gypsy)

(Adrià Gual, Alfred Fontanals, and Joan Solà Mestres, 1914). Barcinógrafo. Script: Rafael Marquina. Design: J. Morales. With E. Beltran (Preciosa), I. Cardala (La Gitanilla), and G. Peña (Juan/Andrés). The great Barcelona playwright and producer Adrià Gual favored literary works, here turning sequences from Cervantes's moving novella of the same name into a three-reel (1,000-meter) romantic adventure.

La Gitanilla is a young and beautiful woman introduced to middle-class wealth by the gypsies, becoming her wandering tribe's mascot. When a young nobleman falls in love with her, he also accepts the peripatetic mode of life of her people. Things take a turn for the worse when he is forced to kill another in a quarrel, and he is condemned to death. La Gitanilla pleads for his life, and her gypsy band rescues him from the gallows.

### La gran jornada (The Big Journey)

(David Howard, 1930). Fox. Script: Francisco More de la Torre. Photography: Sidney Wagner. With Jorge Lewis (Colman), Carmen Guerrero (Isabel), and Antonio Moreno. A great deal of effort and money was spent to come up with the Spanish-language version — and a Raoul Walsh production — of Walsh's spectacle *The Big Trail* (1930), the first 70-mm film in the studio's history. It was filmed in Oregon, and resulted in a beautifully scenic story of an over-whelming 19th century migration across a continent. The film was released in Spain as *Horizontes nuevos*.

### Los guapos de la vaquería del parque (The Handsomest Guys at the Park's Dairy Shop)

(Fructuoso Gelabert, 1905). Empresa Diorama. Script: Gelabert. Photography: Gelabert. Design: Vicenç Raspall. With Carme Vital, Joan Morales, Joan Alarma, Antoni Riba, José Vico, Joan Solsona, Josep Parera, and Josep Pineda. This early comedy short, which was shot on location in Barcelona, was a huge hit over a stretch of several months. It is about a group of young men who hope to attain a fortune after a newspaper item catches their attention. Filmmaking pioneer Gelabert's 250-meter comedy, wrote a critic years later, tends towards the kind of "ballet" found in

René Clair's classic *The Italian Straw Hat* (1927).

## Gulliver en el país de los gigantes (Gulliver in the Land of the Giants)

(Segundo de Chomón, 1903–1904). **Photography:** Chomón. One of the trick-film pioneer director's earliest efforts is this free and very abbreviated version of the second part of Swift's classic tale. Chomón's inspiration was Méliès's *Gulliver's Travels* (1902). The 150-meter film showed that Chomón was a technical master of the medium, able to easily sidestep difficulties and produce the first film containing reduced objects and double exposures.

Chomón's recently rediscovered *Le Scarabée d'or* (1907) is an especially striking example of this kind of work. By its extravagant use of colored matter, it blends two subgenres of the "trick film": the "fire film" (pyrotechnical) and the "insect film" (very much in fashion at the time). A supposedly Egyptian sorcerer throws a giant gold scarab (the only blob of bright yellow in a black-and-white setting) into a magic cauldron; as the (yellow) flames work on it, the scarab is transformed in a woman with (blue-green) dragonfly wings. There follows a riot of special effects in which colors fly in all directions. The cauldron is turned into a giant fountain with multicolored jets of water.

## Guzmán el bueno (Guzman the Good)

(Enric Giménez and Fructuoso Gelabert, 1909). Barcelona Films. **Script:** Gelabert. **Photography:** Gelabert. **De-sign:** Joan Morales. **With** Margarida Xirgu, Enric Giménez (Guzmán), and Enrique Guitart. A neoromantic historical drama (based on the four-act work by Antonio Gil y Zárate) is a tragic recital on the subject of national history. It signaled a technical revolution in film-making, for it was one of the first productions in world cinema to contain real sets rather than curtains of painted scenes. It is a tale about the conflict between duty to family and duty to country. The 350-meter Barcelona production is set in the time of El Cid, when Guzmán's son is held hostage by the Moors, who threaten to put him to death if his father does not surrender his city. Guzmán deals with the depression produced by his decision to sacrifice his son with gradually strengthening resignation.

Filmed at a studio within a tower and castle (owned by Martí Codolar), the production was one of the earliest Spanish films shown widely abroad, in France, Portugal, Latin America, and the United States.

## La hermana San Sulpicio (Sister San Sulpicio)

(Florián Rey, 1927). Perseo Films. **Script:** Rey. **Photography:** José María Beltrán. **Design:** José María Torres. **With** Imperio Argentina (Gloria), Ricardo Núñez (Ceferino Sanjurjo), Modesto Rivas, Erma Becker, and María Anaya. Rey's first great comedy was a scenic 82-minute triumph. In Andalusia, the physician Sanjurjo is on a long stay to recover his health. He spots and falls for a pretty nun, follows her to Seville, gets her out of the convent — and marries her. The humorous work is based on the short story by Armando Palacio Valdés. A 3-minute fragment survives.

## La historia de un duro (Tale of a Five-Peseta Piece)

(Sabino A. Micón, 1927). Luna Film. **Script:** Micón. **Photography:** Juan Pacheco. **With** Carmen Rico, Manuel Montenegro, Ignacio Caro, and Manuel Blanco. The short, experimental — and now legendary — film is a fable in which a coin is the central element. A fishmonger finds a pot of gold coins, which feeds his greed. When the pot drops, one of the coins breaks away. The 1.5 ounce coin, in picaresque fashion, is shown making its way through the hands of a money lender, a thief, a pianist, and a young child — their hands signifying greed, avarice, joy, and hope — their stories ranging from the sublime to the ridiculous. The only face shown is that of Carmen Rico in silhouette. In the end, the coin ends up where it began — under a rock.

## Al Hollywood madrileño (Hollywood in Madrid)

(Nemesio M. Sobrevila, 1927). Madrid Film. **Script:** Sobrevila. **Photography:** Agustín Macasoli. **Design:** Sobrevila. **With** Elisa Ruiz Romero, Soledad Martín, José Montenegro, and Julio Rodríguez. An early experimental satire that employed special optics and effects, the film is divided into several stories about the crazy process of filmmaking. A young girl and her father, enamored with the new art of filmmaking, decide to create their own version of Hollywood in Madrid by finding backers

to film five sketches about varying lifestyles. The film, which contains animation that touches on cubism, symbolism, and futurism, was reedited with additional scenes the following year and retitled *Lo más español* (*The Most Spanish Thing*). After this production, the director retired from films.

## Un hombre de suerte (Lucky Man)

(Benito Perojo, 1930). Paramount. **Script:** Pierre Collings. **Dialogue:** Pedro Muñoz Seca. **Photography:** Harry Stradling. **With** Roberto Rey (Luciano Barbosa), María Luz Callejo (Urbaba), Carlos San Martín (Digno), Amelia Muñoz, and Helen D'Algy. This Paris production enabled influential Perojo to make his way to Hollywood. The lucky film he directed in Paris was the studio's eagerly awaited debut Spanish feature out of the French capital.

It is a comedy about a man who locates a fortune behind a wall. Rey, playing the lucky man, was also lucky with this hit film: it helped make him a Spanish-language star and led to an invitation to Hollywood. Perojo's film was based not, as has been widely reported, on Robert Florey's Hollywood melodrama *A Hole in the Wall* (1929), but rather on Paramount's French-language comedy *Un Trou dans le mur* (1930).

## Humanidad

(Domènec Ceret and Alfred Fontanals, 1916). Studio Films. **Story:** Jaime Ardèvol. **With** Lola Paris, Alberto Martínez, Tina Jordi, Carolina López, Vincenç Ciurana, and Trino Cruz. A social drama about a poor family and its tribulations in a harsh culture, the sweeping film was one of the most ambitious and costly of its time. The two-part (3,000-meter) film had scores of feature players and thousands of extras — and ran into trouble with censors in Barcelona and Madrid, who labeled it a threat to the established order.

## La incorregible

(Leo Mittler, 1930). Paramount. **Script:** George Abbott. **Adaptation** and **dialogue:** José Luis Salado. **With** Enriqueta Serrano (Evelyn), Tony D'Algy (Roy), Antonia Arévalo, and Gabriel Algara (Mr. Albee). In Paris, German director Mittler filmed this 94-minute Spanish-language melodrama, which was based on the Hollywood version *Manslaughter* (1930), the tale of a woman who accidentally kills an officer. In order to increase interest in the film, Paramount changed the title to emphasize the nature of the protagonist rather than the crime she commits.

## Los intereses creados (Vested Interests)

(Jacinto Benavente, 1918). Cantabria. **Adaptation:** Benavente. **Photography:** Francisco Oliver. **With** José Buchs (Arlequín), Ricardo Puga (Crispín), Raymonde de Bach (Leandro), Teresa Arróniz (Silvia), and Isabel Faure (Colombina). The production company's first venture — an attempt to film a classic of Spanish literature — is a festive Mediterranean comedy directed by a man who would win the 1922 Nobel Prize for literature. Based on Benavente's 1907 play of the same name, the production was ambitious and expensive, costing 150,000 pesetas.

In a small town in 17th-century Spain, in a setting akin to the sunny, ancient Italy of Shakespeare's comedies, the film centers on a pair of traveling picaros: Crispin and his slightly more honest protégé, Leandro. Crispin's latest get-rich-quick scheme is to convince everyone that his companion is, in fact, "Signor Leandro," a wealthy nobleman, traveling incognito. The scheme works, and soon Leandro, who is the toast of the town, is set to wed Silvia, daughter of a wealthy merchant. Her father, however, opposes the match, and is aided in his opposition by an unfriendly judge. The plot then revolves around whether Crispin can get the pair to the church on time — before the bills come due and everything comes unglued. In this successful hit, Buchs, playing a poet, was assistant director in his first film.

## Julieta compra un hijo (Juliet Buys a Son)

(Louis King, 1935). Fox. **Supervisor:** Gregorio Martínez Sierra. **With** Catalina Bárcena, Gilbert Roland, Luana Alcañiz, and Anita Campillo. The great Barcena's seventh and final Spanish-language production from Hollywood is an adaptation of a similarly titled play by Gregorio Martínez Sierra and Honorio Maura, a feminist tale of a wealthy young woman who, disillusioned with men, dreams of raising a child. Her solution is to marry a down-and-out aristocrat — and "buy" a baby. After the child is born, the father abandons the family. "People ... will be entranced by Bárcena's performance," wrote *Cine-Mundial*.

## Las de Méndez (The Méndez Women)

(Fernando Delgado, 1927). R.A.F.E. **Script:** Delgado. **Photography:** Enrique

Blanco. **Design:** Agustín Espí. **With** Carmen Viance (Soledad), Javier de Rivera (Juan), Lina Moreno (Julia), Isabel Alemany (Irene), and Juana Espedo (Gertrudis Méndez). Directed by one of the pioneers of Spanish cinema, the powerfully poetic and moving melodrama about class conflict, which was also distributed by Pathé under title *Diario de una enfermera* (*Journal of a Nurse*), signified the peak of Delgado's career. His 3,400-meter production is the tale of the widow Méndez and her three daughters, Soledad, Julia, and Irene, and their rise and escape from poverty. That happens thanks to Soledad's efforts at obtaining work in a sanitarium as well as the help of a powerful and sympathetic official.

### Las joyas de la condesa (The Countess' Jewels)

(Domènec Ceret and Joan Solà Mestres, 1916). Studio Films. **Script:** Ceret and Mestres. **With** Pepe Font (Morson), Consuelo Hidalgo (the countess), Alberto Martínez (the detective), Lola Paris, and Baltasar Banquells. A mischievous adventure about an ingenious theft and the detective who uncovers the criminal and locates the goods. The Barcelona-produced, 1,600-meter film was appreciated enough to be screened in Britain.

### El Lazarillo de Tormes (Little Lázaro of Tormes)

(Florián Rey, 1925). Atlántida. **Script:** Rey. **Photography:** Alberto Arroyo. **Design:** Antonio Molinete. **With** Alfredo Hurtado (Lázaro), Manuel Montenegro, José Nieto (José), and Carmen Viance (Soledad). This melodrama is a morality tale based on the 16th century classic of the same name, attributed to Diego Hurtado de Mendoza (1503–1575). However, it is set in the 20th century. The film served two purposes: As a critique of social conditions in Spain, and as an example of Rey's ability to anticipate later attempts by filmmakers to transpose stories, legends, and myths to contemporary times.

In this tale of an orphaned youth whose only goal is survival, that is, to fill a realistically hungry stomach, the main action shows the little boy's travels around Spain and his work for vain, stupid, egotistical, and self-centered adults. He is hired out to a blind beggar, a miserly sacristan, a penniless nobleman, and an itinerant actor. But the boy's fortunes takes a turn for the better during the rivalry between contending villages (Romeral and Romerilla) for the right to possess an image of the Virgin Mary. A miracle sets things right—and when Lázaro unites two young lovers on opposite sides of the dispute, they adopt him.

### El León de la Sierra

(Alberto Marro, 1914). Hispano Film. **Photography:** Jordi Robert. **With** Jaume Borràs (Montalvo) and Luisa Oliván. A four-part (1,600-meter) silent along the lines of the popular Film d'Art, the Barcelona production concerns a woman who, having been dishonored, joins a band of outlaws who are led by the man known as the "Lion of the Sierra." The film's basis is José M. de Guevara's *Narración de la vida e historia de Roberto Montalvo, el León de la Sierra*.

The film is the second in the four-film *Serie de oro del arte trágico* (*The Golden Classics of Tragedy*), a combination of adventure and melodrama featuring well-known theatrical performers. The other films in the series are *Los muertos hablan* (*Dead Men Speak*), *La tragedia del destino* (*Tragedy of Fate*), and *La queja del pasado* (*The Complaint of the Past*).

## La llama sagrada (The Sacred Flame)

(William McGann, 1931). Warner Bros. **Script:** Guillermo Prieto Yeme. **With** Elvira Morla, Luana Alcañiz, Martín Garralaga, and Juan de Homs. The studio's second Spanish-language film from Hollywood is based on Somerset Maugham's wrenching play as well as *The Sacred Flame* (1929). An interesting, emotionally intense drama that evolves from a dinner scene, the seven-reel film concerns a mother and her two sons, one of whom is a crippled war hero whose life is ended by a family member.

## Lo mejor es reír (Better to Laugh)

(Emmerich W. Emo, 1931). Paramount. **Supervisor:** Florián Rey. **Script:** Benno Vigny. **Adaptation:** Pedro Muñoz Seca. **Dialogue:** Luis Fernández Ardavín and Claudio de la Torre (unaccredited). **With** Tony D'Algy (Paul), Imperio Argentina (Gaby), Rosita Díaz Gimeno (Margarita), Marguerite Moreno (Bijou), José Brujo (Bernard), and Carlos San Martín (Henri Gilbert). This was a superbly cast, 70-minute Spanish production out of Paris, a version of Harry D'Arrast's *Laughter* (1930), the sophisticated Depression-era comedy about making a fast buck.

Emo shot the film on the same set, using the same technicians and designs as the other Paris versions of the story, but that is where the similarities end (save for Emo's Portuguese version). Supervisor Rey, along with his writers and the director, crafted an original film by emphasizing the singing and dancing abilities of Imperio Argentina (who plays a Paris artist) and by tightening the running time by 30 minutes. They refashioned the story into the kind of film Latin audiences adored—a musical comedy—and produced a smash hit. This second Spanish success out of Paris, after *Su noche de bodas* (1931), was shown in Madrid in January 1932 and in Los Angeles that September. Director D'Arrast, who was of Spanish descent, ranked this production the best of Paramount's Spanish renditions based on Hollywood versions.

## Los que danzan (Those Who Dance)

(William McGann, 1930). Warner Bros. **Supervisor:** Henry Blanke. **Adaptation:** Baltazar Fernández Cué. **With** Pablo Alvarez Rubio, Antonio Moreno, María Alba, and Tito Davison. This beautiful and stylish Spanish version of the gangster thriller *Contre-Enquête* (1930) was the Hollywood studio's first Spanish-language film. The seven-reeler screened at the Callao theater in Madrid in September 1932. *Cine-Mundial* made note of the film under the title *Fin de fiesta*, and the film was also called *Aquellos que bailan*.

## Las luces de Buenos Aires (The Lights of Buenos Aires)

(Adelqui Millar, 1931). Paramount. **Screenplay:** Alfredo Le Pera, Manuel Romero, and Luis Bayón Herrera. **Photography:** Ted Pahle. **With** Carlos Gardel (Anselmo), Sofía Bozán (Elvira), Gloria Guzmán (Rosita), Pedro Quartucci (Pablo), Vincent Pedula, Carlos Martínez Baena (the impresario), and Jorge Infante (Romualso). Carlos Gardel's debut in sound was an eagerly anticipated 85-minute musical romance, an original Paris production shot in three weeks. The engaging tale of a talent agent who discovers a beautiful girl contains Gardel's lovely "El Rosal ("The Rosebush") and a tango he composed himself, "Tomo y Obligo" ("Drink, I Make You Drink"). The latter song expresses a classic theme — the rejected lover drowning his sorrows.

The production was called a "good picture" by *Variety*, with "excellent tango music, snappy Spanish dialogue … good comedy, principally by Gloria Guzman, songs by Argentine's champion tango crooner … and [Julio de] Caro's orchestra in good form." *Cine-Mundial* concurred, applauding all the parties involved. Other critics described the film as "one of the best musical comedies the sound cinema has yet realized." Shown in Los Angeles in late 1931, the tender tale was still playing to Spanish-speaking crowds three years later.

## Mama

(Benito Perojo, 1931). Fox. **Supervisor:** Gregorio Martínez Sierra. **Adaptation:** José López Rubio. **With** Catalina Bárcena (Mercedes), Rafael Rivelles, Andrés de Segurola, and Carmen Jiménez. Wrote *Cine-Mundial*, "They did what they thought no one could do" in this $100,000 Spanish-language drama from Hollywood. This little miracle of adaptation and artistic simplicity, based on Martínez Sierra's 1912 play of the same name, was, continued *Cine-Mundial*, a "Hollywood-level" production. Further, it was a breakthrough: of Hollywood's Spanish-language productions, the film was nearly irreproachable from all points of view.

This tale of a woman addicted to gambling because her marriage isn't working reflects one of the problems then at the heart of Spanish middle-class life, and it may well have convinced Fox to continue producing Spanish-language films. The director "keeps his characters stepping briskly most of the time," wrote the *New York Times*. Bárcena "makes her role appear quite authentic."

## Mefisto (Mephisto)

(Joan María Codina and Joan Solà Mestres, 1918). Studio Films. **With** Lola Paris (María), Bianca Valoris (Zizí), Baltasar Banquells (Mefisto), Josep Balaguer, Julián de la Cantera, Ramon Quandrény, and Joan Oliva. A 12-episode (9,500-meter) adventure serial produced on a grand scale in Barcelona. Deception and a false inheritance are the plot ingredients in this production, which was (like earlier efforts by the filmmakers) inspired by French models.

## Los misterios de Barcelona (The Barcelona Mysteries)

(Joan María Codina and Alberto Marro, 1915). Hispano Films. **Script:** Marro. **Photography:** Jordi Robert.

With Franceso Aguiló, Joaquim Carrasco, Joan Argelagués, Joan and Josep Durany, Pierre Smith, Clara Wilson, Emília de la Mata, and Angeleta Blanco. Also called *Barcelona y sus misterios*, this was an excellent example of the era's adventure series, an expensive, hugely popular, and ambitious eight-part (8,000-meter) serial — inspired by the French models. Based on the 1880 novel of the same name by Antoni Artadill, it was comparable in expertise to the best French and U.S. serials, made by a dynamic group that had a feel for the medium.

Shot in well-known cosmopolitan locations, the melodrama's episodes range from *Sports, Contraband, Inheritance, Shoeshines,* and *Counterfeiters* to the *Wishes of a Dying Man, Return of a Jailbird,* and *Death of Diego Rocafort.* The production was successful enough to inspire the six-part sequel *El testamento de Diego Rocafort* (*Diego Rocafort's Will*), released the following year.

## Monsieur le fox

(Hal Roach, 1931). MGM. **Adaptation** and **dialogue:** Roberto Guzman. **Design:** Cedric Gibbons. **With** Gilbert Roland (Luis Le Bay), Rosita Ballesteros (Nedra), Lillian Savin (Woolie Woolie), and Barbara Leonard. This 66-minute Spanish-language version of the atmospheric tale of the Canadian wilds, *Men of the North* (1930), signaled the Spanish-language debut of Hollywood matinee idol Roland. "Atención, muchachas," exclaimed *Cine-Mundial.*

It was also the first Hollywood film for Spanish import Ballesteros, and the attractive señorita made the most of it. While the theme is lighter and more transparent than a spiderweb, *Film Daily* noted, "There is lots of action and colorful stuff ... including a dog team dash through the wolf country." This version, which Roach shot simultaneously with his English, French, and Italian versions, was also released as *El Zorro.*

## La Mujer X (Madame X)

(Carlos Borcosque, 1931). MGM. **Script:** José López Rubio and Eduardo Ugarte. **Design:** Cedric Gibbons. **With** Rafael Rivelles (Luis), María Fernanda Ladrón de Guevara (Jaquelina), and José Crespo. "Another magnificent Spanish-language production," wrote *Cine-Mundial* about this 78-minute Hollywood mystery, based on Lionel Barrymore's powerful drama *Madame X* (1929) as well the play by Alexandré Bisson. Of the plot about a woman who kills to avoid blackmail, and who at her murder trial is defended by a young man unaware of the fact that she is his real mother, *Variety* wrote, "Works like this confound the reformers, elevate the name of pictures, and tell the world that there is an art in film making."

## Olimpia

(Juan de Homs and Chester M. Franklin, 1930). MGM. **Adaptation:** Miguel de Zárraga. **Photography:** William Daniels. **With** José Crespo (Captain), Elvira Morla, María Alba, Juan de Homs, and Carmen Rodríguez. The studio's first Spanish-language production out of Hollywood, it had *Cine-Mundial* proclaiming, "What a difference between professional and amateur actors!" Based on Ferenc Molnár's romantic *Olympia,* the heartrending play about a princess who falls in love with a commoner, the film's eight reels can lay claim to the expertise of the stars, which overshows the first ten stagy minutes of the production.

On its release in Madrid and Los Angeles, *Variety* wrote, "as a production, the superiority of the Hollywood touch is immediately apparent.... It is bound to impress internationally." *Cine-Mundial* agreed, calling the dramatic production, a "jewel of Spanish art, technique, and aesthetics."

## El otro (The Other)

(Joan María Codina, Joan Solà Mestres, and Eduardo Zamacois, 1919). Studio Films. **Photography:** Solà Mestres and Alfred Fontanals. **With** Zamacois, Bianca Valoris, and Ramon Quadrény. Inspired by the fact that the work of Spanish writer Vicente Blasco Ibáñez was successfully being adapted to the screen, the novelist and journalist Zamacois followed suit. His celebrated novel (published in 1910) became a haunting, extraordinary metaphysical tale of murder, with the attendant guilt and punishment.

At the start, a man writes letters to a dead woman. These are left on her tomb, where they disappear at night and return as white butterflies. The woman was Adelina Vera, mistress of Baron de Nhorres ("the other"). The two had conspired to murder her husband, doctor Riaza. But having done the deed, they can find no peace: Riaza's ghost torments them. At the moment when the baron is in Madrid, Juan Enrique Haldera tries to shoot Rhiaza's ghost, but instead kills Adelina. The film, which was not released in Barcelona for a year because of censorship problems, was a huge hit in South America.

## Para el ideal (For the Ideal)

(Domènec Ceret and Joan Solà Mestres, 1916). Studio Films. **Script:** Ceret. **Photography:** Solà Mestres. **With** Ceret, Consuelo Hidalgo, Lola Paris, Rosa Barco, Josep Font, and Samuel Hipson. A drama about a painter whose idealized portrait of a noblewoman leads to trouble, the Barcelona-produced 1,100-meter film was a huge hit (in Spain, France, Italy, and Argentina) thanks to Ceret, and became the first of a series of productions featuring the actresses Paris and Hidalgo.

## La Pasionaria (The Passion Flower)

(Joan María Codina and Joan Solà Mestres, 1915). Condal Film. **With** Tórtola Valencia and Gerardo Peña. A three-part (1,500-meter) drama that marked the debut of the beautiful and elegant performer Valencia. She plays a young woman, dishonored by a nobleman, who becomes a famous ballerina in America—and then gets her revenge. The Barcelona film (the first in a series starring Valencia) was distributed abroad by London and Counties Film Bureau, Ltd.

## A la pesca de los 45 millones (To Search for 45 Million)

(Domènec Ceret and Joan Solà Mestres, 1915). Studio Films. **Script:** Ceret and Solà Mestres. **Design:** Ceret. **With** Ceret (Don Raimundo), Josep Font (Sir John), Lolita Arellano, Héctor Quinanilla, and Visitació López (Zuri). This comedy adventure out of Barcelona was one of the earliest examples of the genre, about a father who wants one of his daughters to marry into wealth. The groom: a rich American. The 800-meter film (distributed by Eclair) was to have been the precursor of *El resultado de los 45 millones* (*The Result of 45 Million*), but the latter was never filmed.

## El pilluelo de Madrid (The Brat from Madrid)

(Florián Rey, 1926). Atlántida. **Script:** Rey. **Photography:** Carlos Pahissa. **Design:** Antonio Molinete. **With** Elisa Ruíz Romero (Carmen), Alfredo Hurtado (Juan/Manuel), Manuel Montenegro, and Ricardo Núñez (The Duke). An excellent two-part comedy and satire by the highly regarded Rey about the twins Juan and Manuel, opposites in temperament, whose adventures in a circus and in a band of thieves lead people to mistake one for the other.

## Poderoso caballero (Big Guy)

(Enrique Blanco, 1916). A farce about three men with swelled heads bearing the names of great Iberians — Magellan, Cortés, and Pizarro. Reduced to making a living by begging and similar methods, their fortunes change when they get hold of a winning lottery ticket. The adventure of their lives begins — it includes "gentleman" crooks and the fascinating woman Mercedes — after which they're left with just enough money to set up a shoeshine stand.

## El presidio

(Ward Wing, 1930). MGM. **Supervisor:** Edgar Neville. **With** Juan de Landa (Butch), José Crespo (Morgan), Tito Davison (Montgomery) and Luana Alcañiz (Anne). Made in Hollywood, the realistic 88-minute Spanish-language version of the Wallace Beery prison vehicle *The Big House* (1930), directed by George F. Hill, was a big hit. Directed by Theda Bara's brother-in-law, it features the highly regarded Landa who, wrote *Cine-Mundial*, "in spite of the artistic insignificance of the character ... created the most difficult Butch."

As the killer, "Landa does not imitate Beery. He's too much of an artist to simply imitate." When the film premiered in Spain alongside the English, French, and German versions, filmgoers ranked Juan de Landa's performance on a par with Beery's. *Cine-Mundial* called de Landa's performance the superior achievement.

## Primavera en otoño (Spring in Autumn)

(Eugene J. Forde, 1932). Fox. **Supervisor:** Gregorio Martínez Sierra. **Adaptation:** José López Rubio and John Reinhardt. **With** Catalina Bárcena, Raúl Roulien, Mimi Aguglia, and Luana Alcañiz. This Spanish-language drama, which is based on a 1911 play by Martínez Sierra, was Bárcena's second Hollywood production, shot in 17 days at a cost of $80,000. The beautiful lead plays an Andalusian actress who ignores her husband and child for her art. Late in life, she recovers her past and makes of fall another spring, that is, wife and estranged husband reunite to plan their "primavera en otoño." The woman's reincarnation is so convincing that few could doubt her triumphant return.

## El príncipe gondolero (The Gondolier Prince)

(Edward Venturini, 1931). Paramount. **With** Rosita Moreno, Roberto

Rey, Andrés de Segurola, Manuel Arbó, Juan de Homs, Elena Landeros, and Luis Llaneza. An eight-reel Spanish-language musical romance in which, against a colorful background, wrote *Film Daily*, the "cast, direction, and all-around handling are of a high order." The Hollywood film met a reception all too common for foreign-language films out of the film capital: a blind eye from some critics.

Countered one Paramount executive: "I don't understand the hostile reaction from certain sectors of Spanish public opinion…. The patriotic feelings expressed are quite often contrary to what you might expect of them…. If in Hollywood, movies are made in Spanish, they should be proud of the fact. Wasn't this the land where the Spaniard Friar Junipero Serra undertook his most humanitarian work, where the architecture ranging from the far-off mission-style to the more recent Spanish style is part of Hispanic culture, and where today's legendary figures called Zorro or Ramona were created?"

Wrote *Cine-Mundial*, "Bárcena's development has intensified the pure simplicity of the primitive play, making it pulsate with more life, more force, and more power of suggestion." The film's natural dialogue, according to reviews, has the unmistakable elegance associated with all works of art, and it ranked with the best Spanish films Fox produced.

## *El proceso de Mary Dugan (The Trial of Mary Dugan)*

(Marcel de Sano, 1931). MGM. **Adaptation:** José López Rubio. **Design:** Cedric Gibbons. **With** María Fernanda Ladrón de Guevara, Elvira Morla, María Tubau, Celia Montalvan, Ramón Pereda, Rafael Rivelles, Juan de Landa, José Soriano Viosca, Julio Villarreal, Paco Moreno, Lucio Villegas, and José Crespo. The studio's 88-minute Spanish version of its first sound film, *The Trial of Mary Dugan* (1929), stars, wrote *Cine-Mundial*, "the whole constellation" of Spanish actors in Hollywood. Marcel de Sano's suicide, shortly after its completion, hurt the film at the box office.

## *La pura verdad (The Naked Truth)*

(Manuel Romero, 1932). **Supervisor** and **dialogue director:** Florián Rey. **Adaptation:** Pedro Muñoz Seca. **With** Enriqueta Serrano (Emilia Lamberti), Manuel Russell (Roberto), María Brú (Mrs. Lamberti), and José Isbert (Mr. Lamberti). Manuel Romero's second film out of Paris, which was supervised by one of Spain's finest directors, is a risqué 89-minute Spanish comedy about a scandal swirling around the fund raising activities of executives of the Association for Social Action Against Nudity. Shot in the evenings over a three-week period in June 1931, the production was based in name only on Paramount's *Nothing but the Truth* (1929).

## *Rosa de Francia (Rose of France)*

(Gordon Wiles, 1935). 20th Century–Fox. **Script:** José López Rubio. **With** Rosita Díaz Gimeno (Louisa Isabelle of Orleans), Rita Cansino/Hayworth, Antonio Moreno, Enrique de Rosas, María Calvo, Tito Davison, and Jinx Falkenburg. The newly-formed studio's third and last Spanish-language film in Hollywood is a lavish, free, and improvised version of a 1923 play by Eduardo Marquina and Luis Fernández Ardavín. The 70-minute historical drama was filmed in a scant 15 days. Louisa is the object of desire of Louis, the son of King Philip V, founder of the Bourbon Dynasty in Spain. Elegant and witty is the tale of the monarch who abdicates his throne in 1724 in the hopes of succeeding to the throne of France — thereby allowing his son to become king and marry "Rose of France." The film was described as "handsomely made" by *Film Daily*.

## Salga de la cocina! (Come Out of the Kitchen!)

(Jorge Infante, 1931). Paramount. **Script:** Herman J. Mankiewicz. **Adaptation** and **dialogue:** Luis Fernández Ardavín. **Photography:** René Guissart. **With** Roberto Rey (Carlos), Miguel Ligero (Burnstein), Ampara Miguel Angel (Alicia), and Enriqueta Soler (Rosario). This 76-minute Paris comedy about the complications faced by a brother and sister when they rent their southern home to a northerner gave Spanish-language filmgoers a rare look into America. It is based on Alice Duer Miller's 1916 novel of the same name and the 1930 Hollywood production *Honey*.

## El secreto del doctor (The Doctor's Secret)

(Charles de Rochefort, 1930). Paramount. **With** Eugenia Zuffoli, Félix de Pomès, and Tony D'Algy. The Spanish version of the hit 1930 Hollywood film of the same name was one of Paramount's earliest films out of Paris.

## Señora casada necesita marido (A Married Woman Needs a Husband)

(James Tinling, 1934). Fox. **Supervisor:** Gregorio Martínez Sierra. **Adaptation:** José López Rubio. **With** Catalina Bárcena, Antonio Moreno, and José Crespo. The sexy Spanish-language comedy was the very able, versatile, charming, and incomparable Catalina Bárcena's next-to-last Hollywood film. She and Moreno play the young, out-of-step couple who need the "jealousy treatment" to prevent their divorcing. With action — including a Mae West bit — that kept spectators entertained until the end, the film (based on Hungarian Eugene Heltai's 1907 novel) was called by *Cine-Mundial* "a great comedy which does honor to director and supervisor." It was remade in English (without Bárcena) under the title *The Lady Escapes* (1937).

## Sevilla de mis amores

(Ramón Novarro and Carlos Borcosque, 1930). MGM. **With** Novarro (Juan de Dios Carbajal), Conchita Montenegro and Rosita Ballesteros. The 95-minute version of *Call of the Flesh* (1930) was the first Spanish-language film out of Hollywood whose subject matter and stars were entirely Spanish. It is the tale of a young opera singer who attains musical acclaim in his native tongue.

In charge, for the first time, of a film in the language of his birth, Novarro managed to enjoy comparative immunity from official studio supervision that had so often wrecked the artistic intent of many a director. Said one observer during filming, "It will be well worth a critic's time to look up the Spanish replica that he is about to conjure forth and compare it to the English version." Novarro created a sentimental tale spiced with comedy, and handled the mix of Spanish and Mexican players— they were extraordinarily touchy as to rank and perquisites—with tact and firmness. He dances a number that recalls his famous tango in *The Four Horsemen of the Apocalypse* and, in the finale, sings the famous "Ridi Pagliacci." Also called *La Sevillana*, "the new Novarro film," wrote a critic, "should be a riot in the Latin countries."

### Sombras del circo (Shadows of the Circus)

(Adelqui Millar, 1931). Paramount. **Script:** George Abbott. **With** Tony D'Algy (Ned), Amelia Muñoz (Greta Nelson), Miguel Ligero (Slim), Antonia Arévalo (Mrs. Elsie), and Félix de Pomès (Nick). A Paris show business drama that centers around a circus-based love triangle (trapeze artists) and an "accidental" death. Based on Paramount's *Half-Way to Heaven* (1930), the film (whose working title was *En mitad del cielo*) was shown in Spain in April 1931.

### Soñadores de la gloria (Dreamers of Glory)

(Miguel Contreras Torres, 1932). Imperial Art Films. **With** Lia Torá and Contreras Torres. United Artists backed the making of one of only two Hollywood-made Spanish-language films in 1932. The man behind it was the Mexican renaissance man Contreras Torres, an author, producer, actor, and director. In 1930, when Spain passed from a monarchy to a republic, he shot war scenes in Morocco and Spain, and completed filming in the Tec-Art Studios in Hollywood in 1931. The 110-minute film was hailed by *Cine-Mundial* as a "triumph of Spanish cinema," while The *New York Times* wrote that the production "Gives a pretty good idea of a few years ago when Spain was warring against rebellion in Morocco. Filled with episodes in the bullring ... this film holds the spectators interest."

### Los sucesos de Barcelona (The Events in Barcelona)

(Josep Gaspar Serra, 1909). Gaumont. Also called *Semana trágica* (*Tragic Event*) and *Semana trágica de Barcelona*, this nonfiction short, which documents political change, was greatly admired abroad. The director took extraordinary risks, filming highlights of an early 20th century revolution. His film became one of the most exported of early Spanish productions, especially to Russia, which took more than 100 copies.

### Sueño o realidad (Dream or Reality)

(Baltasar Abadal, 1919). Lotus Films. **Story:** Ricardo Llonch. **Photography:** Jordi Robert and Abadal. **With** Margarida Miró, Ricardo Llonch, Pau Prou de Vendreil, and Sofia Solande. A representative of Méliès and a pioneering filmmaker since 1899, Abadal founded his own production company in Barcelona to put out this many-peopled and much-heralded four-part (6,000-meter) melodrama of intrigue, deception, tragedy, and death.

## Su noche de bodas (Her Wedding Night)

(Louis Mercanton, 1931). **Supervisor:** Florián Rey. **Script:** Henry Myers. **Dialogue:** Luis Fernández Ardavín. **Photography:** Enzo Riccione. **Music:** Charles Borel-Clerc and Richard Whiting. **With** Imperio Argentina (Gisèle Landry), Helen D'Algy, Miguel Ligero (Adolphe Latour), Rosita Díaz Gimeno (Loulou), and José (Pepe) Romeu (Claude Mallet). This 83-minute musical comedy became a smash. It is based on Paramount's risqué Hollywood hit *Her Wedding Night* (1930), starring Clara Bow.

In order to enhance the appeal for Latin audiences, supervisor Rey added what Spanish audiences love best: musical numbers, which did not exist in either the original Hollywood version or Mercanton's French-language version, *Marions-nous* (1931). The numbers include "Blancaflor," "Cantares Que el Viento Llevo," "A la Mujer a Quien Digas," and "Entre Todas Te Busque." It was shown in Madrid in April 1931.

## Su última noche (His Last Night)

(Chester M. Franklin, 1931). MGM. **Script:** Eduardo Ugarte and José López Rubio. **Adaptation:** Miguel de Zárraga. **With** Ernesto Vilches (Mario), Conchita Montenegro (Luisa), Juan de Landa, and María Alba. As the 75-minute Spanish version of John Stahl's domestic comedy-drama *The Gay Deceiver* (1926), this is one of a number of stage and screen themes involving a central male character who, wrote *Variety*, "has been a gay old boy, a gay old roue, a gay old lover and ... 'a gay deceiver.'" The Hollywood film was also called *Toto*.

## Tengo fe en ti (I Believe in You)

(John Reinhardt, 1937–1940). Victoria Films. **Adaptation:** José López Rubio. **Photography:** Arthur Martinelli. **With** Rosita Moreno, José Crespo, Emilia Leovalli, and Carlos Villarías. This 66-minute production was the brainchild of actress Rosita Moreno. Completed at a cost of $60,000 and distributed by RKO, it had the distinction of being just about the last Spanish-language film out of Hollywood.

In the sentimental dance drama, narrated in the first person, with several flashbacks and no subtitles, the vivacious Moreno plays a Hungarian ballet dancer who forsakes her high-brow career for more popular dancing. Moreno's teacher-husband, played by Crespo, is uncomfortable with her choice, so after she dies, he teaches their daughter ballet and hopes to see her become the kind of classical star her mother briefly was. Like her mother, however, the young woman rejects ballet for something else — and in the end father and daughter are reconciled. *Variety* found "Miss Moreno in particular exhibiting plenty of reason for her popularity.... She's nifty in the ballet work and in pop dancing and warbling."

## Tierra baja (Lowlands)

(Fructuoso Gelabert, 1907). Barcelona Films (Diorama). **Photography:** Gelabert. **Script:** Joan Morales. **With** Enric Giménez (Manelich), Enrique Guitart (Sebastian), Maria Llorente (Marta), Emília Baró (Nuri). A tragedy based on complex play of the same name

(also called *Marta of the Lowlands*) by
Angel Guimerà (1845–1924), the 400-
meter film represents Gelabert's first attempt to turn literature into film.

He enthusiastically filmed principal scenes of the evocative, tender, and
highly moving peasant story whose author was known as the poet of Catalonia.
It is a realist drama set in a remote
province in Spain where Marta, a beautiful maiden, has become the mistress of
a powerful landowner. He manipulates
her into marrying Manelich, a goat herd
from the mountains, in order to marry
another and inherit a fortune. The two
slowly awaken to the treachery that has
befallen them. An honest affection grows
between them, and they end by turning
against their common betrayer. The
film's success, as well as its message that
the free spirit of the mountains will
overcome the age-old servitude of the
peasants of the valley, spurred Gelabert

to film Guimerà's *Maria Rosa* the following year.

### Toda una vida (A Whole Life)

(Adelqui Millar, 1930). Paramount.
With Carmen Larrabeiti, Félix de
Pomès, Isabel Baron, Tony D'Algy, and
Luis Peña. An early Paris production by
the studio, this highly sentimental Spanish version of *Sarah and Son* (1930)
retells the tale of the 14-year separation
of a mother and her child. Larrabeiti is
the tragic heroine and opera singer;
Baron the wealthy woman who does her
best to hold onto the adopted child she
and her husband are smothering with
kindness. "The director manages to keep
his characters from tarrying too long in
one spot," wrote the *New York Times*.
"The film has a certain interest, although there is never any doubt as to the
outcome."

## La traviesa molinera (The Mischevious Miller's Wife)

(Harry D'Arrast, 1934). **Script:** D'Arrast. **Dialogue:** Edgar Neville. **Photography:** Jules Kruger. **Art direction:** Ricardo Soriani. **Music:** Rudolf Halftner. **With** Eleanor Boardman, Hilda Moreno, and Allan Jeayes. Harry D'Arrast's final film of his career is a work of art, a sardonic production based on a well-known 18th-century folk tale about how an affair between a mayor and a miller's wife (Moreno) causes the miller to take up with the mayor's wife (Boardman). The story is told mostly in mime, with an almost continual musical accompaniment and a good deal of spirited dancing.

*Opposite and this page:* Eleanor Boardman in scenes from *La traviesa molinera* (*The Mischevious Miller's Wife*), the comedy directed by her husband (Harry D'Arrast, 1934).

Its making reflected D'Arrast's background and his need to be free of Hollywood pressures. Born in Argentina and educated in Paris and Switzerland, the multilingual American Harry D'Arrast left Hollywood for Madrid in mid–1934, and went to work under less than ideal conditions. Though lacking efficient production facilities and experienced actors, he and his art director formed a production company and put together their cast (headed by D'Arrast's wife, Eleanor Boardman) and crew, and lined up United Artists, which agreed to release the 67-minute production — the first Spanish film to get worldwide distribution — except in the only place it really mattered: the United States. In Britain the film was called *It Happened in Spain*, and in France, *La Meunière debauchée*.

D'Arrast had overcome production delays (and a strike that held up the Madrid premiere) to make a sharply limned and spare-dialogue film that Chaplin ranked as one of his favorites. *Cinema News* in London praised the "brilliant and sensitive handling of simple and hearty situations" and the film's "pervasive lyric quality mingled with rich and delicious touches of humor and characterizations, enhanced by superb pictorial compositions of authentic Spanish sun-drowsy village and pastoral scenes." D'Arrast was called a director "who exemplifies Shakespeare's dictum that the hand of least employment hath the keenest touch. Every one of the few films he has made has been worth seeing. But none of them is so worth seeing as this exquisite picturization of Alarcon's poetic farce." In the end, the richness of the film may have been its undoing. "The pity of it," concluded *Cinema News*, "is that its appeal resides so much in the beauty of setting, pictorial perfection, rich characterization and a pervasive lyrical quality; it is so much above the heads of the average patrons as to be definitely out of the popular box-office class." London's *Cinema News* praised the "brilliant and sensitive handling" of the tale.

## La verbena de la Paloma (The Fair of la Paloma)

(José Buchs, 1921). Atlántida. **Script:** Buchs. **Photography:** Alberto Arroyo and Joan Solà Mestres. **Design:** Emilio Pozuelo. **With** Elisa Ruiz Romero (Susana), Florián Rey (Julián), José Montenegro (Don Hilarión), and Julia Lozano (Casta). The prolific director Buchs preferred historical subjects, and here made a comedy (based on Tomas Breton and Ricardo de la Vega's well-known "zarzuela," or operetta) about a lovers' spat that takes place during the most famous celebration of its time: the fair in the Madrid of the 1890s on the saint's day of the Virgin of the Dove (La Paloma).

An old, would-be Don Juan takes two pretty dressmakers to the fiesta — to the great indignation of a handsome young painter. For the first time in Spanish cinema, a street celebration was recreated within the studio, where the ambiance of the era and picturesque nature of the period are beautifully brought to life. The atmospheric, gracious, and well-done 1,800-meter work was a huge hit in the Spanish-speaking world.

## Una viuda romantica (A Romantic Widow)

(Louis King, 1933). Fox. **Supervisor:** Martínez Sierra. **Adaptation:** Jardiel Poncela and José López Rubio. **With** Catalina Bárcena, Gilbert Roland, Mona

Maris, María Calvo, Mimi Aguglia, Fernando de Toledo, Juan Toreno, and Julio Pena. The great Spanish-language romantic comedy, based on Martínez Sierra's 1920 play *Sueño de una noche de agosto*, tells the tale of a charming young lady who favors equality of the sexes. She very much wants to work, but her conservative brothers urge her to marry and live a more traditional life. Simple in scope, the story allows for considerable amusement and action.

Wrote *Cine-Mundial*: "There is action because there is overflowing life that exhibits movement and excitement until the point of insanity." Bárcena's protagonist, while not immune from the conventions and anxieties of her time, wrote the critics, feels the impulses of independence, liberty, and romantic abandonment. Fantastically, she finds her dream lover, and, like the true person she is, takes charge by making him hers. "Bárcena," continued *Cine-Mundial*, "doesn't act any more, she lives and she lives intensely, vehemently and overflowingly, with a naturalness that captures us and elevates our eyes above other performers." That's not to say that Roland, Maris, and the three playing her brothers—Fernando de Toledo, Juan Toreno, and Julio Pena—were not fine; or that María Calvo and Mimi Aguglia were not their usual exceptional selves. It's just that Bárcena stood apart. The Fox film, a great success in its time, was also called *Una viuda difícil*.

## Viva Madrid, que es mi pueblo! (Hooray for Madrid, My Village!)

(Fernando Delgado, 1928). Producción Exclusivas Orozco. **Script:** Delgado. **Photography:** Enrique Blanco. **Design:** Agustin Espí. **With** Marcial La-Landa (Luis), Carmen Viance (Lucia), Celia Escudero (Ana María), and Eduardo G. Maroto. This comedy was one of Spanish cinema's greatest commercial and critical successes of the era. For the first time in Spanish cinema, panchromatic stock was used — to great effect — in a number of sequences, with exteriors shot in the Plaza de Chinchón. Initially called *La conquista de Madrid*, the film (financed by Madrid bullfighter LaLanda as a present to his wife) is based on the three-act *El roble de la Jarosa* (1915) by Pedro Muñoz Seca (1881–1936), about a famous bullfighter, his young lover, and a dangerous femme fatale. A 55-minute portion survives.

## La voluntad del muerto (The Dead Man's Wish)

(George Melford, 1930). Universal. **Script:** Baltazar Fernández Cué. **With** Lupita Tovar, Antonio Moreno, María Calvo, and Andrés de Segurola. This 87-minute Spanish rendition of Hollywood's highly successful mystery *The Cat Creeps* (1930) was the studio's first Spanish-language production. While the English version was shot during the day, the Spanish film was shot—appropriately for the film's atmosphere—at night. Both films are, in turn, sound remakes of Paul Leni's silent classic *The Cat and the Canary* (1927).

Inherently fantasmagorical, with murder, shadow, noise, and a mysterious hand, the Spanish film — directed by the same man who did the extant Spanish rendition of *Drácula* (1931)— relates the story of greedy relatives who assemble at midnight in an old house to hear the last will and testament of an eccentric. In the process, a young heroine, heir to a fortune, is threatened.

### Wu Li Chang

(Nick Grindé, 1930). MGM. **Adaptation:** Salvador de Alberich. **With** Ernesto Vilches, Angelita Benítez and José Crespo. In Hollywood the great Spanish star Vilches hoped to realize a great success when he made in this seven-reel Spanish version of the 1914 stage play *Mr. Wu* and the 1927 silent of the same name. It is a story about a daughter of the Mandarin Wu who is seduced by a young Englishman. Tradition demands that Wu kill his daughter and then kill the seducer or seduce his mother. When all indicators point to Wu's triumph, Wu equivocates at the key moment, taking poison that ends his diabolical scheme at vengeance.

Though *Cine-Mundial* called his role an "insuperable creation," Vilches felt otherwise. "There is no common sense in choosing casting" in Hollywood, he said. Further, the film was edited so as to make it appear that Vilches failed to give his work "the correct ambiance." And having a producer "suppressing details," said Vilches, the film remains "a skeleton, a body without soul."

### Yo, tu, y ella (Me, You, and Her)

(John Reinhardt, 1933). Fox. **Supervisor:** Martínez Sierra. **Adaptation:** José López Rubio and John Reinhardt. **With** Catalina Bárcena, Gilbert Roland, Mona Maris, and Rosita Moreno. In Hollywood's Spanish-language adaptation of Gregorio Martínez Sierra's 1924 play *Mujer*, the scintillating Bárcena plays the woman who makes her adulterous husband beg to take him back. The story begins in Paris, shifts to other French and Italian sites, and finishes in Madrid. There she is a woman remade, more sophisticated and stylish, and — as an indicator of her progress — she takes up smoking. Her more defiant stance toward life is shown most clearly when refuses to permit her husband to return — but filmgoers understand that she is punishing him and will eventually relent.

# Sweden

In 1912, the year August Strindberg died, the golden age of Swedish film began. Led by directors Mauritz Stiller, Victor Sjöström, and John W. Brunius, the Swedish cinema peaked by the early 1920s. It emphasized the home market: Swedish films for Swedish audiences. Making use of good lighting and camera work, Swedish cinema was "first in intelligence, first in force, and first in imaginative zeal," noted a critic. But the lure of Hollywood, the pull of international productions, and the transition to sound changed everything. By the end of the decade, Swedish cinema's finest talent — Garbo, Sjöström, Stiller, Lars Hanson — was in the film Mecca. The introduction of sound was an even greater shock to the Swedish industry, as evidenced by its first "sound" film, the synchronized *The Dream Waltz*, starring Edvin Adolphson, which was hurriedly released in late 1929.

Paramount in Paris capitalized on the changing technology by producing some of the first Swedish sound films. In 1930 the studio made five Swedish-language films, while the entire Swedish film industry produced nine. When Paramount released its first such production, *När rosorna slå ut* (1930), it came in for praise: "Paramount handily won the race to give the public the first 100% Swedish talkie. The idea of making sound films in a multitude of different versions is a good one," wrote a Swedish critic, "and the fact that this major American studio has opted for the language of honor and heroism is indeed likely to bolster our Swedish self-esteem." Still, Paramount's first Swedish production was not free of problems: the synchronization was off and the microphones were visible. However, "these are mere technical flaws that will be eliminated with improved tecnology and greater experience," wrote the critic, "and they certainly did not seem to have had a negative effect on the happy 'premiere' mood.... The Swedish film industry has been born."

In all, Paramount in Paris produced 14 Swedish-language features and one musical revue in the period 1930–1932. Three of these productions are not versions of Hollywood films, while the others, starring some of Sweden's finest talent, were made as distinctively Swedish as possible. Two are extant: *Vi två* (*We Two*) (John W. Brunius, 1930) and *Längtan till havet* (*Longing for the Sea*) (Alexander Korda, 1931).

## Dödskyssen (The Kiss of Death)

(Victor Sjöström, 1916). Svenska Bio. **Script:** Sjöström and Sam Ask (A.V. Samsjo). **Photography:** Julius Jaenzon. **With** Sjöström (Lebel), Mathias Taube (Dr. Adell), and Albin Lavén. A kind of *Rashomon* in its day, Sjöström's experimental film is unique in his career, an original, rigorously structured psychological drama (also known as *Ingenjör Lebels aventyr* [*Engineer Lebel's Adventure*]) about a man in the depths of depression. Lebel, an engineer, is in prey to a crisis. Forced by his doctor to go on a rest cure, he finds himself a double, a look-alike, and charges him with making sure his engineering work goes well.

To this drama teeming with improbabilities, director Sjöström (playing two roles) placed technique at the service of the tale. In order to bring it to a successful conclusion, he had to conjure away the implausible. He did this through the use of a relatively new technique for its time: flashbacks. Each flashback is used to shed light on an episode of the adventure of which the hero has become a victim.

The director was equally skillful in his use of lighting to highlight the drama. He left a large part of space in shadow, and often had the main characters emerge from darkness somewhat like ghosts materializing out of thin air. Finally, Sjöström made the personalities of the engineer and his double just different enough so that spectators remained aware of who was who.

Filmgoers took to the film, of which Louis Delluc said, "The dream is quite comfortable in this film. The atmosphere is made more mysterious by the perfection we sense in it. These beauties did not surprise me. I was more surprised by the respect shown by the public."

## Den Farliga leken (The Dangerous Game)

(Gustaf Bergman, 1930). Paramount. **Script:** Elsa af Trolle. **With** Jenny Hasselquist (Ellen Brenton), Ragnar Widestedt (George Farland, attorney), Elsa Wallin (Alice), Rune Carlsten (Harry Brenton), Olga Andersson (Mrs. Playgate), Stellan Windrow (Bob Dugan), and Ragna Broo-Juter. Based on Alfred Sutro's play *The Laughing Lady*, which premiered in London in 1922, and Victor Schertzinger's sophisticated *The Laughing Lady* (1929), starring Ruth Chatterton and Clive Brook. This Swedish-language production, the fifth in Paramount's series out of Paris, represents a rarity: it had no French-language equivalent and was also Paramount's first Swedish comedy. The impression that this production made in Sweden can be summed up as "fairly good at times, and very good in a few instances," wrote a critic. "Let's try to be generous," wrote another critic, "and call it a generally acceptable comedy of manners about love, marriage, presumed love affairs, actual love affairs and divorce, even if its failings and dull stretches are hard to ignore."

## Doktorns hemlighet (The Doctor's Secret)

(John W. Brunius, 1930). Paramount. **Script:** Per Stille. **With** Ivan Hedqvist (Dr. Bolton), Pauline Brunius (Lady Lillian Gardner), Olaf Sandborg (Richard Gardner), Hugo Björne (Hugo Paton), Erik Berglund (Mr. Redding), Anne-Marie Brunius (Annie), and Ragna Broo-Juter. Paramount's third Swedish production from Paris is based on the 1930 English-language melodrama starring Ruth Chatterton. The cast is headed by two former silent-screen directors, Ivan Hedqvist and Pauline Brunius, as the pair that shares a secret. It was shown in Stockholm in November 1930, when critics noted the melodrama's "strongly concentrated, evocative plot, which takes place over a mere half hour, engages us with its dramatic vigor ... and the dialogue is elegant and well thought out."

## Farornas paradis (Paradise of Dangers)

(Rune Carlsten, 1931). Paramount. **With** Elisabeth Frisk (Anita), Ragnar Arvedson (Mr. Jones), Knut Martin (Davis), and Oscar Textorius (Mr. Schomberg). The eleventh in Paramount's series of Swedish films out of Paris is based on Joseph Conrad's popular *Victory,* as well as Maurice Tourneur's 1919 drama of the same name and Paramount's English-language *Dangerous Paradise* (1930), directed by William A. Wellman. In this melodrama, set in the tropics, violinist Anita comes into trouble with the sharp, acerbic crime boss Mr. Jones. Paramount went to great pains to recreate a realistic setting, including evocative scenery and musical natives. Everything takes place in a languorous, humid atmosphere. When the film reached Stockholm in October 1931, Swedish critics found that it "tends a bit too heavily toward a live theatrical performance."

## Fiskebyn (The Fishing Village)

(Mauritz Stiller, 1920). Svenska Bio. Script: Bertil Malmberg and Stiller. Photography: Henrik Jaenzon. With Karin Molander (Martina), Lars Hanson (Thomas Rilke), Carl Helleman, and Egil Eide (Jacob Vondås). Also called Chains, the five-reel (1,800-meter) drama of revenge is based on Georg Engel's 1905 work Im Hafen (In the Harbor).

## Generalen (The General)

(Gustaf Bergman, 1931). Paramount. Adaptation: Bergman. Photography: Philip Tannura. With Edvin Adolphson (General Platoff), Karin Swanström, Inga Tidblad (Maria Sabline), Paul van der Osten (Viktor Sabline), Karin Swanström (Alexandra), and Knut Martin (Glinka). Paramount's eighth Swedish film from Paris is based on Lajos Zihaly's Hungarian play A Tabornok (1928) and the studio's First World War tale The Virtuous Sin (1930). It afforded the handsome and commanding Adolphson a magnificent physical role.

In Caucasian dress uniform and beautiful waistcoat, "with its poniards, sabres and silver cartridges across the chest," wrote a critic, Adolphson makes a dashing Russian officer known as "Iron Face" who must decide the fate of a pacifist under his command. Tidblad plays the young woman trying to save her pacifist husband, while Swanström plays a bordello madam. In the cast are Russian extras, including Grand Duchess Maria, Prince Wilhelm's estranged wife. The Swedish melodrama was filmed at night one week and during the day the next, alternating with the German production starring Conrad Veidt. Shown in Stockholm in April 1931, Bergman's film, a critic pointed out, has more camera movement and close-ups than his earlier Paris efforts, but its dialogue "has been thinned out in an artificial and theatrical manner." He "continues to think of talkies as filmed theater ... with the emphasis on diction, dramatic pauses and elaborate pacing."

## Halvvägs till himlen (Half-Way to Heaven)

(Rune Carlsten and Stellan Windrow, 1932). Paramount. With Elisabeth Frisk (Greta Nelson), Haakon Hjelde (Ned Lee), Edvin Adolphson (Nick), and Karin Swanström (Madame Jenny). Paramount's thirteenth Swedish-language feature out of Paris can be considered the most Scandinavian of the series because the dialogue is a mix of Swedish, Danish, and Norwegian. Based on Paramount's Half-Way to Heaven (1929), starring Jean Arthur and Paul Lukas, the film is set in Chicago. During a circus act one trapeze artist drops his rival during a "catch" and then tries to win the favor of his rival's lover. The acting is especially good, wrote a Swedish critic, particularly that of the comedienne Swanström and the hero Adolphson "who can really speak the language of film." His "character delineations are packed with meaning." Shown in Stockholm in January 1932, the film represents one of Paramount's last adaptations of an earlier Hollywood version.

## Hämnaren (The Avenger)

(Mauritz Stiller, 1915). Svenska Bio. Script: Martin Jörgensen and Louis

Levy. **Photography:** Hugo Edlund. **With** Karin Molander (Emma), Richard Lund (Josef), John Ekman (Jakob Kahn), Edith Erastoff (Ester), and Wilhelm Hansson (Georg Vide). A stark, three-reel (1,000-meter) masterwork about racial conflict that begins when Georg, a student, falls in love with the young Jewish woman Ester. Anti-Semitism leads to tragedy and revenge.

### Hjärtats röst (Call of the Heart)

(Rune Carlsten, 1930). Paramount. **With** Margit Manstad (Brigit Storm), Richard Lund (Stanley Vanning), Ivan Hedqvist (Cyril Brown), Ragnar Billberg (Jim Grey), Mathias Taube (John Ashmore), Stellan Windrow (Wells). This 80-minute tearjerker represents Paramount's fourth foreign rendition of Arzner's *Sarah and Son* (1930), the tale of a vaudeville dancer's path to stardom and the long struggle to find her abducted boy. Margit Manstad stars in Ruth Chatterton's part and Billberg (the handsomest of the men in any of the versions) plays the worthless husband. The great Richard Lund appears as the young attorney who sets things right.

This Swedish film by Paramount in Paris (though not up to the technical standards of the French version) did well enough in New York in June 1931 "because there have been no Swedish pictures in months," wrote *Variety*. In Stockholm the critics noted that the film "represents a definite step forward." Most of the credit belonged to Rune Carlsten "under whose steady direction the story comes shining through at a brisk pace. The camera moves with the same mobility as in silent films, thus eliminating the impression of bad, static theater that plagues so many talkies."

### Kampen om hans hjärta (The Fight for His Heart)

(Mauritz Stiller, 1916). Svenska Bio. **Script:** Georg Wiinblad. **Photography:** Henrik Jaenzon. **Design:** Axel Esbensen. **With** Karin Molander (Emma Reuter) and Richard Lund (Robert Walter). An exquisite 50-minute (900-meter) experimental work with racy elements.

### En Kvinnas morgondag (A Woman's Tomorrow)

(Gustaf Bergman, 1931). Paramount. **Photography:** Fred Langenfeld. **With** Vera Schmiterlöw, Paul van der Osten, Ragnar Widestedt, and Mathias Taube. This production, which was Paramount's tenth Swedish-language film out of Paris, is based on Paramount's Hollywood drama *The Devil's Holiday* (1930), the tale of a woman trying to make amends for past misdeeds. Shown in Stockholm in May 1931, the film elicited this response from a critic: "The Swedish actors and actresses blossom in this script which, despite all its failings, is full of the sense of human possibility ... Osten and ... Widestedt play their parts well, much better than in previous Paris films." Lead actress Schmiterlöw delivers her lines as a vamp and as a shaken, repentant woman well enough, but fails as a highly touted tragedienne, laboring without enough "passion or fire."

### Kärlek måste vi ha (We've Got to Have Love)

(Gustaf Bergman, 1931). Paramount. **Script:** Torsten Quensel. **Photography:**

Fred Langenfeld. **Music:** W. Franke Harling. **Lyrics:** Gösta Stevens. **With** Margit Rosengren (Olive Dangerfield), Nils Ericsson (Charles Dangerfield), and Isa Quensel (Cora). A Paris comedy based on Paramount's Hollywood musical *Honey* (1930), this Swedish production is that rare glimpse of America. In this tale of mistaken identity, a brother and sister are forced to play the butler and maid in the southern home they rent to a northerner.

Paramount's sixth Swedish production out of Paris, shown in Stockholm in January 1931, "does provide a pleasant and enjoyable mixture of farce and operetta — it is a pretty good movie," wrote a critic. The studio "has succeeded in assembling an exceptional Swedish cast ... successfully portraying youth, burlesque and resolve." Another reviewer noted that the film's program, including the original authors of the novel and play on which the film is based, "lists a total of ten cooks. However, you couldn't say that they had spoiled the broth." On the contrary, their combined efforts produced a pleasant and appealing blend of fairly conventional operetta direction "with men and women who sing well and with good humor."

### De Landsflyktige (The Exiles)

(Mauritz Stiller, 1921). Svensk Filmindustri. **Script:** Stiller and Ragnar Hyltén-Cavallius. **Photography:** Henrik Jaenzon. **With** Carl Nissen, Karin Swanström, Jenny Hasselquist (Sonia), Lars Hanson (Michailov), Ivan Hedqvist (moneylender), John Ekman, and Edvin Adolphson (revolutionary student). Stiller's "Russian film" was a well-crafted production, in which the "great sets convey no suspicion of the studio" in telling the tale of one of the most beautiful and noble of characters, Princess Sonia.

Released in the U.S. under the title *In Self Defense*, the five-reel production, based on the novel *Zoja* by the Finno-Swedish author Runar Schildt, is, observed a critic, an "exceptionally strong drama" that, "unlike the majority" of the studio's productions — and the work on which it is based — "has a happy ending." In pre–Revolutionary times, a young woman of aristocratic birth is instrumental in saving Alexander Michailov, "a son of the people," from her country's brutal internal security forces. During the Russian Revolution, he returns the favor, saving her and her family from fellow Bolsheviks. Then, after he is forced to flee turbulent Russia, he locates Sonia and her family in exile in Finland. Matters turn from bad to worse when Sonia's father gets involved with a moneylender who soon turns up dead. Sonia is accused of the deed because she had spurned the underhanded banker's attentions, though it is Michailov who killed the scoundrel, who was actually a "traitor." However, if Michailov admits to the deed, many others will suffer. Knowing this, Sonia consents to go on trial for murder.

"Throughout, the acting is amongst the best ever seen," wrote a critic. "The characters live." Hasselqvst "gives a sterling performance ... and the entire cast is miles ahead of 99 per cent of picture players."

### Landshövdingens dotter (The Governor's Daughters)

(Victor Sjöström, 1915). **Script:** Sjöström and Marika Stiernstedt.

Photography: Henrik Jaenzon. With Alfred Lundberg (Salta), Jenny Tschernichin-Larsson (Mrs. Salta), Lili Bech (Elvine/Daniela), Richard Lund (Henrik Pasch), and Margit Sjöblom (Daniela's mother). Based on two of well-known writer Marika Stiernstedt's works, this is a three-reel drama about half-sisters Elvine Salta, who is legitimate, and Daniela, who is illegitimate.

## Lika inför lagen (Equals Before the Law)

(Gustaf Bergman, 1931). Paramount. Adaptation: Frederick Lindh. Photography: Jacques Montéran. With Karin Swanström, Gustaf Bergman, Knut Uno Henning, Ragnar Widestedt (attorney), Margita Alfvén and Lillebil Ibsen (Sonja). As the seventh of Paramount's Swedish-language productions out of Paris, the film, shown in Stockholm in March 1931, broke new ground, its dramatic development more dynamic than in previous Swedish productions. "The velvet sofas and plush chairs have been stowed away," wrote an observer, "and there is space and light in the scenes. The camera captures spacious apartments and courtrooms in sweeping panoramas, and no longer clings to a single person or piece of furniture."

The melodrama is based on the Hollywood production Manslaughter (1930). This is another version of the tale of a woman, accused of vehicular homicide, whose lover is the prosecuting attorney. Attempting to shed light on middle class perceptions of justice, the film tries to make the case that truth and right prevail. "The prospect of a brush with the law is explored in a number of generally successful dialogues," noted a critic. In fact, the young middle-class woman is punished.

## Madame de Thèbes

(Mauritz Stiller, 1915). Svenska Bio. Script: Martin Jorgensen and Louis Levy. Photography: Julius Jaenzon. With Ragna Wettergreen (Ayla), Nicolai Johannsen (Robert), Albin Lavén (von Volmar), and Karin Molander (Louise). A psychological drama of life and manners that was released as A Son of Fate in the United States.

## Minlotsen (The Mine Pilot)

(Mauritz Stiller, 1915). Svenska Bio. Script: Sigurd von Koch. Photography: Hugo Edlund. With Lili Bech (Maria), Nicolai Johannsen, and Sven Bergvall (Murray). With the war as a backdrop, Stiller filmed a 40-minute (750-meter) drama (subtitled En Händelse fran krigets dagar i tre akter) set among the bare rocks and blowing winds of the outer skerries.

## När rosorna slå ut (When the Roses Bloom)

(Edvin Adolphson, 1930). Paramount. Script: René Barbéris. Adaptation: Edvin Adolphson and Gösta Stevens. With Karin Swanström (Charlotte), Knut Uno Henning (André), Nils Wahlbom (Greven), Margita Alfvén (Marguerite), Sven Gustafson (Anatole), and Else de Castro. This was Paramount's initial Swedish production out of Paris. It was shot at Gaumont's Paris studio, which had double soundproofed walls, because Paramount's own studios were under construction. The film has nothing to do with Robert Florey's Hollywood melodrama *A Hole in the Wall* (1929). Rather, it follows the storyline of Paramount's debut feature out of Paris, *Un Trou dans le mur* (1930), which is based on Yves Mirande's hit play.

In the 86-minute romantic comedy, the adventurous young lawyer André seeks out a treasure buried behind a wall in the Palace Brignolles in Paris. Along the hunt, he finds love in the form of the beautiful Marguerite. He also meets Charlotte, the indomitable lady of the house played by Swanström, whom critics singled out as "a real performer." "An agreeable and light-hearted cast moves through the leisurely narrative," wrote the *New York Times*, when the film was shown in New York in February 1931. "The emphasis is on dialogue rather than action." The Paris production was a hit in Sweden, and to make the film attractive in Denmark and Norway, Paramount emphasized that Viking Ringheim and Else-Marie Hansen were in the cast.

### Det Omringade Huset (The Surrounded House)

(Victor Sjöström, 1922). Svensk Filminspelning. **Script:** Sjöström and Ragnar Hyltén-Cavallius. **Photography:** Henrik Jaenzon and Axel Lindblom. **Advisor:** S. T. Buchanan. **With** Meggie Albanesi (Mary Lixton), Uno Henning (Jeff Gordon), Ivan Hedqvist (Major Cyril Ward), Richard Lund (Harry Lixton), Edvin Adolphson, Sjöström (Capt. Davies), Hugo Björne, Ragnar Arvedson, S. T. Buchanan, Nils Brambeck, and Arthur Natorp. A five-reel confessional, based on Pierre Frondaie's 1919 play *La Maison Cernée* that was Sweden's first

postwar "international" picture. By moving away from purely Swedish film and introducing the international element, Sjöström was making Swedish movies look more like Hollywood. That's something which would eventually help destroy the Swedish film industry.

The action takes place in Palestine during its occupation by the Turks in 1917. Jeff Gordon is a young officer in love with Mary, the wife of his commanding officer. He is captured and accused of espionage for having secretly entered the officer's house at night. He lets the accusation stand so as not to compromise the one he loves. But to prevent the young man from being shot, the wife confesses to the truth. The drama, nonetheless, ends in the best way possible, with the death of the husband, wounded in battle. Before dying, he asks his wife to marry the young officer to reward the heroism he showed.

### Paramount Stjerneparade

(1930). Paramount. **With** Ernst Rolf and Tutta Rolf. Paramount's Swedish-Danish all-star revue along the lines of *Paramount on Parade* (1930), filmed in Paris.

### Studenter i Paris (Students in Paris)

(Louis Mercanton, 1932). Paramount. **Photography:** Harry Stradling. **Music:** Raoul Moretti and André Cadou. **With** Meg Lemonnier (Jacqueline Cordier), Henri Garat (Jacques Dombreval), Aino Taube, and Else de Castro. The fourteenth and last of Paramount's series of Swedish-language features out of Paris represents the other version of Mercanton's French hit *Il est charmant*

(1931), based on the elegant little musical comedy by Lorens Marmsted.

This film too is a slightly risqué operetta with catchy and typically Parisian songs, "sung in a pleasant and entertaining manner" by Garat, as the distracted Sorbonne student, and by young woman he is chasing, the beautiful and charming Lemonnier. An original Paris production (not based on a Hollywood version), the film was shown in Stockholm in April 1932, with the critics noting "a few familiar Scandinavian faces ... hidden among the large French cast — among them ... Aino Taube. We would gladly have seen and heard more of them, and of the equally talented and captivating heroine."

### Trådlöst och kärleksfullt (Wireless with Love)

(Frederick Lindh, 1931). **Script:** Lindh. **Photography:** Ted Pahle. **With** Paul van der Osten, Karin Swanström, Margita Alfvén. and Ragnar Widestedt. Lindh's only film and Paramount's ninth Swedish production from Paris is a romantic drama about a young, penniless inventor of a television apparatus who would have been swindled out of his discovery but for the actions of his girlfriend. His electronic device is used to show newsreel footage of exotic North African camel troops, dance numbers from Paris revues, and Kashmir's gondola-filled rivers. Although this is not based on an original Hollywood version, it is one of the many renditions of the French-language *Magie moderne* (1931). Critics commented that "Paramount used to be able to afford to spend suitable amounts of money on their films." In a caricature of a cleaning woman, Swanström "gives an honest effort and comes across well, as she always does when she tries." Shown in Stockholm in April 1932.

# The United States of America

The United States has suffered the least number of lost films out of 40,000 features made since 1896, but that is not to say that significant material has not vanished. Take the work of the little remembered J. Gordon Edwards, a mainstay of Fox until his death in 1923. He directed Theda Bara and the great Danish actress Betty Nansen. Much that he — and his stars — made is gone, as are films by Tod Browning, Josef von Sternberg, Ernst Lubitsch, Marshall Neilan, Erich von Stroheim (not surprisingly), and films starring John Barrymore, Rudolph Valentino, Clara Bow, Laurel and Hardy, and Lillian Gish.

### The Air Circus

(Howard Hawks and Lewis B. Seiler, 1928). Fox. **Script:** Seton I. Miller and Norman McLeod. **With** Arthur Lake

(Speed), Sue Carol (Sue Manning), David Rollins (Buddy), and Louise Dresser. This was Hawks's first aviation tale, a 118-minute comedy-drama that was hailed as "an exceptionally fine specimen … bright entertainment that exudes the spirit of youth…. It carries one along … it captivates the attention." The film was the studio's first part-talking feature and its making demonstrated Fox's division of labor: Hawks handled the nontalking exterior shots while Seiler (the director of Tom Mix Westerns) took care of the talking sequences. Actor and stage manager Charles Judels "staged" the dialogue in the film.

It is set at a California training ground and school for pilots, where Buddy, a young man from Ypsilanti, and Speed vie for the attention of Sue. Buddy comes to doubt his abilities to become an aviator because of acrophobia. The instructor, Sue — a young woman who is quite an expert at handling a plane — encourages him in his dreams, and inadvertently plays a part in resolving his doubts. At the crucial moment, Buddy (having promised his overly cautious mother that he would forego flying) takes control of a plane in trouble and saves Sue's life and that of daredevil friend Speed. The film's dialogue is "pretty good," wrote the *New York Times*.

Hawks's film, which was made in silent and sound versions, hit the right note with middle America theater owners, who called it, "Excellent. Though this is not a special, it is one of the best program pictures on the market. The youth of the characters and the able direction make it a most entertaining picture"; and "A sweet little picture, sure to please near 100 per cent. Has everything, thrills, comedy, romance and a few tears."

## *The Angel of Contention*

(John G. O'Brien, 1914). Majestic. **Script:** Will L. Comfort. **With** Lillian Gish, Spottiswoode Aitken, George Seigman, and Raoul Walsh. "The years 1912 to 1915 found the screen engaged in strivings to escape from its one-reel bondage," wrote film historian Terry Ramsaye. Responding to impetus from abroad (especially films from Italy), the independent production concern Majestic produced this two reeler featuring Gish in the rough Western environment of the cattle range. As an angel of mercy and understanding, she gives a peerless performance as the lover of a big-hearted sheriff who must contend with mean-spirited hombres and restless Indians. Gish, wrote *Moving Picture World*, "in her exquisite characterization and mental revelations, lifts this old melodrama … into a play of deeper human interest." An atmosphere of sweetness and nobility "beautifies and warms" the short film.

Stills: *Moving Picture World* (July 25, 1914)

## *Anna Karenina*

(J. Gordon Edwards, 1915). Fox. **With** Betty Nansen and Edward José (Alexis Karenin). Returning from Europe, where he studied film production, stage director Edwards directed the great Danish stage actress Betty Nansen (already famous for her imported productions) in her second American film. Edwards was instrumental in signing Nansen to a Fox contract in Copenhagen. In the five-reel adaptation of

Tolstoy's tragedy, she gives a restrained performance as the unhappy heroine, doing "some splendid work," observed a critic. "It is only a question of time before she develops a bigger following in picturedom." *Motion Picture News* noted that Nansen, in the un–Hollywood-like fashion of the era, was an exponent of the "repressed emotion school of acting."

## Anne of Green Gables

(William Desmond Taylor, 1919). Realart. **With** Mary Miles Mintner, Frederick Burton, Marcia Harris, Leila Romer, and Russell Hewett. Launched by Adolph Zukor, Realart Pictures often featured Mary Miles Mintner and a secondary line of stars. The stories of L. M. Montgomery brought forth the beloved character of Anne, and Mintner — long associated with Mary Pickford — portrays the orphan rescued from an asylum by a kindly farmer and his sister. Humor, pathos, melodrama and romance are the "reliable ingredients" of the six-reel tale. Anne "keeps the rural community into which she is brought pretty well agitated while she is blossoming into the belle of the town," wrote a critic. In the end she becomes loved by everyone "especially the young man picked for the final fade-out."

*Motion Picture News* noted that "orphan stories have perhaps had an overrun.... But ... the last two reels, where Anne grows up and carries the whole burden of the household on her slender shoulders, makes the whole worthwhile sitting through. Mary Miles Minter is lovely in this episode, which augurs well for her brilliant future. She should, however, be careful to avoid any suggestion

of affection in her portrayals; her very sincerity, for Miss Minter is a very sincere little girl, may have brought up this difficulty." The director (an English soldier of fortune) was praised for bringing much of the story's rural atmosphere naturally to the screen. His murder in 1922 set off a scandal — and cast a shadow over his films.

Stills: *Photoplay* (January, 1920)

## The Aryan

(William S. Hart, 1916). Triangle. **Supervisor:** Thomas Ince. **Script:** C. Gardner Sullivan. **Photography:** Joseph August. **With** Hart (Steve Denton), Bessie Love (Mary Jane Garth), Charles K. French ("Ivory" Wells), and Gertrude Claire. In a five-reeler that he said fit him "like a glove," the popular Hart played an out of character loner. No longer young at 42, Hart cut an enigmatic figure for a Western hero — dour, humorless, sentimental, playing a hard man who has lost a fortune in gold to a band of cutthroats.

When Steve Denton, rich from years of prospecting, is cheated out of his money, he kidnaps the person he believes most responsible — a woman — and makes her his slave in a desert hideaway — and he refuses to come to the aid of a wagon train of farmers in trouble in the desert. That holds true until he meets the beautiful Mary Jane.

Critics credited the "subtle artist and powerful craftsman" Thomas Ince with making the production (which cost $13,500) a reality. Hart, however, exerted his own influence on the film. He had sought Mae Marsh for the lead, but when she was unavailable, D. W. Griffith suggested Bessie Love. "When I saw her

The Vengeful Hart opens his heart to Bessie Love in *The Aryan* (William S. Hart, Triangle, 1916).

I grabbed her — she didn't have a chance to escape," said Hart. He characterized her performance in her first hit as "one of the very finest ... I have ever seen on the screen." He shot more than 15,000 feet of film, which he edited down to a third of that. "It proved to be a gripping story," Hart said, "one of the best Westerns ever made."

## Bardelys the Magnificent

(King Vidor, 1926). MGM. Adaptation: Dorothy Farnum. With John Gilbert (Bardelys), Eleanor Boardman (Roxaianne), Roy D'Arcy (Chatellerault), John T. Murray (court jester), Arthur Lubin (Louis XIII), and Lionel Belmore (DeLavedan). In this 93-minute, swift-moving, swashbuckling romp set in the court of Louis XIII, Bardelys — a braggart and womanizer — wagers he can woo the demure but very irresistible Roxaianne. Under disguise, he accomplishes the deed, but is arrested for treason by his archenemy Chatellerault. *Variety* noted that Gilbert more than met the challenge of being a dashing heartthrob, doing everyone of the "kicking-over tricks and climbing stunts" that were the trademarks of Fairbanks and Barrymore. And Vidor, recognized in the 1920s as an "artist at the work of making pictures" brings out, in black and white, the beautiful points and situations (of Rafael Sabatini's spirited story) just as easily and convincingly. At the same time, Vidor put some "novel touches to the romantic portions which other directors can well take cognizance of." One of these takes place on a lake, where Bardelys is rowing and Roxaianne is reclining in a boat. Weeping willows sweep over the vessel and, for a fraction of second, obscure each other's view. In the climax, Bardelys, having escaped the gallows, is running from his enemies. He grabs a canopy covering, turns it into a parachute, and quietly descends 100 feet to the ground and, of course, lands on his feet. "It's a wow of a shot," wrote *Variety*, "and possibly the most outstanding." *Moving Picture World* commented

that the vigorously mounted, amorous thriller "is not intended to be taken seriously but ... should provide genuine pleasure for all who go to the movies solely for entertainment."

Stills: www.mdle.com/ClassicFilms/PhotoGallery/bardelys.htm; www.mdle.com/ClassicFilms/PhotoGallery/gilbert5.htm.

## The Battle Cry of Peace

(J. Stuart Blackton, 1915). Vitagraph. **With** Norma Talmadge, Charles Richman, and numerous public officials. "New York Shelled on 'Movie' Screen," read a review for this jingoistic vehicle. As the first film to note that the Great War might be America's war, it was

The "enemy" brings war to the streets of America in *The Battle Cry of Peace* (J. Stuart Blackton, Vitagraph, 1915).

based on munitions manufacturer Hudson Maxim's diatribe entitled *Defenseless America*. In the film, an animated and lurid call to national defense and preparedness, an unnamed enemy urges cuts in U.S. military appropriations, stresses peace talks, and launches a sneak attack on the Capitol Building in Washington. The production names no one in particular, "but they ceretainly are not Portuguese," wrote a critic. Instead, it paints a picture of the horrors that might befall America — akin to the atrocities visited by the Germans upon Belgium. Screen gossip had it that a certain extra by the name of Leber Bronstein was in fact Leon Trotsky.

The producers and especially director Blackton hoped to show this call to war to 75 million Americans. Trying to drum up support, they sought the cooperation and endorsement of the War Department, which, to its credit, stated that it was "not the policy" of the Department to review films. The film, however, was released at military installations and veterans' gatherings. It made money — and caused a national uproar. It received raves from citizen Theodore Roosevelt, was denounced by Henry Ford, and led Thomas Ince to note that there was a market for the other side of the argument. Ince's antiwar *Civilization* (1916) also turned a box-office profit.

Stills: fileroom.aaup.uic.edu/FileRoom/documents/Cases/72battleCryofPeace.html

## The Battle of Gettysburg

(Thomas Ince, 1913). New York Motion Picture Corp. Ince's first feature is an ambitious, grandiose, large-scale five-reeler shot (in Santa Ynez Canyon) during the 50th anniversary of the historic three-day battle that became a turning point in the war. It is the kind of "smoke and din and clash of conflict" picture for which Ince became famous. "It isn't history," wrote a critic, "but it's smashing, thrilling warfare.... Considering the almost constant haze of battle smoke ... the photography ... is excellent."

Examples of the film's ambitious scale can be gauged from Mack Sennett's one-reeler, *Cohen Saves the Flag* (1913), a film of the period that made use of the props and sets, as well as the number of mob extras, from Ince's film.

## Battle of the Sexes

(D. W. Griffith, 1914). Mutual. **Story:** David Goodman. **With** Donald Crisp (husband), Robert Harron (son), Lillian Gish (daughter), Owen Moore, Fay Tincher (Cleo), and Mary Alden (wife). After five years at Biograph, D.W. Griffith is "now with Mutual Movies," announced the trade journals in late 1913. At the studio, which became famous because of the slogan, "Mutual Movies make time fly," Griffith plunged into activity. His film (working title, *The Single Standard*) went into production overnight, and he had it ready for release in seven days. A five-reel tale of infidelity and scandal, the film "is a fine, big object lesson," noted *Variety*. "It may patch up many a broken home, and ... will be blessed by thousands of women ... besides telling fathers to stay at home, even if the attraction is further away than across the hall."

## Beau Sabreur

(John Waters, 1928). Paramount. **Story:** Tom J. Geraghty. **Photography:**

A Confederate soldier faces the wrath of Northerners in *The Battle of Gettysburg* (Thomas Ince, New York Motion Picture Corp., 1913).

C. E. Schoenbaum. **With** Gary Cooper (Major Beaujolais), Evelyn Brent (Mary Vanbrugh), Noah Beery (El Hamel), and William Powell. This 67-minute tale of colonial intrigue and the ingratiating swashbuckler (and handsome swordsman) who must deliver an agreement — while saving a beautiful young woman — is the sequel to the North African hit *Beau Geste* (1926). The film begins with a note of marching feet and laughter at the plight of three soldiers of the Foreign Legion, and ends with many a life lost, many an Arab and Frenchmen floundering and dying in the desert. Adapted from Pervival Wren's 1926 story, the production was called "magnificent … beautiful and intelligent…. It is not a film one cares to turn away from, not even for the fraction of a second," wrote the *New York Times*. Previews of the expensive, action-packed film survive.

Handsome Gary Cooper receives his award for saving the day, and the woman, Evelyn Brent, in *Beau Sabreur* (John Waters, Paramount, 1928).

## Beyond the Rocks

(Sam Wood, 1922). Paramount. **Adaptation:** Jack Cunningham. **Photography:** Alfred Gilks. **With** Gloria Swanson (Theodora Fitzgerald), Rudolph Valentino (Lord Bracondale), and Alec B. Francis (Capt. Fitzgerald). Based on a story by popular British author and screenwriter Elinor Glyn, this emotional, actionless drama, which is set in the mountains, is about sacrifice. In this rarity for Valentino, no great physical heroics enter into the tale of three people allowed to give sway to their feelings. An older, less attractive man literally gets out of the way when his beautiful wife falls in love with a handsome stranger. Swanson "can wear clothes. So can ... Valentino," wrote the critics. More to the point, "the talents of each are given full play."

Stills: www.mdle.com/ClassicFilms/PhotoGallery2/gloria2.htm.

## Butterflies in the Rain

(Edward Sloman, 1926). Universal. **Script:** Charles Kenyon. **Photography:** Gilbert Warrenton. **With** Laura La Plante (Tina), James Kirkwood (John Humphries), and Dorothy Cummings. England and Spain furnish the background for this sensitive tale of emotional turmoil, which was made by a British director most of whose films have long since disappeared. "The evil genius of this story is a woman who wears a monocle. She's quite a snob," wrote a critic. However, Tina, the young Englishwoman who admirers the Bohemian life, thwarts attempted blackmail, and saves her marriage by being honest about her past. She and her husband then hope to make a new life for themselves in America. The inspirational production is said to have a "number of interesting scenes." However, the production's atmosphere, a critic wrote, "is rather that of Hollywood."

## The Case of Lena Smith

(Josef von Sternberg, 1929). Paramount. **Technical advisor:** Hans Dreier. **Script:** Jules Furthman. **Photography:** Harold Rosson. **With** Esther Ralston (Lena), James Hall, and Gustav von Seyfferitz. Taking a chance in the closing days of the silents, von Sternberg directed a 70-minute production that, a critic noted, "holds nothing to captivate the frivolous fan mass." It is a humorless, bitter indictment of Austria's late 19th century ruling class. In effect, von Sternberg's meaningful, artistic work about a village girl who marries an officer from Vienna only to be crushed by class prejudice (the lead actress ages several decades in the story) suggests that plenty was gained in eliminating such a prewar culture.

The film's distribution was cut short by the arrival of sound films, and it soon vanished.

## The Celebrated Scandal

(J. Gordon Edwards and James Durkin, 1915). Fox. **Script:** Elaine Sterne. **With** Betty Nansen (Teodora), Edward José (Don Julian), Walter Hitchcock, Stuart Holmes, Wilmuth Merkyl, and Helen Robertson. This drama is based on the 1881 play *El Gran galeoto* by José Echegaray, the leading Spanish dramatist of the last quarter of the 19th century (and cowinner of the 1904 Nobel Prize in literature). The five-reel adaptation, set in Spain, features Denmark's famous stage actress Betty Nansen in her first American production. She was called the "idol of Europe" and her nation's Sarah Bernhardt, having portrayed Hedda Gabler, Nora, and Rebecca in the premieres of Ibsen's plays at Copenhagen's Royal Theater. She was signed to a Fox contract of $1,000 per week by director Edwards. Studio head William Fox noted that she had "proven her worth before the camera" in ten successful Danish features in the period 1913–15. She was royally treated on her arrival in America and Hollywood.

In the film, in which scandal and duplicity lead to near disaster, the winsome and attractive Betty Nansen plays a young woman rumored to be cheating on her husband (Don Julian) who has been named ambassador to England. To make matters right, two duels, one by her husband, another by a loyal friend, are fought to save her honor. *Motion Picture News* reported that the "producers have been wise in selecting such as vehicle" for Nansen's American debut. "It has afforded her some of the best opportunities in which to exercize her world renowned ability to interpret tragic roles."

## Clarence

(William de Mille, 1922). Paramount. **Script:** Clara Beranger. **With** Wallace Reid, Agnes Ayres (governess), Adolphe Menjou, and May McAvoy. Based on Booth Tarkington's delicately subtle Broadway hit of the same name, the film features a now-forgotten matinee idol, Wallace Reid, in one of his last roles. He plays a handsome young war veteran and former professor of entomology — a mule driver during the war — who lands a job within a family-owned business. What he actually winds up doing is becoming a peacemaker, patching up domestic quarrels within the discordant family before running off with the governess and returning to his college chair.

The director, wrote Robert E. Sherwood, "managed to retain the charm, the grace, and the gaiety of Mr. Tarkington's play." Reid "fits into the part of the meek, yet exceedingly competent Clarence, with apparent ease and is able ... to indulge in the light comedy pantomime at which he is adept," wrote a critic. Within a year Reid was dead of a drug overdose, and the shock spurred his wife to make *Human Wreckage* (1923).

## Cleopatra

(J. Gordon Edwards, 1917). Fox. **Story:** Adrian Johnson. **With** Theda Bara, Fritz Lieber (Caesar), Thurston Hall (Antony), and Henri deVries (Octavius). One of the blockbusters of the era, Theda Bara's film was said to be as big in scenery and fanciful depiction as it is long. At 11 reels, it cost $500,000 to produce and had a cast of thousands and a story to back it up. In California and New Jersey J. Gordon Edwards recreated settings of the Roman Forum, Alexandria, the North African desert, the Sphinx and the Pyramids, as well as the battles of Actium and Alexandria — all of it loosely based on Shakespeare and Victorien Sardou.

It is the film that had the critics commenting, "of all the vampires of screen there's none so bare as Theda." The exposure of so much flesh caused a furor and helped to make the film a huge success. Archival footage is in the George Eastman House.

Stills: www.mdle.com/ClassicFilms/PhotoGallery/index2.htm.

## Confessions of a Queen

(Victor Sjöström, 1925). MGM. **Adaptation:** Agnes Christine Johnston. **Design:** Cedric Gibbons. **With** Alice Terry (Queen Fredericka), Lewis Stone (King Christian), John Bowers (Prince Alexei), and Helen D'Algy (Sephora). The Swedish director's third American film, based on Alphonse Daudet's *Kings in Exile*, contains Sjöström's stock-in-trade beautiful scenic effects and the un–Hollywood-like emotionalism of his Swedish films. It stars the leads from Rex Ingram's *The Prisoner of Zenda* (1922). Sjöström's work is an 1,800-meter tale of uneasy heads of state, especially one royal woman under stress. In the mythical kingdom of Illyria, on the Adriatic coast, a revolution ensues, and the king and queen flee to Paris. They are not yet out of the woods: The king has taken up with a mistress and is the target of assassins. Only by renouncing his claim to the throne in favor of his son — and giving

up the other woman — will he, and she, be safe. It is up to the queen to show him what he must do.

## A Connecticut Yankee at King Arthur's Court

(Emmett J. Flynn, 1921). Fox. **Adaptation:** Bernard McConville. **Photography:** Lucien Andriot. **With** Harry C. Myers (Sir Boss), Pauline Starke (Sandy), Rosemary Theby (Queen Morgan le Fay), William V. Mong (Merlin), and Charles Clary (King Arthur). When Douglas Fairbanks turned down the lead in the first screen rendition of Twain's satire, a splendid 8,300-feet filming of the classic that contains nods to modernization, critics noted the "lack of perspective on the part of some people." Harry Myers, it was observed, "bids fair

to cause Doug to step in time, providing he is given stories of this calibre."

The film was hailed as one of the "exceptional photoplays" of the year. Martin Cavendish wants to marry his mother's secretary rather than the young woman his mother has chosen for him. One night, while reading a book about chivalry, the young man is knocked unconscious by a burglar and, in a dream, he finds himself in Camelot in the 6th century.

The adaptation follows the outline of events in Twain's novel, with abundant contemporaneous touches added to the screenplay — Sir Boss introduces to Camelot the telephone, electricity, plumbing, cars (made from armor), and the clock. Thus the production steers clear of the novel's misanthropy in favor of the comedy and the rescue of the beautiful Lady Alisande. The director

*Above:* A knight in action in King Arthur's realm in *A Connecticut Yankee at King Arthur's Court* (Emmett J. Flynn, Fox, 1921). *Opposite:* Theda Bara in her most famous role in *Cleopatra* (J. Gordon Edwards, Fox, 1917).

was credited with keeping "the action and suspense in the foreground at all times," and his entertaining production, a hit on release, contains "some corking exterior shots," effective scenes of Arthur's Court, and the showstopper: the Yankee (when recalling his history) saving his life by commanding the night to fall in the middle of the day.

Stills: *Motion Picture News* (February 26, 1921).

## The Conqueror

(Raoul Walsh, 1917). Fox. **Script:** Henry C. Warnack. **Photography:** Dal Clawson. **With** William Farnum (Sam Houston), Jewel Carmen (Eliza), Charles Clary, and J. A. Marcus. Walsh's tale of action and romance is the story of a bigger-than-life Texas hero and the reluctant beauty called "the fairest rose of Tennessee." The eight-reel film was immediately hailed as one of the "masterpieces of the screen." Replete with drama, picturesque settings true to the "period," "big scenes," and a dramatic rescue of a damsel in distress, the production lauds a man who climbed his way to the top and into a woman's heart, concluding when he is asked, "Can a former governor find in me a worthy wife?"

## Damaged Goods

(Richard Bennett and Thomas Ricketts, 1914). Mutual. **With** Richard Bennett (George Dupont), Adrienne Morrison (streetwalker), Maud Milton (Mrs. Dupont), Olive Templeton, and Florence Short (nurse). Until the advent of sound, this seven-reel film, made at a cost of $40,000, was the last important picture of its type — the vice-curse theme. It is based on Académie Française member Eugene Brieux's eye-opening play of the same name (produced in New York in 1913, starring Richard Bennett). The film became one of the most celebrated of its day on a subject of great social and moral concern: syphilis.

Straightforward and honest, it starkly presents one of the major social problems in American life. "Twenty percent of the population ... is infected with this dread disease," it notes, and calls for early treatment while denouncing quack therapy. The story begins at a bachelor party where a young man, engaged to a prominent society belle, has sex with a prostitute. This leads to disastrous consequences for him, his future wife, and their child, whose birth is "a little too strong, too realistic, perhaps, but nothing else." Included in the film is a hospital visit to sufferers of the disease, as well as close-ups of medical illustrations of its effects. Bennett, wrote *Variety*, "has turned out a fine picture, photographically as well as lyrically." He is conspicuous throughout, "giving a credible performance of a rather difficult character." Perhaps most important, he maintains a certain sympathy, said a critic, for the story makes no one a scapegoat, "even vindicating, as far as possible," the prostitute. The film, which was rereleased in 1915 and 1917 in reedited versions, grossed an astonishing $600,000.

## A Daughter of the Gods

(Herbert Brenon, 1916). Fox. **With** Annette Kellerman. The sequel to

*Opposite:* Annette Kellerman as the half-naked beauty in a tale about a harem in *A Daughter of the Gods* (Herbert Brenon, Fox, 1916).

Brenon's box-office hit *Neptune's Daughter* (1914) is the tale of harem life in the palace of a sultan. The ten-reel production was filmed in Kingston, Jamaica, where, for two-thirds of a year, employing 20,000 extras, using 2,000 feet of lumber and 2,500 barrels of plaster, Brenon created an even vaster, fantastic, sun-drenched setting: a Spanish fort, a Moorish city, a tower for Kellerman's famous dive into the sea at the end. The director shot 22,000 feet of film, thereby blowing his budget, but gained great attention for the film's apparent nudity and his daring tracking shots. Wrote a critic on the film's premiere: "Audrey Munson, as exhibited … in 'Purity,' has nothing on Miss Kellerman, and as it has been elsewhere observed, neither has Miss Kellerman." In an important sidelight, when Brenon and company returned to the United States his studio seized his film in order to do its own editing. But when Fox removed Brenon's name from the credits the director sued. Brenon eventually received his due for his most lavish silent film. Just as significantly, Brenon established a reputation for independence and helped create the conditions under which directors received contracts that stipulated proper attribution. One reel survives, in the archives of Gosfilmofond, Moscow.

### The Devil's Pass Key

(Erich von Stroheim, 1920). **Photography:** Ben F. Reynolds. **With** Mae Busch, Sam De Grasse, Clyde Fillmore (the Captain), Maude George, and Una Trevelyn. After his successful first venture directing *Blind Husbands* (1919) — the only film in his career over which he had complete control — the "cinemati-cian" Stroheim went "beyond his achievements" in this drama (based on his own story "Clothes and Treachery"). It is a dark, 12-reel tale of American innocents abroad.

A married woman is compromised and almost suffers serious consequences. The wife of an American playwright in Paris, she becomes ensnared in the seductive wiles of an American Army officer, but her devotion to her husband convinces the officer to try to extricate her from the gossip and scandal that have ensued. The near tragedy was heralded as a "work in moving pictures." Neither subtitles, nor spectacle, nor beauty or tricks of the stars, nor the sentiment or surprise of the story are the chief element in this Paris-based tale, wrote the critics. Rather it is "the moving pictures that have meaning," the montage that helps to expose something unexpected in character or plot. The film ends happily — thanks to studio interference.

### The Divine Woman

(Victor Sjöström, 1928). MGM. **Adaptation:** Dorothy Farnum. **Photography:** Oliver Marsh. **With** Greta Garbo (Marianne), Lars Hanson (Lucien), Lowell Sherman, and John Mack Brown. The director's sixth film from America is his only cinematic effort with Garbo. Taking as its starting point Gladys Unger's stage play *Starlight*, which is set in Brittany, Sjöström's film is suggestive of, if not entirely accurate about, the life of the legendary Sarah Bernhardt, who died in 1923. "The photography is perfect," noted *Variety*, "and the scenic ambitions seem directed at realism rather than magnificence." A fragment (clips of

Garbo and Hanson) survives of this tale of a woman who forsakes the theater for love; and the fact that the film was made is ironic in light of the fact that Sjöström's colleague Stiller had wanted to direct Garbo in Hollywood, and never did.

Stills: www.mdle.com/ClassicFilms/PhotoGallery/index2.htm.

## A Doll's House

(Maurice Tourneur, 1918). Artcraft. **With** Elsie Ferguson (Nora Helmer), H. E. Herbert (Helmar), and Ethel Terry. Based on the 1879 classic about a wife who forges her father's name and leaves her husband, French-born Tourneur's splendid five-reel (one-hour) adaptation, containing quotations for captions, "held most consistently to the Ibsen theme," said a critic. "He took no licenses.... The picture holds far more tension than first imagined." In addition to the staging, the film was singled out for its acting. The star called upon her famed histrionic ability "to send the screen characterization over with realism and naturalness.... She is at home ... before the camera."

## The Dragnet

(Josef von Sternberg, 1928). Paramount. **Script:** Jules and Charles Furthman. **With** George Bancroft (Two-Gun Nolan), Evelyn Brent (The Magpie), and William Powell (Dapper Frank Trent). This swift and tense film was called a model of editing — and the production that redeemed the director after the failure to release his *The Sea Gull* (1926), produced by Chaplin. The 70-minute underworld film opens with action — the murder of a stoolie about to testify at a murder trial — and never lets up. It is said to have compared favorably with von Sternberg's earlier classic *Underworld* (1925). Oliver Garret's story is the inspiration for this tale of a gang, led by the cynical Powell, that frames a police captain for the murder of one of his own men when the police attempt to clean up "Gangville."

## Dry Martini

(Harry D'Arrast, 1928). Fox. **Script:** Douglas Z. Doty. **Photography:** Conrad Wells. **With** Mary Astor (Elisabeth Quimby), Matt Moore, Albert Gran (Willoughby Quimby), and Jocelyn Lee. Director D'Arrast "is just simply proving again what a master of cinematic expression he is, one to whom triteness and banalities are poison." His sophisticated, distinctive 77-minute comedy — his last silent — could have been called "Wry Martini." Set during Prohibition, it begins in a Paris bar, where a white-haired American expatriate named Quimby is drowning his sorrows. His adventurous daughter is arriving in town, and he supposes he will have to mend his ways. The young woman (a keen lover of hats) puts her dallying father through a trial by fire, however, when she demonstrates she is as modern as any man in the French capital. As an example, she elopes with an artist at the drop of a hat. Quimby deems it his duty — in fact, his honor is at stake — to try to save her from this mistake. In the starring role, Astor "flings plenty of appearance around," wrote a critic.

## The Escape

(D. W. Griffith, 1914). Mutual. **Script:** Paul Armstrong and Griffith.

Photography: Billy Bitzer and Karl Brown. With Mae Marsh (Jennie Joyce), Donald Crisp ("Bull" McGee), Robert Harron (Larry Joyce), Blanche Sweet (May Joyce), and Owen Moore. While in preparation for *Birth of a Nation* (1915), Griffith directed this tale of a severely dysfunctional family during which the famous director steps into the "below the line stuff now and then," noted a critic. "Why put so much misery on the screen when no one is looking for it?" asked the reviewer.

The seven-reel production became one of Griffith's most unusual works, and one of his most ignored films. Based on Paul Armstrong's play of the same name, it deals with the Joyces, a family from the Lower East Side of New York, and their attempts to escape to a "fine place uptown." In presenting the reality of their dismal, violent-prone lives, Griffith "will take the most awful chances!" wrote an observer. The director even allowed an actor "to stand in the presence of death without removing his hat." The cleverly done film, said another observer, "shows an interestingly told story of what ... the producers believe to be the haphazard way in which human beings select their mates," their mismating, and subsequent difficulties. The real escape, Griffith implies, involves more than a change of neighborhood.

### The Exquisite Sinner

(Josef von Sternberg, 1925). MGM. Adaptation: Sternberg. Photography: Maximilian Fabian. With Conrad Nagel (Dominique), Renée Adorée (gypsy), Paulette Duval, and Frank Currier. Sternberg's second film in his career (partially reshot by Phil Rosen) is a fanciful, wild, and romantic drama of a rich young man seeking to sew his oats. The gypsy he meets "runs away with the picture…. She steals every scene" of the 70-minute work. The director "is good," wrote *Variety*. "He transgresses good taste," however, "when he shows too much flesh and a bit of irreverence during a funeral.

### The Flaming Frontier, or The Indians Are Coming

(Edward Sedgwick, 1926). Universal. With Hoot Gibson (Langdon), Dustin Farnum (Custer), Anne Cornwall, Kathleen Key, Noble Johnson (Sitting Bull), and George Fawcett. This melodrama was released on the 50th anniversary of Custer's Last Stand. At 101 minutes, it was Hollywood's attempt to revive interest in cowboys and Indians.

Costing a walloping $400,000 to produce, it begins with the Indians being swindled out of their homelands during the Grant administration, then moves on to a romance involving one of Custer's scouts. The scout (played by Gibson) receives an appointment to West Point, but after he runs into political intrigue, he is back in the West — at just the right historical moment. The film concludes at the Little Bighorn. The scout becomes "one of the few to escape death in the battle," wrote a critic. "Two titles, two cowboy stars, two sweethearts, and too late," said another critic.

### Flaming Youth

(John Francis Dillon, 1923). First National. With Colleen Moore (Patricia Fentriss), Myrtle Stedman, and Milton Sills (Cary Scott). "When the sex text,"

Hoot Gibson plays the scout who survives "Custer's Last Stand" in *The Flaming Frontier* (Edward Sedgwick, Universal, 1926).

wrote film historian Terry Ramsaye, "passed to psychoanalysis and the new assertiveness of youth, bobbed hair and the flappers," film art moved along in stride. One example is this extremely risqué, roaring '20s romance about a jazz-devoted, saucy flapper interested in her late mother's lover. "The censor," wrote a critic, "possibly with an eye on the artistic photography and settings, appears to have exercised unusual leniency with this photoplay." Set in a splendid mansion as well as aboard a yacht, the production was singled out for a number of scenes. In one, a bedroom is shielded from the gaze of the curious by barely filmy lace. In a swimming scene, the guests are shown in semi-silhouette, "disrobing, revealing their undergarments," the men in knee-length garments, the women in lace-decoration. In a third, the star is seen in rather exotic pajamas.

The fast paced film sent a message about the vapidness of the unexamined life.

Stills: www.mdle.com/ClassicFilms/ PhotoGallery3/flapper4.htm.

## Forty Winks

(Frank Urson and Paul Irbe, 1925). Paramount. **Script:** Bertram Milhauser. **With** Viola Dana (Eleanor), Raymond Griffith (Adam Chumley), Theodore Roberts (Butterworth), Cyril Chadwick (Gaspar la Sage), Anna May Wong (Annabelle Wu), and William Boyd. Culled from David Belasco and Henry C. De Mille's farcical success, called *Lord Chumley*, the 68-minute updating gave the dapper, top-hatted Raymond Griffith one of the best roles of his career. Here he plays a lovable, foppish Englishman suspected of being an interloper and spy. Secret plans vanish, Chumley faces a court-martial, and the price for their return is the hand of Chumley's bethrothed, Eleanor. The spinning out of the tale, which blends thrills and comedy, results in a "corking" melodrama directed by a "deft" hand; the lead is "capital," Dana "charming," while Wong, Chadwich, and Boyd "give adequate delineations of their … roles," said a reviewer.

## Four Devils

(F. W. Murnau, 1928). **Adaptation:** Berthold Viertel. **With** Janet Gaynor, Charles Morton, Nancy Drexel, Barry Norton, and Mary Duncan. German filmmaker F. W. Murnau, called "that artist among directors," was responsible for one of the best productions at the close of the silent era. Based on a novel, his two-hour, silent tragicomedy (five minutes of dialogue were later added), which was his second for Fox, is about orphans who become known as "The Four Devils," trapeze superstars in the Cecchi Circus in Paris. His "indoor circus is superb," wrote *Variety*, "and no circus on the screen, under canvass or under roof has approached the semblance of bigness Murnau has given here." That includes Dupont's classic circus tale, *Variety* (1925). Murnau handled the actors with his characteristic and unrivaled skill, and provided another example of photography that is soft and seductive while calling subtle attention to "the realism and art that pass in turn before the onlooker," wrote a critic. "It is the unfaltering manner in which Mr. Murnau attacks his scenes that is responsible for this picture's greatness. One forgets the actors and thinks of the characters."

Stills: http://falbala.f h-bielefeld. de/fb4/murnau/fwmframe.htm

## The Garden of Allah

(Rex Ingram, 1927). MGM. **Photography:** Lee Garmes. **Design:** Henri Ménessier. **With** Alice Terry, Ivan Petrovich, and Marcel Vibert. Veteran director Ingram had less Hollywood support than ever when he began shooting this film in the North African desert in early 1927. An 8,200-meter adaptation of a novel, the production was close to Ingram's heart. "I have been interested in things Arabic," he said, "and have always had a profound respect for Islam. I admire much in Islam as I do in Christianity and Buddhism but my sympathy for Islam is rather a question of philosophy of life than faith." His fourth film abroad, it is the tale of a distressed monk (Ivan Petrovich) who flees to the world of the Arabs, where he marries an Englishwoman (Terry). When the two are trapped in a sandstorm, he vows that if they are spared, he will return to his religious order. He gets his wish, but his wife remains in North Africa to raise their son alone. Ingram highlighted the story through the use of authentic designs of a monastery and the casbahs of Arab towns. *Variety* noted, "the story has body and share of fame behind it to lift it above the usual screen tale."

## Gentlemen Prefer Blondes

(Malcolm St. Clair, 1928). Paramount. **Story** and **adaptation:** Anita Loos. **Photography:** Harold Rosson. **With** Ruth Taylor (Lorelei Lee), Alice White (Dorothy Shaw), Mack Swain, and Chester Conklin. This "sweet picture dips in an out of the original," said a critic, maintaining enough risqué material to give a "slap at the national reform movement." An eyefilling, sweet Lorelei for the men, dressed to the hilt for the women, Ruth Taylor reprises the role that made June Walker famous in the stage comedy. It concerns a young woman heading out into the world to make good. Beginning in Arkansas, where Lorelei has just shot her boyfriend, then to the film capital, to New York, and finally Europe, where Lorelei and Dorothy meet the rich and corner the market on diamonds, St. Clair's 75-minute film was tabbed "de luxe program fare."

## The Great Love

(D. W. Griffith, 1918). Artcraft. **Script:** Griffith and Stanner Taylor. **With** Lillian Gish (Susie Broadplains) and Robert Harron (Jim Young). Griffith's English war film, which circulated primarily in Britain, stars the same lovers as in his earlier *Hearts of the World* (1918). In this tale of a Canadian and the daughter of an Australian clergyman who are seeking meaning in the war, Griffith made use of wartime footage to tell a romantic but no less patriotic story of lovers stirred into action because of reports of German atrocities. Long since vanished, the eight-reeler, built around scenes of actual war-time conditions in England and France, contains footage of air raids and fighting at the frontlines, but also scenes of royal personages and historic sites. Griffith's flair for melodrama, spectacle, and romance combine with documentary footage to display the "deftness with which he can link fact and fiction in an almost continuous chain, wrote a reviewer." "It is true that sometimes there seem to be missing links ... but when one remembers that the producer had to deal with the inflexible material of actual occurrences, the difficulties of this task are appreciated and his degree of success becomes much more prominent."

## The Greatest Thing in Life

(D. W. Griffith, 1918). Artcraft. **Script:** Griffith and Stanner Taylor. **Photography:** Billy Bitzer. **With** Lillian Gish (Jeanette), Robert Harron (Edward), Elmo Lincoln, Adolphe Lestina, and David Butler. Lillian Gish called this work "one of Mr. Griffith's best films and one of his most neglected." The 80-minute, seven-reel drama was made from the 86,000 feet of film that Griffith shot while in England and France during the First World War. The visually affecting tale (whose title was suggested by Gish) contains unusual, even shocking elements for its time. A southern officer (who loves a pretty young Frenchwoman) and a black American soldier

A moment of peace during a time of war in *The Great Love* (D. W. Griffith, Artcraft, 1918).

find themselves in the same foxhole during battle. When the white man is wounded, the black soldier comes to help him but is shot. As he lies dying, the black man calls out for his mother, and the white man responds by kissing him on the lips. Griffith, wrote a critic, "produces his pictures just a little better than most directors, and spares no expense in the matter of minute details. His photographer is in a class by himself."

## Hats Off

(Hal Yates, 1927). MGM. **Supervisor:** Leo McCarey. **With** Laurel and Hardy, James Finlayson, Anita Garvin, and Dorothy Coburn. A two-reeler in which Laurel and Hardy (in their signature outfits) are door-to-door washing machine salesmen. It's the "story," goes the titles, "of two boys who figure that the world owes them a living — but is about thirty-five years behind in the payments." One customer (naturally) lives at the end of a very long and tall stairway, and, undaunted, the boys drag their wares all the way up. When it turns out to be no sale, chaos — especially the antics of plenty of hats being knocked off — ensues. The well-received film vanished soon after release, but the theme was reworked in their hilarious Oscar-winning *The Music Box* (1932).

The silent film's cutting continuity is on file at the Library of Congress.

Stills: fpr10.maths.strath.ac.uk/LH/HATS.HTM.

## The Haunted House

(Benjamin Christensen, 1928). First National. **Script:** Lajos Biró. **Photography:** Sol Polito. **With** Thelma Todd, Montague Love, and Chester Conklin. Danish director Christensen's fourth American film, containing sound effects and a musical score, is based on Owen Davis's 1926 novel *The Haunted House: An American Comedy in Three Acts.* Combining comedy and horror, his 70-minute film concerns four heirs to a millionaire's fortune. Each of them is instructed to keep sealed a letter until the benefactor's death. Of course they all open their letters, which reveal the whereabouts of a fortune, hidden in a house of ghosts and ghouls, and inhabited by a bizarre cast of characters, including a mad doctor, a sleepwalker, an undertaker, and a beautiful maiden. It's all a litmus test — a device Christensen favored in several of his films — to reveal character. The *New York Times* found that the film's "camera angles are more than slightly reminiscent" of Paul Leni's classic thriller that established the genre, *The Cat and the Canary* (1927).

## Hawk's Nest

(Benjamin Christensen, 1928). First National. **Photography:** Sol Polito. **With** Milton Sills. The director's third American film was the first of his so-called mystery comedies, an 80-minute tale about a disfigured owner of an establishment called the Hawk's Nest. In order save a friend from the electric chair, he infiltrates the Chicago underworld. To do that he disguises himself (undergoing plastic surgery) and along the way finds romance. "Struggling ... in the melodramatic labyrinth of underground passages, Chinese ex officio judges and cabaret habitues is the girl," wrote the *New York Times*. "The reason for her presence is a mystery.... But the picture gets along nicely."

## Hollywood

(James Cruze, 1923). Paramount. **Script:** Frank Condon and Tom J. Geraghty. **Photography:** Karl Brown. **With** Monta Bell, Hope Drown (Angela Whitaker), Luke Cosgrove, G. K. Arthur, and Ruby Lafayette. When Cruze completed this film (also called *Joligud*), he had made one of the first satires of the film capital, inspired by scandal swirling around the film Mecca. At the time he was the world's highest paid director, earning $6,000 a week (thanks to the success of *The Covered Wagon*, 1923), and decided to take a bite at the hand that was feeding him. He directed a 90-minute fantasy about an average girl of average beauty from a small town from nowhere who does *not* get the job. Imagining herself a film star, Angela heads for Hollywood — bringing along Grandpa. There he finds work while she meets one disappointment after another.

Director Cruze kidded his subject from start to finish, especially the fact that Angela is quite hapless. He introduced elements of absurdity, such as Angela's entire family coming to Hollywood and finding work in film, while she

A Hollywood star meets an admirer in *Hollywood* (James Cruze, Paramount, 1923).

winds up marrying the pants presser from back home. Cruze managed to bring in 80 of his studio's stars and directors, including J. W. Kerrigan, Charles de Rochefort, William S. Hart and Pola Negri, who had roles in a ridiculous dream by the pants presser that involves slow motion and double exposure.

There is also this scene in the film: An unemployed actor approaches a casting director, who points to a sign that reads, "No Work Today." The actor turns to face the camera: It is Fatty Arbuckle (uncredited), the comedian whom the studio had dropped from the lead in

Cruze's *One Glorious Day* (1922) because of the scandal that rocked the industry. In 1924, Cruze directed another comedy about the film capital — this time a male has the selfsame desire — called *Merton of the Movies*. That film is also lost.

## The Honeymoon

(Erich von Stroheim, 1928). Paramount. **Screenplay:** von Stroheim. **Photography:** Hal Mohr and Ben Reynolds. **Editor:** Josef von Sternberg. **With** von Stroheim, ZaSu Pitts, Fay Wray, and Matthew Betz. This silent is the followup (or Part II) to von Stroheim's two-hour

Stroheim as the prince and ZaSu Pitts as the bride in *The Honeymoon* (Erich von Stroheim, Paramount, 1928).

*The Wedding March* (1926). Released only in France in 1931 as *Mariage de prince*, the 70-minute contains a 20-minute summary of the action thus far — two women seeking marriage to an aristocrat — and continues the drama about a prince trying to reunite with his real lover. It concludes unfinished — von Stroheim had hoped to end the prewar Vienna tale on a happy note — but its subject matter — class conflict, decadence, and sexuality — was close to von Stroheim and is another example of the director's mordant style, his deliberate and intense closeups, and long and slow scenes. Reportedly the only copy of the film — it was never shown in the U.S. — was destroyed in a fire at the French Cinematheque in the late 1950s.

## House of Horror

(Benjamin Christensen, 1929). First National. **Photography:** Sol Polito. **With** Thelma Todd, Chester Conklin, Louise Fazenda, and William V. Mong. The Danish director's sixth — and last — American film is a 65-minute tale of the strange. Containing dialogue only in the first few minutes, it is a story of a "bachelor" and his "spinster" sister, living in Ohio, who undertake a journey, at the request of a "mystery man," to "Uncle Abner" in New York. The unreal doings, comings and goings take place in an old house in a cosmopolitan setting where the cast of characters includes reporters in search of lost jewelry, a reclusive old man, and — at the heart of this mystery — the so-called mystery man himself.

## Human Wreckage

(John Griffith, 1923). **Story:** C. Gardner Sullivan. **Photography:** Henry Sharp. **With** Dorothy Davenport/Mrs. Wallace Reid (Ethel MacFarland), James Kirkwood (Alan MacFarland), Bessie Love (Mary Finnegan), and George Hackathorne. A one-hour exposé, based on events of the period, of the dangers of drug use, starring the wife of Wallace Reid, star of *Clarence* (1922). Reid had died of a drug overdose, though no reference is actually made to Reid or his fate in this film "As an educator for the purpose of suppressing the drug habit," wrote *Variety*, the film is "an enlightener. The young can see … things they should not know…. The best impression … is that of a ghostlike hyena stalking through every scene where drugs come in to wreak their worst."

## The Immortal Alamo

(William F. Haddock, 1911). Méliès/ Star Film. **Photography:** William Paley. **With** William A. Carroll (Lt. Dickinson), William Clifford (Travis), Francis Ford (Navarre), Gaston Méliès (Padre), and Edith Storey (Lucy Dickinson). This early rendition of the great Texas battle

of 1836 (also called *Fall of the Alamo*) contains "all the movements of interest of a war picture," noted *Moving Picture World*. The production marked the historic event's 75th anniversary (the battle lasted from February 23 to March 6, 1836) in "a realistic manner."

Students from Peacock Military College took on assignments as major and minor historical figures, with Miss Storey, in particular, in a small part, making "the most of it, as usual," and giving a "convincing presentation of a woman in utter despair." Her film company, wrote the trade journal, "deserves the highest commendation."

## Just Another Blonde

(Alfred Santell, 1926). First National. **Script:** Paul Schofield. **Photography:** Arthur Edeson. **With** Louise Brooks (Diana), Dorothy Mackaill (Jeanne), Jack Mulhall and William Collier. Even though Brooks was one of Famous Players–Lasky's up and coming talents, the studio wasn't averse to lending her out for the right price. An offer from rival studio First National led to this feature (tentatively titled *Even Stephen*). For the period of the loan (26 July to 22 August 1926), First National paid Famous Players–Lasky $1,000 a week. Not that Brooks was aware of these financial details; she continued to receive her standard salary of $250 per week. In contrast to the mayhem of a shoot such as Sutherland's *It's the Old Army Game* (1926), First National's crew and actors were models of efficiency. Director Santell was taken with Brooks (just as Sutherland had been) but he kept the production on schedule and expertly marshaled a huge team of extras.

And the female lead, Dorothy Mackaill, was a studious professional actor from England and one of First National's most valued properties.

In this appealing six-reeler (based on a short story by Gerald Beaumont), Jack Mulhall and William Collier are a pair of Bowery gamblers, while Mackaill and Brooks are their love interests. The men are best friends and agree to split everything down the line (even Stephen) and let no woman pull them apart. When the gamblers set up shop on Coney Island, the Kid falls for the nearby gallery sharp shooter, played by Brooks. Before the lovers can "come out," the pact between the Kid and Jimmy needs to be unglued a bit. This can best be done by getting Jimmy and Jeanne together. Only towards the end does the matchmaking come to fruition and Jimmy and Jeanne attest to their love while plummeting to earth in an out-of-control bi-plane, thinking the end is near.

By far the most physical and action-filled of Brooks's films to date, *Just Another Blonde* includes a front seat on a Coney Island roller coaster, aerial photography, and a shocker of a plane crash. (In fact, there were two plane crashes. In the first, Dorothy Mackaill was doing a test for the flying sequences in an open-cockpit two-seater. Because

Dorothy Davenport/Mrs. Wallace Reid gives herself a dose of heroine in this warning about drug abuse in *Human Wreckage* (John Griffith, 1923).

of the heavy camera equipment on the plane, landing was difficult and the plane crashed, killing the pilot. Mickaill was thrown free and escaped serious injury. The episode was hushed up and re-shot.) *Harrison's Reports* noted that there is an "aeroplane wreck that for realism ... has never been approached in any picture.... The aeroplane is shown striking a telegraph pole, tearing off its landing gear. Afterwards ... making a landing without the wheels ... and rising on its nose and summersaulting."

## The Kaiser, the Beast of Berlin

(Rupert Julian, 1918). Renowned Pictures Corp. **Script:** Julian, Elliott Clawson, and Erich von Stroheim. **With** Julian (Wilhelm II), Elmo Lincoln (Marcus), Harry von Meter (Capt. von Hanck), Lon Chaney (Bethmann-Hollweg), Jay Smith (Hindenberg), Alfred Allen (Gen. Pershing), and Erich von Stroheim. Rabid propaganda, a "masterpiece," wrote *Motion Picture News*, and a record-breaking film in its day, this film has become one of the AFI's "ten most wanted" lost films.

During the war years, Hollywood's mood was summed up in a 1917 editorial in *Motion Picture News*, which proclaimed that "every individual at work in this industry wants to do his share ... through slides, film leaders and trailers, posters, and newspaper publicity." They "will spread that propaganda so necessary to the immediate mobilization of the country's great resources." Movies like *The Kaiser, the Beast of Berlin*, *Wolves of Kultur*, and *Pershing's Crusaders* flooded American theaters. One picture, *To Hell with the Kaiser*, was so popular that Massachusetts riot police were summoned to deal with an angry mob that had been denied permission to see it.

The seven-reel *The Kaiser, the Beast of Berlin* was promoted throughout America as an "amazing expose of the intimate life" of Germany's leader and "a picture to make your blood boil." It begins with a prologue: The world is at peace before that fateful day in August 1914. But the Kaiser (vilified as "the mad dog of Europe") is shown as bent on conquest. The action centers in Belgium. In Louvain, the Germans pillage the town, but the blacksmith Marcus (though wounded) saves his daughter from the clutches of the enemy. After the sinking of the *Lusitania* (by submarine Capt. von Hanck), America and the Allies gain the upper hand, eventually capturing the Kaiser and the Imperial Palace in Berlin. He is taken to Louvan as a prisoner, and his jailer is none other than the blacksmith. "Great applause marked the finale," wrote *Moving Picture World*. "In this scene were introduced ... Generals Pershing, Haig, Joffre, and Diaz." The photography and lighting effects "are good," wrote another critic.

## Kliou (The Tiger)

(Henri de la Falaise, 1936). Bennett Pictures. **Photography:** William H. Greene. **Music:** Heinz Roemheld. **With** Dhi (the girl), Bhat (the boy), Nyan (the brother), Khan (the father), Henri de la Falaise, and Charles Carney. This 55-minute tale of the wild was the first all–Technicolor film shot in the jungles, in Annam, in Indo-China. Absent sound effects, the film uses titles to help relate the tale of the Moi people who are at the mercy of a killer, man-eating tiger. The animal is eventually tracked down and killed by a young man with poison-tipped arrows. There is also a love story as subplot. The director shot 30,000 feet of film, thanks to the cooperation of French colonials and a local rajah, and his work was praised for its outstanding cinematography.

## A Knickerbocker Buckaroo

(Albert Parker, 1919). Fairbanks Pictures. **Story:** Douglas Fairbanks. **Photography:** Victor Fleming. **With** Douglas Fairbanks (Teddy Drake), Marjorie Daw (Mercedes), William A. Wellman (Henry), and Frank Campeau. The film begins by stating its intentions: Douglas Fairbanks is shown mixing ingredients labeled Mystery, Adventure, Romance, Comedy, Pep, and Ginger to create a cake iced with the film's title.

Heeding the advice of a famous man that he go West, New Yorker Teddy Drake runs into more than he bargained for. That includes highwaymen and a pretty girl — though of course he does his amazing stunts and feats "with all the ease and éclat with which the average man crosses Fifth Avenue with the policeman's permission." This costly six-reel production, which was elaborately staged, was directed "with a good eye for scenic effects," said the *New York Times*. It costars future director Wellman in his acting debut.

## Ladies of the Mob

(William A. Wellman, 1928). Paramount. **Script:** John Farrow. **Photography:** Henry W. Gerrard. **With** Clara Bow (Yvonne), Richard Arlen (Red), and Helen Lynch. Based on a story by Ernest Booth (a convicted bank robber serving a life sentence for murder), the melodrama features Clara Bow in one of her most unusual roles. She plays the daughter of a man who was put to death in the electric chair. Married to a bank robber named Red, she tries to lead him away from a life of crime (after a robbery). The 6,800-feet film ends with the handcuffed lovers being sent to prison. The closing titles stress that they intend to lead productive lives after serving their time. Containing an "elemental idea of excitement," the story is told in such a way as "almost to glorify the crooks," noted a critic.

In this film, real bullets were used; the stars suffered minor injuries from ricochets.

## The Last Moment

(Paul Fejos, 1927). Fine Arts. **Script:** Fejos and George McCall. **Photography:** Leon Shamroy. **With** Otto Mattiesen (Pierrot), Julius Molnar (young Pierrot), Georgia Hale (second wife), and Lucille La Verne (innkeeper). This 55-minute drama was hailed as perhaps Fejos's greatest film and the first experimental feature in American cinema. "Out here in Hollywood, over in London, Paris, or Berlin," said Fejos, "we who tell the tales revel in them no less than those who hear and see them, for after all, the flower of fairyland is in spinning the yarn. Those who listen are necessarily limited by what others have to tell, while those who make them are bounded only by their imaginations." Fejos's imagination led him to take chances, and before Orson Welles, Fejos could claim that rare thing in motion picture production: total control and supervision of a production, the freedom to make your own film.

Shot in two weeks, his film contains no explanatory titles; only subjective photography relates the significant episodes in the protagonist's life. In the prolog, a jumble of events — a series of last reflections—flashes before a drowning man's eyes. After which the film picks up his life, beginning with his boyhood, recounting his unsentimental two marriages, and carrying it through to his life's end at a still pond. "The grip of the story," said *Variety*, "lies in the development of the unrelated incidents.... It demonstrates that stern realism can be made absorbing on the screen." The prolog is repeated at the end of the film, and "the whole business ... has a kick." Photographer Shamroy supplied the capital (a bankroll of $4,000), the stage space, and the film laboratory that permitted Fejos to film this lost classic.

## Legion of the Condemned

(William A. Wellman, 1928). **Adaptation:** Monk Saunders. **With** Fay Wray (Christine), Gary Cooper (Gale Price), Barry Norton, and Lane Chandler. From Wellman and Saunders, who collaborated on *Wings* (1927), came another suspenseful and successful drama, as well as a magnificent pictorial display. It is the tale of warriors of the clouds—the heterogeneous First World War aviators and spies of the Lafayette Escadrille. The members of this group, known for their bravado, include a dueling Argentinean, a reckless Britisher, a gambler from Monte Carlo, and the courageous Gale Price, called one of "the rarin', tearin', galoots, who aim to die in their tall, brown boots." After delivering the beautiful Christine behind enemy lines, Gale and his charge are captured. They face an enemy firing squad, but "the arrival of Gale's colleagues is quite a rousing climax" to the 6,700-feet drama, wrote a reviewer.

## Life Without Soul

(Joseph W. Smiley, 1915). Ocean Film. **Script:** Jessie J. Goldberg. **With** Percy D. Standing (creature), William W. Cohill (Victor), Lucy Cotton, and George de Carlton. A five-reel version of the Frankenstein tale, but with a difference. Here the supernatural events turn out to be only the imaginings of Victor, the young medical student. *Moving Picture World* called it a "photoplay which appeals to the emotions and ... of distinct merit. Great diversity of incidents and scenes, of views of deep chasms, wild glades, desert sands and the ocean's wide expanse, are intermingled with glimpses of the young scientist bending over his creation in his laboratory." The characterization of the soulless creature was called "awe-inspiring, but never grotesque.... At times, he actually awakens sympathy."

Stills: *Moving Picture World* (December 4, 1915).

## Life's Whirlpool

(Barry O'Neil, 1916). Brady. **Adaptation:** O'Neil and E. M. Ingleton. **With** Holbrook Blinn (McTeague), Fania Marinoff (Trina), Walter Green (Marcus), Phil Robson (Mr. Sieppe), and Julia Stuart (Mrs. Sieppe). At five reels, this was a much more modest work than von Stroheim's 1923 adaptation of the same material, Frank Norris's *McTeague*. A tale of a young man seeking fame and fortune who winds up killing his wife, the film was called "intensely dramatic." The real star of the film is the emotional Marinoff, "a foreign artist. She gives the entire picture a continental atmosphere."

Holbrook Blinn exhibits his wrath to Fania Marinoff in *Life's Whirlpool* (Barry O'Neil, Brady, 1916).

## London After Midnight

(Tod Browning, 1927). MGM. **Script:** Waldemar Young and Browning. **Design:** Cedric Gibbons. **Photography:** Merritt B. Gerstad. **With** Lon Chaney (Burke), Marceline Day (Lucille Balfor), Conrad Nagel, (Arthur Hibbs), and Henry Walthall. The first American vampire film is this Tod Browning work, a seven-reel (65-minute) mystery that contains his stock-in-trade supernatural elements, a set of unearthly characters, and an eerie atmosphere. From the foggy British capital, Scotland Yard inspector Burke is called in—five years after the fact—to take another look at an apparent suicide. In an old castle, the mystery sleuth disguises himself as a vampire and makes use of hypnosis on several suspects to track down a murderer. The impression lingers at the end, though, that some elements of the case will always remain open to interpretation. *Photoplay* called the drama "marvellously sustained." In 1935, Browning directed a sound rendition, called *Mark of the Vampire*, in which pseudovampires again unmask a killer.

Stills: www.mdle.com/ClassicFilms/ PhotoGallery/index2.htm; www.mdle. com/ClassicFilms/PhotoGallery/lam2.ht.

## The Lotus Eater

(Marshall Neilan, 1921). First National. **Subtitles:** George Ade. **With** John Barrymore, Anna Q. Nilsson, Colleen Moore and Wesley Barry. Containing subtitles only "where they are needed," this is a satirical fantasy that is "different ... jollily heretical," wrote an ecstatic critic. Whimsical hero Barrymore, after falling in love with a self-centered married woman (for whom he is not rich enough), leaves on a long trip across the Pacific. His plane crashes, and he finds himself on a strange, remote South Seas island. Having no awareness of Western culture, the inhabitants of the island worry not a whit about money, clothing, status, and the like. Their lives are simple and they exhibit only friendship and interest in others. Our hero meets a beautiful young maiden, with whom he falls in love. At this point in the seven-reel film — the tale is not a dream — the hero departs for New York. But soon enough, he decides lotus eating is what he wants — and returns to his paradise. Civilization, he decides, will just have to get along without him, and he without civilization. Fluctuating from drama to tragedy to comedy, which may be "disturbing to the spectator," the film and its "good parts ... are so enjoyable that its less satisfactory portions leave no feeling of annoyance," wrote a reviewer.

## The Man from Blankley's

(Alfred E. Green, 1930). Warner Bros. **Adaptation:** Harvey Thaw. **Photography:** James Van Trees. **With** John Barrymore (Lord Strathpeffer), Loretta Young (Marge Seaton), and Emily Fitzroy. An example of Barrymore's wild range of talent and a sophisticated satire about class differences, particularly of the mores of the middle class, Green's film revolves around the romance between former lovers. An evening of mishaps and embarrassments leads to the humorous ending in this 65-minute production.

Barrymore was rarely seen during these early days in anything less than doublet and hose, so it was a surprise when he decided to try his hand at a modern-day comedy. Although the cast is American, someone must have worked very closely with them to firm up their British accents, as they are virtually without flaws. Barrymore is a muddle-headed peer who wanders into the wrong house when he drinks a bit too much. The hostess of the home has planned a gala dinner and only has 13 guests, so she's hired a professional company, Blankley's, to supply her with someone befitting the other attendees at the dinner. She thinks it's Barrymore and invites him in.

The film makes sport of the American guests and is a sharp satire with some fine slapstick scenes. Barrymore dominates the proceedings as the pomposity of parvenus is punctured. Fitzroy is the hostess and Carver is hilarious as a noisy Chicago matron who alternately slaps backs and hoots, then settles down in a vain attempt to act as a classy dowager.

"How they got an American cast to reproduce with exactitude the Anglicisms of British speech is another wonder of Hollywood," said a critic." But the remarkable part of it all is that Barrymore should take a fancy for this sort of thing when nobody knows better than he that the Don Juan and General Crack are his meal ticket."

## *Merton of the Movies*

(James Cruze, 1924). Famous Players–Lasky. **Adaptation:** Walter Woods. **With** Glen Hunter (Merton Gill), Viola Dana (Sally Montague), DeWitt Jennings (Jeff Montague), Elliott Roth, Charles Selion, and Charles Ogle. Cruze's second satire of Hollywood was called "the greatest piece of film" to come from the studio since *The Ten Commandments*, and "as far above the rank and file of features as New York City is beyond Kalamazoo." Thanks to director Cruze and star Glen Hunter, "the laughs roll along with the ease of a waterfall and with the staccato frequency of machine gun fire," wrote *Variety*. The 80-minute film is based on George Kaufman and Marc Connelly's play (which starred Hunter) about a clerk who yearns to makes it in Tinsel Town. The comedy opens with a scene of the "great open spaces where men are men." Merton is astride a horse on a cliff watching bandits about to attack a young maiden. Heroically, he descends by rope and confronts the badmen as he rolls a cigarette. With William S. Hart–like movements, he gets the upper hand. The scene then dissolves into reality: Merton is in the backroom of a grocery, his arm around a dummy. How the ingenuous young man gets his chance to see his name in lights — if not exactly in the kinds of films he imagines — is the heart of this gem of a film. "Nothing is exaggerated," wrote the *New York Times*. "There is all the humor and pathos it is possible to extract from the story, the various nuances being beautifully balanced. The assembling of the scenes is accomplished effectively, and the dissolves, fade-outs and flashbacks come as pleasant surprises.... This is such a good picture that we intend seeing it again." It ranked as one of the ten best of the year.

## *The Miracle Man*

(George Loane Tucker, 1919). Mayflower/Paramount. **With** Betty Compson (Rose), Thomas Meighan, and Lon Chaney. The film that made Compson, Meighan, and Chaney stars was directed by the man whose ten-reel *Traffic in Souls* (1913) had demonstrated the tremendous box-office value of sex. Tucker repeated his success in a different kind of film six years later. His nine reel (8,200 feet) *The Miracle Man* is a fast-action, well-acted, and "uncommonly interesting photoplay," said a critic, that "will please movie enthusiasts and convert a few more." In fact, the film, based on Frank L. Packard's novel of the same name (and not on George M. Cohan's stage adaptation), was so well received it once ranked alongside *Intolerance* and *Broken Blossoms*. Former bathing beauty Compson attains her own "miracle" in the tale of an old village faith-healer's exploitation by a couple of swindlers. Especially noteworth is the scene in which a cripple, thrilled by the spectacle of a "cure," casts away his crutches and walks up the path into the healer's arms. "It is a breathless moment from which ... every atom of excitement is wrought," wrote the *New York Times*. The film's success seems to have been due to the strong dramatic elements — loosely based on the director's own miraculous recovery from illness thanks to Christian Scientists — and the decision to forego stars in place of film value.

Stills: www.mdle.com/ClassicFilms/PhotoGallery2/chaney17.htm

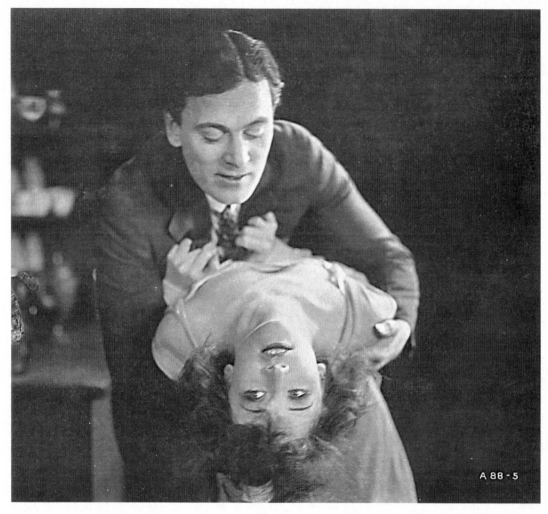

Betty Compson receives treatment from *The Miracle Man* (George Loane Tucker, May-flower/Paramount, 1919).

## *Mockery*

(Benjamin Christensen, 1927). MGM. **Script:** Christensen. **Photography:** Merritt Gerstad. **With** Lon Chaney (Sergei), Barbara Bedford (Tatiana), Ricardo Cortez (Dmitri), and Mack Swain. The Danish director's second American film marked the 10th anniversary of the Bolshevik Revolution. It is silent about a rather unattractive peasant who risks his life to save a beautiful aristocrat during the cataclysmic period in Russian history. Christensen's 70-minute story of terror and revolution contains elements of cinematic concerns that had intrigued him for the last 15 years: historical sweep, repression, chaos, uprising, and honor. The estimable Lon Chaney, as the hare-lipped, greasy, muscular, long-haired savior, gives a performance that was characterized as strikingly painstaking. He called Christensen a "truly great" director who had "finer values" than other Hollywood directors.

Stills: www.mdle.com/ClassicFilms/PhotoGallery2/chaney18.htm.

## Now I'll Tell One

(James Parrott, 1927). Hal Roach Studios. **With** Laurel and Hardy, Charley Chase, Edna Marian, Lincoln Plumer, and Will R. Walling. This two-reel short was generally considered a Charley Chase comedy with Stan Laurel listed as a supporting cast member. In 1989, footage of the film was located in the collection of British film collector David Wyatt, and from that copy it was determined that Oliver Hardy also had a role in the film. Though the two do not play together as a comedy team — Stan plays Charley's lawyer and Ollie plays a policeman — their joint appearance makes this a Laurel and Hardy work.

## One Glorious Day

(James Cruze, 1922). Paramount. **Script:** James Cruze. **With** Will Rogers (Ezra Botts), Lila Lee (Molly), John Fox (Ek), Alan Hale, and Emily Rait. "Can anything imaginative come out of Hollywood?" asked a critic in the early 1920s. "It can. It has," in the form of a witty, stylistic, and fantastic five-reel spiritistic spree (which was supposed to star Fatty Arbuckle, until the scandal broke). It is an uproarious work about Ek, an unborn spirit who gets tired of waiting in the line where unborn spirits dwell and slips away to earth, looking for a body to inhabit. When a stork just beats him to a baby he has in mind, he skips about the earth until he finds an awkward professor who lectures on spiritism. At the moment that the pro-

fessor puts himself in a trance and sends his own spirit out of his body, in comes Ek. Instantaneously, the mild-mannered professor is a new man. The Ek-static Botts goes on a rampage: He cleans out a political smoke-filled back room, rescues his girlfriend, and turns into a real lover. Meanwhile Botts's own spirit is wandering aimlessly, looking for its own body. He knows his body won't be able to stand too much more of Ek, and finally Ek departs. But for one day, Botts was a hero, and from then on he manages to live up to his new reputation. Will Rogers, wrote a critic, "is a revelation." He can be a "good deal more on the screen than just himself." The production involved almost continuous double exposure, and some exceedingly difficult feats. "But there doesn't seem to be a missed shot in it. It is a skillful and ingenious work." Summing up, the critic wrote, "although you may say that Hollywood is not noted for its imagination, remember that *One Glorious Day* is an Ek-ception."

## The Patriot

(Ernst Lubitsch, 1928). Paramount. **Adaptation:** Hanns Kräly. **Photography:** Bert Glennon. **Design:** Hans Dreier. **With** Emil Jannings, Lewis Stone (Phalen), Vera Veronina, and Florence Vidor. With the tenth anniversary of the Bolshevik Revolution still in the news, three Germans — an actor, scenarist, and director — fashioned what the critics termed "a mighty picture" set in Russia at the end of the 19th century. Lubitsch's 12-reel tragicomedy was one of his last silents and one of the most sought-after of lost films, based on the stage play by Alfred Neumann. It centers on the life and death of Czar Paul I. It was voted one of the best films of the year, the *New York Times* proclaiming that "Jannings outshines his performances in *Variety* and *The Last Laugh* as the mad czar.... The motion picture is a credit to the screen." Others crowned Lubitsch as the world's finest director, his film the "Hamlet of the screen." Preview scenes survive.

## Pied Piper Malone

(Alfred E. Green, 1924). Paramount. **Story:** Booth Tarkington. **Adaptation:** Tom Geraghty. **Photography:** Ernest Haller. **With** Thomas Meighan (Malone), Lois Wilson (Patty), Emma Dunn, Charles Stevenson, and Brian Keith. This small-town comedy-drama was written for the screen by the popular novelist Tarkington, and is an example of a film that is "100 percent clean ... no sexy stuff," wrote a critic, "but still a picture that is sure to get the crowds." The 77-minute drama concerns an upstanding young man named Malone — the 13th offspring in the family — who heads out to sea to make a life for himself, leaving his girl back home. He is the first officer on board and, during a typhoon in the China Sea, his ship founders. Word reaches home that during the crisis, Malone was drunk and in dereliction of his duties. It is then up to Malone to vindicate himself and win back his girl.

## The Popular Sin

(Malcolm St. Clair, 1926). Paramount. **Script:** James A. Creelman. **With** Florence Vidor (Yvonne Montfort), Clive Brook (Corot), Greta Nissen (La Belle Toulaise), Philip Strange (Montfort), André Beranger, Iris Gray, and Gladys Quatero. St. Clair's "highly intelligent satires," said the *New York Times*, "rivaled only by those of Lubitsch." The director looks at the foibles of the rich when it comes to love. Ignored by her husband, Yvonne falls in love with Corot, a writer, and seeks a divorce. After their marriage, her new husband falls for the beautiful and charming Toulaise. Corot obtains a divorce from Yvonne to marry his latest love, after which his new wife falls for Montfort. This 5,800-feet comedy concludes when the writer, once again seeking his lawyer's office, is told "you ... ought to know where it is."

## Purity

(Rea Berger, 1914). American Film/Mutual. **Story:** Clifford Howard. **Photography:** Robert Phelan. **Art director:** Edward Langley. **Dance director:** Geneva Driscoll. **With** Audrey Munson (Purity/Virtue), Nigel de Brullier (Thornton Darcy), Alfred Hollingsworth (Claude Lamarque), and William A. Carroll (Evil/Luston Black). The film stars a woman whose sculpture graced San Francisco's Panama Pacific exposition in 1915. It is an allegory around the theme "to the pure all things are pure," and concerns an artist's model who serves as inspiration for great poetry and art in the contemporary landscape garden of a California millionaire. In the seven-reel drama, Munson walks before the camera about every 300 feet "clad mostly in a smile" or in the same state of undress "as she would be on entering her morning tub," reported *Variety*. Her film (which was involved in censorship disputes and caught the attention of Anthony Comstock) was as

Audrey Munson as an artist's model in *Purity* (Rea Berger, American Film/Mutual, 1914).

big a box-office hit as the scandalous *The Hypocrites* (1915).

## The Queen of Sheba

(J. Gordon Edwards, 1915). Fox. **Story:** Virginia Tracy. **Camera supervisor:** John Boyle. **With** Betty Blythe, Fritz Lieber (Solomon), George Nichols (David), and Claire de Lorenz. The peak of Fox's spectacle making, with lavish costumes, massive sets, and great mob scenes, was Edwards's greatest film. The well-known story made

Betty Blythe, the studio's new vamp, a star — her charms and attributes were clearly evident — though the special effects, particularly Tox Mix's staging of the chariot race that concludes the first half of the production, nearly upstaged her. "The Queen, at no time," observed a critic, "is unnecessarily overburdened with clothes ... Miss Blythe possessing the required visionary assets." In presenting King Solomon without a beard, "Edwards enabled himself a creative historian," wrote Terry Ramsaye, "on the ground that 'no motion

Betty Blythe in the role that made her a star and Fritz Lieber as the beardless Solomon in *The Queen of Sheba* (J. Gordon Edwards, Fox, 1915).

picture audience would stand for Sheba falling in love with a set of whiskers.'"

## Ravished Armenia

(Oscar Apfel, 1919). W. N. Selig. **With** Aurora Mardiganian, Anna Q. Nilsson, Eugenie Besserer, Irving Cummings, Lillian West, and George Melikian. At eight reels, this was the first personal film account of the annihilation of a people by the forces of the Ottoman Empire in the years 1915–1918. It is founded on the actual terrifying events in the life of 17-year-old Mardiganian, the only one of her family of seven to come out alive.

As a tale of survival in the face of genocide, the production is "a rare feat to so faithfully reproduce a representation of the Far East," said *Variety*, "and have it convincing, both as to the locales and the personnel." As for depicting the atrocities that Mardiganian, her family, and the Armenians faced at the hands of the Turks, Kurds, and Circassian bandits, the film only suggests the "actualities." Titles, instead, refer to firsthand, official reports by Viscout Bryce and Robert Morgenthau. The highly touted production was sponsored by the American Committee for Relief in the Near East, and was called "superfine … with the direction and photography no small part."

## Red Hair

(Clarence Badger, 1928). Paramount. Captions: George Marion, Jr. **With** Clara Bow ("Bubbles" McCoy), Lane Chandler, William Austin, and Jacqueline Austin. This "gay and dashing" production of a red-haired Lorelei Lee is based on a story by the excellent British writer Elinor Glyn, whose material helped turn Clara Bow into the *It* girl. Early in this 6,300-feet lighthearted tale, a splash of color is introduced so that audiences can get an idea of the Titian-haired star. She contributes a "stellar performance" fending off a number of admirers (but not their gifts) at the seashore, wrote the *New York Times*. The film became the "best picture in which Bow has been featured." Excellently captioned, the film includes the line, "If you've seen one raindrop, you've seen them all."

Stills: www.mdle.com/ClassicFilms/PhotoGallery/index2.htm.

## Riddle Gawne

(William S. Hart, 1918). Paramount. **Script:** Charles A. Selzer. **Photography:** Joe August. **With** Hart (Jefferson Gawne), Lon Chaney (Hame Bozzam), and Katherine MacDonald (Kathleen Harkless). Based on the published serial *The Vengeance of Jefferson Gawne*, this popular film was called "an ideal" story for Hart, "who does well directing himself." "Riddle" Gawne is a saturnine individual who spends his time hunting down the cattle-rustling murderer (Hame Bozzam) of his brother. He also raises his niece because her mother has fled with her husband's killer. This five-reel archetype of the genre contains "some exceedingly exciting gunplay," and is "an altogether satisfactory Hart release."

Stills: www.mdle.com/ClassicFilms/PhotoGallery4/hart15.htm.

## The Rogue Song

(Lionel Barrymore and Hal Roach, 1930). MGM. **Story:** Frances Marion and

John Colton. **Photography:** Percy Hilburn. **With** Lawrence Tibbett (Vegor), Catherine Owen (Pricesss Vera), Laurel and Hardy. John Barrymore's all-color musical, based on Franz Lehar's operetta *Gypsy Love*, features the popular baritone Lawrence Tibbett in his first sound film. It is the story of a Russian princess kidnapped by a bandit. MGM promoted the film as "The picture that will change motion picture history! A powerful, tremendous, amazing panorama of love and life dominated by a dramatic personality — the greatest dramatic and romantic star that has emblazoned the screen in this generation. Drama flaming with passion — sparkling spectacular scenes — scintillating with glorious music — sparkling with riotous comedy! It will live forever."

Highlights of the 100-minute production are Tibbett's grand numbers, including "When I'm Looking for You," and eight comedy routines by Laurel and Hardy — their first appearance in a color production — directed by Roach. In the sequences Hardy wears a long rose-pink smock, Laurel a purple satin doublet with red flannel underwear showing at neck and sleeves. Tibbett's "flair for giving numbers a climax," wrote the critics, "makes the finish of this picture something to wait for." This early sound film was a test of Hollywood's production methods in fitting the powerful singer to a microphone: it was placed 15 feet back, with the orchestra anchored, and director Barrymore instructing, "Fire when ready, Larry."

The reason this film, like so may of the period, is missing is that the old two-strip Technicolor film stock was apparently more unstable than standard B & W nitrate film. Also, early talkie musicals were rarely revived — almost all were too creaky — and became dated almost overnight. With apparently no later rereleases of this film, there never was any reason to transfer the film's sound track to optical sound, or to make new prints with the sound-on-film process. (The film's soundtrack exists on 78 records. Films that were not rereleased or redone didn't even make it to early television; so there were no prints ever made on safety film.) Three minutes of film are extant.

Stills: fpr10.maths.strath.ac.uk/LH/ROGUE.HTM.

## Roped

(John Ford, 1918). Universal. **With** Harry Carey (Cheyenne Harry) and Neva Gerber. This is a Ford Western with a new angle: A millionaire cowboy comes to, of all places, New York, to get married — and afterward he finds he is no longer home on the range. He becomes a father, while his mother-in-law tries desperately to separate the unsuited pair. Literally "roped," he is made a nonentity by those around him. The state of affairs is symbolized by "tablecloths ... dresses, and furniture coverings [that] blow about in the wind," noted a critic about the six-reeler.

## The Rough Riders

(Victor Fleming, 1927). **Script:** John Goodrich. **With** Frank Hopper (Roosevelt), Charles Farrell (Steward van Brunt), Charles E. Mack, Mary Astor, Noah Beery (Hells Bells), and George Bancroft (Happy Joe). Before he directed *Gone with the Wind* (1939), Fleming

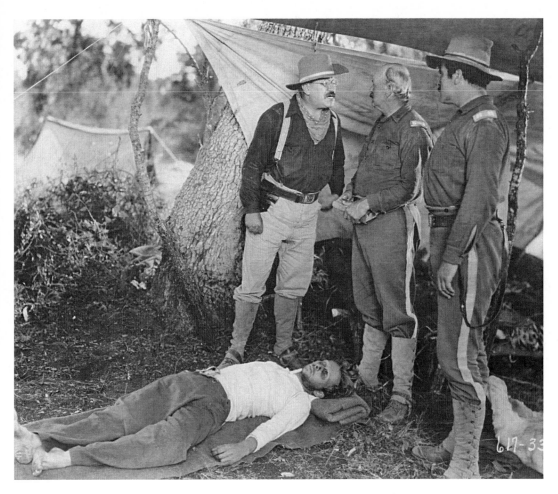

Frank Hopper as T.R. recruits *The Rough Riders* in Texas (Victor Fleming, Paramount, 1927).

made this war picture and rendition of Roosevelt's famous band of Spanish-American War heroes. The comedy-drama was billed as "bully" entertainment. Containing newsreel footage, recreations of dress of the day, and depictions of the "peculiar methods of warfare," the production is also notable for its casting of the lead. He was a Los Angeles book agent whose resemblance to the real man was called "extraordinary." Further, in its glimpses of the recruiting of the Rough Riders and their training in Texas, "the picture excels," said a critic.

## Salome

(J. Gordon Edwards, 1918). Fox. **Script:** Adrian Johnson. **With** Theda Bara, Albert Roscoe (John the Baptist), G. Raymond Nye (Herod), and Vera Doria. This production, said an observer, "for richness and extent of pageantry, sumptuousness of setting, and color of detail has few equals."

When Herodias divorces her husband and marries his brother Herod Antipas, governor of Judea, the prophet John the Baptist protests and is imprisoned.

Salome, daughter of Herodias and both niece and step-daughter to Herod, dances seductively and wins the prize of anything she asks of Herod. What she asks for is, of course, the head of John the Baptist.

Theda Bara is "every bit the vampire in manner and movement and expression." Loosely based on the writing of Josephus — the director is said to have followed "the best historical guides" — "there is much on the screen that could not be included" in either Strauss's opera or Oscar Wilde's play of the same name. What is included in this vivid eight-reel representation of ancient Jerusalem and its people is a "freshly barbered" John the Baptist, the prophet of the wilderness, "carrying a cross."

## Saved from the Titanic

(Etienne Arnaud, 1912). Eclair. **With** Dorothy Gibson (Dorothy), Alec B. Francis (Father), Miss Stuart (Mother), Jack Adolfi (Ensign Jack), William H. Dunn, and Guy Oliver. Designed to capitalize on the public's appetite for news of the *Titanic*, this was the first *Titanic* film, a one-reel production that came as close to verisimilitude as possible: it was filmed onboard the *Titanic's* sister ship, the *Olympic*, and starred one of the first-class passengers from the *Titanic*, Dorothy Gibson.

Gibson had been the first person to enter a lifeboat (#7), which was also the first lifeboat to be lowered. She was one of the first to escape the sinking ship. One month to the day following the sinking, she was in her first starring role. In the film, rather than being one of the first off the sinking ship, Gibson is one of the last. She comes across as both a damsel-in-distress and as a strong, decisive woman unafraid of the terrifying events going on about her. The film enjoyed several weeks of great popularity, then vanished from the circuit. Gibson went on to make several other films that year.

That same year, in June, Continental Kunst-Film in Berlin released its own *Titanic* story, *In Nacht und Eis* (*In Night and Ice*), which it called a "true-to-life drama of the sea based on authentic reports." The 30-minute work, the earliest extant production of the *Titanic* tragedy, was directed by Mime Misu.

## The Sea Gull

(Josef von Sternberg, 1926). Charles Chaplin Film Corp. **Script:** von Sternberg. **Photography:** Eddie Gheller and Paul Ivano. **With** Edna Purviance, Eve Southern, Charles French, Raymond Bloomer, and Gayne Whitman. Also called *A Woman of the Sea*, this melodrama represents Chaplin's attempt to save the film career of Edna Purviance, his longtime leading lady in comedy. Sensing that her comedy days were behind her, Chaplin assigned her to a production about a woman who almost loses her husband to her free-spirited sister. Exacting director von Sternberg (in only his fourth work) put Purviance through numerous takes and multiple reshootings to try to get the right lighting. The seven-reel film was shown in mid–1926, "then promptly returned to Mr. Chaplin's vaults," said von Sternberg. Of the few who actually saw the film, John Grierson labeled it "beautiful and empty," and Georgia Hale said it would have been a box-office dud. Seven years later, Chaplin managed to take a tax write-off for the film — and reportedly destroyed the negative. Stills survived in the private papers of Edna Purviance.

## Señorita

(Clarence Badger, 1927). Paramount. **Script:** John McDermott. **Photography:** William Marshall and H. K. Martin. **With** Bebe Daniels (Francisco/Francesca), James Hall (Roger), William Powell (Ramon), and Josef Swickard (Don Francisco Hernandez). A highly diverting comedy (with accompanying music) in which the agile Daniels satirizes the heroics of Douglas Fairbanks and Tom Mix. Set in South America, the 6,600-feet film became one of Badger's and Daniels's best. It revolves around a young fellow, a Zorro of sorts, who is helping his grandfather do battle against a rival family. The trouble is, the old don, who was there at the birth of his grandchild, doesn't know that the boy he hoped for is a girl. Twenty years later, she arrives at his hacienda — dressed as a male, with whiskers, sword, and daring. Despite her size, she makes pincushions of the enemy. "Miss Daniels is mischeviously ready for all emergencies," wrote a critic, "being both hero and heroine," and

Bebe Daniels playing a Zorro of sorts in *Señorita* (Clarence Badger, Paramount, 1927).

the film is "extravagant and always interesting."

## Service for Ladies

(Harry D'Arrast, 1927). Paramount. **Script:** Ernest Vajda and Benjamin Glazer. **With** Adolphe Menjou (Albert), Kathryn Carver, and Charles Lane. D'Arrast's directorial debut signaled the arrival of a sophisticated filmmaker and "a [6,200-feet] work as close to perfection as any screen or stage audience has a right to expect," wrote a critic. His light, atmospheric comedy is about a supremely knowledgeable headwaiter of a posh Paris restaurant. Its numerous light touches and the delicious performance by Menjou as the man with the knack for offering the right service, in word or deed, reminded the critics of the gentle elements in Chaplin's *The Gold Rush* (1926) and *A Woman of Paris* (1923)—two films D'Arrast had a hand in.

## Should a Mother Tell?

(J. Gordon Edwards, 1915). Fox. **Script:** Rex Ingram. **Photography:** Arthur D. Ripley. **With** Betty Nansen (Rose), Stuart Holmes (Gaspard), Stephen Gratten, Kate Blankley, and Arthur Hoops. This morality tale was a departure for the great Danish actress Nansen. It is about a murder that a young mother is witness to, and contains elements of blackmail, theft, and prison. The film also hints at sexual difficulties. Her fourth film for the studio since coming to America that year, the production contains a "cast that is one of the best that has ever been seen in a Fox production," observed a critic. Nansen, wrote *Moving Picture World*, "could not be im-

proved upon" and "her almost entire absense of gestures deserves special remark." Further, "the direction of the picture is faultless," making for "a decidedly virorous and sensationally effective photoplay," wrote the trade journal. Edwards, who was the director of all of her American films, handled the story "with the easy command of a technical expert who has been given a free hand and a large expense account." Ingram's script helped to make the five-reel film a critical success.

## Siege

(Sven Gade, 1925). Universal. **Adaptation:** Harvey Thew. **With** Virginia Valli (Fredericka), Eugene O'Brien (Kenyon Ruyland), Mary Alden (Augusta Ruyland), Marc McDermott (Norval Ruyland), and Harry Lorraine. "It would be a blessing indeed ... if more pictures were produced along the lines of Siege," wrote the *New York Times*. Danish actor-director Gade's American film (based on Samuel Hopkins Adams's story) contains forcefully drawn characters and a theme audiences could appreciate: one generation's passing and another taking its place. It made a strong enough impression to have the critics noting that "only too rarely does one see a worthy strong drama on the screen ... of unusual merit and one which we hope will lead other producers to appreciate the value of intensive characterization and a natural and plausible theme."

## Sin

(Herbert Brenon, 1915). Fox. **With** Theda Bara (Rosa) and William E. Shay. In this "unusual and quite artistic" five reeler, wrote *Moving Picture World*, the director "has made good use of excited street mobs and has succeeded in suggesting the spirit of religious frenzy." It is the story of a man who, jilted by his lover in Italy, follows her to New York. To prove his love, he steals religious ornaments (during the Festival of the Madonna) from an East Side church and gives them to her. This leads to disaster: outrage by priests and congregants; the innocent young woman's "terror and ... insanity" when she envisions her soul is damned; and the young man's suicide. Despite the startling title and content, the film was less sensuously frank than earlier Theda Bara productions depicting women of strong emotional temperament. That's because a number of "promising love passages" were cut. Still, Bara was called "thoroughly at home in the Italian character" and her production "away from the usual love affair, bring[ing] with it a different climax and a natural finale."

## So Big

(Charles Brabin, 1925). First National. **Script:** Adelaide Heilbron. **Photography:** Ted McCord. **With** Colleen Moore (Selena Peake), Joseph De Grasse, Wallace Beery, Jean Hersholt, Frankie Darrow (Dirk), and John Bowers. Studio executives were reluctant to hire someone known as a comedienne for the dramatic lead character (who ages over 40 years during the story), but Colleen Moore had earned so much for them in the popular movie *Flaming Youth* (1923) that they could not refuse her the part.

Delivering an "astonishingly fine performance," Colleen Moore is the personification of the stolid woman living for her son. Everything in her life is taken in stride in this 8,600-feet adaptation of Edna Ferber's well-known novel. For two decades and especially in widowhood, she raises her son Dirk, who is "so big," first on the farm and then in High Prairie, around Chicago. The director (who garnered credit for his handling of *Driven*, 1923) is "resourceful and imaginative," wrote Mordaunt Hall, in his depictions of the old costumes, high bicycles, wide streets, and the low structures and houses of the era.

## The Song of Hate

(J. Gordon Edwards, 1915). Fox. **Script:** Rex Ingram. **With** Betty Nansen (Flora Tosca), Arthur Hoops (Baron Scarpia), Dorothy Bernard, and Claire Whitney. This was Danish actress Nansen's last American film and the final film of her career. The celebrated performer who was called "the greatest emotional actress appearing in photoplays" ended her Hollywood career at her peak with this melodramatic adaptation of Victorien Sardou's *La Tosca*. Some critics objected to the great number of closeups in the six-reel production, which apparently reduced the number of emotional "scene-chewing" possibilities of the tragedy. "Repression should be cast aside for heaving bosom stuff," wrote *Variety*. Nonetheless, when Tosca stabs the villainous police chief Scarpia, "audiences applauded strenuously," wrote the trade publication. The film, which was scripted by Ingram, was touted as "one of the finest features ever released," by *Variety*. *Motion Picture News* called it "the most tragic piece of dramatic art that the writer has ever laid eyes on. There is not one faint glimmer of happiness in it ... Nansen plays her role to the last hilt of dramtic skill." The film was Nansen's most successful American effort, and earned the studio a hefty return on its investment. In her five American films, wrote an observer, "Nansen's tears have coursed over 25,000 feet of celluloid." When she returned home, *Photoplay* referred to her as the "Vikingess."

## Sporting Life

(Maurice Tourneur, 1918). **Script:** Winthrop Kelley. **With** Ralph Graves (Earl of Woodstock), Warner Richmond, Charles Eldridge, and Henry West. Based on Henry Hamilton and Seymour Hicks's play about upper crust Britishers and villains being foiled at the eleventh hour, this action-filled, suspenseful, comedy-drama culminates in the running of the English Derby. Lord Woodstock, a sporting man in financial straits, hopes to see his horse Lady Love win the Derby. But there's a plot afoot to keep the horse, if not Winthrop, out of competition. Thieves steal the horse — after which Winthrop is himself kidnapped. Escaping and recovering his prize possession, he has to make a last-minute dash to the Derby to enter the horse into the race. Containing Tourneur's highly regarded sense of effect and lighting, "the (seven-reel) film will make an attractive special release and ... give satisfaction to any audience," wrote a critic. Tourneur remade the film in 1925 for Universal, starring Myrna Loy.

## The Street Angel

(Frank Borzage, 1928). Fox. **Script:** Marion Orth. **Photography:** Ernest Palmer. **With** Janet Gaynor (Maria), Charles Farrell (Angelo), and Natalie Kingston. Borzage's late silent melodrama about transcendence stars one of the most famous duos of the late 1920s: Gaynor and Farrell. Gaynor plays a poor Neapolitan who is forced into crime to stay alive, while Farrell is a struggling artist who meets her at the circus. Enchanted, he has her pose for his painting of the Madonna. But his faith in her is shaken when she is picked up by the police — and her past is exposed.

This sentimental work by director Borzage, who was following up his 1927 "film of the year," *Seventh Heaven*, cemented the pairing of six-foot-two Farrell with the five-foot Gaynor. So charmed were film audiences by these two all–American performers that they were accepted in whatever roles they undertook. The 9,200-feet film earned Oscar nominations for Best Cinematography and Best Interior Decoration.

## The Street of Sin

(Mauritz Stiller, 1928). Paramount. **Story:** Josef von Sternberg and Benjamin Glazer. **Script:** Chandler Sprague. **Photography:** V. Milner and Harry Fischbeck. **With** Emil Jannings (Basher Bill), Fay Wray (Elizabeth), and Olga Baklanova (Annie). One of Mauritz Stiller's finished American films is this drama about the desperate, disturbing lives of the poor. It is the kind of production that helped make Stiller's cinematic reputation in Sweden. The camerawork in the one-hour film, said *Variety*, "aptly caught the intended filth of the locale with Stiller's direction particularly to the fore."

## Suzanna

(F. Richard Jones, 1923). United Artists. **Supervisor:** Mack Sennett. **With** Mabel Normand, George Nichols, Walter McGrall, Evelyn Sherman, and Leon Barry. A love story about a poor girl raised in wealth, the film, set in Spanish California in the early 1880s, was a marked change for filmmaker Mack Sennett. Not once does he "veer into blugeon-like comedy.... As we did not have to sit through the custard pie stages, the film was a relief and we were ... pleased," wrote a critic. While the story of the eight-reeler is slight, there are plenty of love scenes, along with the appropriate ambiance, set changes, and bullfight scenes to make one yearn for yesteryear.

"*Suzanna* made a lot of money, part of which I got," recalled Mabel Normand.

## Tess of the D'Urbervilles

(Marshall Neilan, 1924). MGM. **Adaptation:** Dorothy Farnum. **With** Blanche Sweet, Stuart Holmes, Conrad Nagel, and Joseph Dowling. This famous

Blanche Sweet as the heroine in a contemporary adaptation of Hardy's great novel *Tess of the D'Urbervilles* (Marshall Neilan, MGM, 1924).

tale by Hardy is daringly set in modern times. To add verisimilitude to the production, Neilan shot the exteriors in Wessex County, England, in Stonehenge and other places described by Hardy. The beautiful Blanche Sweet plays the pure girl-woman, daughter of a drunkard, who is ravished by an aristocrat. With more sexuality and less innuendo or seduction than the character is given in the novel, Sweet "is beautiful every inch of the film," wrote a critic. Neilan's 88-minute film graphically shows the tragic, shocking effects of the assault on her. She is hanged at the end. The *New York Evening World* wrote that Neilan "has retained all the power, the appeal and beauty of the original and has invested the dramatic progress of the story with pictorial beauty." Hardy was said to have been pleased with the film.

## That Royle Girl

(D. W. Griffith, 1925). Famous Players–Lasky. **Story:** Edwin Balmer. **With** W. C. Fields (Mr. Royle), Carol Dempster (Daisy Royle), James Kirkwood (Fred Ketlar), and Harrison Ford. Any film with W.C. Fields is worth recovering, even if he had only a minor role in it. This one, which cost $600,000 to pro-

W.C. Fields can't help making them laugh in *That Royle Girl* (D. W. Griffith, Famous Players–Lasky, 1925).

duce, was a departure for D.W. Griffith and one of Fields's best silents. He plays a bibulous, reprobate father. In one scene he makes an appearance in a dress suit with a short white waistcoat and black suspenders; in another scene he sticks a candle rather than a cigar into his mouth. More often than not he is unaware that his beautiful young daughter, who is in love with a married band leader, is in trouble. When the music man's wife is killed by gangsters, and he is framed, she sets out to catch the real killers. In doing so, she is called upon to emulate the acrobatics of Tom Mix, Douglas Fairbanks, and Richard Dix. "There is no denying," wrote the critics, "that she gives a splendid account of herself in these wild passages, especially when she escapes from a building hand-over-hand along a painter's ladder." Griffith's two-hour drama ends in an even wilder fashion: an old-fashioned cyclone bears down on everyone. Griffith's "work on this subject," wrote an observer, "proved for the most part a satisfactory entertainment." The film grossed $900,000.

## The Three Passions

(Rex Ingram, 1928). **Script:** Ingram. **Photography:** L. H. Burel. **Design:** Henri Ménessier. **With** Alice Terry and Ivan Petrovich. Ex-patriot Ingram's first directorial effort free of Hollywood's influences (and Terry's last film) is a serious-minded drama of a well-off couple trying to make sense of the world. This encompasses the liberal times in which they live (the Jazz Age), the open class conflict between labor and management at a shipyard, and the couple's own traditions of religion. In Nice, where Ingram owned his own studio, he spent a year making the 70-minute film (based on the novel by Cosmo Hamilton). *La Liberté* called his effort "powerful, intelligent ... and must make the viewers think"; and *Le Soir* said it is "sumptuous and powerful. The details are evocative," and Burel's "camera angles reveal astonishing technique." In the U.S. the reaction was quite different. *Variety* ranked it "not a bad picture 20 years ago."

## Thunder

(William Nigh, 1929). MGM. **Script:** Byron Morgan and Ann Price. **Photography:** Henry Sharp. **With** Lon Chaney (Anderson), Phyllis Haver, and James Murray. In his next-to-last film, Chaney plays a crusty, highly dedicated old engineer whose motto is that the trains run on time, no matter what. Made in the closing days of the silents, the nine-reel film focuses on railroad procedures and contains the "sundry mutterings and moanings when trains are speeding across the country." The tale is about the old pro who loses his job when he causes a wreck that kills his son. He redeems himself by piloting a Red Cross train to flood victims in the South.

Stills: www.mdle.com/Classic Films/ PhotoGallery2/chaney29.htm.

## Time to Love

(Frank Tuttle, 1927). Paramount. **Script:** Pierre Collings. **Photography:** William Marshall. **With** Raymond Griffith (Raymond Casanuova), Vera Veronina, William Powell (Marquis de Daddo), and Josef Swickard. A fast-paced farce (based on a story by Alfred Savoir) starring the zealous comedian Griffith. Despondent, he casts himself from a bridge and lands in a gondola —

and into the lap of the woman (momentarily engaged to his best friend) whom he will ultimately marry. Before the ending of the 50-minute production, the quaint little Griffith fights what seems to be an endless series of duels, rescues the girl he loves at a wedding ceremony, has a high-speed auto chase, and goes aloft in a hot-air balloon wearing a silk hat and accompanied by the charming heroine. "Nice interiors set the action off," wrote *Variety*, "and a pip of a sport Renault for transportation."

## Too Much Johnson

(Orson Welles, 1938). **Script:** Welles. **Photography:** Paul Dunbar. **With** Joseph Cotten, John Houseman, Virginia Nicholson, Arlene Francis, Marc Blitzstein, John Berry, and Rith Ford. A silent based on William Gillett's play, Welles's film is a madcap comedy, comprised of a 20-minute introduction and two 10-minute episodes, which concern lovers spying on, and trying to get the better of, each other. Welles shot 25,000 feet of film in New York and Yonkers, and intended to use some of the footage in the stage play — a combination of live action and film in theater. Just as he was putting together the finishing touches, Paramount notified him that *it* owned the rights to the play; then Stony Creek Theater, where Welles intended to premiere his work, told him it wouldn't run a nitrate film. Put on the back burner by the ever more busy Welles, the film was reportedly destroyed in a fire in Welles's Madrid villa in 1970.

## The Tower of Lies

(Victor Sjöström, 1925). MGM. **Adaptation:** Agnes Christine Johnston and Max Marcin. **Photography:** Percy Hilburn. **With** Lon Chaney (Jan), Norma Shearer (Glory), Ian Keith, William Haines, David Torrence, and Claire MacDowell. Directing the stars of his *He Who Gets Slapped* (1924), Sjöström came up with perhaps his most Swedish film from Hollywood, if not his best American effort. His fourth work from the film capital finds him in the company of characters whose mentality and behavior he knew well.

The film is based on Nobel Prize–winning author Selma Lagerlöf's fantasy *The Emperor of Portugalia*, about the longing for happiness. The story is set in the Swedish countryside in the bosom of a family of farmers who are struggling to raise their daughter above their means. Jan's daughter Glory, whom he lovingly calls "The Empress of Portugalia," leaves for the city in order to earn a living and help her parents pay their debts. She succeeds, but does not reveal how to her parents. When she returns home after a long absence, she finds her father has gone mad. She could stay and make a life with a lover who has remained faithful to her, but the hostility of the villagers, who have discovered the truth, is too much for her to bear. She leaves by boat, thus causing her father to drown when he tries to stop her.

Sjöström's 6,500-feet production ends on a happier note, imposed by the studio. Glory, desperate, returning to the fold, marries the man who has not stopped loving her and at whose side she would become a good farmer's wife. Nevertheless, the film was called "different … an attempt to tell the story … through the powers of suggestion." It is a "sincerely made picture," said *Variety*, that is "excellent from the artistic and literary viewpoints." "The acting is aces and the direction is masterful," noted the trade journal, and the film fades out against a sunset effect in the manner of a Millet mural.

Stills: www.mdle.com/ClassicFilms/PhotoGallery3/shearer7.htm.

### Treasure Island

(Maurice Tourneur, 1920). Paramount. **Script:** Jules Furthman. **Photography:** René Guissart. **With** Shirley Mason (Jim Hawkins), Lon Chaney (Pew/Merry), Charles Ogle (Long John Silver), Josie Melville, and Wilton Taylor. This "wonderfully photographed and effectively acted" screen adaptation of Stevenson's classic adventure contains swift movement and sharp action right from the first scene. "There's always something doing," wrote a critic, while "the choice of locations, lighting effects and attention to detail are so expertly attended to as to leave all but those on the lookout unable to guess just what it is they miss." In addition, if the "sons of hell" who roamed the Spanish Main

Shirley Mason as Jim Hawkins in this lost adaptation of Stevenson's classic *Treasure Island* (Maurice Tourneur, Paramount, 1920).

as pirates aboard the *Hispaniola* resembled the cast, "let us be duly grateful they caught Captain Kidd and his crew and hanged them," pointed out the reviewers.

Vivid, disturbing scenes of the six-reeler include "Two pirates in a death struggle with the thumb of one slowly gouging out the eyeball of his mate," wrote the critics, "two gentlemen of fortune killing a third before a deep blue background, and racing down to the sea waving their blood-stained cutlasses. And last a whole ship's company dangling in the wind from the yards of their vessel — black bundles against a vivid blue sky.... A buccaneer is pinned to the cabin door by a knife through his chest, and there he hangs stiff and dead with the blood spot widening on the door behind him."

Stills: www.mdle.com/ClassicFilms/ PhotoGallery2/chaney30.htm.

## Vanity Fair

(Hugo Ballin, 1923). **Script:** Ballin. **With** Mable Ballin (Becky Sharp), George Walsh (Rawdon Crawley), Hobart Bosworth (Lord Steyne), Harrison Ford, Eleanor Boardman (Amelia Sedley), and Willard Louis (Joseph Sedley). Thackeray's novel was transferred to the screen almost whole in this atmospheric, elaborate, detailed, and very complete story of the world of a 19th-century gold-digger, starring the director's very attractive wife. "Infinitely more entertaining and far better done than many other films," wrote a critic, this is also a carefully constructed costume drama, most notably in those scenes of soldiers going off to do battle against Napoleon's forces.

## Village Blacksmith

(John Ford, 1922). Fox. **Script:** Paul H. Sloane. **With** William Walling (John Hammond), Virginia Boardman (Mrs. Hammond), Virginia Valli (Alice), Bessie Love (Rosemary Martin), Dave Butler (Bill), Tully Marshall, and Carolina Rankin. Ford's production "gets an audience in the throat in the beginning and never releases its grip until the final minute," wrote a critic. It is loosely based on Longfellow's poem, and in fact makes use of his poetry in the subtitles. The immortal words "under the spreading chestnut tree" convey the strength of a blacksmith's idyllic family, who are shown in opposition to the troubled family of a jealous squire, who had once sought the hand of the blacksmith's wife. The fate of the children of both families is the heart of the tale. The culminating scenes of the six-reeler are ones of great emotional turmoil, and are signaled by a walloping storm — similar in kind to those in Ford's *Hurricane* (1937). One reel survives.

## Wedding Bill$

(Erle Kenton, 1927). Paramount. **Adaptation:** Grover Jones, Keene Thompson, and Lloyd Corrigan. **Titles:** George Marion, Jr. **With** Ann Sheridan, Raymond Griffith (Algernon Schuyler van Twidder), Vivian Oakland, and Edgar L. Kennedy (detective). This farce features the now-forgotten Raymond Griffith in one of his zaniest films. The one-hour film's rattling flip captions only added to the thrills. It's about a man called upon to be the best man at three weddings on the same day. At one of these affairs, he must retrieve a valuable necklace snatched by a bird and deposited atop a skyscraper. This adaptation of a man doing Harold Lloyd is "neat, clean, steady amusement," said a critic. "Griffith plays smoothly and likably ... a debonair fixer."

## A Woman's Resurrection

(J. Gordon Edwards, 1915). Fox. **With** Betty Nansen (Katusha Maslova), Edward José (Simonson), Stuart Holmes, and William J. Kelly (Prince Dimitri). Danish theatrical actress Nansen (who specialized in Ibsen) had become the equal of Sarah Bernhardt with her performance of Katusha in Tolstoy's 1899 tragedy *Resurrection*. In America, Fox went all out in Nansen's third film for the studio, an adaptation of the literary classic about suffering lost souls in Siberia.

Prince Dimitri, a Russian nobleman serving on a jury, discovers that the young woman on trial, Katusha, is someone he once seduced and abandoned and that he himself bears responsibility for reducing her to crime. He sets out to redeem her and himself. As one of the earliest screen adaptations of Tolstoy's work, the five-reel film brought accolades to the star. "Miss Nansen has a number of opportunities which she handles convincingly," wrote *Variety*. In the end, she dies for her sins.

## The Young Rajah

(Phil Rosen, 1922). Famous Players–Lasky. **Script:** June Mathis. **Set and Costume supervision:** Natacha Rambova. **With** Rudolph Valentino (Amos Judd), Wanda Hawley, and Robert Ober. Based on the novel and play of the same name, this Valentino-Mathis-Rambova film represents Valentino's attempt to transcend his *Sheik*-style glossy star vehicles. It is a mystical tale about an heir to a far off kingdom. When the throne in India is seized by a usurper, Harvard-educated Amos Judd, in glorious costume, returns home. Despite death threats and disturbing visions of doom, he vows to overthow the despot and save his people. In the process, he forsakes his American lover. In the epilog, the Rajah is in his garden, mourning for his love, "but the vision of prophesy, which has never been wrong, appears to show that ultimately they will be reunited," wrote *Variety*. A two-minute Czech trailer survives.

Stills: www.mdle.com/ClassicFilms/PhotoGallery4/rudy12.htm.

# Selected Bibliography

*American Film Institute Catalogues 1911–1920, 1921–30,* and *1931–1940* (1993).

Bishoff, Ruud. *Hollywood in Holland: De Geschiedenis van de Filmfabriek Hollandia, 1912–1923.* Amsterdam: Thoth, 1988.

Brismee, Jean. *Cinéma : Cent Ans de Cinéma en Belgique.* Mardaga, 1995.

*Catalogue des Film Française de Long Métrage, 1929–1939.* Cinémathèque Royale de Belgique.

*Catalogue des Films de Fiction de Première Partie, 1929–1939.* Paris: Archives du Film de Centre National de la Cinématographie, 1988.

*Cinegraph.* Lexikon zum Deutschsprachigen Film, 1984.

Daisne, Johan. *Filmographic Dictionary of World Literature,* 1977.

*Deutsche TonFilme,* vols. 1–3. Deutschen Bibliothek, 1988.

*Dizionario del Cinema Italiano,* vol. 1, 1930–1944. Rome.

Donaldson, Geoffrey. *Of Joy and Sorrow.* Amsterdam: Filmmuseum, 1997.

*Encyclopedia dello Spettacolo.* Rome, 1954.

Engberg, Marguerite. *Registrant Over Danske Film 1896–1914.* Copenhagen: Institut for Filmvidenskab, 1977–1982.

*Film Directors Annual* (1930).

Fritz, Walter. *Geschichte des Österreichischen Film.* Vienna: Bergland Verlag, 1949.

____. *Kino in Österreich, 1896–1930.* Vienna: Österreichischer Bundesverlag, 1981.

González López, Palmira. *Catálogo del Cine Español,* vol. 1. Filmoteca Español, 1993.

____. *Els anys daurats del cinema classic a Barcelona (1906–1923).* Publicacions de l'Institut del Teatre de la Diputacio de Barcelona, 1987.

*Histoire du Cinéma Française, 1929–1935.*

Jordaky, Lajos. *Az erdelyi nemafilmgyartas tortenete, 1903–1930.* Bucharest: Kriterion, 1980.

Kreimeier, Klaus. *The Ufa Story.* New York: Hill and Wang, 1996.

Leprohon, Pierre. *The Italian Cinema.* New York: Praeger, 1972.

Mitropoulos, Aglae. *Découverte du cinéma grec, histoire, chronologie, biographies, films.* Paris: Seghers, 1968.

____. *Notes sur le cinéma de Grèce: 1912–1975.* Cinémathèque Quebec, 1975.

Mitry, Jean. *Filmographie universelle.* Paris: Institut des Hautes Etudes Cinématographiques, 1963–1987.

Nemeskurty, Istvan. *Word and Image: History*

*of the Hungarian Cinema.* Budapest: Corvina Press, 1974.

Noizet, René. *Tous les Chemins Mènent á Hollywood: Michael Curtiz.* Paris: L'Harmattan, 1997.

*Polskie Filmu Fabularne, 1902–1988.* Warsaw: 1990.

Ribeiro, M. Felix. *Filmes, Figuras e Factos da História do Cinema Português.* Lisbon: Cinemateca Portuguesa, 1983.

*Svensk Filmografi,* vols. 1, 2, and 3, 1930–1939. Svenska Filminstitutet, 1982.

Thomas, Paul. *Un Siècle de cinéma belge.* Ottignies, Belgium: 1995.

Surowiec, Catherine A., ed. *The Lumiere Project,* 1996.

Usai, Paolo C., and Lorenzo Codelli, eds. *Prima di Caligari.* Biblioteca dell' Immagine, 1991.

Visscher, Wim. *Amsterdam in de Film: Een Filmografie van 1896 tot 1940.* Amsterdam: Gemeentearchief, 1995.

# Index